Canons and Contexts

CANONS AND CONTEXTS

Paul Lauter

New York   Oxford
Oxford University Press
1991

Oxford University Press

Oxford   New York   Toronto
Delhi   Bombay   Calcutta   Madras   Karachi
Petaling Jaya   Singapore   Hong Kong   Tokyo
Nairobi   Dar es Salaam   Cape Town
Melbourne   Auckland

and associated companies in
Berlin   Ibadan

Library of Congress Cataloging-in-Publication Data
Lauter, Paul.
Canons and contexts / Paul Lauter.
p.   cm.   ISBN 0-19-505593-4
1. American literature—History and criticism—Theory, etc.
2. Criticism—United States—History—20th century.   3. English
philology—Study and teaching (Higher)—United States.
4. Educational innovations. 5. Canon (Literature) I. Title.
PS25.L38   1991   810.9—dc20   90-42019

1   3   5   7   9   8   6   4   2

Printed in the United States of America
on acid-free paper

For my mother, Lillian Roberts
"O body swayed to music, O brightening glance"

Preface

Poverty and homelessness, industrial stagnation and meaningless work, racial and sexual discrimination, drugs, violence, pollution, and crime—what relationship has education to such social issues? Or to the cataclysmic changes going on in Eastern Europe, Central America, and Southern Africa? The answers remain very conflicted, and seldom clearly debated.

A traditional American view, voiced periodically by public calls for reforming schools and colleges, is that education is a source of change, and in fact a major weapon in overcoming problems from unemployment to teen pregnancy. At the very least, those holding this view contend, schooling has been a primary agent of individual upward mobility. To be sure, almost all credible research denies the connection between education and social change, but that has not noticeably affected the passion with which Americans of virtually every class turn to the schools to resolve public issues.

On the other side are those who view educational institutions simply as expressions of existing social arrangements. Far from influencing society, they hold, schools are altogether its products, reflecting and conveying dominant values, teaching young people to internalize as personal norms unequal economic and cultural relationships based on class, gender, and race. From this perspective, education is hardly a resource to use in achieving social mobility. At the "high end" it is more of a consumer good, such as compact discs and vacations at Club Med, displaying one's social class position by virtue of the kind of education one can afford to buy. At the other end, it is a device for separating, socializing, and controlling the workforce on behalf of a changing American capitalism.

Both of these views seem to me naïve and potentially dangerous. The first, ignoring the very substantial evidence not only of research but also of everyday experience, places excessive faith in education . . . and then proceeds to blame teachers for their alleged "failure" to live up to such exaggerated expectations. Thus it fosters the love-hate relationship between Americans and their schools that has helped undermine what education can reasonably accomplish. The other position expresses what I think is a morbid understanding of theories of cultural and social "hegemony"—viewing power as if it were immutably fixed, and social relations as frozen into irremediable class structures. Often, this view is based upon a mechanical interpretation of the distinction between economic "base" and cultural "superstructure," an interpretation that argues that only the transformation of the base can significantly affect the superstructure and that influence flows strictly in one direction, from society *to* education and culture. This outlook, it seems to me, leads to political paralysis, especially when it is also argued that even those struggling against oppression and marginalization can do so only within the discourse of the powerful. If nothing can be changed meaningfully until everything "fundamental" is transformed, then the cultural world truly is embedded in Kurt Vonnegut's *ice-nine*.

From my perspective, education—like other cultural institutions—is an arena for struggle, and what is decided there significantly affects the political economy and important social arrangements. To be sure, the contestants in this arena are not equal, since he who pays the piper will most often be able to call the tune. But the players in education, in writing, and in the arts are never mechanical creatures activated by coins and springs. Nor is power merely the accumulated weight of dollars. In fact, culture—from the history textbook to the picket line chant, from Shakespeare's *Henry IV* to "Subterranean Homesick Blues"—is a significant way of constructing and mobilizing power. It is, indeed, serious work that, as E. B. White's dialogue between "John D.'s grandson Nelson" and Diego Rivera reminds us, might usefully be viewed with a smile.

> "And though your art I dislike to hamper,
> I owe a *little* to God and Gramper,
>   And after all,
>   It's *my* wall . . ."
>   *"We'll see if it is," said Rivera.*
>
> ("I Paint What I See")

The features and the language will differ, but those of us who are cultural and educational workers will always be engaged in struggles over what can be placed upon the institution's wall and in its books.

Within colleges and universities this contest for authority takes a number of forms. In this book I concentrate on two: First, the issue of changing the literary canon and the related curricular questions, such as the value and possible content of general education courses. And second, the questions of institutional purpose raised in the 1970s by management practices like widespread "retrenchments," and in the 1980s by the string of studies and polemics seeking to prescribe for higher education's supposed ills. While the sites of these differing struggles have varied, the underlying issues remain consistent, as the identity of the contestants suggest. Some commentators, seeing the future modeled by the past, propose a highly structured set of postsecondary options and general education curricula consistently focused on the presumed "monuments of unaging intellect." They have spoken primarily to a general public and to political leaders in language that ranges from the stagnant commonplaces of foundation study committees to the heated sermons of William Bennett and Allan Bloom. Others, generally the more established members of the professoriat, concentrate on writing large the needs of professional specialization on the canvas of higher education as a whole. They offer ever more refined analyses, informed by one or another sophisticated "theory," in what is too often an all but impenetrable dialogue with a small number of colleagues. Their concern is to preserve space for humanistic study, however esoteric, in a world increasingly committed to "bottom-line" calculations of value.

The third party to this contest, a kind of loosely constituted "Left" comprised of feminists, black scholars, gay and lesbian academics, educational progressives, and cultural radicals, wishes to reconstitute curricula around the central perception of difference—especially of race, gender, class, and sexual orientation—and to open colleges to more democratic participation and decision-making. Too often, no doubt, they have spoken primarily to the converted when they have not been engaged in arguments with one another. But interesting coalitions have been emerging with the new decade, perhaps as the political urgency created by Reagan administration policies and appointments overcomes the conflicts that a concern for difference generates.

As is the case elsewhere in American politics, the lines between these three "parties" are not clearly drawn and, as some of these essays indicate, odd and temporary coalitions can emerge. Many on the Left as well as on the Right seem to agree that certain kinds of study *ought* to be required of all college students—though they disagree radically over what. The Right argues for the putative "classics"; the Left calls—at a minimum—for adding works by women and minorities generally excluded from that category, and has increasingly sought to demonstrate how the category, "classic," is itself an historically constructed mask for unacknowledged power relationships. Many academic liberals as well as conservatives seem uncomfortable—if not altogether horrified—with basic questions about thus widening the established literary canon; similarly they express scepticism, if not fear and loathing, over doubts raised by advocates of affirmative action about traditional personnel standards. Still, as I try to make clear, these three "parties," or centers of intellectual and institutional gravity, do project quite different conceptions of society, as well as of educational institutions and literary study.

What has come to be called "the question of the canon" is one front in this cultural battle, a particularly vital one. By "canon" I mean the set of literary works, the grouping of significant philosophical, political, and religious texts, the particular accounts of history generally accorded cultural weight within a society. How one defines a cultural canon obviously shapes collegiate curricula and research priorities, but it also helps to determine precisely whose experiences and ideas become central to academic study. If one reads few, if any, works by writers of color, as was the case when I went to school, then "their" lives likely will remain marginal to "your" literary experience. Moreover, defining what is "central" and what is "marginal," a basic function of canonization, will itself help decide who studies, who teaches, and who has power in determining priorities in American colleges. If increasing numbers of texts *by* women enter the canon, then those who have historically been concerned with such texts, primarily women, will gain more entrée to the institutions, such as colleges and text publishing, that study and perpetuate canons. The question of the canon, that is, not only shapes the academic course of study but is closely connected to (though not identical with) issues of affirmative action and related processes of university governance. Moreover, as the controversies over William Bennett's curricular proposals and E. D. Hirsch's notions of "cultural literacy" suggest, debating the canon turns out to be a symbolic way of arguing a variety of other social and political issues—basically, who has power and how it is exercised.

If the question of the canon is one focus of debate, issues of academic governance and priorities provide the other. During the past two decades, many of the major "service" professions have been undergoing a significant restructuring. Power over the institutions in which they work has gradually been shifting from medical personnel, including doctors, to health-care administrators; from social workers to organizational administrators; and from professors to collegiate managers. Such processes are not altogether new, nor are they simple to chart; but they bring with them profound changes in culture and in institutional priorities. For people who see themselves as managers generally share far more with their peers in other fields—into which they may well move—than with the professionals whose work they administer. Indeed, with their M.B.A.s and doctorates in academic administration, and with their predominantly cost-conscious approaches to defining and solving problems, they participate deeply in the broader managerial culture of American business.

Now it may seem peculiarly Utopian to challenge the market-oriented thinking of this culture, particularly right now as even the most hardened Leninist policy-makers appear to be waltzing down that distinctly capitalist road. Yet this is precisely what I wish to do. It is not my intention to enter into the wider debate over the virtues and limitations of market mechanisms in motivating human productivity and in distributing the world's goods. I think theorists are only at the beginning, rather than at the end, of that debate. What I will argue, however, is that whatever the virtues of a marketplace approach to *some* areas of human enterprise, the notion that such thinking is appropriate to governing *all* areas of activity is not only banal but dangerously authoritarian. With respect to colleges and universities, this book argues, the managerial governing strategy has blocked rather than enhanced the faculty and student creativity needed to seize the vast opportunities being created in this wonderfully-changing world.

Why? Marketplace ideology casts students into the role of "consumers" of the "products" offered in the grand store of the collegiate curriculum. Teachers thus become suppliers of products that, if they are not bought, must naturally be cleared from the shelves. And managers, as those entrusted with "responsibility" for the production of education, must then determine which product lines and which workers to eliminate and which new ones to stock. To be sure, the more idiotically rigid application of this doctrine seems less common today than it did a decade ago, but such bottom-line thinking still pervades most enrollment-driven institutions, which a huge portion of today's students attend. The notion that young (or even older) students should ultimately be responsible through their "choices" for the design of collegiate education strikes me as a perversion of even the most extreme individualistic ethos. It is one thing to offer true freedom of choice in the kinds of institutions students might wish to attend or the kinds of majors they might wish to pursue; it is quite another matter to place in the hands of such "consumers" determinative power over the content of such courses of study. Young people are not incompetent to make reasonable choices, despite the efforts of American society to infantilize our youth; but those choices are but one factor in the construction of a coherent educational program. Besides, as I suggest later, students are by no means offered anything like "free" choice over the kinds of colleges they may attend or the collegiate careers open to them. They are, in fact, "channeled" through particular doors—to use the image made notorious in the 1960s by General Hershey, head of the Selective Service.

What this managerial/marketplace model comes down to was perhaps more honestly expressed by the 1950s slogan that "what's good for General Motors is good for America." What its managers said was "good" for General Motors has *not* turned out to be particularly good for America—as the movie *Roger and Me* so vividly dramatizes—or even, in fact, for General Motors, or at least for its workers, much less for Wayne State University and its sister institutions. The effort to adapt authoritarian corporate models to higher education has resulted, I will argue, not only in inefficient, bureaucratic institutions, but also in the demoralization of precisely those, the faculty, who must identify their futures with these blundering university dinosaurs if they are to be truly productive. The alienation of faculty in the last decade has become notorious; it may be inevitable given the corporate transformation of college institutions. But I see no more reason to accept that authoritarian "inevitability" than, finally, to have accepted the former government of Romania.

To be sure, the particular scholarly interests of individual professors by themselves provide no more steady guide to the formulation of collegiate policy than either the managerial imposition of a marketplace ideology or the changing expression of student preferences. To teach merely what we wish to specialize in can produce only another form of narrowed curriculum—or, what has been more the case, the miscellanies of unrelated courses and works that have constituted most academic programs of study for the last two decades.

What I think we need to learn from the recent history not only of American education but of Eastern Europe is the limitation both of fundamentally individualistic and of centralized totalitarian models for organizing institutions. The alternative, I believe, emerges from a process that might best be called *democracy*. It is a term now often appropriated to describe formal nationwide elections or the consumer marketplace. But it seems to me more accurately applied to the process in which the maximum number of people participate, discuss, and decide central questions about the direction and configuration of an institution's programs. If forms of democratic, participatory decision-making are difficult, perhaps impossible, at the level of nation-states, they remain viable, I believe, in the departments, divisions, and schools that make up colleges and universities. Democratic decision-making is time-consuming and sometimes contentious, but it offers the only possibility that I know of for those who do the work of education to take responsibility for its character and quality. Increasingly, commentators across the political spectrum have come to see that goal as the sine qua non for reinvesting educational institutions with energy and values.

For such reasons, then, this book questions the market-oriented management strategies prevalent in much of American higher education, just as it rejects the idea that any single discourse—even what is called "Western civilization"—can constitute the dominant core of academic curricula. It suggests, rather, that *difference,* manifest in race, gender, class, and certain other categories of experience and analysis, can and should provide a central way of thinking about collegiate educational programs. And it urges that what is done in colleges should be based not simply on what students are willing to "buy" at any passing moment, but upon what the people in differing institutions and in different places, with differing constituencies and missions, determine are the values, and the social and intellectual objectives for which they want the institution to stand. I do not offer any grand formulae, for core curricula or for managerial strategy, precisely because I do not believe *any* such formulae are appropriate to any and all circumstances. On the contrary, I would argue that the development of democratic and inclusive processes for reconstructing academic programs will be at least as important as the precise products that emerge.

That is, of course, an argument rather more appealing to some faculty members than it might be to managers, collegiate or industrial, or even to many first-generation-to-college students, for whom general education requirements seem to be hurdles, and for whom difference is precisely what they wish to escape. It would be disingenuous to pretend that the forms of academic governance and the nature of the curricula for which I argue do not serve particular group interests, including my own. But that is as true of the proposals offered by commentators like Allan Bloom and William Bennett, and the practices pursued by college managers. No such set of practices and proposals stands apart from specific interests. But it seems to me that a democratic polity and a curriculum that values, indeed focuses upon, difference opens a genuinely broader college education to far more citizens than any monologue, however well-intentioned.

It opens something else as well, I believe, and that is the possibility of reenergizing American society to face and honestly contend with the kinds of problems I named in the first sentence of this Preface. I find it impossible to believe that the drab, shopworn, business-as-usual platitudes that pass for political discussion in the United States are all that can be fielded in response to a worldwide revolution of rising hope. I refuse to accept the notion that grudging, minimal change—stale slops from a military trough—is the best that American political leaders can offer a people increasingly desirous of housing the homeless, treating the drug-addicted and the disease-ravaged, cleansing the air we breathe and the water we drink, and creating work that joins the power of technology to the values of a heterogeneous democracy. Every week I revive to hope and struggle reading and teaching Toni Morrison and Frances E. W. Harper, Rolando Hinojosa and Tillie Olsen, Charles W. Chesnutt and Louise Erdrich, Henry David Thoreau and Alice Walker. I find my students, like students a quarter century ago, eager for the challenge of rebuilding a democratic, varied, and equitable society—not in Lithuania but here, in the United States. They read Thomas Paine and Thomas Jefferson and David Walker and William Lloyd Garrison and Angelina Grimké and Harriet Beecher Stowe and Herman Melville and Frederick Douglass; they think of the long struggle for freedom; and they cannot help but wonder whether the unique opening now before us will be foreclosed by dull, arrogant, visionless men of affairs, who have no language but that of war and no object but that of control.

When I teach Thoreau's "Plea for Captain John Brown," I like to call my students' attention to a passage that, I think, explains the vehemence of his rhetoric as well as the objective of his writing:

> Our foes are in our midst and all about us. There is hardly a house but is divided against itself, for our foe is the all but universal woodenness of both head and heart, the want of vitality in man, which is the effect of our vice; and hence are begotten fear, superstition, bigotry, persecution, and slavery of all kinds. We are mere figure-heads upon a hulk, with livers in the place of hearts. The curse is the worship of idols, which at length changes the worshipper into a stone image himself.

I believe the primary goal of study, and particularly of literature, is to shatter that "woodenness," to open our heads and hearts to what needs doing in a world near the beginning of its better history. If this book encourages you along that road, it will have made its small contribution.

New York, N.Y.   *P. L*
July 1990

Acknowledgments

Earlier versions of a number of the essays in this book have been published, in part or in different form, in the following books or periodicals: "Society and the Profession, 1958–1983," *Publications of the Modern Language Association;* "Race and Gender in the Shaping of the American Literary Canon," *Feminist Studies;* "Reconstructing American Literature—Curricular Issues," *Reconstructing American Literature* (The Feminist Press); parts of "Teaching Nineteenth-Century American Women Writers," *Legacy;* parts of "The Two Criticisms," *Literature, Language and Politics* (University of Georgia Press); "Canon Theory and Emergent Practice," *The Politics of Literature: Toward the Year 2000* (Columbia); "Retrenchment—What the Managers are Doing," *Radical Teacher;* "A Scandalous Misuse of Faculty—Adjuncts," *Universitas;* "Beyond Consciousness Raising—Changing Institutions," *Face to Face: Fathers, Mothers, Masters, Monsters* (Greenwood); "University Reform—Threat or Opportunity," *Thought and Action;* parts of "Looking a Gift Horse in the Mouth," *Social Text; San Jose Studies;* parts of "The Book of Bloom and the Discourse of Difference," *The Trinity Reporter.* I wish to thank the (often anonymous) editors for their help, and also to express particular appreciation for the equally anonymous reader for Oxford University Press, who helped me rethink every part of this volume.

Many of my friends and colleagues have read and commented on one or more of these essays. I wish to acknowledge my debt to Kate Adams, Elizabeth Ammons, Houston Baker, Miller Brown, Juan Bruce-Novoa, Selma Burkom, Johnnella Butler, Cynthia Butos, Héctor Calderón, Ellen Cantarow, Sergei Chakovsky, Jules Chametzky, Jan Cohn, Constance Coiner, Joel Conarroe, Peter Conn, Michael Cowan, Betty Jean Craige, Lennard Davis, Joanne Dobson, Richard Flacks, Shelli Fowler, Ellen Friedman, Diana Hume George, Alfred Habegger, Marie Harris, Elaine Hedges, Allison Heisch, Reamy Jansen, Amy Ling, Meg McGavran Murray, Bella Mirabella, Malcolm Nelson, Judith Newton, Richard Ohmann, Susan O'Malley, Alicia Ostriker, Raymund Paredes, Deborah Rosenfelt, LaVonne Brown Ruoff, Michelle Russell, Jose Saldívar, Catharine Stimpson, Jane Tompkins, Aleksandr Vashchenko, Linda Wagner-Martin, Sam Wakshull, John Walter, Joyce Warren, Mary Helen Washington, Susan Waugh, M. Elizabeth Wallace, Andrew Wiget, Richard Yarborough, Olga Zernetskaya, and Yasen Zasursky. Many of the virtues of this book derive from the comradely criticism of these people;

I did not always follow their advice, but I was always the better for having had it. I particularly wish to thank Tucker Farley, who forced me to rethink and clarify the last group of essays.

Support for the research and writing of sections of this book was provided by a fellowship from the National Endowment for the Humanities.

Three people have read all the essays herein: Peggy Gifford, Louis Kampf, and Ann Fitzgerald. The language of appreciation provides very little to express what their ideas and encouragement have meant to me. To Annie, in particular, my fiercest critic and most indefatigable promoter, this book is an expression of love.

Contents

Part I

"We'll build in sonnets pretty roomes"

The Canon and the Literary Profession

Society and the Profession, 1958–83

> The question that he frames in all but words
> Is what to make of a diminished thing.
> > Robert Frost, "The Oven Bird"

> When your women are ready and rich in their wish for the world
>   destroy the leaden heart,
>   we've a new race to start.
> > Muriel Rukeyser, "More of a Corpse Than a Woman"

When I was asked to write about the impact of society on our profession over the last twenty-five years, it occurred to me that the period also measures my own lifetime as a professional. I took up full-time teaching in 1957, the year before I received my doctorate. I gave my first paper at a Modern Language Association convention around that time, participated in producing two sons, and published my first article. I left one job, joined in antinuke, anti-ROTC, and prounion activities, and got fired from the second job. I remember complaining to my graduate school director, en route to a third job, how painfully remote upstate New York seemed from everything I valued. Said he, flatly, "You can publish your way out of any place." Perhaps that was so, then; certainly I acted on that instruction. But I never really put it to the test, for somehow my career swerved that splinter and never returned quite to the groove.

In 1963 I went to work for the Quakers, promoting peace studies and learning about political economy. Then, in 1964, I traveled to Mississippi to teach in Freedom Schools and discovered the profound limitations of my graduate school education. With deliberation, among a group of my students from Smith, I went off to jail in Montgomery. Later, as the peace movement brought the war home, I was provided with a more impromptu visit to the Baltimore pokey after trying to protect a Vietnam vet from an outraged policeman. For a number of years I sported a little red button that said "A

This paper was originally commissioned for the Centennial issue of *PMLA,* and it appeared there—99 (May 1984): 414–426—in slightly different form.

free university in a free society"—an idea on the basis of which I tried to conduct my life. In due course, I became an active feminist, involved in efforts, like The Feminist Press, to change education and thus society. That pattern of life was not, of course, precisely typical of members of our profession—though more people than we now acknowledge participated in it one way or another. I speak of my life because it reflected, in a sense became a vehicle of, the forces for social change I am to write about here.

In other respects, however, my career has been quite typical. For although I began in private, elite institutions, in the 1970s I found myself, like many in our profession, scraping along in a new, public institution, one that had not even existed in 1958. Unlike many of my colleagues, I did not teach what are euphemistically called "skills"—reading and writing, that is. But that was a function not of my students' needs, which were overwhelming, but of peculiar institutional rigidities. In fact, what I taught was limited only by my own inventiveness—and by the severe restrictions imposed by my students' earlier miseducation. So some courses were a yearly joy and others regularly disastrous. Free but numbed, I found myself nodding agreement to each of my epigraphs. And in explaining the social phenomena that have reshaped our professional world, I discovered that I was also accounting for my personal experience—and perhaps that of many of you—as well.

I want to consider the wider impact of the two social and economic phenomena that have molded my life: first, the political movements for equality of the 1960s and early 1970s and, second, the economic expansion of that period and the subsequent stagnation of the last decade. I argue that our profession, like other primarily cultural institutions, has been especially sensitive to these forces and that they have pushed us in opposite directions: toward openness and variety, on the one hand, and toward rigidity and self-absorption, on the other. This contradictory motion helps to explain the high degree of drift, tension, anxiety, even animosity that so many of my colleagues find in our profession, yet its continuing pull on us.

I

Consider, then, the 1958 MLA convention, held, as it almost invariably was in alternate years, in New York. The convention lasted two and a half days; its twenty-two-page program listed a total of eighty-seven sessions, including three general assemblies and the meetings of seventeen affiliated organizations. The sessions were essentially divided between large "sections" and "discussion groups," among which were those on American literature. This arrangement, by the way, had been developed at the beginning of the 1920s and persisted for almost fifty years. Today the program contains over one hundred large-sized pages, listing nearly eight hundred sessions during the three days of the convention, including meetings of ninety-two affiliated organizations. In 1958 women were but 22, or 9.6 percent, of the 228 paper presenters or discussion leaders at the convention; they constituted approximately 19 percent of the 9,239 members of the association. By 1982 women made up 39.7 percent of the over 2,000 presenters or discussion leaders, while they constituted some 44 percent of the approximately 27,000 members; the proportions are higher now.

In 1958, as I need hardly report, none of the papers or sessions was devoted to the work of a black writer—much less of a Native American, Asian-American, or other "ethnic" writer. There was, of course, a session devoted to Spanish-American Literature; characteristically, the papers concerned subjects like the second phase of *modernismo* in Chile and German literature in Mexican periodicals of the late nineteenth century. A discussion group for thirty-five people treated the new subject of Hispanic area studies, but nothing in the program suggested a concern for the writings of Chicanos or Puerto Ricans. Nor was there much interest in the writing of women. The topic for the American Studies Association was "Modern Novelists and Contemporary American Society"; the novelists considered were, predictably, Hemingway, Faulkner, and James Gould Cozzens. The Contemporary Literature group focused on "Thematic and Technical Modernism in the Novel," with papers on Lawrence's *Rainbow,* Ford's *Parade's End,* and, once again, Faulkner. Like a great deal else in 1958, Literature and Society (General Topics 6) was involved with social responsibility: Mark Schorer spoke on the social responsibility of the "man of letters," Hiram Haydn on that of the publisher, and Carlos Baker on that of the critic. But perhaps the best expression of 1958 are the titles of the papers of the American Literature group: sandwiched around a luncheon address by Max Lerner, they were as follows: "Criticism as History: A Problem for the Study of American Literature," by Roy Harvey Pearce; "American History and Literary History," by Richard K. Ludwig; "Some Undercurrents in American Literature," by John Henry Raleigh; "Bibliographical and Textual Studies and American Literary History," by Lewis Leary; and "The New Criticism and American Literary History," by Leon Howard.

A few other signposts gleaned from the *PMLA*s of the period: The convention registration fee in 1958 was $1.00 (compared with $55–$90 now); but then, New York subway tokens were 15¢ and cabs 25¢ for the first fifth of a mile. The first woman president of the Modern Language Association, Louise Pound, died in June 1958. Given impetus by Sputnik, the association was pressing forward with a major foreign language program, whose goal was to develop integrated sequences for language study from the earliest elementary grades through graduate school. One does not discover from *PMLA* that 1958 marked the founding of Motown Records in Detroit or the first annual Puerto Rican Day parade in New York. But in 1959 one finds that the American Friends of Vietnam issued a request for back issues of *PMLA* for the University of Hue.

What is one to make of the changes between 1958 and now? To begin with the obvious, the profession grew enormously in the decade after 1958, as a result, of course, of the rapid enlargement of college and university enrollments produced by the baby boom and the expanding economy. The growth of the Modern Language Association and certain of its functions, like publications, its computer, the job exchange, is even more vivid. Membership tripled in less than fifteen years (though it fell off somewhat during the late 1970s), but the staff of the association increased from about eleven in 1958 to about seventy-five in the mid-1980s, and, as I have indicated, the formal parts of the convention have multiplied even more rapidly—despite the temporary decline in membership. Our lives and our work, like those of most Americans, are increasingly carried on in the context of large bureaucratic organizations.

The association, the specialized society, the union—these absorb more and more of our time and of our salaries. We depend more on them because academe is no longer a world of individual entrepreneurs. The organizations have also become increasingly formal and complex, and, given recent economic constraints, they compete for membership, often by trying to satisfy the interests of newer constituencies. That process had begun in 1958 with consideration, for example, of the need for the MLA to encompass languages other than those traditionally included, but it accelerated in ways that were hard to imagine thirty years ago.

This expansion of the association is best revealed in today's convention program. The incredible diversity of concerns listed therein, literary and otherwise, reflects several historical forces, apart from sheer growth. First and foremost are the social movements of the 1960s and early 1970s, which brought us developments like black studies, women's studies, and Chicano studies. My discovery in Mississippi in 1964 that I knew virtually nothing of black culture or history has become, among white academics, more or less commonplace—though what follows from that discovery is perhaps less clear than it was two decades ago. At any rate, these growing disciplines have sought various forums for expression, of which the annual convention of the Modern Language Association is only one. But on the MLA they have had a major impact. For it is not simply that the old association of 1958 or 1933 has expanded to encompass new concerns. Rather, the character of the association—and of the underlying profession—has been transformed as profoundly, I think, as it had been around 1920. At that time, the old, gentlemanly gathering was absorbed into a far more elaborate organization of professionals, with their greater specialization, more ambitious projects, more formal entry requirements, and—a point to which I will return—their sense of the importance of their work. Over the last two decades, the MLA has become an umbrella for, and on occasion a coalition of, many diverse groups and individuals. We do not all teach; and even those of us who do, teach at wildly different institutions. We do not all do literary research or criticism; and if we do, we may concentrate on figures who would have been unknown to or scorned by our peers a quarter century ago.

The changed convention clearly reflects these changes in the profession. Indeed, one might interpret as signs of progress the striking increase in the proportion of white women and minority professors on the program and the equally apparent increase of papers devoted to the work of minority and white women authors. And they are; I want to be explicit in praise of the association's responses to some of the imperatives for equality (though it was only at the MLA's centennial that an ongoing discussion group on African-American literature was established). But to stop at that tribute would, I fear, be a misleading oversimplification. For the very meaning of giving a presentation at the MLA convention has itself changed, a fact testified to by the surprisingly large number of people listed in the program who did not actually show up. In 1958 little short of galloping consumption would have excused default on an MLA paper. Giving a paper was a benediction on one's career by the powers that were in the profession: a rite of passage for a young scholar and a significant accolade for an established citizen. Now, while we still in some degree accumulate credits toward professional recognition, reading a paper often means getting together with a few specialists in one's narrow area or even with a few friends and onlookers. Or, even more crassly, it means that one is willing to invest over one hundred dollars joining and registering. In the years after 1968, the doors of the convention were, in effect, flung open, and it has become rather like a *Grande Jatte* on which people of every cultural persuasion perform their chosen rituals.

I do not by any means intend such a comment to demean the event. But we should not be deluded that the appearance of women and minority men at a workplace simply means *progress*. That most bank tellers are now women or minority men testifies to the routinization, computerization, and general decline in the status of that job. The position once might have led upward in the financial world; it is now slightly elevated above that of the supermarket checkout clerk (and not a lot better paid). Speaking at the MLA convention once meant advancement in the hierarchical structure of the profession. It occasionally still may. But mainly it means that the convention and the association have been reorganized to give at least some space and a modest voice to those at the bottom of the profession, as well as to those at the top. The shape of the program does *not,* however, mean that women and minority professors are now, in significant numbers, at the top of the hierarchy, much less that the hierarchy has itself been altered. On the contrary, the profession remains as stratified as ever; the statistics on the status of women and minority men provided by the Commission on the Future of the Profession bear out that fact in painful detail.[1]

Just as the hierarchy of the profession remains fundamentally unaltered, so—as yet—does the hierarchy of what we value. We call that the literary "canon." It is only within the last decade and a half that the term has come to be seriously discussed; I believe the first session at an MLA convention on the question of the canon was the one I organized in 1973 at Chicago. Within a few years, a large forum focused on the subject, and by the 1982 convention at least half a dozen sessions explicitly or implicitly concerned the canon and its revision.

The question of the canon grows directly from the impact of the social movements of the 1960s on the profession. They asked of our courses, our texts, our research, "Where are the blacks?" "Where are the women?" Most of us, certainly myself included, on first hearing those questions looked blank. I'd never studied a black writer and, until the early sixties, hardly read more than a novel each by Baldwin, Ellison, and Wright—even though I had joined the NAACP in 1949. Social justice was one thing, my career another. As for women, there were, of course, a few—Austen, Eliot, Woolf, and Dickinson, mainly, with perhaps a baseball poem by Marianne Moore and "The Jilting of Granny Weatherall." For the most part they were "minor" or "regionalist," were they not—and I was a New Yorker gone to the School of Letters and Yale.

The question of what we taught and what we read was pressed on us both by a changing student population—increasingly vociferous about what it wanted to know—and by the extraordinarily rapid process of discovery in new fields like black studies and women's studies. Answers to those questions began to emerge: the women, the blacks, the Chicanos were there, all right, though often forgotten and buried under our critical terminology and procedures. As the power of writers like Frederick Douglass, Mary Wilkins Freeman, Charles Chesnutt, Kate Chopin, and Zora Neale Hurston became apparent in the seventies, the issue has shifted from "Who are they?" to "Whom do you want to replace?" In the twenties, it was said, our predecessors had pushed over the busts of Lowell and Holmes to make room for Melville and Thoreau. But the Hall of Fame, like our classes and texts, had only so many niches. "Are you serious that you teach 'The Yellow Wallpaper' and *no* Henry James in your introductory American literature course?" The gods frown; foundations tremble; then the Norton anthology opens to Douglass and Chopin. A sigh of relief runs round the profession—we have done the right thing and can return to the classics, slightly augmented.

That amounts to altering the hand-me-downs, not stitching a new suit. In 1981 I collected about 100 syllabi for introductory American literature courses to see if curricula had seriously responded to scholarly developments in black studies and women's studies. The results, for those interested in change, were discouraging.[2] With few exceptions, even instructors who used the then-new Norton anthology, with its inclusion of Douglass' *Narrative* of his life, did not teach Douglass. Through the 1980s I collected hundreds more American literature syllabi, and the pattern largely remained. The signals of change abound, but not yet its manifestations. Indeed, a certain resistance has emerged. In the 1970s we were challenged to produce our new classics; now we are engaged in a struggle for precedence.

It is a struggle embittered, I believe, both by economic dislocation and by some of the legacies of the 1960s' expansion of the profession. For the issue of the canon involves not only taste and values—as if they were not sufficiently weighty—but jobs and power. Accepting Freeman, Chopin, Wharton, Cather, Glasgow, and, yes, Stowe, as central to American fiction[3] implies the centrality of women's experience and women's culture. And what if we also perceive Douglass' *Narrative* as a paradigmatic text in American literature? What does all that say about the values, and the value, of the writers who have given expression to white male lives, "our" lives? Are "we" being reassessed, along with Franklin, Nick Adams, Nick Carraway, Hemingway, and Mailer? And haven't we enough trouble already with the dean, who wants to retrench the eighteenth century in favor of Mortuary Science and Funeral Service? The social movements of the 1960s and 1970s placed the issue of the canon high on the agenda of our profession. And the academic wings of those movements have begun to produce answers, practical and theoretical, to the questions so raised. But it has become clear that the old walls will not crumble because we march round them blowing the trumpets of Hurston and LeSueur. Change in our profession, if we read history correctly, has come about because our predecessors organized to produce it. Still, none of them faced a period of decline and conflict quite like ours. The struggles to end poverty, racism, war, unemployment, and meaningless work, sparked by the movements for change, have been beset by economic, social, and, to be frank, intellectual retrenchment. Can the issue of the canon, with everything it represents, be happily resolved if the three R's become recession, retrenchment, and righteousness? To understand the tensions of our profession—represented by my two epigraphs—I want to look closely at the more troublesome aspects of the 1960s and at the emergent social structure of our profession.

II

The rapid growth of higher education in the 1960s created jobs, mobility, a decent pay scale, and the illusion that the professional hierarchy was flattening out, or, at least, becoming permeable. We played donnish Horatio Algers, and some of us did, indeed, end up at Yale, Berkeley, or even Texas, with a two-course load and a $75,000 contract. Far more of us, as my own experience suggests, settled into what were formerly teachers' and technical schools or branch campuses newly expanded into liberal arts colleges and giant graduate institutions. To these campuses came a large, diverse, and seemingly unruly student population, significantly different in class, race, and—somewhat later—gender composition from the student population of the 1950s. Expansion and the changing student body brought with them problems as well as virtues. The problems grew when, with the war-produced economic stagnation of the 1970s and the contraction of the traditional college-going cohort of young people, the boom collapsed. The humanities, our profession among them, became particularly vulnerable to the forces of economic and social change.

As teachers of English and modern languages we had always been cultural and therefore social gatekeepers. When I taught at Indiana, an open-admissions university in the 1950s, the three-term composition sequence was, and was expected to be, one of the major flunk-out courses. We had a set of elaborate grammatical commandments, and three violations meant failure of a paper. I recall one of my students, a young black man from Gary, who so far as I could then see was never able to understand the past tense. He flunked

paper after paper, and ultimately the course, largely because he seemed
incapable of grasping the high importance of "-ed." I was my duty, as I
understood and was taught it, to fail such students, and fail them I did. But
the social and cultural consensus that informed that duty disintegrated in the
1960s. The causes were complex: the sense among many new students that
they were left out of that consensus, mistrust of traditional American values
produced by our war on Vietnam, the movements for change themselves.

The dislocation of an intellectual consensus paralleled the disintegration
of the 1950s political consensus. Between 1960 and 1963 I taught at Hobart
and William Smith Colleges, which were nominally affiliated with the Epis-
copal church. I was a member of the staff for the required courses in "Western
Civ." The subtext of those courses was nicely stated in their formal title: The
Origins of Christian Civilization. As I came to understand the ideology
of the courses, expressed in excellent staff briefings and seminars, well-
developed lectures, and home-devised texts, I found myself becoming increasingly restive. I began to argue that the history as presented left out too
much, especially Jews. In true liberal fashion, the response was to propose
that I give a lecture on intertestamental literature, the specifically Jewish
context for the development of what became identifiable Christian ideas. I
was Jewish and I was concerned, so I was tapped. I found myself launched
into a vast and, to me, quite unknown scholarly world, from which I emerged
frantic with at least two hours of notes and wonderful texts to be stuffed into
an hour's lecture. In a way, giving the lecture helped; in another way, it
served simply to silence me, for the organization and weight of the course
did not change, nor did its ideology. And while people complimented me on
my lecture, no one was about to consider fundamentally altering the course
on the basis of my, or a few students', malaise. But the consensus was weak-
ening. It rapidly crumbled with the increasing numbers of students and faculty
who did not feel a part of it and with the growth of militance, especially
arising from the civil rights movement, which encouraged opposition. What
in 1962 could be taken as my personal idiosyncrasy would be seen in 1968 as
cultural (racial, sexual) politics. And if we could no longer agree on what an
educated person should know, how could we impose required courses on
reluctant students, especially as we ourselves turned from teaching such requirements toward specialties offering greater professional rewards?

No one factor produces cultural change, and one may differently weigh
the reasons for the disintegration of the 1950s consensus. But the effects were
clear by the early 1970s. First, the language and literature requirements that
had kept many of us in business were rapidly being abandoned, particularly
in the newer institutions. It was not only that students seemed intent on a
career focus for their higher education, though many did, and especially first-
generation-to-college students. As I suggest below, they remained unper-
suaded—not without reason—of the value of what we offered in the humanities.[4] But also, in many institutions, and again especially the newer ones,
there existed no firmly established, and certainly no agreed-on, tradition of
liberal education; thus there reigned a marketplace conception of education,

with students as consumers and deans as store managers. We did not then sufficiently understand how that conception also entailed a shift in academic power from faculty to managers, managers whose jobs depended on sustaining not an idea of a university but a given level of student FTEs at a given cost. As the general education constituency evaporated and managers placed such courses on back shelves, the rationale for English and language majors also diminished. These majors had never offered wide career possibilities, and now jobs in publishing and teaching, for example, were rapidly dwindling. For students whose social and economic position provided adequate margins, the literature or language major might remain attractive, a genteel transition to law school, say, but such students were mostly in a few elite institutions. At the rest, majors disappeared, as did the students whose requirements had brought them into our courses. Baffled and defensive, we found ourselves increasingly assaulted by the body counters.

And then there was the question of literacy. Whenever colleagues used to tell me about the decline of writing skill, I would recite for them a sentence I memorized from a theme of one of my students in 1955: "The slope of her shoulders flowed gently down her sides to her hips, there to form a perfect contrast." In turn, they would tell me that they would be pleased if their students wrote as well. In a way, we were both right. The expansion of higher education in the United States has meant that we are enrolling and trying to maintain in college far more people, like my student from Gary, whose linguistic traditions differ and whose culture, however verbal, does not emphasize the written word as, by and large, literary professors' do. In a way, we are engaged in a grand experiment in mass higher education, an effort to provide postsecondary schooling for well over half the population of this country. But it is a commonplace that most of us do not experience that task as very grand; on the contrary, it seems a massive chore imposed by the need to retain our jobs as enrollments in literature courses plummet. However we experience the task of teaching literacy, it contrasts starkly with the vision of the literary life to which most of us in the profession, and particularly those of us who join the Modern Language Association, were bred. Graduate school provided little but on-the-job training in teaching literacy, a circumstance that said something about the academic status of that duty, and the hierarchical structure of the profession still further diminished the value of the task. After all, who performed it?

Economists conventionally see the labor force as divided between "primary" and "secondary" sectors.[5] Those in the primary sector enjoy job mobility, good working conditions, and high wages; those in the secondary sector suffer from unstable employment and low wages. Some economists suggest further that the differences derive from a fundamental distinction between "core" and "peripheral" sectors of the American economy or even, within a particular sector, between core and peripheral firms or organizations. The primary work force is associated with core industries or core companies within an industry; the secondary work force with peripheral sectors. Thus, in the past, workers in steel, a core sector, have been relatively better off than those, for example, in service industries. Similarly, in publishing, major firms like Doubleday and Random House at one time constituted a core, within which the more permanent work force enjoyed significant financial and social advantages over employees of marginal firms. This model provides some useful insights, though it does not fit the academic world, or our profession, in some important respects.

The "core" of our stratified profession consists of a small cadre of professors of literature, mainly critics in style, at elite graduate and a few undergraduate institutions. Surrounding this cadre are acolytes nervously clinging to the fringes of hope, for, far below them, at the "periphery," struggles an increasing army of unemployed or seldom employed professionals, picking up an adjunct course here, a year's replacement there, and, almost invariably, teaching literacy—writing, reading, basic skills. Two features of the work of these "marginal" teachers lend a quality of desperation to the struggle to stay out of their ranks: the status of what they teach and the "proletarianization" of their lives. The word is more bitterly appropriate than when some of us began to use it, in perhaps unconsidered ways, twenty years ago. The work has little glory and fewer rewards. For it is by no means apparent that the society wants or, as presently constituted, can really use a thoroughly literate work force. In the 1950s my task at Indiana was clear: to separate out a portion of the aspirants for college degrees; I was supposed to flunk twenty percent or more and to make them believe, as indeed I then did, that failure was a result of their own inadequacies.[6] Today the rhetoric of literacy teaching holds that our goal is to equip every interested student with the tools necessary to get through a college education. But in fact there is not a university in the country that provides the resources necessary to accomplish anything close to that goal. And the low status and worse salaries and working conditions of many of those who teach literacy register the social priorities very clearly.

The vast majority of us are not, of course, at the core or at the periphery but in the great middle class of our profession. Yet the conflict I have been sketching between our aspirations, both literary and social, and the realities of teaching deeply affects us as well. Teaching, as most of us do, in elephantine bureaucratic institutions, we may try to cling to our tweeds and the remnants of control over our work. But such institutions, increasingly dominated since the early 1970s by academic managers and outside politicians, allow little room for the genteel illusions that, in 1958, would have helped mask the conflicts and the slippage of our place in the academic hierarchy. In a sense, the validation heretofore provided by the central role of literary study and its practitioners in the American academy has slid away. The financial rewards, the expectations of growth currently belong to people in computers and management. For many of us, the work we do comes more and more to resemble that of our colleagues at the periphery of the profession. Indeed, within our own institutions, we hold jobs that, while celebrated as central, are paid and often largely staffed as peripheral. No wonder many of us feel like some long-term New York City apartment dwellers: rent control ensures affordable and sometimes internally pleasant quarters, but outside, the night is hostile, the subways cruel, and the job . . . Ah, well, the job. Like those apartment dwellers, we cannot afford to move—or even to risk, were there a risk to take. Tenured but stuck. It is certainly not the life of the academic migrant, the adjunct; compared with life among the lowly, it is a good life, in fact. But it is experienced as a "diminished thing."

In explaining the malaise I encounter among a majority of those in our profession—and it is still a white and male majority—I have cited a number of factors: most of my colleagues are as yet unmoved by, even somewhat antagonistic toward, the enormous energy generated by women's studies (and black and ethnic studies) practitioners; they are experiencing real declines in their financial and academic status; they feel pushed into forms of teaching that almost everything within the profession has led them to disdain. I want to add one further factor, and that is the nature of literary study practiced at the core of the profession, among that small group of academic critics. Again, the MLA conventions provide a point of reference. In recent years there seem to be two centers of energy at the conventions: formalism and feminism.[7] The program often lists more sessions on literary criticism and theory than on any other subject—even twentieth-century American literature. And I suspect there are still more sessions on women's studies in language and literature, though they are not listed separately in the subject index. In general, formalist and feminist sessions are the best attended, and, give or take some overlap, their constituencies are largely distinct.

At one of the most crowded sessions on criticism at the 1982 convention three rather complex, not to say obscure, papers were presented. At the end, with an unusual amount of time left, the chair asked for comments or questions. A heavy silence spread through the room. No one spoke. People shifted disconsolately. The session finally ended. In the circumstances, the silence needs some explanation. Formalism is the culture of our professional elite, the core. Going to papers on literary criticism and theory, however impenetrable they may be to the naked ear, is more than an "in" thing, more even than a matter of reflected status. Its importance is displayed in the terminal silence. Speaking up presents far too high a risk. To ask a question might imply the inadmissible: that you do not understand part, or even all, of a paper. Worse, perhaps, a question might inadvertently reveal your ignorance of a subtle hermeneutical point. Who knows how such a feather could weigh in the scale held by those who might balance you against some equally qualified candidate for a job? And a question might be taken, even characterized, as a vulgar attack on the Brahmin sensibilities of the advanced. Better silence, gravity, and pretense.

My point is not that criticism is today more obscure than it was in the days of R. P. Blackmur or Kenneth Burke. I think it is, in fact, but certainly it's entitled. Rather, I want to make two other points, one about power, the other about function and substance. In 1958 the wave of formalist criticism was building to its crest but had by no means yet swept the seats of academic respectability.[8] Today, criticism is the language of power, as surely as British was in colonial India. You speak one of its dialects or remain unheard. You cite its viceroys to frame your arguments. You learn to play in its phrases— or you give up forever any hope of entering the core of the profession. Geoffrey Hartman, arguing for scope to enable speculative critics to do their thing, insists that "literary criticism is neither more nor less important today than it has been since the Renaissance."[9] An accurate statement, no doubt, if spoken by God. But in this world, how you weigh importance depends on the chair in which you sit—indeed on whether you have a chair or are peering in from the snow. The form of work done at the profession's core weighs heavily on us all. And its importance derives not necessarily from its inherent value—whatever that might be—but from the institutional status and power of those who do it.[10]

What, beyond reinforcing status, is the function of criticism? In 1958 formalist criticism, for all its ambiguous politics, lighted the path of young literary practitioners back to texts we loved and could now share with our students. It illuminated classrooms. Can that be said of criticism today? As I argue in a subsequent chapter, I think not. Indeed, speculative critics reject that function as making criticism inferior to other literary forms.[11] Nevertheless, criticism confers value, privileging certain texts as it performs its pirouettes. As Hartman says, "the literary works analyzed and quoted by the New Critics are a special selection from literary history, as are those analyzed and quoted by Derrida or Barthes or Heidegger" or de Man or Hartman.[12] Indeed, they are "special," if not altogether precious, Gallic crystals, which resonate to the elitism of the enterprise. What is included in and excluded from the "text-milieu" of speculative criticism? An index test of Hartman (or any of his colleagues) resurrects familiar questions: "Where are the women?" "Where are the blacks?"[13] As criticism departs from the real social milieu in which most of us live and work, it becomes increasingly self-referential, suffering from the Boudingi syndrome, named after the fabulous bird that flies in ever-decreasing concentric circles until it violates its own anatomy. The latest books of criticism seem to be, in the main, about neither literature nor life but about other criticism.

It is no defense to assert that as a literary form criticism has the right to define its own subjects, including the language it uses, or to say, in effect, that criticism does not mean, it is. For we must then ask of it, as literature, of what value are the experiences it encodes and what are its social functions? Criticism long since surrendered the function Arnold saw for it, the education of a new and powerful class.[14] Ever retreating from ravening social conflict down the path marked by Eliot and Tate, criticism now increasingly rejects the narrowly "practical" task of illuminating texts, though at its best it wrestles them round in clouds of language. Too often, however, criticism becomes an exercise in romantic self-assertion, valorizing (ghastly word) its performers, mainly white academic men from elite universities. Riding the intellectual shuttle between Paris and New Haven, isolating themselves in studious despair from the mass of students *and* colleagues, speculative critics at the profession's core have rarely spoken persuasively to the need for jobs and meaningful work or to the reawakening concern for an education rooted in humane values.

The issue can be posed in one fundamental question: What is "the life of the mind"? The play of intellect, protecting itself from the encroaching demands of politics and society? Or the struggle of intelligence to grasp and change the world? To put it more narrowly: we have always promoted our profession as one concerned with literacy and values. Those objectives, we said, were sufficiently central to college education to justify entrusting every student to us for a term, a year, perhaps two years; we were further able to insist that those students had to learn our terms, our discourse, or fail. And yet our work has wandered far from a concern with literacy and values. Advancement in our profession has increasingly depended on commitment to and performance in formalist rhetoric. Indeed, we have erected a set of interlocking intellectual systems, privileging those texts that give criticism scope and usefulness and privileging also those individuals most deft in working the lingo. I am mildly overstating, to be sure. But the basic point cannot be overstated: no profession can indefinitely survive such fundamental contradictions. It is not only the economy, the passing of the baby boom, the changing interests of job-oriented students that are catching up with us. It is ourselves.

III

I have tried to sketch some of the large-scale changes that have shaped the profession during the last twenty-five years and also some of the particular conflicts that have soured many of our colleagues on their work. But disillusion, discouragement, and anger contend in our profession, and often within a single person, with hope, aspiration, freshness. However we may seem to be drifting toward academic deserts, we are not likely to die in a blizzard of computer chips. In fact, the past two and a half decades can be read as a movement toward new possibilities as well as away from old sureties. It is not my goal here to prescribe for the future. But I want to underline the implications of certain trends that provide a more hopeful cast to that future.

During the past two decades many of us have invested heavily in learning to teach literacy. Except for the success of individual students, the investment has not been remunerative. Now we hear from the National Collegiate Athletic Association, state legislatures, and alumni committees that "limited" collegiate resources should no longer be "wasted" on teaching skills to "marginal" students. Hardy is the soul who publicly contradicts the appeal to old standards, however rooted in nostalgia and a false construction of the past it may be. And it is, of course, reasonable to wish that students learn to read, write, and cipher in elementary and secondary schools. Some high school students have begun to take a more conventional and structured set of courses. But I doubt that the literacy problems our profession has faced will simply evaporate.

Two trends militate against that possibility. One is competition for fewer students among more colleges. While a minority of institutions may be able to raise enrollment standards, partly in fact by limiting enrollments and cutting staff, most will continue to feel pressure to sustain present numbers by broadening and varying traditional standards. Second, standardized tests—generally promoted by advocates of "raising standards"—continue to be criticized as limiting the opportunities of low-income and especially minority students, because they do not accurately predict the performance of these students and do not take into account the inadequacies of their prior education. Those who wish to keep colleges open to the more diverse constituency we now serve have generally resisted testing methods that, if rigidly applied, would eliminate many of the gains made by nontraditional students since the late 1960s. Throughout this period, indeed for most of the MLA's lifetime, the problem has been how to institutionalize and provide reasonable levels of support for the teaching of language skills. We can, and no doubt should, try to spread the teaching of literacy across the curriculum, but I wouldn't expect much from our colleagues in physics and psychology. Oddly, the rhetoric developed recently by collegiate managers and overseers calling for higher levels of literacy among students presents the profession with an opportunity it has not often had to reduce the gross conflict between the importance attributed to literacy and the lack of material support given its teaching. I am not suggesting that we can suddenly right this ancient wrong by pointing out the justice of providing as well for those who teach our students to read with intelligence as for those who teach them to manage with profit. But in the 1970s I think our profession began to understand the need for organizing to achieve goals on which we agree. That is why the MLA has increasingly been encouraged to be "political," to lobby, to pressure. Whatever the relation of "publish" and "perish," we are beginning to comprehend a central working-class slogan: "Don't mourn, organize."

A different kind of opportunity derives from the efforts to reestablish some forms of core curricula or liberal arts requirements. Most of these changes have been thinly disguised attempts to shore up enrollments in certain areas of the humanities and social sciences—when they have not been nostalgic gestures toward that long-dissolved consensus about what an educated person should know. The growing diversity of our own profession has taught us to define the problem differently. The question is not how to impose a narrowly construed (white, Western, male, Christian) tradition on all comers. It is, rather, how to explore, celebrate, and understand the differing cultures and traditions that shape real life in these United States. We no longer view American literature, for instance, as many did even in 1958—an inferior and parvenu branch of British letters. Instead we have come to see the differences and interactions of the many cultures of America and have sought ways to organize our scholarship and teaching to illuminate that variety. We have tried to understand the "thickness" of the values and forms diverse cultures have generated.[15] In this connection, we may need to consider shifting our attention from the implicit alliances of speculative criticism with philosophy and linguistics and to affirm the fundamental correlation of our work with that of the historical disciplines.

During the past two decades, scholars in women's and minority studies have concentrated on identifying and editing key texts, charting historical and cultural relations, and examining critical methodologies and aesthetic standards to find inherent ideologies. Now attention has been turning to what was initially described as "integrating" the fruits of such scholarship in a wide range of departmental offerings. As the decades of scholarship proceeded, it became clear that adding a course in women writers, or even adding a few women or minority male writers to the survey course, would not adequately reflect the broad intellectual landscape that the new scholarship has revealed. Rather, basic reconstruction of departmental and general education curricula has seemed necessary, and a significant number of projects designed to achieve such transformations on individual campuses and in whole professional areas, perhaps hastened by the emergence of a female majority among undergraduates, have been funded by public and private foundations. It is far too early to know what impact these efforts will have. But it is important, I think, to note the directions of change that were set in motion by the social movements of the 1960s and 1970s.

Finally, however, we must return from the academic elaborations of those movements to their core of values. In 1958 the executive secretary of the MLA could portray the profession, and the association, as playing a critical role in preparing Americans to speak, think, and work effectively in other languages and cultures and thus in enabling them to carry out the international roles of the United States. Further, he could write optimistically that the purpose of the Cooperative English Program is "to develop in the members of the English teaching profession an awareness of their total responsibility to the educational system of this country in preparing students for participation in a complex democratic society and in transmitting the cultural heritage upon which that society is founded."[16] Most of all, he could locate our work in the humanist tradition, which not only involves the recovery of the past but emphasizes the evaluation of things recovered as a way of seeing, with clarity and wholeness, their present relevance. Similarly, in the 1920s, the new professors of American literature justified their study of that previously scorned subject as vital to understanding the character of an emerging world power.

Are such aspirations merely quaint and ill-founded, the rhetoric of an era as bygone—and as happily dispensed with—as La Belle Epoque? The rhetoric of our profession, like that of any group with special interests, takes on certain self-justifying qualities. Since a good deal of what we do has a narrow, sometimes antiquarian, cast to it, we pose ourselves in as broadly humanistic terms as we can and when possible hitch our special wagons of scholarship and criticism to the stars of national aspiration. Along that path, we follow *PMLA* to the University of Hue. And we grow cynical about the humanizing function of cultural study—after all, ran an argument I remember from the 1960s, the Nazis listened to Beethoven at Auschwitz and read Goethe at Berchtesgaden. So, the argument continued, perhaps we'd best stay with the forms and structures literature takes, the ways in which it encodes and transmits values, and leave the values themselves to other auspices.

I cannot be satisfied with that view, and I have to confess to a certain sympathy not with the politics of that 1958 portrait of our profession's value but with the statement's two underlying ideas: that our work can be significant in shaping consciousness and even behavior and, more fundamentally, that the importance of what we do derives from the social values we help to further. I do believe that teaching literature in ways that emphasize its impact on students' values and lives will provide widening opportunities for meaningful work.

The most profound teaching experience I had took place in a hot, echoing Mississippi church basement in 1964. I sat in a circle with a white friend and a group of young black students, ranging in age from perhaps twelve to nineteen, talking about Richard Wright's *Native Son*. The students had read the book hungrily, for they had nothing like it in their own schools. And in the freedom school class they struggled with what it made them learn, lessons not so much about their society and its racism, for that they knew, but about their own scary feelings toward it, toward us, toward themselves. "What did Bigger want?" I found myself asking, insistently. "What do you want?" The questions were, in a way, the conventional freedom school ones, and perhaps I was too easily satisfied with the answers. But the point for me, finally, wasn't the questions I asked or the answers I got, but the demands art was making on our lives, the nourishment it was providing our intellects. I had never encountered the tension of life in a literature classroom; neither, it seemed, had the students. But they insisted that it be there; otherwise, why read and talk of books?

Had I then known Frederick Douglass, I might next have asked them to read his *Narrative*. He writes of the fruit of his struggle to learn to read at about age twelve:

> I got hold of a book entitled "The Columbian Orator." Every opportunity I got, I used to read this book. Among much of other interesting matter, I found in it a dialogue between a master and his slave.... In ... [it] I met with one of Sheridan's mighty speeches on and in behalf of Catholic emancipation. These were choice documents to me. I read them over and over again with unabated interest. They gave tongue to interesting thoughts of my own soul, which had frequently flashed through my mind, and died away for want of utterance. The moral which I gained from the dialogue was the power of truth over the conscience of even a slaveholder. What I got from Sheridan was a bold denunciation of slavery, and a powerful vindication of human rights. The reading of these documents enabled me to utter my thoughts, and to meet the arguments brought forward to sustain slavery.... It was this everlasting thinking of my condition that tormented me. There was no getting rid of it. It was pressed upon me by every object within sight or hearing, animate or inanimate. The silver trump of freedom had roused my soul to eternal wakefulness. Freedom now appeared, to disappear no more forever.[17]

Douglass' point is not, of course, that reading has power in general; rather, it is that literacy and the particular works he read liberated his mind from the oppression of slavery. The moment he discovered—from his master, Mr. Auld—why a slave was forbidden to learn to read, he "understood the pathway from slavery to freedom" (p. 49). In our lives, what the social and political movements of the 1960s kindled was not simply a new set of academic disciplines—black studies, women's studies, and the like. Neither does the value of these endeavors derive just from their capacity to interest students or to reinvigorate our scholarship—however useful such functions may be—much less to provide new grist for the mills of criticism. The movements for change after the postwar political and intellectual ice age reconstituted a vision of possibility and developed concrete efforts to achieve justice and peace. The meaning of these efforts has more to do with Montgomery and the bus boycott than with the demand a decade later for black studies programs. The work of the 1960s was the equivalent of Douglass' work: his education of fellow slaves, his escape, his career as an abolitionist leader and speaker and human rights activist. Freedom school, 1834 or 1964, was about freedom. I watched my students go out in the afternoon to canvass the neighborhood for adults willing to risk their jobs and safety to register to vote. And I began to understand that it was the pulse of their work that had filled that basement, opened the pages of our books, and taught us to take seriously what it is we too can do.

Notes

1. MLA Commission on the Future of the Profession, "Report of the Commission on the Future of the Profession," *PMLA* 97 (1982), 940–956.

2. Fifty survey courses were compared in our survey. Black women writers simply do not appear in these fifty courses, except for one period in one course devoted to one poem by Phillis Wheatley. White women and black men are very little more in evidence. And, of course, a traditional stream of forty-two white male writers dominates each course. Only one woman, Emily Dickinson, and no black men appear among the twenty most popular writers. Mark Twain, for example, figures in thirty of the fifty courses (the other twenty mainly cover a different period); Dickinson in twenty. The next most popular women, Edith Wharton and Kate Chopin, appear in but eight of the fifty courses; the most popular black man, Ralph Ellison, in seven. Of the fifty-three most widely assigned authors, only six are women (in addition to Dickinson, Wharton, and Chopin, Sarah Orne Jewett and Anne Bradstreet show up in six courses and Flannery O'Connor appears in four) and four are black men (Ellison, already mentioned, and Richard Wright, Charles W. Chesnutt, and Langston Hughes, each assigned in four courses).

3. See, for example, Elizabeth Ammons, "Women and Realism in Turn-of-the-Century America: Notes Toward the Definition of a New School," paper, 1978.

4. Barbara Kessel, "Free, Classless, and Urbane?" in *The Politics of Literature,* Louis Kampf and Paul Lauter, eds. (New York: Pantheon, 1970), pp. 177–193.

5. See, for example, David M. Gordon, *Theories of Poverty and Underemployment* (Lexington, Mass.: Heath, 1972).

6. See Burton R. Clark, "The 'Cooling-Out' Function in Higher Education," *American Journal of Sociology* 65 (May 1960), 569–576.

7. "Formalism" may no longer be the most appropriate label for all that is now being put into the bottles of criticism. Certainly, poststructuralist, hermeneutic, speculative, philosophical, or theoretical modes of criticism are different from those of the New Criticism and its various successors. Still, even the practitioners of the newer modes of literary criticism have trouble knowing what to call it. It's rarely theory and, say philosophers, it isn't philosophy. Maybe it should be called Ludic, since it spends lots of time at play. I prefer "formalism" since it accepts the formalist stance by analyzing texts, including its own, primarily as autonomous objects isolated from their social origins or functions. Frank Lentricchia presents a similar view: "Whether New-Critical or poststructural, the formalist critic is concerned to demonstrate the history-transcending qualities of the text" [Frank Lentricchia, *After the New Criticism* (Chicago: University of Chicago Press, 1980), p. 185.]

8. When I was a graduate student at Yale, I worked as the TA for Charles Feidelson during the term—in 1957, I believe—in which he first replaced Stanley Williams as lecturer for the big introductory American literature course. A measure of how far the course moved away from traditional literary history toward the content of symbolism and American literature were the incredibly low grades earned by students who did not come to class but relied on the old cribs to prepare for the first exam.

9. Geoffrey Hartman, *Criticism in the Wilderness* (New Haven, Conn.: Yale University Press, 1980), p. 227.

10. In applying the work of Michel Foucault to the literary profession, Lentricchia makes a similar analysis.

> to probe the source of a speaker's authority is very quickly, as Foucault shows, to discover impregnable interlocking institutions which force expression into certain thoroughly architected places of confinement. A medical doctor will have a degree from a university which is overseen and accredited by professional associations and governmental agencies; furthermore, there will be an institutional site of speaking, a laboratory, a hospital, from which the doctor makes his discourse, and from which this discourse derives its legitimate source and point of application. . . . " The analogy with the literary critic is plain. He will, at a minimum, have a Ph.D. in literature, and preferably from one of a small group of celebrated universities. He will need a university appointment or a position at a small "respected" college. . . . And his books and articles will speak from institutionally sanctioned sites: a university press, a scholarly journal, but again this is only minimal, for to be critically *dans le vrai* in 1980 is to speak under the imprimatur of certain preferred presses and journals. Above all, certain doctrines will be paid reverence.
>
> Frank Lentricchia, *After the New Criticism* (Chicago:
> University of Chicago Press, 1980), pp. 198–99.

11. In *Criticism in the Wilderness* Hartman presents perhaps the best summary of the attack on speculative criticism as well as one of the most spirited cases for its autonomy. For example, he writes:

> There have been charges that a new elitism is creeping into literary studies. It is said to show itself in the growing breach between sensible literary commentary and hermeneutic cerebration. The objection bears this time not only on the verbal style of the interpreter but also on his general attitude toward the text. Instead of subordinating

himself to the literary work, he puffs his own activity until criticism becomes a rival of literature. Because of its allusive, dense, intertextual quality, this new *écriture* is hermetic rather than open.

These charges are based on simplification and historical ignorance. There is no reason why all criticism should be of the reporting or reviewing kind. Even if we prefer plain-style writing, should we reduce critical prose to one pattern or delude ourselves that a purely utilitarian or instrumentalist mode of communication is possible? (p. 236).

... criticism is a relatively free, all-purpose genre, and closely related to the personal or familiar essay. It is a literary genre, of a special sort, although I mean by this not that it should aim to be prose-poetry, but simply that it shares its text-milieu with other forms of literature while struggling with its own generic pressures of style.

(*Ibid.*, p. 233).

These are sensible and clarifying comments. Unfortunately, they perhaps gloss over the cultural significance of obscurantism in texts of any sort and the real social roles of critics.

12. Cf. Hartman, p. 245: "philosophical criticism ... has its own preferred writers, texts and positions. Nietzsche's emphasis on the will, for example, and Valéry's on the act of 'construction' that is common alike to imaginative and scientific thought are important. Anything that blows the cover of reified or superobjective thinking is important." And Hartman 299: "I am inclined to argue that every literary theory is based on the experience of a limited canon or generalizes strongly from a particular text-milieu."

13. The index to Hartman's *Criticism in the Wilderness,* for example, cites 230 men and seven women—and almost all the women are mentioned casually in the book. At least one other woman cited in the text doesn't make the index. I do not mean to single out Hartman; the same test applied to any one of his colleagues produces almost identical results. Oddly, criticism that argues for the autonomy of speculative writing almost never cites Virginia Woolf, and books that plead for the importance of theory hardly ever refer to Raymond Williams.

14. For a detailed version of this argument, see Louis Kampf and Paul Lauter, *The Politics of Literature* (New York: Pantheon, 1970), pp. 14–22.

15. That has been one of the objectives of the project on Reconstructing American Literature, which I have directed since its inception in 1980, and which produced in 1990 the canon-broadening *Heath Anthology of American Literature,* 2 vols. (Lexington, Mass.: D.C. Heath, 1990).

16. George Winchester Stone, Jr., "The Modern Language Association and the Shape of Things to Come," *PMLA* 73.5.2 (1959), 87.

17. Frederick Douglass, *Narrative of the Life and Frederick Douglass, An American Slave, Written by Himself* (New York: Signet, 1968), pp. 54–55.

Race and Gender in the Shaping
of the American Literary Canon
A Case Study from the Twenties

In its original form this chapter was delivered at a late-1970s forum sponsored by the Commission on the Status of Women in the Profession of the Modern Language Association. It had a kind of underground, mimeographed existence for a few years before seeing print in *Feminist Studies* in 1983. It has made its way and continues, I think, to be useful for those studying the canon. I have therefore not undertaken to change it.

Judith Fetterley has raised one important criticism of the piece. In her fine introduction to *Provisions: A Reader From 19th-Century American Women* (Bloomington: Indiana University Press, 1985, pp. 18–19) she argues that the exclusion of nineteenth-century women writers from the literary canon began far earlier than the 1920s, in fact during the nineteenth century itself. There is significant evidence to support that contention. John Macy's 1911 volume *The Spirit of American Literature,* for example, devotes its sixteen chapters to sixteen white men, though his "Preface" expresses admiration for the work of Jewett, Freeman and Wharton, and even passingly for Stowe. Brander Matthews' similar volume, *An Introduction to the Study of American Literature* (1896, rev. 1911), focuses fifteen chapters on individual white men and then devotes one to "other writers," including Whitman and Stowe. These very likely reflected the state of much academic opinion, though volumes like *An American Anthology, 1787–1900* (ed., Edmund Clarence Stedman, 1900) and Mildred Cabell Watkins' young adult primer, *American Literature* (1894) offer countervailing evidence. And, of course, as I outline in the article, other older academics like Fred Lewis Pattee and Arthur Hobson Quinn offered a far wider version of American letters. Fetterley thus provides what I think is a useful corrective to broad generalizations about academic canons, especially with respect to early and mid–nineteenth-century writers.

Feminist Studies 9, no. 3 (Fall 1983).

But the central point, in my view, is that dominantly male academic accounts of the American canon were far less weighty around the turn of the century than they became in and after the 1920s. In the earlier period, their authority was balanced—offset, I think—by that of other cultural institutions, from the vast network of women's literary clubs to the magazines that spoke to primarily female audiences. Later, these academics and their allies among the more popular critics became increasingly dominant and remained so for fifty years. Another way of saying this is that differing versions of an American canon contested for visibility and power during the decades prior to the First World War. After, an essentially new, academic canon emerged and exerted an increasingly hegemonic force in American culture. A more detailed study of the *institutions* critical to canon formation will help clarify these processes; this article remains a contribution to that goal.

The map of American literature which most of us have used was drawn sixty years ago. Its mountains, bumps and flats were charted; its deserts certified unfit for cultural habitation. Only during the past decade, in response to the movements for change of people of color and of women, have we begun to face the task—not systematically undertaken since the 1920s—of resurveying the territory.

That task, the revision of the literary canon, has been necessary because in the 1920s processes were set in motion that virtually eliminated black, white female, and all working-class writers from the canon. Institutional as well as theoretical and historiographic factors were involved in that exclusion, and I shall describe some of these shortly. But why is the literary canon of importance and what precisely was the history of its development in the 1920s?

I mean by the "American literary canon" that set of authors and works generally included in basic American literature college courses and textbooks, and those ordinarily discussed in standard volumes of literary history, bibliography, or criticism. Many such books are also available in widely marketed paperback series of "classics." Obviously, no conclave of cultural cardinals establishes a literary canon, but for all that it exercises substantial influence. For it encodes a set of social norms and values; and these, by virtue of its cultural standing, it helps endow with force and continuity. Thus, although we cannot ascribe to a literary canon the decline in attention to the concerns of women in the 1920s, the progressive exclusion of literary works by women from the canon suggested that such concerns were of lesser value than those inscribed in canonical books and authors. The literary canon is, in short, a means by which culture validates social power.

A study of the origins of the American literary canon, then, is not simply an antiquarian exercise. Changing the canon has over the past fifteen years become a major objective of literary practitioners of women's studies, black studies, and other "ethnic" studies—the academic wings of the social movements of the 1960s and 1970s. Fundamental alteration of the canon to include significant numbers of minority and white female writers will both reflect and help spur a widening revaluation of the significance of the experiences with which such writers are often concerned. But the American literary canon will be changed only by conscious literary and organizing efforts. This study is, therefore, part of the groundwork for that effort, an attempt to understand the processes which created the literary canon as most of us know it even today.

What was the history of the canon in the twenties? In his 1916 preface to *The Chief American Prose Writers,* Norman Foerster wrote that "the nine writers represented in this volume have become, by general consent, the American prose classics."[1] Over forty years later, with—I must believe—a certain sense of irony, Foerster wrote in the preface to *Eight American Writers:* "In the consensus of our time eight writers—Poe, Emerson, Thoreau, Hawthorne, Melville, Whitman, Mark Twain, and Henry James—constitute our 'American Classics.' "[2] Only Poe, Emerson, and Hawthorne were common to both lists. We are relatively familiar with the changes of taste that, largely in the decade following World War I, devalued Benjamin Franklin, Washington Irving, James Fenimore Cooper, William Cullen Bryant, James Russell Lowell, Henry Wadsworth Longfellow, Oliver Wendell Holmes, as well as John Greenleaf Whittier, Sidney Lanier, William Dean Howells, to name but a few. Those changes of taste also rescued Melville from obscurity, elevated Twain and James, as well as Thoreau—particularly certain of their works—and eventually focused serious attention on Emily Dickinson. Less familiar is the literary or canonical history of white women and black and working-class writers of both sexes.[3]

The 1920s witnessed, as we know, a flourishing of literary work by black as well as by white writers. African-Americans, as is often forgotten, had previously produced a substantial body of literary art, in the form of songs, tales, and slave narratives, as well as in more "formal" styles.[4] Newly crowded into urban ghettos, pushed back from the activism of a decade of struggle for civil and political rights, subjected to white curiosity about their supposed "exotic" qualities, black authors and singers generated a significant literary renaissance in the 1920s. Substantial collections of black writings were issued in that decade and during the thirties,[5] and at least some black writers managed to make a living from their trade. These facts were in no way reflected in the teaching of American literature, in general anthologies, or in most critical discussions by whites of the literature of the United States.

It would have been no great revolution to include black writers; even Edmund Clarence Stedman had printed five spirituals and six poems by Paul Laurence Dunbar in his *American Anthology, 1787–1900* (Boston: Houghton Mifflin Co., 1900). Nevertheless, of twenty-one major classroom anthologies (and their numerous revised editions) produced between 1917 and 1950, nine contained no works by black artists; three included only a few spirituals; four contained one black writer each (Dunbar; Phillis Wheatley, twice; Richard Wright); two printed some spirituals and one black writer (W.E.B. Dubois; Countee Cullen—who is dropped in a revised edition). Only three somewhat unusual anthologies included the work of more than one black writer—never more than three—as well as a few spirituals or work songs.[6] General and classroom poetry anthologies reveal a similar pattern. Conrad Aiken's Modern Library volumes, *Twentieth-Century American Poetry* (1927, 1944) and *A Comprehensive Anthology of American Poetry* (1929, 1944) included no black poets, although the latter was advertised as "a newly edited anthology that includes every American poet of note from the 17th century to the present day. . . . " Oscar Williams' "Little Treasuries" (Scribner's) of *Modern Poetry* and of *American Poetry* (1946, 1952) similarly omitted black poets, although the latter did include a section devoted to "American Indian Poetry." F. O. Matthiessen's 1950 version of the *Oxford Book of American Verse* eliminated the one black poet, Dunbar, who had been included in Bliss Carman's 1927 version.

The most notable exceptions to this pattern are Alfred Kreymborg's 1930 *Lyric America* (Tudor Publishing; also called *An Anthology of American Poetry*), which included the work of seven black men, and Louis Untermeyer's *Modern American Poetry* (Harcourt, Brace & Co.). Untermeyer's editing exemplifies the rise and fall of interest in black writers. His first two editions (1919 and 1921) contained poems by Dunbar, joined in the 1925 version by Countee Cullen, James Weldon Johnson, Claude McKay, and Alex Rogers, and then later by Langston Hughes and Jean Toomer. By the 1942 sixth edition, however, only Dunbar, Johnson, Cullen, and Hughes remained; the seventh edition witnessed the elimination of Dunbar. The general and poetry anthologies uniformly omitted all black women with the solitary and rare exception of Phillis Wheatley.

Similarly, Jay Hubbell's 987-page history, *The South in American Literature: 1607–1900*, consciously excludes black writers as "northern" and outside the book's chronology, although it includes other distinctly northern and twentieth-century writers. The index conveys the operative view of African-American writing: apart from a few miscellaneous entries, the index is limited to "See also Abolitionists, folk songs, folklore, and slavery."[7] More recent anthologies and critical works do, of course, include some black writers, but fundamental organizing principles have seldom been altered to accommodate the fact that the significant literary work of African Americans cannot be understood as an expression of "European culture" in an "American environment"—to use Norman Foerster's formulation.[8]

The position of white women writers in the formation of the canon is rather more complex: some perspective is gained by examining the work of one of the earliest professors of American literature, Fred Lewis Pattee. Pattee's anthology, *Century Readings for a Course in American Literature*, first published in 1919, reflects his appreciation of women writers; it includes work by Harriet Beecher Stowe, Mary Wilkins Freeman, Sarah Orne Jewett, Helen Hunt Jackson, Rose Terry Cooke, Constance Fenimore Woolson, and even Emma Lazarus, among many other women writers. In *The New American Literature* (1930), Pattee praised Willa Cather, Edith Wharton, Ellen Glasgow, and Zona Gale, in particular. "The work of these women marks the highest reaches to which the novel of characterization and manners has attained in America during our period. Perhaps no literary phenomenon in our history," he continued, "has been more noteworthy than this feminine assumption of leadership. The creation of fiction in most of its areas has proven to be an art adapted peculiarly for the powers of women. Feminine success has, however, come also from another peculiar fact: woman has surpassed her male competitors in workmanship, in artistry, in the quality of work toiled over and finished—she has been compelled to do this because of an age-old conception or prejudice. Her success," Pattee concludes, "has raised fiction-writing during the period to the rank of a new regular profession for women."[9] A few years later, another member of the older generation of professors, Arthur Hobson Quinn, in his 1936 *American Fiction,* devoted chapters to Gale, Mary Austin, Dorothy Canfield, and Susan Glaspell, as well as substantial sections to Cooke, Stowe, Elizabeth Stoddard, Rebecca Harding Davis, and Elizabeth Stuart Phelps.[10]

Nevertheless, the first edition of Howard Mumford Jones and Ernest E. Leisy's *Major American Writers,* which was issued in 1935, contains no work by women whatsoever, although it includes such luminaries as William Byrd, Philip Freneau, Bret Harte, and Sidney Lanier, as well as all the traditional schoolroom poets of New England. In later editions, Jones and Leisy admitted Dickinson to their canon, joined in solitude by Glasgow.[11] By 1948, when the National Council of Teachers of English (NCTE) reviewed American literature in the college curriculum, only three women appeared in the ninety syllabi of survey courses studied. Dickinson appeared in twenty-four of these courses; that placed her seventeenth on the list, tied with Holmes and Cooper, but behind Whittier, Lowell, Bryant, Longfellow, and others. The other women were the last two writers listed; Wharton (number thirty-six) appeared in five courses of the ninety surveyed; Cather (number thirty-seven) appeared four times. Before both of them came Frank Norris, Hamlin Garland, Theodore Dreiser, Mather (presumably Cotton), William Bird, Abraham Lincoln, Bret Harte, and Jonathan Edwards.[12] Ben W. Fuson's 1952 study of twenty-seven American literature anthologies shows significant representation of only six women among seventy authors whose works are substantially covered. In all, women represent no more than 13.7 percent and as little as 3.2 percent of the writers in these anthologies, on average about 8 percent. The proportion of women is often related to the proportion of what Fuson calls "borderline" or non-*belles lettres* items.[13] One 1950 collection, edited by Lyon Norman Richardson, G. H. Orians, and H. R. Brown, recognized that a need already existed for giving "special attention to a reconsideration of the works of our women authors."[14]

These academic opinions and statistics reflect a cultural reality which had developed perhaps a decade before. Interest in many of the novelists praised by Pattee and Quinn had begun to decline some time before the critics of the 1920s wrote about them. After all, to cite a reversed instance of the lag between social change, cultural consciousness, and academic revision, it took fifteen years after *Brown v. Board of Education* and a decade after the sit-ins began to achieve even token representation of black writers in contemporary anthologies.[15] The essentially nineteenth-century tastes of Pattee and Quinn and their concerns for gentility did not survive the 1920s.[16] Since women were seen as the preservers of gentility and women writers as its promoters, the change in literary taste helped ensure their exclusion from the canon.

Thus, as the NCTE survey accurately shows, by the end of the 1950s, one could study American literature and read no work by a black writer, few works by women except Dickinson and perhaps Marianne Moore or Katherine Anne Porter, and no work about the lives or experiences of working-class people.

How can we account for such a development? Three important factors may be responsible: the professionalization of the teaching of literature, the development of an aesthetic theory that privileged certain texts, and the historiographic organization of the body of literature into conventional "periods" and "themes."

The proliferation of American literary anthologies that began in the twenties was a product of the expansion of higher education generally. More particularly the anthologies reflected that American literature had become a legitimate subject for academic study only after the First World War. Courses in American literature had seldom been taught in schools and colleges before the last decade of the nineteenth century; classroom anthologies and American literature texts began to appear only after the turn of the century. The dominant view of the cultivated was that American letters were a branch— a shaky one at that—of the British stock.[17] In the decade prior to 1915, there were four articles on American literature out of perhaps 250 in *The Publications of the Modern Language Association (PMLA)*. The American Literature Group, now one of the Modern Language Association's largest, began in 1921 with a meeting attended by only a handful of professors. By 1928, however, that group had been responsible for publishing the influential *Reinterpretation of American Literature;* and by 1929, for starting the magazine *American Literature*. Although the subject remained something of an academic stepchild, it was a major topic of concern for literati from H. L. Mencken to Virginia Woolf.

The survey courses, the anthologies, the professional specialization all contributed to the academic institutionalization of reading choices. What had been the function of individuals, of families, or of literary clubs and certain magazines—choosing books to be remembered and read, building culture and taste—became the purview of the classroom. Even on college campuses prior to 1920, and certainly in communities, a good deal of literary study, particularly of contemporary authors, was carried on within literary societies, mainly female. (The campus men's societies were concerned primarily with debating and oratory; off campus men's clubs, whatever else they were, were *not* literary.) My own research indicates that on campus in the 1920s reading choices were increasingly "suggested" by professors; indeed, formal courses began to absorb what had earlier been talked about "in society." By the 1930s, if they still existed, campus literary societies met to play bridge and to get up theatre parties. Community literary societies continued, much diminished, but the taste of participants was likely to have already been formed in college. Thus, in significant measure, influence over reading shifted before the 1930s from women who were not academic professionals to academics, the great majority of whom were white and male. And reading choices moved significantly away from the range of female writers—Mary Austin to Sigrid Undset—who had been a staple of most women's literary clubs.[18]

Demographic factors were also at work, as historian Laurence Veysey has pointed out. The proportion "of the mature working-age population in America" who were college and university professors and librarians was rising "spectacularly" in the decades leading to 1920—especially in relation to older, static learned professionals, like doctors, lawyers, and the clergy. Although they constituted only a tiny portion of people at work, professors had enormously larger impact "as the universities increasingly took over training for a wide variety of prestigious occupations. . . . " In fact, Veysey writes,

> the social effect of intellectual specialization [occurring in universities among other areas of American life] was to transfer authority, most critically over the printed word and what was taught in colleges to sons and daughters of the elite, away from the cultivated professions considered as an entirety and toward a far smaller, specially trained segment within them, those who now earned Ph.D. degrees. . . . Concretely, this meant vesting such authority in a group that, as of 1900, numbered only a few hundred persons spread across the humanistic fields. The immediate effect was thus the intensification of elitism as it was transferred onto a new academic basis. A double requirement was now imposed—intellectual merit, at least of a certain kind, defined far more rigorously, as well as a continuing expectation of social acceptability.[19]

In short, the professoriat exercised increasing control of the definition of a "literate" reader, including those who were to become the next generation's writers.[20]

The social base of that professoriat was small. The professors, educators, critics, the arbiters of taste of the 1920s, were, for the most part, college-educated white men of Anglo-Saxon or northern European origins. They came, that is, from that tiny, elite portion of the population of the United States which, around the turn of the century, could go to college. Through the first two decades of the new century, this dominant elite had faced a quickening demand for some power and control over their lives from Slavic, Jewish, Mediterranean, and Catholic immigrants from Europe, as well as from black immigrants from the rural South. Even women had renewed their demand for the vote, jobs, control over their bodies. The old elite and their allies moved on a variety of fronts, especially during and just after the First World War, to set the terms on which these demands would be accommodated. They repressed, in actions like the Prohibition Amendment and the Palmer raids, the political and social, as well as the cultural, institutions of immigrants and of radicals. They reorganized schools and professionalized elementary and secondary school curriculum development, in significant measure as a way to impose middle-class American "likemindedness" on a heterogeneous, urban, working-class population.[21] Similarly, calling it "professionalization," they reorganized literary scholarship and teaching in ways that not only asserted a male-centered culture and values for the college-educated leadership, but also enhanced their own authority and status as well.[22]

The Modern Language Association, for example, underwent a major reorganization just after the First World War, the effect of which was to concentrate professional influence in the hands of groups of specialists, most of whom met at the annual convention. The convention thus took on much greater significance, practically and symbolically, in terms of defining professional leadership. As professionalism replaced gentility, the old all-male "smoker" at the convention was discontinued. With it also disappeared a female and, on occasion, modestly feminist institution: the ladies' dinner. We do not fully know how, or even in this instance whether, such institutions provided significant support for women scholars, nor do we know what was lost with their disappearance in the 1920s.[23] Clearly, women were left without any significant organizational base within the newly important convention. For when, in 1921, specialized groups were established for MLA conventions, women's roles in them were disproportionately small, minor, and largely confined.[24] If the men gave up the social institution that had helped sustain their control, they replaced it with professional authority in the new groups. Not only were women virtually excluded from leadership positions in them and given few opportunities to read papers, but they also appear to have been pushed toward—as men were certainly pushed away from—subject areas considered "peripheral" to the profession. For example, folk materials and works *by* women became particularly the province *of* women—as papers, dissertation topics, and published articles illustrate.[25]

As white women were excluded from the emerging scholarly power structures, and blacks—female or male—were kept almost entirely ghettoized in black colleges, "their subjects," women and blacks, remained undeveloped in a rapidly developing profession. For example, in the first ten years of its existence, *American Literature* published 24 full articles (as distinct from Notes and Queries or Reviews) by women scholars out of a total of 208. Nine of those appeared in the first two volumes, and a number of women published more than once. An article on Dickinson appeared in volume 1, and others in volumes 4 and 6. These apart, the *only* article on a woman writer until volume 10 was one on American comments, mostly by men, on George Sand. In volume 10 one finds a piece, by a male scholar, on Cather, as well as another trying to show that Ann Cotton derived her material from husband John. It is not, I should add, that the journal confined itself to "major" writers or to authors from the early or mid-nineteenth century. Quite the contrary, it ran pieces on stalwarts like John Pendleton Kennedy, not to speak of *Godey's Ladies' Book,* as well as articles dealing with a number of twentieth-century male authors.

While professionalization was thus erecting institutional barriers against women, their status was being attacked in other ways. Joan Doran Hedrick has shown how the ideology of domesticity and the bogey of "race suicide," which reemerged around the turn of the century, was used during the next thirty years to attack women teachers, both the proverbial spinster school-marm and the female college professor.[26] The extent to which such attacks arose from the pressure of job competition, general political conservatism, antisuffrage backlash, or other factors is not yet clear. It was true, however, that women had not only been competing more and more effectively for positions in the humanities, but also that the predominance of women students in undergraduate literature courses had long worried the male professoriat. In 1909, for example, the chairman of the MLA's Central Division had devoted his address to the problem of "Coeducation and Literature." He wondered whether the predominance of women taking literary courses "may not contribute to shape the opinion that literature is preeminently a study for girls, and tend to discourage some men. . . . This is not yet saying," he continued, "that the preference of women turns away that of men. There are many factors to the problem. But it looks that way." How, he asked, can we deal with the problem that the "masculine ideal of culture" has largely rejected what the modern languages, and we as its professors, have to offer? "What may we teachers do more or better than we have done to gain for the humanities as represented by literature a larger place in the notion of masculine culture?"[27]

Something of an answer is provided in an unusually frank way in the *Annual Reports* of Oberlin College for 1919–20. In the section on the faculty, Professor Jelliffe, on behalf of Bibliography, Language, Literature, and Art, urged the hiring of an additional teacher of composition. He writes:

> In my opinion the new instructor, when appointed, should be a man. Of sixteen sections in Composition only three are at present being taught by men instructors. This is to discredit, in the opinion of our students, the importance of the subject, for despite the excellent teaching being done by the women of the English faculty, the students are quick to infer that the work is considered by the faculty itself of less importance than that to which the men devote their time.[28]

Such ideas, the institutional processes I have described, and other historical forces outside the scope of the paper, gradually eroded the gains women had made in higher education in the decades immediately following the turn of the century. By the early 1920s, women were earning 16 percent of all doctorates; that proportion gradually declined (except for the war years) to under 10 percent in the 1950s. Similarly, the proportion of women in the occupational category of college presidents, professors, and instructors rose from 6.4 percent in 1900 to 32.5 percent around 1930, but subsequently declined to below 22 percent by 1960.[29] The proportion of women earning advanced degrees in the modern languages and teaching these subjects in colleges was, of course, always somewhat higher, but the decline affected those fields in a similar way. Because more women were educated in these fields, they were particularly vulnerable in the 1930s to cutbacks ostensibly instituted to preserve jobs for male "breadwinners" or to nepotism regulations newly coined to spread available positions among the men. Not surprisingly, by the 1950s only 19 percent of the doctorates being earned in the modern languages were awarded to women,[30] a proportion higher than in fields like sociology, history, or biology, but significantly lower than it had been thirty years earlier. As a result, the likelihood of one's encountering a female professor even in literature—and especially at elite male or coeducational institutions—was perhaps even slighter than the chances of encountering a female writer.

Blacks, female or male, faced a color line that professionalization did nothing to dispel. Black professors of literature were, for the most part, separated into their own professional organization, the College Language Association, and into positions at segregated black colleges. The color line persisted in *American Literature* so far as articles on black writers were concerned, until 1971, when the magazine printed its first piece, on James Weldon Johnson. The outlook apparently shared by *American Literature's* editors comes clearest in a brief review (10 [1938]: 112–113) by Vernon Loggins, then at Columbia, of Benjamin Brawley's collection of *Early Negro American Writers*. "The volume . . . gives a hint of American Negro literature before Dunbar, but scarcely more than a hint. Yet it should be of practical value in American literature courses *in Negro colleges*. Professor Brawley obviously had such an aim in mind in making the compilation" (emphasis added). Over the years a few articles appeared on images of blacks in the writings of white authors, but in general, as such reviews and notes on scholarly articles make clear, those interested in black writers were effectively referred to the *Journal of Negro History* or to the *College Language Association Journal*.[31]

Although the existence of such black professional organizations and periodicals reflected the pervasiveness of institutional racism in American life, such black-defined groups and magazines like the *Crisis* had at least the advantage of providing to black writers and scholars outlets for and encouragement of their work. Women, especially white professional writers, faced rather a different problem in this period: one can observe a significant shift in cultural authority from female-defined to male-defined institutions—in symbolic terms, one might say, from women's literary societies to *Esquire* magazine. The analogy may, at first, seem farfetched, but it is probably more accurate than the cartoon view of women's clubs with which we have lived since the twenties. In fact, the taste of the older generation of "genteel" professors and magazine editors largely accorded with that of the female literary clubs; the outlook of the new professoriat and *Esquire*, the *Playboy* of its day, largely coincided, at least with respect to the subjects and writers of fiction, as well as to certain conceptions of male camaraderie and culture.[32] To understand why, we must now turn to the aesthetic theories which helped to shape the canon.

Two aesthetic systems, ultimately in conflict, came to dominate literary thought in the 1920s and 1930s. One set of critics viewed literature—or at least some books—as important to reconstructing a "usable past" consonant with the new role of the United States as a dominating world power. To one degree or another, all the scholars who developed American literature as a field of study were devoted to this objective. Another critical school emphasized the "aesthetic" or formal qualities of literature—literature as *belles lettres*—above whatever historical interest it might have, or even the values presumably conveyed by it. Indeed, later formalist critics came to disparage the very idea that art—or even criticism—"conveyed" anything at all. Both nationalist and formalist aesthetics, however disparate, produced a *narrowing* of the canon.

The American literature professors of the twenties were, as I have suggested, a serious group that asserted national responsibilities. And they presented the tasks of American literature in broad moral terms. In his introduction to *The Reinterpretation of American Literature,* Norman Foerster posed the work of literary professionals in the context of the international role of the United States. "The power of America renders it perilous to remain in the dark as to what she really is." Literature would reveal our culture, for, as Harry Hayden Clark added, "in the life of the past, as mirrored in literature, there exists a reasonable and dependable guide for a troubled present. . . . "[33] For such aspirations, a focus on domesticity and family, on education and marriage, even on "love and money," to use Jane Austen's formula, would not do, they felt. The tension for the "new woman" between work life and family life would also not suffice as a topic of high national seriousness. Women were liberated, it was said, by the vote, a relaxed style of dress, labor-saving devices, a new sexual openness. They could enter most male professions—it was up to them. So the concerns of "feminist fiction" were no longer relevant.

Besides, a central problem with American literature, or so some seemed to feel, was its "feminization." Joseph Hergesheimer, a then-popular if rapidly dated novelist, had attacked "The Feminine Nuisance in American Literature" in a *Yale Review* article of 1921. Literature in the United States, he claimed (pp. 719–720), "is being strangled with a petticoat," written primarily for women, without a "grain of masculine sand." Hergesheimer's definition of the truly masculine hero provides, in its crude exaggerations, a useful reflection of a developing literary ideal.

> I must return to the word vitality, for that alone explains my meaning: such men have perceptibly about them the air, almost the shock, of their force. It is a quality, at bottom, indescribable, without definition, subconscious; and we can do no more than recognize its presence. Such men are attended by a species of magic; they go in direct lines through the impotent turnings of sheep-like human tracks; and as their stay, they have principally that unshakable self-confidence which is condemned as conceit by lesser spirits. It is, therefore, unavoidable that the man I am describing should be, from the absolute standard of normality, abnormal; any wide imagination, any magical brain, is abnormal, with necessities, pressures, powers, altogether beyond the comprehension of the congenital clerk. . . . Does anyone

think that, laying an arm across the shoulders of his devoted wife, he would explain how he had repudiated the dishonest offer of the Mikado of Japan? Can you see him playing auction bridge in a room twittering like an aviary?[34]

The Bookman, more than any other periodical responsive to the interests of women readers and literary clubs, quickly ran a response from "the feminine nuisance."[35] Frances Noyes Hart chided Hergesheimer as ungrateful, in view of his large female readership, and pointed out that she knew of

> no group of masculine authors who deal less in manufactured sunshine or specious sweetness and light than the large group of women who are now at the head of their profession in England and America—Ethel Sidgwick, Willa Sibert Cather, Rebecca West, May Sinclair, Edith Wharton, Katharine Fullerton Gerould, Dorothy Richardson, Anne Douglas Sedgwick, Sheila Kaye-Smith, Clemence Dane—I take the names at random; there are at least a score more. They face life in varied ways—some nervewracked and tense, some grateful and ironic, some lusty and ruthless, some shadowed and mysterious, some bitter and defiant—but unquestionably they all face it, with scant truckling to any public thirsting for spurious joy and the conventional happy ending.

By the end of the decade, however, even *The Bookman* had joined the antifemale parade, featuring in its March 1929 (vol. 69) issue a piece by another forgotten novelist, Robert Herrick, somewhat more subtly called "A Feline World." Herrick begins with what he conceives to be a discovery: that younger women novelists have come to "disregard the tradition that this is primarily a man's world and have taken to describing boldly their own primary interests, among themselves, for themselves." He does not, he claims, "deplore" the tendency; rather, he misses "the stir of the old-time, standard fiction" of men, "above all, the talk about politics and bawdy and religion and the reorganizing of our bad, old world . . . mature talk even when the characters were very young" (p. 2). George Meredith, Herrick argues, did not confine his fiction "to the tea table or boudoir or night club . . . ," and Hardy was not solely preoccupied "with emotional subtleties, subjective illusions. Certainly never with purely social reactions and complications. . . . " With [Arnold] Bennett, Herrick continues on page 3, "we have moved farther along toward feminization. . . . even the males are feminized; they act and usually talk like women and their chief preoccupations are the petty daily affairs belonging in general to the home."

Herrick's final argument, in a magazine read mainly by women, takes an ugly turn. Women novelists are, he claims, particularly occupied with sex, not bluntly, like their brothers, but with more erotic effect. "Women," he continues, "know the neurotic sides of sex, which do not eventuate in either marriage or maternity, as well as what once was called (with a hush) the perverted side, the wooing of one's own sex. A disturbing number of recent stories by women deal with this taboo and are not overly vague in the handling of it. We must assume that it interests many of their readers." Thus the interest of women in women novelists becomes primarily a manifestation of lesbianism. It is only a short step from there to using the label "feline" to cover everything that manly intellectuals and activists must deplore; the female, "feline" world becomes identified with intellectual and social reaction, with a rejection of idealism and experimentation, and even with militarism. To be sure, the absurdities of Hergesheimer and Herrick can be dismissed along with Hawthorne's competitive jealousy of that "damned mob of scribbling women." Yet they express a widely held set of attitudes, both about women generally and about art. They reflect the other side of the professoriat's concern that a truly American art be attractive to, embody the values of, masculine culture. For, as professors and male novelists seemed to perceive it, the problems of the United States were not to be encountered over the cup of proverbial tea, in reading novelists at once genteel and sensual, or in fretting over village life in Maine or Louisiana. America needed the grand encounters with nature of Melville or even Thoreau, the magical abnormalities of Ahab, the deeper possibilities for corruption Twain and even James in their different ways established. I do not want to overdraw the picture. But as Hergesheimer and Herrick illustrate, I am afraid that I could not. The strenuous nationalism of even the most professional scholars, the masculinist attitudes of otherwise refined novelists, defined the issues for the art of the time as fundamentally distinct from the concerns of the domestic sphere which, it was insisted, were to occupy most women, including most female writers.

These attacks on "gentility" and "domesticity" centered, for the most part, on the subject matter of an earlier generation and sought to substitute a more "masculine" content for art. Still, academic scholars continued to view art as a guide to conduct, although the conduct and values being extolled were quite changed. On the other hand, the generation of literary critics who, following T.S. Eliot, began to come to prominence in the 1920s, were doubtful—if not altogether suspicious—of the power of art to shape behavior at all. Indeed, these writers, led by the American "New Critics," felt that civilized values were well on the way to being overwhelmed by "mass society," and that the functions of the artist and the "man of letters" in the modern world were much more defensive than shaping, protective of the remnants of culture rapidly being ground under. What could be defended, if anything, was the value of art itself, and what needed emphasis was not the behavior a work of art promoted, or its subject matter as such, but its language and form, which represented and sustained the best achievements of human creativity.

On the face of it there appears to be no reason why such a formalist aesthetic should narrow the canon in the ways I have indicated. But there are a number of reasons why that was in fact the result. There is, first, the basis on which the "best" achievements of human creativity are defined. Allen Tate, for example, argues that the presence of "tension"—"the full organized body of all the extension and intension that we can find in it"—accounts for the quality of great poetry.[36] Such a definition sets at a discount art which strives for simplicity, transparency, and unity in its effects.[37] Obviously, it leads to the preference of "A Valediction: Forbidding Mourning" over "Roll,

Jordan." No doubt, the spiritual lacks the complex language and ambiguity of John Donne's poem; but then "A Valediction" has never inspired many thousands to survive tyranny. Formalist criteria of excellence developed in the 1920s by critics like John Crowe Ransom, Cleanth Brooks, R.P. Blackmur, and Tate have emphasized complexity, ambiguity, tension, irony, and similar phenomena; such standards are by no means casual. They place a premium on the skills of the literary interpreter: *He* shall unpack the ambiguities and tensions to the uninitiated students, the products of a degraded "mass education." Such criteria are thus directly related to the status of the literary critic. To say it another way: what the American Scholar may have lost with the decline of the ability of the educated classes to establish standards of conduct shall be rescued by reinvesting "the man of letters in the modern world" with authority at least over standards of language.

> "His critical responsibility is thus . . . the recreation and the application of literary standards. . . . His task is to preserve the integrity, the purity, and the reality of language wherever and for whatever purpose it may be used. . . . The true province of the man of letters in nothing less (as it is nothing more) than culture itself. . . . It is the duty of the man of letters to supervise the culture of language, to which the rest of culture is subordinate, and to warn us when our language is ceasing to forward the ends proper to man. The end of social man is communion in time through love, which is beyond time."[38]

Such critical "authority" over culture has, to be sure, proved illusory, but with respect to the canon it did play a significantly narrowing role.

A second and closely related factor leading to a narrowed canon derives from the critical emphasis upon "masterpieces," rather than "tendencies," to use Van Wyck Brooks's 1918 formulation. Focusing on the formal qualities of discrete works of art gradually eroded the earlier scholars' concern for tendencies, for the social and cultural context within which all art is born.[39] In the late 1930s, anthologies like Jones and Leisy's *Major American Writers* began to reflect the narrowing focus to fewer "major" works by fewer "major" writers. Successive editions of the highly successful anthology edited by Norman Foerster also show the influence of this trend: between the second and third editions such writers as Stowe, Richard Henry Dana, William Gilmore Simms, Mary Noailles Murfree, Wharton, and Dorothy Canfield Fisher were eliminated, as were most of the "cultural" pieces, including excerpts from the Bay Psalm Book and the New England Primer. Obviously, critics did not propose as a dictum that only white men could be "major" writers, but it was preeminently the works of white males like themselves that they selected.[40] Further, the tide toward certain "masterpieces," once it set in, could hardly be reversed except through the intervention of forces from outside the literary profession. For two generations or more, literary professionals, brought up under the influence of formalist criticism, knew little or nothing of the work of writers outside the hardening canon and thus had few alternative models—or standards—for determining noncanonical masterpieces, much less for understanding tendencies.

Both critics and scholars of the period would no doubt have joined in rejecting such an argument on the grounds that literary masterpieces have the ability to create their own audiences, to break through existing limits of taste and perception and to open readers to new experience. In some measure they would be correct in this rather Romantic conception of the power of art. Yet people survive, in part, by excluding from awareness much of what presses on their senses. They selectively screen out these most recent victims of starvation, that student's persistent difficulties, this critic's passion for Gwendolyn Brooks, that writer's evocation of plantation or domestic experience. It is natural to do so—one cannot physically or psychologically respond to all stimuli. But *what* one screens away is by no means natural or inevitable. Rather, it is a product of particularities of nationality and time, of class and race and gender, as well as elements of private life.

The arbiters of taste, scholars and critics alike were, as I have pointed out, drawn from a narrow stratum of American society. Their experience seldom included the lives and work about which black writers, for example, wrote. Indeed, upper-class white Americans in the 1920s acknowledged the lives of black people, and the work of black writers, only in "their place"— as "exotic," like a taste for Pernod or jazz, a quaint expression of the "folk." It was very well to visit Harlem, but decidedly inappropriate to include blacks in the anthology or the classroom, much less in the Modern Language Association. As we have come to learn with the overthrow of the doctrine of "separate, but equal," if people need not be dealt with physically, socially, seriously, their experiences are not likely to be seen as providing a basis for significant art.[41] The literary canon does not, after all, spring from the brow of the master critic; rather, it is a social construct. As our understanding of what is trivial or important alters in response to developments in the society, so our conception of the canon will change. But that perception has itself been forced on us only by the movements for social change of the 1960s and 1970s. Sixty years ago, the dominant scholars and critics were able to dismiss lives and art beyond their experience, concentrating instead on scrutinizing with considerable ingenuity a narrow range of work. But part of the price was a constricted canon.

The third factor on which I shall touch is historiographic: the conventional definitions of periods in American literature, which were, in the twenties, formulated by men such as Foerster, Brooks, and Clark. Many generations of their students were trained in a sequence involving the "Puritan Mind," "Romanticism," the "Frontier Spirit," the "Rise of Realism"—categories which provide the basis for *The Reinterpretation of American Literature*. Such phrases have been widely, if loosely, used, both as historical frameworks and as cultural classifications, and while their popularity diminished in some respects with the rise of formalist criticism and the decline of literary history after the 1930s, they have remained surprisingly influential. They shape significantly the ways in which we think about culture, emphasizing works that fit given frameworks, obscuring those which do not.

In the 1920s, literary historians acknowledged that their work was perhaps a decade behind that of American historians; they used the historians' structures to frame the study of literature and thus the canon. A similar situation exists today: feminist and Third World historians have demonstrated that historical epochs are experienced differently by women and men, by whites and by people of color. To quote Gerda Lerner, for example:

> neither during or after the American revolution nor in the age of Jackson did women share in the broadening out of opportunities and in the political democratization experienced by men. On the contrary, women in both periods experienced status loss and a restriction of their choices as to education or vocation, and had new restraints imposed upon their sexuality, at least by prescription.[42]

The usual divisions of history according to wars or political events turn out to be more relevant to the lives of men than of women; moreover, such divisions are often used less to understand the dynamics of history than as convenient pigeonholes in which to place works in syllabi or anthologies. To review the canon, we must create a usable past, as Brooks advised in 1918. Simply eliminating historical frameworks, as some anthologists and scholars have done in response to the inadequacies of traditional categories, leaves us viewing discrete works in a historical void. New categories can bring into focus, rather than obscure, the experience and culture of people of color and of white women. They allow us to illuminate the interrelationships of culture and other historical forces. And from a practical standpoint, they help us construct new courses and anthologies—like that developed by the project on Reconstructing American Literature and published by D. C. Heath, designed to present and to validate the full range of the literatures of America. Finally, alternative categories provide useful perspectives on the limitations of the traditional formulations by suggesting how different a canon posed in their terms would be. But in a way, we have little choice about proposing different literary categories, for the seams of the old ones simply cannot contain the multitude of previously ignored literary works.

As a historical category, "Puritanism" has been used to exaggerate the significance of New England, and particularly the male, theocratic portion of it, within the complex tableau of American colonial experience. Focusing on Puritanism, a socioreligious construct, seems largely to have led to the study of the ideology by which a narrow group of male divines construed and confirmed their dominant roles in New England society. Implicitly, the category did not readily lend itself to exploration of the broader contexts of New England family, political and business life, much less to comparisons with cultural development in other English as well as non-English settlements. Emphasizing Puritanism as religious ideology distorted understanding of the witchcraft trials, Anne Hutchinson, colonial family and sex life, and the sys-

tematic extermination of "Indians." Imposing the label of "Puritanism" on
the culture of early New England also obscures the important dynamic of
colonization and decolonization, possibly a more helpful tool for framing
colonial American history, as V. F. Calverton pointed out sixty years ago.[43]

The colonies embodied many now-familiar aspects of settler societies.
These included exploitative, if not altogether genocidal, attitudes toward the
indigenous population, provincial exaggerations of imported social patterns,
and increasingly ambivalent relationships to the parent society. These aspects
were reflected in colonial culture, from the myths about the native Americans
and the captivity narratives, to the terrors of Charles Brockden Brown, and
the late-coming calls for literary decolonization contained in works like Emerson's "The American Scholar" and Margaret Fuller's "American Literature."[44] I do not pose colonization and decolonization as the only "correct"
historical frameworks for analyzing seventeenth- and eighteenth-century
white culture. The terms do seem to me, though, a useful way to understand
the general development of culture in the young United States, as well as to
illuminate the social origins and functions of Puritan intellectual writings
generally examined only in relation to one another. And the concept of
colonization and decolonization contains, I think, some inherent intellectual
safeguards against the abuses to which the concept of "Puritanism" seems to
have been open.

As an ahistorical cultural category, Puritanism also came in the 1920s to
represent a legacy of repression embodied in grim Salem shades and proper
Cambridge ladies. Critics like Ludwig Lewisohn celebrated Freudianism as a
liberating ideology, enabling a natural sexuality to flourish in life as in literature. The counterposition of Puritanism to Freudianism not only distorted
history—for the Puritans were hardly celibate—but often emphasized a finally
puerile issue of libido: "Does she or doesn't she?" That may give prominence
to Henry Miller or some of the sillier parts of Hemingway; but it obscures
books like Kate Chopin's *The Awakening,* Edith Summers Kelley's *Weeds,*
Agnes Smedley's *Daughter of Earth*[45] more broadly concerned with the contexts for and consequences of sexuality, with the implications of contraception
and abortion, the problems of childbearing, the tension between sexuality
and work.

Both as a category of history and of culture, then, "Puritanism" helped
produce a distorted canon. A similar problem exists with respect to the category of the "Frontier Spirit." The phrase came to be defined in terms exalting
male individualism, physical courage, and the honor code of the "lone cowhand" heroically confronting and triumphing over savagery. Although literary
historians achieved some distance on this image of the frontier, they continued
to focus on books that described human relationships with nature in terms
of confrontation, conquest, and exploitation; that omitted what was left back
east, where most people still lived; and that produced distorted images of
Native American "savages," and white female bearers of "civilization." They
canonized works that obscured the historical reality of the "trail of tears,"
of Indian starvation, of women's loneliness and self-sufficiency. Although

recent feminist and Native American scholarship has quite altered under-standing of the history of the frontier, it is not at all clear that a category like the "Frontier Spirit" could, even now, be freed of its chauvinist cultural baggage and be used to validate a significantly different canon.

By contrast, "urbanization" provides a still-relevant historical focus. The major period of urbanization in the United States stretched over the 80 to 100 years during which European and Asian immigrants came to this country, contributing, along with native-born emigrants from the South and other rural areas, to the swelling population of its cities. That process continues today, as Puerto Rican, Haitian, Dominican, Vietnamese, other Hispanic, and Asian immigrants come to the United States. The life-styles, values, and family structures of rural peoples have been and continue to be challenged and changed as they attempt to assimilate to more homogeneous, sophisticated urban styles and to survive economically in an urban industrial environment. That clash of values, that struggle for survival is a central subject of some of this country's best (yet noncanomical) books: Upton Sinclair's *The Jungle,* William Attaway's *Blood on the Forge,* Harriette Arnow's *The Dollmaker,* and Tillie Olsen's *Yonnondio.*[46] Further, although an emphasis on the frontier helps submerge the lives and roles of women (one escapes them to "light out" for the "territory"), urbanization is a lens that brings into clear focus the doubly changing roles of women in the family and in work. It provides a fuller vision than the 1920s' emphasis on the frontier, which may have served the purpose of distinguishing the United States from Europe but which also obscured the experience of women, as well as of urbanized immigrant and minority men.

I have suggested two different categories of historical and cultural coher-ence—colonization/decolonization and urbanization. I wish to add a third cultural category that has characterized all of American history; it is embodied in W.E.B. DuBois's comment that "the problem of the twentieth century is the problem of the color line." To focus on the color line is to recognize, in the first place, that among the earliest indigenous literary forms in the United States were those produced by people not of European but of African origins: namely, slave narratives, work and "sorrow" songs, dialect and other oral tales. These literary works were based in particular historic contexts—slavery, reconstruction, northern migration. That they continue to live is not only a measure of their artistic vitality, but also an indication that the struggles brought alive in Frederick Douglass' *Narrative* of his life, in Charles Chesnutt's stories, and in Gwendolyn Brooks's Bronzeville continue. The art of the color line also produces an especially rich and recurrent image—invisibility. The central metaphor of Ralph Ellison's *Invisible Man,* it is also the theme of Chestnutt's "The Passing of Grandison," and important to Nella Larsen's fiction.

The canon that might have developed from categories like colonization and decolonization, urbanization, and the color line differs substantially from the one that did, in fact, emerge from the categories of the twenties. Although a few of the books and authors I mention as illustrations, like *The Awakening,* have been incorporated into the canon—or at least into anthologies—most have not; some works are even out of print. But the major issue is not assimilating some long-forgotten works or authors into the existing categories; rather, it is reconstructing historical understanding to make it inclusive and explanatory instead of narrowing and arbitrary.

To the extent that the categories I have criticized are historically valid, they raise another issue; the very conception of periodicity. Dividing experience chronologically tends to accentuate the discontinuities rather than the continuities of life. It is something like imagining the world as it is presented in a tabloid newspaper, with its emphasis on the exceptional, rather than upon the commonplace, the ongoing. In some measure, women's lives in patriarchal society have been more fully identified with continuities—birthing, rearing, civilizing children; maintaining family and cultural stability. Indeed, there is some evidence to suggest that the rituals of female experience— regular, periodic, sustained—are culturally distinguishable from those of males. In this regard, emphasizing distinct chronological or literary periods may be one-dimensional, obscuring what is ongoing, continued. The color line persists, although its conventions and the forms of its literary expression are different in colonial and in modern, urbanized society. Urbanization is surprisingly similar over time. The point is simply that social and cultural continuities need to be understood as clearly as the periodic categories that seem to remain useful if the canon is not to be distorted in yet another way.

I have tried to outline a number of the factors that shaped the American literary canon into the rather exclusive form it had even as late as the 1960s. Certain other significant forces—for example, publishing decisions and changes in the publishing industry or the shorter-term impact of popular critics—remain to be examined in detail. But I have found nothing thus far that conflicts with the patterns I have sketched. Indeed, the one dissertation that has examined processes shaping the canon viewed literary scholars in their roles as teachers and anthologists as far more influential than publishers or critics.[47]

It is also important to understand that processes of institutionalization such as I have discussed, development of heavily capitalized anthologies and national marketing of texts—not to speak of academic tradition and inertia— all contribute to the difficulty of changing a canon once it has been formed. For about two decades now feminist scholars and scholars of color, participants in broad social movements for human rights, have tried to reconstitute the canon. From one point of view, certain progress has been made: even standard anthologies, for example, now include Frederick Douglass' *Narrative* and Kate Chopin's *The Awakening,* among other previously buried works. But it is not so clear that the institutional, aesthetic, and historiographic factors which had once served to exclude such works have yet been sufficiently scrutinized, much less fundamentally altered. Thus, what is here presented must be seen as part of a work in progress toward not only a more representative and accurate literary canon, but also toward basic changes in the institutional and intellectual arrangements that shape and perpetuate it.

Notes

1. Norman Foerster, ed., preface to *The Chief American Prose Writers* (Cambridge, Mass.: Riverside Press, 1916), p. iii.

2. Norman Foerster and Robert P. Falk, eds., preface to *Eight American Writers* (New York: W.W. Norton & Co., 1963), p. xv.

3. I will not, primarily for reasons of space, deal with working-class literature in this chapter; I do so in the next. Some of the earlier anthologies contained sections of popular songs and ballads of the Revolution and the Civil War, an occasional work song, and perhaps a selection from Jack London or Upton Sinclair. But little or nothing of working-class or socialist culture of the nineteenth and early twentieth centuries was taken seriously as art. Not until the 1930s, with the resurgence of left-wing cultural institutions in the United States and the development of theories of "proletarian literature," were the real experiences of working people validated as a basis for literature. And even then, much of what working-class writers themselves produced, in the way of songs and other occasional writings, for example, remained marginal even to progressive literary theorists. Questions concerning the basic characteristics, value, and functions of working-class literature remain vexed today. They are discussed in Raymond Williams, *Culture and Society, 1780–1950* (New York: Harper, 1960); Martha Vicinus, *The Industrial Muse* (New York: Barnes & Noble, 1974); Paul Lauter, "Working-Class Women's Literature: An Introduction to Study," *Women in Print 1*, ed. Joan Hartman and Ellen Messer Davidow (New York: Modern Language Association, 1982), 109–34; and Dan Tannacito, "Poetry of the Colorado Miners, 1903–1905," *Radical Teacher*, 15 (1980).

4. See, for example, the useful but not exhaustive "Select Chronology of Afro-American Prose and Poetry, 1760–1970" in *Afro-American Writing*, eds. Richard A. Long and Eugenia W. Collier (New York: New York University Press, 1972) 1: xix–xlii; Dorothy B. Porter, *North American Negro Poets: A Bibliographical Check-List of Their Writing (1760–1944)* (1945; reprint, New York: Burt Franklin; 1963); Ora Williams, *American Black Women in the Arts and Social Sciences: A Bibliographical Survey*, rev. and enl. ed. (Metuchen, N.J.: Scarecrow Press, 1978); Ann Allen Shockley, *Afro-American Women Writers 1746–1933: An Anthology and Critical Guide* (Boston: G. K. Hall, 1988); and the Bibliography on "Afro-American Literature" in *Redefining American Literary History*, A. La Vonne Brown Ruoff and Jerry W. Ward, Jr. eds. (New York: Modern Language Association, 1990).

5. For example, Robert T. Kerlin, *Contemporary Poetry of the Negro* (1921; reprint, Freeport, N.Y.: Books for Libraries Press, 1971); James Weldon Johnson, ed., *The Book of American Negro Poetry* (New York: Harcourt, Brace & Co., 1922); Robert T. Kerlin, *Negro Poets and Their Poems* (Washington, D. C.: Associated Publishers, 1923); Newman Ivey White and Walter Clinton Jackson, eds., *An Anthology of Verse by American Negroes* (Durham, N.C.: Trinity College Press, 1924); Countee Cullen, ed., *Caroling Dusk* (New York: Harper & Row, 1927); Alain Locke, ed., *Four Negro Poets* (New York: Simon & Schuster, 1927); V. F. Calverton, ed., *An Anthology of American Negro Literature* (New York: Modern Library, 1929);

Otelia Cromwell, Lorenzo Dow Turner, and Eva B. Dykes, eds., *Readings from Negro Authors* (New York: Harcourt, Brace & Co., 1931).

6. The anthologies consulted are the following: W. R. Benét and N. H. Pearson, eds., *The Oxford Anthology of American Literature* (New York: Oxford University Press, 1938); Walter Blair, Theodore Hornberger, and Randall Stewart, eds., *The Literature of the United States* (Glenview, Ill.: Scott, Foresman, 1946); Percy H. Boynton, ed., *Milestones in American Literature* (Boston and New York: Ginn & Co., 1923); Oscar Cargill, Robert E. Spiller, Tremaine McDowell, Louis Wann, and John Herbert Nelson, eds., *American Literature: A Period Anthology*, 5 vols. (New York: Macmillan Co., 1933); Joe Lee Davis, John T. Frederich, and Frank L. Mott, eds., *American Literature* (New York: Charles Scribner's Sons, 1948); Milton Ellis, Louise Pound, and George Weida Spohn, eds., *A College Book of American Literature* (New York: American Book Co., 1939); Norman Foerster, ed., *American Poetry and Prose* (Boston: Houghton Mifflin, 1923, 1934, 1947, 1962); James D. Hart and Clarence Gohdes, eds., *American Literature* (New York: Dryden Press, 1955); Jay B. Hubbell, ed., *American Life in Literature* (New York: Harper & Brothers, 1936, 1949); Howard Mumford Jones and E. E. Leisy, eds., *Major American Writers* (New York: Harcourt, Brace & Co., 1939, 1945); Ludwig Lewisohn, ed., *Creative America* (New York: Harper & Brothers, 1933); Alfred E. Newcomer, Alice E. Andrews, and Howard Judson Hall, eds., *Three Centuries of American Poetry and Prose* (Chicago: Scott, Foresman, 1917); Fred Lewis Pattee, ed., *Century Readings for a Course in American Literature* (New York: Century Co., 1919, 1922, 1926, 1931); L. W. Payne, Jr., ed., *Selections from Later American Writers* (Chicago: Rand McNally, 1926); Henry A. Pochmann and Gay Wilson Allen, eds., *Masters of American Literature* (New York: Macmillan, 1949); Arthur Hobson Quinn, Albert Baugh, and W. D. Howe, eds., *The Literature of America* (New York: Odyssey, 1926); Franklyn B. Snyder and Edward D. Snyder, eds., *A Book of American Literature* (New York: Macmillan, 1927, 1935); William Thorp, Merle Curti, and Carlos Baker, eds., *The Library Record*, vol. 2 of *American Issues* (New York: Lippincott, 1941); Harry R. Warfel, Ralph Henry Gabriel, and Stanley T. Williams, eds., *The American Mind* (New York: American Book Co., 1937); W. Tasker Witham, ed., *Masterpieces of American Literature*, vol. 2 of *Living American Literature* (New York: Stephen Daye Press, 1947).

By contrast, Bernard Smith's *The Democratic Spirit* (New York: Knopf, 1941) includes work by Frederick Douglass, W.E.B. DuBois, James Weldon Johnson, Claude McKay, Countee Cullen, Langston Hughes, and Richard Wright. Smith, who was active on the Left, saw "democratic writers" as constituting the central literary tradition of the United States.

7. Jay Hubbell also devotes ten pages to that eminent "southerner," Ralph Waldo Emerson, as well as chapters to Stowe and the white dialect "humorists." *The South in American Literature, 1607–1900* (Durham, N.C.: Duke University Press, 1934). The seventeen-volume *Library of Southern Literature,* ed. Edwin A. Alderman, Joel Chandler Harris, and Charles W. Kent (Atlanta: Martin and Hoat, 1907–23) contains many "dialect stories" by white writers like Harris, Thomas Dixon, and Thomas Nelson Page, but no work by a black person. Frederick Douglass is included in the "Biographical Dictionary of Authors," but not in the bibliography of works or in the Historical Chart. The index contains references to "Negro Dialect, Life, Character, and Problems (see also Slavery)" and "Negro Song (verse)," which turns out to be a single poem, but no other reference to a black author.

8. Norman Foerster, "American Literature," *Saturday Review of Literature* 2 (April 3, 1926): 678.

9. Fred Lewis Pattee, *The New American Literature* (New York: Century Co., 1930), p. 268.

10. Arthur Hobson Quinn, *American Fiction* (New York: D. Appleton-Century Co., 1936). Quinn had been working on this book for many years; it thus reflects a taste formed some decades earlier.

11. Howard Mumford Jones and Ernest E. Leisy, eds., *Major American Writers*, rev. and enl. ed. (New York: Harcourt, Brace & Co., 1945). It was suggested privately to me by a person who knew the editors that the choice of Glasgow was influenced by an editor's friendship with her.

12. Committee on the College Study of American Literature and Culture, William G. Crane, chairperson, *American Literature in the College Curriculum* (Chicago: National Council of Teachers of English, 1948), p. 27.

13. Ben W. Fuson, *Which Text Shall I Choose for American Literature? A Descriptive and Statistical Comparison of Currently Available Survey Anthologies and Reprint Series in American Literature* (Parkville, Mo.: Park College Press; distributed in cooperation with the College English Association, 1952).

14. Lyon Norman Richardson, G. H. Orians, and H. R. Brown, eds., *The Heritage of American Literature* (Boston: Ginn & Co., 1951).

15. The lag in secondary schools, where bureaucratic forms and political control were established early and elaborately, is far greater, as was attested by the three or even four generations of American schoolchildren for whom "the modern novel" was represented by *Silas Marner, The Rise of Silas Lapham,* and *Ethan Frome.*

16. In reviewing Carl Van Doren's *American Literature: An Introduction* (Los Angeles: U.S. Library Association, 1933), for example, Pattee writes:

> It seems to be the fashion now to exclude from the roll of American authors of major importance all who were not . . . shockers of *hoi polloi* readers who are old-fashioned in taste and morals. Van Doren's little volume excludes Bryant, Longfellow, Whittier, Holmes, Lowell, Stowe, Harte, and the like, and fills one fourth of his space with Emily Dickinson, Henry Adams, Mencken, Cabell, Dreiser, Lewis, Paine, Poe, Melville, Thoreau, Whitman, Mark Twain, and Emerson. . . .
>
> *American Literature* 5 (January 1934): 379–80.

17. American letters, wrote Henry S. Pancoast (in *An Introduction to American Literature* [New York, 1898], p. 2) are only "the continuation of English literature within the limits of what has become the United States, by people English in their speech, English to a considerable extent by inheritance, and English in the original character of their civilization." Pancoast quoted in Howard Mumford Jones, *The Theory of American Literature,* rev. ed. (Ithaca N.Y.: Cornell University Press, 1965), p. 98. Even Virginia Woolf pointed out that Emerson, Lowell, and Hawthorne "drew their culture from our books." See Woolf, "American Fiction," *Saturday Review of Literature* 2 (August 1, 1925): 1. On the early development of courses in American literature, and the resistance to them, see, for example, Fred Lewis Pattee, *Tradition and Jazz* (New York: Century Co., 1925), pp. 209–219.

18. These generalizations are based upon research I have been conducting for a book on the origins of the American literary canon. At this writing, I have examined the papers of over a hundred such literary societies as well as materials from and for such clubs provided by periodicals such as *Bookman.*

19. Laurence Veysey, "The Humanities, 1860–1920," typescript of paper for volume on the professions, c. 1974, 21, 24.

20. Pattee remarks that "American literature today is in the hands of college-

educated men and women. The professor has molded the producers of it." See Pattee, *Tradition and Jazz*, p. 237.

21. Barry M. Franklin, "American Curriculum Theory and the Problem of Social Control, 1918–1938" (Paper presented at the Annual Meeting of the American Educational Research Association, Chicago, April 15–19, 1974), ERIC, ED 092 419. Franklin quotes Edward A. Ross, *Principles of Sociology* (New York: Century Co., 1920): "Thoroughly to nationalize a multitudinous people calls for institutions to disseminate certain ideas and ideals. The Tsars relied on the blue-domed Orthodox church in every peasant village to Russify their heterogeneous subjects, while we Americans rely for unity on the 'little red school house.' "

22. Whatever its ostensible objectives, in practice, professionalization almost invariably worked to the detriment of female practitioners—and often female "clients" as well. The details of this argument have been most fully worked out for medicine; see, for example, Barbara Ehrenreich and Deirdre English, *Complaints and Disorders: The Sexual Politics of Sickness* (Old Westbury, N.Y.: Feminist Press, 1973), and *For Her Own Good: One Hundred and Fifty Years of the Experts' Advice to Women* (New York: Pantheon, 1979). See also Janice Law Trecker, "Sex, Science, and Education," *American Quarterly* 26 (October 1974): 352–366; and Margaret W. Rossiter, *Women Scientists in America: Struggles and Strategies to 1940* (Baltimore: Johns Hopkins University Press, 1982), especially the chapters titled "A Manly Profession," pp. 73–99, which includes a wonderful discussion of the professionally exclusionary function of the male "smoker," and "Academic Employment: Protest and Prestige," pp. 160–217.

23. The ladies' dinner had disappeared by 1925. A good deal of work on female cultures of support has recently been published, beginning with Carroll Smith-Rosenberg, "The Female World of Love and Ritual: Relations between Women in Nineteenth-Century America," *Signs* 1 (Autumn 1975): 1–27. In another professional field, history, women apparently felt so excluded from the mainstream and in need of mutual support that in 1929 they formed the Berkshire Conference of Women Historians, an institution extended in the 1970s to include sponsorship of a large conference on women's history. In most academic fields, however, while the proportion of *individual* women obtaining doctorates might have increased or been stable during the 1920s, female-defined *organizations* seem virtually to have disappeared–and with them, I suspect, centers for women's influence.

24. From 1923 on, the MLA gathered in what was called a "union" meeting, rather than in separate conventions of the Eastern, Central, and Pacific divisions—another indication of the new importance of the convention. That year 467 registered as attending the session. Fifty-nine women attended the ladies' dinner; some of the women were probably wives and other women members probably did not attend. About 24 percent of the MLA members were female; very likely a smaller proportion attended the convention. Among the divisions and sections there were 37 male chairpersons, and 1 female, Louise Pound, who chaired the Popular Culture section. There were 29 male secretaries, and 1 woman, Helen Sandison, served as secretary for two sections. Of the 108 papers, 6 were delivered by women.

In 1924, 978 persons registered, and 121 women went to the ladies' dinner. There continued to be 1 female chairperson, Louise Pound, and now 43 men. The female secretarial corps had increased to 5, Helen Sandison still serving twice, and "Mrs. Carleton Brown" now serving as secretary for the Phonetics section. Of the 128 papers, 7 were by women.

In *PMLA*, the proportion of women remained, relatively, much higher. In 1924, women were 7 of 47 authors; in 1925, 9 of 47; and in 1926, 11 of 55.

25. For example, of those seven papers delivered by women in the 1924 MLA meeting, two were in Popular Literature, two on Phonetics—where, perhaps not incidentally, women were officers—one in American literature. Similarly, the entry for American literature prepared by Norman Foerster for the 1922 American Bibliography (*PMLA,* 1923) contains one paragraph devoted to works about Native American verse, black writers, and popular ballads. Four of the scholars cited in this paragraph are women, 5 are men. Otherwise, 58 men and 9 women scholars are cited in the article. Of the 9 women, 2 wrote on women authors, 2 are cobibliographers, and 1 wrote on Whittier's love affair.

26. Joan Doran Hedrick, "Sex, Class, and Ideology: The Declining Birthrate in America, 1870–1917," *m.s., c.* 1974. Hedrick demonstrates that many of the sociologists and educators who developed the idea of utilizing curriculum for social control were involved with the supposed problem of "race suicide" and active in efforts to restrict immigration as well as to return women to the home.

27. A.G. Canfield, "Coeducation and Literature," *PMLA* 25 (1910): lxxix–lxxx, lxxxiii.

28. *Annual Reports of the President and the Treasurer of Oberlin College for 1919–20* (Oberlin, Ohio: Oberlin College, December 10, 1920), pp. 231–232.

29. Rudolph C. Blitz, "Women in the Professions, 1870–1970," *Monthly Labor Review* 97 (May 5, 1974): 37–38. See also Pamela Roby, "Institutional Barriers to Women Students in Higher Education," in *Academic Women on the Move,* eds. Alice S. Rossi and Ann Calderwood (New York: Russell Sage Foundation, 1973), pp. 37–40; and Michael J. Carter and Susan Boslego Carter, "Women's Recent Progress in the Professions, or, Women Get a Ticket to Ride after the Gravy Train Has Left the Station," *Feminist Studies* 7 (Fall 1981): 477–504.

30. Laura Morlock, "Discipline Variation in the Status of Academic Women," in *Academic Women on the Move,* 255–309.

31. In 1951, the Committee on Trends in Research of the American Literature Group circulated a report on research and publications about American authors during 1940–1950, together with some notes on publications during the previous decade. For the 1885–1950 period, the report (basing itself on categories established by the *Literary History of the United States*) provided information on ninety-five "major authors." Of these, four were black: Charles W. Chesnutt, Paul Laurence Dunbar, Langston Hughes, and Richard Wright—in context a surprisingly "large" number. Chesnutt is one of the few of the ninety-five about whom no articles are listed for either period; for Dunbar, one three-page article is listed and a "popular" book; for Hughes, there are four articles, two by Hughes himself. Only Wright had been the subject of a significant number of essays. Among "minor authors," as defined by *LHUS,* Countee Cullen had two articles, totaling five pages, written about him; W.E.B. DuBois nothing; and James Weldon Johnson, Claude McKay, and Jean Toomer, among others, were not even listed. Available in Modern Language Association, American Literature Group Files, University of Wisconsin Memorial Library Archives, Madison, Wisconsin.

32. One suggestive illustration:

I was pleased to get your letter and hear about the hunting. I don't know whether you realize how fortunate you people are to live where the game is still more plentiful than the hunters. It is no fun up here where hunting frequently resembles a shooting duel.

I am vastly amused by the report of the situation of the good and important woman who thought we should have more women on our committees in the American Literature Group. . . . Beyond . . . [Louise Pound and Constance Rourke] I cannot think of another

46   *Canons and Context*

woman in the country who has contributed sufficiently to be placed on a par with the men on our Board and committees. If you can think of anyone, for heaven's sake jog up my memory. We must by all means keep in the good graces of the unfair sex.

Sculley Bradley to Henry A. Pochmann, January 12, 1938,
Modern Language Association, American Literature Group Files,
University of Wisconsin Memorial Library Archives, Madison, Wisconsin.

33. Norman Foerster, ed., Introduction to *The Reinterpretation of American Literature* (New York: Harcourt, Brace & Co., 1928), p. vii; Harry Hayden Clark, "American Literary History and American Literature," in *The Reinterpretation of American Literature*, p. 213.

34. Joseph Hergesheimer, *Yale Review*, n.s., 10 (July 1921): 716–25.

35. Frances Noyes Hart, "The Feminine Nuisance Replies," *The Bookman* 54 (September 1921): 31–34.

36. Allen Tate, "Tension in Poetry," *The Man of Letters in the Modern World* (New York: Meridian Books, 1955), p. 71.

37. Susan Sniader Lanser and Evelyn Torton Beck make the same point in "[Why] Are There No Great Women Critics?" in *The Prism of Sex: Essays in the Sociology of Knowledge,* Julia A. Sherman and Evelyn T. Beck, eds. (Madison: University of Wisconsin Press, 1979). Deborah Rosenfelt adds: "Because the New Criticism valued works that could be analyzed as autonomous, self-contained structures without reference to the artist or to the historical era, certain genres (like poetry and fiction) became more highly regarded than others (like autobiography or essay)." See Rosenfelt, "The Politics of Bibliography," *Women in Print 1,* p. 21.

38. Allen Tate, "The Man of Letters in the Modern World," in *The Man of Letters in the Modern World,* pp. 20–22.

39. Frank Lentricchia develops a similar analysis in *After the New Criticism* (Chicago: University of Chicago Press, 1980), especially p. 202:

> Whether it comes from Harold Bloom or traditional historians of American poetry like Hyatt Waggoner and Roy Harvey Pearce, the isolation of Emerson and an Academic 'tradition'... running through Whitman, Stevens, Roethke, and Ginsberg produces a repetitious continuity which celebrates the individual authorial will ('tradition and the individual talent') and which dissolves, in the process, the myriad, changing forces, poetic and otherwise, that shaped the identities of figures as culturally separated as Emerson and Roethke.

40. Compare Rosenfelt's analysis of Perry Miller's introduction to his 1962 anthology in "The Politics of Bibliography," 19–23.

41. A similar problem existed with respect to art that focused on the lives of working-class people. See Alice Kessler-Harris and Paul Lauter's introduction to the books in the Feminist Press series of 1930s' women writers, and Joseph Freeman's introduction to *Proletarian Literature in the United States* (New York: International Publishers, 1935), pp. 9–19.

42. Gerda Lerner, "Placing Women in History: A 1975 Perspective," in *Liberating Women's History,* ed. Berenice A. Carroll (Urbana: University of Illinois Press, 1976), p. 363.

43. V. F. Calverton, *The Liberation of American Literature* (New York: Octagon Books, 1973), pp. 1–6. The original edition was published in 1932.

44. Two key sentences catch the essence of Emerson's and Fuller's outlooks in this respect. Emerson: "We have listened too long to the courtly muses of Europe."

Fuller: "Books which imitate or represent the thoughts and life of Europe do not constitute an American literature."

45. Kate Chopin, *The Awakening* (Chicago and New York: H. S. Stone & Co., 1899); the revived edition was edited by Kenneth Eble (New York: Capricorn Books, 1964). Edith Summers Kelley, *Weeds* (New York: Harcourt, Brace & Co., 1923); a revived edition was first edited by Matthew J. Bruccoli in 1972; it has been reedited, with a previously omitted scene of childbirth, by Charlotte Goodman (Old Westbury, N.Y.: Feminist Press, 1982). Agnes Smedley, *Daughter of Earth* (New York: Coward-McCann, 1929); revived edition edited by Paul Lauter (Old Westbury, N.Y.: Feminist Press, 1973). Chopin's book was out of print from about 1906, Kelley's from about 1924, and Smedley's from about 1937.

46. Upton Sinclair, *The Jungle* (New York: Vanguard, 1905); the book has been available in popular editions since publication. William Attaway, *Blood on the Forge* (Garden City: Doubleday, Doran, 1941); the book has been reprinted with an afterword by Richard Yarborough (New York: Monthly Review Press, 1987). Harriette Arnow, *The Dollmaker* (New York: MacMillan, 1954). Tillie Olsen, *Yonnondio: From the Thirties* (New York: Dell, 1974).

47. The only detailed study of the formation of the canon I have come across concludes that scholars, because they are the teachers of the tradition, are the prime influences on the shaping of the canon. See Joseph Darryl McCall, "Factors Affecting the Literary Canon" (Ph.D. diss., University of Florida, 1958).

The Literatures of America—
A Comparative Discipline

An image has long haunted the study of American culture. It limits our thought, shapes our values. We speak of the "mainstream," and we imply by that term the existence of other work, minor rills and branches. In prose, the writing of men like Franklin, Emerson, Thoreau, Hawthorne, Melville, James, Eliot, Hemingway, Faulkner, Bellow—to name some of the central figures—constituted the "mainstream." Others—writers of color, most women writers, "regional" or "ethnic" male and female authors—might, we said, be assimilated into the mainstream, though probably they would continue to constitute tributaries, interesting and often sparkling, but finally of less importance. They would, we tacitly assumed, be judged by the standards and aesthetic categories we had developed for the canonical writers. At best, we acknowledged that including in the canon writers like Wharton, Cather, Chopin, and Ellison might change somewhat our definition of the mainstream, but the intellectual model imposed by that mainstream image, this Great River theory of American letters, has persisted even among mildly revisionist critics.[1] Such critics have continued to focus on a severely limited canon of "major" writers based on historical and aesthetic categories from this slightly augmented mainstream.

The problem we face is that the model itself is fundamentally misleading. The United States is a heterogeneous society whose cultures, while they overlap in significant respects, also differ in critical ways. A normative model presents those variations from the mainstream as abnormal, deviant, lesser, perhaps ultimately unimportant. That kind of standard is no more helpful in the study of culture than is a model, in the study of gender differences, in which the male is considered the norm, or than are paradigms, in the study of minority or ethnic social organization and behavior based on Anglo-American society. What we need, rather, is to pose a comparativist model

Earlier and less developed versions of this paper were first presented at the United States-Soviet Symposium on the Literatures of American Ethnic Groups, University of Pennsylvania, July, 1985 and published as part of the collection *Redefining American Literary History*, A. LaVonne Brown Ruoff and Jerry W. Ward, Jr., eds. (New York: Modern Language Association, 1990).

for the study of American literature. It is true that few branches of academe in the United States have been so self-consciously indifferent to comparative study as has been the field we call "American literature." While we have, for example, studied Spanish or French influences on American writing, and vice versa, we have seldom been trained in any truly comparative discipline, and the academic journals which serve the American literature professoriat certainly offer no comparative perspective. Nevertheless, only what we might call "comparative American studies" will lead us out of the distortions and misunderstandings produced by the mainstream and tributary framework.

This chapter presents a strategy for approaching the many and varied literatures of the United States. It is not conceived as an overview of what I shall call *marginalized* literatures; it is directed, rather, to certain areas of critical practice that, I think, we must reexamine if we are to contemplate these literatures with accuracy, let alone respond to them with verve. In this sense, what I am presenting may be thought of more as counsel to explorers than as a map of the territory. While parts of the territory are well known, and others are coming into view, what is being found has not yet fully been absorbed or shared. By "marginalized" I designate those writings which, by virtue of their subject matter (e.g., menstruation rather than learning to hunt), function (e.g., "propagandistic," ceremonial, rather than belletristic), formal elements and conventions (e.g., improvisational, epistolary, rather than organic, dramatic), audience (e.g., women, Spanish speakers rather than white, Anglo men), or other factors, have been esteemed relatively less significant to, not at the center of, the definition of a nation's culture. Marginalized works are, largely, the products of groups with relatively less access to political, economic, and social power. To say it another way, the works and authors generally considered central to a culture are those composed and promoted by persons from groups holding power within it.[2] Indeed, only certain forms of creativity are honored with the title "literature" or even, in its narrower definition, "culture."[3] Culture is in this sense a contested ground upon which groups with differing interests contend for priority. Cultural marginalization, I will argue, represents social and political struggle, though the extent to which culture is defined by or redefines politics cannot be stated in the abstract but must be anchored by looking at specific groups in specific time-frames.

The United States in its origins specifically rejected the idea of privilege rooted in birth, race (and national origin), gender, and class; these factors have, nevertheless, come to play fundamental roles in how marginality has been constructed and maintained. Thus we are concerned with the work of women and working-class writers as well as that of minority men. For while there are profound differences between a culture defined significantly in terms of gender and one defined significantly in terms of race or national origin or class, still the burdens and opportunities posed by marginality generate unusually significant parallels.[4] And therefore, finally, we are discussing the writing of a *majority* of the people of this nation, a majority whose creativity,

I would argue, continues to be less than fully understood or appreciated, whose voices are insufficiently heard, by virtue of the factors I wish to examine here.

I want to look, first, at some of the virtues and problems in a comparative approach to the cultures of the United States, then at conceptions of literary history and ideas about the significance of subject which inform historical constructs. Subsequently, I shall discuss differing conceptions of the functions of imaginative writing, and then problems of evaluating differing forms and conventions, including those of characteristic patterns in imagery and language. Finally, I shall turn to audience as problematic. My intent throughout is to illustrate how a comparative approach to the literatures of America can help recast our assumptions about such matters and thus help open marginalized, indeed all, cultures to more adequate study.

I

A primary advantage of a comparative model is that it allows us to discard the notion that all literatures produced in this country must be viewed through the critical lenses shaped to examine "mainstream"—that is, largely white and male—culture. We can then see more clearly that, for example, subjects and forms of African-American writers are influenced not only by the traditions of Anglo-European literature, but by indigenous folk and formal cultures of black communities in the United States and elsewhere, by African models, and by the distinctive rhetorical styles of black churches and podiums. We can note that for many "hyphenated" Americans, the tension between assimilation in and separation from the majority helps define theme and plot— exemplified by the frequent concern with the mulatto, half-breed, greenhorn; with intermarriage; with the sense of cultural loss in the new (or white) world—phenomena largely absent from the work of majority writers. We can perceive that the normative pattern of many Mexican-American and Native American autobiographies, necessarily concerned with the destruction of communities and their values, contradicts the rags to riches design of public, individual stories given prominence by writers like Franklin.

Stepping outside "mainstream" assumptions, we can ask not whether or how any work fits a pre-established cultural pattern or given formal structure,[5] but rather, how it is that people within a particular social group or class— including Anglo-American men—speak, sing, write to one another (and perhaps to others), and what are for them significant concerns, appropriate forms, desirable artistic goals; what, that is, distinguishes their particular discourse. Beyond that, the comparative study of American literatures allows us to reexamine traditionally established works from fresh perspectives provided by minority and white female texts. Frederick Douglass' use of books illuminates in quite new ways Emerson's ideas of the value of letters; Harriet Jacobs' [Linda Brent's] years in an attic cast an oblique light on Thoreau's more comfortable notions of simplification, of where one lives, and what one lives for; the radically similar cultural origins of works by Stowe and Haw-thorne force on us a certain decentering of the latter, a necessary reconstruction of how we understand antebellum fiction. Most of all, a comparative strategy allows us to see Anglo-European male writing as but one voice, albeit loud and various, in the chorus of "American" culture.[6]

Of course, a comparative study brings its own problems. Indeed, one particular difficulty rises as a main bar to this approach: that is the limitation of our own training and knowledge. Marge Piercy offers a cautionary portrait of the blinders often imposed by graduate training:

> English is a hierarchical department. . . . We are taught the narrowly defined Tradition, we are taught Structure, we are taught levels of Ambiguity. We are taught that works of art refer exclusively to other works of art and exist in Platonic space. Emotion before art is dirty. We are taught to explicate poems and analyze novels and locate Christ figures and creation myths and Fisher Kings and imagery of the Mass. Sometimes I look up and expect to see stained-glass windows in our classroom. Somewhere over our heads like a grail vision lurks a correct interpretation and a correct style to couch it in. We pick up the irony in the air before we comprehend what there is to be ironic about.[7]

In these familiar precincts, where the ironic stance precedes the emotional response and art works are held up for arm's length scrutiny, what can become of *The Bluest Eye* or *Winter in the Blood?*

A second set of difficulties arises from the uneven development of the cultures of the United States. "Uneven development" of culture suggests more than the obvious fact that different groups established themselves in this land at quite different times. The term implies, first, a point about chronology: The relationship between the arrival of an immigrant group on these shores and the emergence of a literary (i.e., written) culture (or the beginning of the written articulation of an oral culture) is quite irregular. A literary culture requires, obviously enough, literacy. Only some of the groups which came to this country, or were here, were literate—in their own languages, much less in English. Many immigrants were rural peoples, like this land's original inhabitants, with strongly-established but not literary cultures. At the turn of the century, Jewish—at least Jewish male—garment workers in New York (as well as Welsh miners in Colorado) were among the most "literary" of immigrant workers. That might help to explain the relatively rapid and widespread emergence of a significantly Jewish, as distinct from a Polish or Italian, literary culture.

Then, too, development of a literary culture requires the diffusion through a group of a set of ideas, particularly the notion that it is possible or valid for a person to devote time to the wonderfully arrogant act of artistic composition. Hawthorne had a good deal to say about that in the "Custom House" section of *The Scarlet Letter,* though his reflections, particular to his male, New England, Puritan immigrant heritage, differ strikingly from those of his female contemporaries, like Caroline Kirkland or Fanny Fern, who felt forced by possible social disapproval to discount their own "scribblings." Perhaps it

would be more precise to say that it is the women's *ways* of defending themselves against the ambiguities of a literary life which most clearly reflect the
differences of gender and of their cultural networks. Such ambiguities, and
even more distinct modes of coping, mark the work of recent writers like
Anzia Yezierska in *Red Ribbon on a White Horse,* Tillie Olsen in *Silences,*
Hisaye Yamamoto in "Seventeen Syllables," or Maxine Hong Kingston in
The Woman Warrior. Finally, a literary culture requires the existence of an
audience, a reading public that, on the one hand, resonates to the beat of
the writers' language and concerns and that, on the other hand, serves its
needs by *reading*—and especially reading of a particular kind.[8] An audience
imbued with ideas about the value of producing literary art *may* provide
institutions for supporting artists; these might include offering writers opportunities to concentrate on creation, as well as establishing publishing outlets and means for distributing work. The importance of such material supports
to the evolution of a literary culture can hardly be overestimated.[9] Differences
in literacy, in diffusion of ideas, and in means of support help explain why
the establishment of literary culture in one group does not predict its development in another and why the functions served by reading, or by reading
particular kinds of texts, may be quite diverse.

A second critical point about "uneven development": Literary culture
emerges in a minority or marginalized group in part independently of, in part
in response to, developments in the majority culture. In drawing a distinction
between British working-class and bourgeois culture, Raymond Williams offers one explanation of this phenomenon:

> A culture is not only a body of intellectual and imaginative work; it is
> also and essentially a whole way of life. The basis of a distinction between
> bourgeois and working-class culture is only secondarily in the field of intel-
> lectual and imaginative work. . . . The crucial distinguishing element in En-
> glish life since the Industrial Revolution is not language, not dress, not
> leisure—for these indeed will tend to uniformity. The crucial distinction is
> between alternative ideas of the nature of social relationship.
>
> "Bourgeois" is a significant term because it marks that version of social
> relationship which we usually call individualism: that is to say, an idea of
> society as a neutral area within which each individual is free to pursue his
> own development and his own advantage as a natural right. . . . [Both] this
> idea [of service] and the individualistic idea can be sharply contrasted with
> the idea that we properly associate with the working class: an idea which,
> whether it is called communism, socialism, or cooperation regards society
> neither as neutral nor as protective, but as the positive means for all kinds
> of development, including individual development.[10]

Writing from a British perspective, Williams perhaps underestimates the significance of works of imagination in defining "working-class culture": "It is
not proletarian art, or council houses, or a particular use of languages; it is,
rather, the basic collective idea, and the institutions, manners, habits of
thought and intentions which proceed from this."[11] But his fundamental point
is critical: While broad areas of the culture are common to the working-class

and the bourgeoisie, there remains a "crucial distinction . . . between alternative ideas of the nature of social relationship." This distinction significantly
explains differing "institutions, manners, habits of thought and intentions."
Distinct cultures also help shape ideas about the nature of art, its functions,
the processes of its creation, the nature of the artist and of the artist's social
role.

There is nothing very mysterious about this: people whose experiences of
the world significantly differ, whose material conditions of life, whose formal
and informal training, whose traditions differ—and especially people whose
understanding of their own life-chances and opportunities, their "place,"
differ—will think about things differently, will talk about things differently,
will value at least some things differently, will express themselves to different
people in different ways and about different experiences, at least in some
measure. They will work within distinct linguistic traditions and even languages; they will focus on differing concerns and subjects; and they will speak
to somewhat separate audiences often in popular oral modes rather than in
written forms. Their very opportunities to become writers will differ sharply,
not only because institutions, including those within publishing, extend their
support unevenly, but also because what audiences wish to derive from writing
may or may not be within their capacity or experience to provide.[12] Finally,
the functions of culture in the life of a group of people changes significantly
over time, as social realities and evolving consciousness about them change.

For all these reasons, the literary history of the dominant white and male
culture will only in a limited degree be a useful account of the development
of the varied literary cultures of the United States. A full literary history of
this country requires both parallel and integrated accounts of differing literary
traditions and thus of differing (and changing) social realities.[13] We are only
at the beginning of the creation of such a complex history.[14]

The creation of a new cultural history is, I believe, part of a larger process
of building "an account of the world as seen from the margins," a necessary
prerequisite to transforming the "margins into the center."[15] That is a process
in which writers of color as well as white women and working-class authors
have long been engaged, responding from the very beginnings of "American"
culture to the imperative to speak for themselves and for others like themselves who had been silenced in history. That has entailed defining their own
distinctive voices, creating their own artistic forms and critical discourses,
developing their own institutions, their own foci for cultural work. Different
places, magazines, publishing houses, and anthologies have been central to
certain significant cultural movements. But the issue is less than of "place"
than of power: the power to define cultural form and value. It is to these
issues that I wish to turn.

II

The structures of literary study are based, as Geoffrey Hartman has acknowledged, on limited "text milieux."[16] That is, we derive aesthetic and historical

theories from a selection of works, often lifted from their historical contexts
and quite limited in outlook and even in form. In general, our choice of these
texts is rooted in assumptions based on the particular characteristics of our
class, race, and sex, reshaped, to be sure, by the powerful influence exerted—
especially over those of us from minority or ethnic origins—by the professors
of the dominant culture. From this limited set of texts we project standards
of aesthetic excellence as well as the intellectual constructs we call "literary
history." And once we have developed such constructs, we view other works
in these terms, whether the works originate from that initial text milieu or
from outside it.[17] That commonplace and hardly conscious procedure helps
explain the apparently self-evident character of the canon. It also produces
serious distortions in value judgments (as I shall suggest below) as well as in
historical accounts of literary development.

Consider, as an example of faulty literary history, what was until the mid-
1970s the usual portrait of the evolution of fiction in North America (a portrait
that still shapes curricular choices). Writers such as Charles Brockden Brown,
Washington Irving, and James Fenimore Cooper, it was said, were forerun-
ners, who cleared and plowed the colonial cultural wilderness so that, in the
"American Renaissance," the first generation of major writers—Poe, Hawthorne, Melville—could flourish. They were succeeded by three generations
of fiction writers: Twain and James, who elaborated alternative westward-
looking and eastward-looking subjects and styles; realists and naturalists like
Howells, Crane and Dreiser; and finally, in the 1920s, a new, modernist
renaissance exemplified by the work of Hemingway, Fitzgerald, Dos Passos,
Faulkner, and a host of others.

If this chronology provided a broadly useful historical account, it should
illuminate the texts of writers other than those whose work forms its basis.
What then might it tell us of the first group of black fiction writers? William
Wells Brown's *Clotel* (1853), Frank Webb's *The Garies and Their Friends*
(1857), Martin Delany's *Blake* (1859), and Harriet Wilson's *Our Nig* (1859)
are roughly contemporaries of *The Scarlet Letter* (1850) and *Moby-Dick*
(1851), as are Frederick Douglass' novella "The Heroic Slave" (1853) and
Frances Ellen Watkins Harper's story "The Two Offers" (1859). Read in
terms of Hawthorne's and Melville's works they may seem underdeveloped,
in places even crude and propagandistic. But to view them in such a perspective would be, I think, unhelpful and an error in historical understanding.
In one sense these writers are more the contemporaries of someone like
Cooper, and share many of his shortcomings—and virtues. For these black
writers are only beginning the process of establishing a novelistic style for
their culture and of elaborating in that style fictional material of consequence
to the audience to which they aspire. In another, metaphoric, sense these
texts reach back to the semi-autobiographical fictions of Elizabethan and
Jacobean writers.

But the comparisons with *The Last of the Mohicans* or *The Unfortunate
Traveler* are in other respects equally misleading since they would obscure
what were undoubtedly the major cultural influences on these books: the well-

established tradition of black slave narratives, the African-American oral tradition of tales and legends, and the publication of *Uncle Tom's Cabin* (1852). The narratives and Stowe's novel helped establish and broaden an audience for which reading and writing was integrated with social activism; an audience which responded to images of heroic and adventurous black men and women and was willing to confront the complex realities of the oppression, particularly sexual, of black women; an audience which also accepted the very idea of a black *writer*—a problematic conception for many people, even some blacks, in antebellum America. Further, a historical account to which the slave narratives, Stowe, and the black oral tradition are integral helps us understand, as Richard Yarborough has suggested, that a central project developed in the nineteenth century by black writers was the effort to assert through fiction the potential of black people in America and, at the same time, to document and preserve their history.[18]

As the older accounts of American fictional history left us asking "where were the blacks?" so they provoked the parallel question "where were the women?" The work of critics like Elizabeth Ammons, Nina Baym, Hazel Carby, Barbara Christian, Kathy Davidson, Josephine Donovan, Judith Fetterley, Annette Kolodny, Jane Tompkins, Mary Helen Washington, and Sandra Zagarell has begun to answer that question. These critics often pose Stowe as a key figure,[19] in a sense a "bridge" between the earlier female writers both of realistic and of romantic narratives—Susanna Rowson, Catharine Maria Sedgwick, Caroline Kirkland, Fanny Fern, Susan Warner, E.D.E.N. Southworth—and the next generations of realistic writers, white women like Rebecca Harding Davis, Elizabeth Stuart Phelps, Rose Terry Cooke, Sarah Orne Jewett and Mary Wilkins Freeman. These authors turned neither "east" nor "west" but at their finest, focused eyes keen for detail on the constricting material and often on the dominantly female communities they inhabited in New England, New York, and the South. In turn, building consciously on the accomplishments of that previous generation, the white women writers of the early twentieth century—Chopin, Wharton, Mary Austin, Glasgow, Cather—produced many of the most significant novels of the period by engaging the burning questions of the time concerning social, political, and sexual equality for females.

In fact, an account of changing patterns of nineteenth-century women's— and some men's—fiction can be constructed around questions of gender, race, creativity, and power. The domestic authors of the earlier generation—the subjects of Nina Baym's *Woman's Fiction*—wrote success tales, in which virtue, in the form of constancy; often self-denial; and sometimes devotion to craft, generally brought about happy endings for the heroines and the communities which, in effect, they had gathered around themselves. Alcott and Stowe continued to present domestic values as key to ethical life, to public virtue, as well as, in a story like Alcott's "Psyche's Art," to the creation of good art. While women's and men's spheres are separate, the subordination of hearth to countinghouse has not yet, fictionally at least, taken place; indeed, Stowe offers both fictive and theoretical validations of the kitchen as value center. In Jacobs' *Incidents in the Life of a Slave Girl,* while the form of self-denial is even more profound, both the meanings of "constancy" and the happiness of the ending are made problematic by virtue of how white American society construed black women as commodities, whether of the kitchen or the countinghouse. In Phelps, the contradictions between countinghouse and the sphere of women remain harsh, if different, for in *The Silent Partner* women are excluded from the sources of economic power, and while Sip and Perley, the two heroines, continue trying to improve the lives of workers, it is not clear whether that project can reach beyond the consolations of Christian charity. In Phelps' later work, like *The Story of Avis* and *Dr. Zay,* the conflicts between domesticity and a woman's art or work heighten. Such conflicts remain but are less central than race to the instructional program of Frances Harper's *Iola Leroy.* Jewett sustains the values of an elaborated, extended domestic sphere; indeed, *The Country of the Pointed Firs* emerges as a kind of mythic center of family strength, to which an urban inhabitant may travel for renewal, though she cannot stay. Freeman is even less optimistic, for while many of her women are strong and independent, they are so in a narrowing world, at its bleakest in a story like "Old Woman Magoun," but constricting even in the triumphant "The Revolt of 'Mother.' " The arc of this fictional history can thus be tracked, as it were, from the successes of *Ruth Hall* and Capitola in *The Hidden Hand,* to the contrasting fates of the heroines in *The Awakening* and *The House of Mirth.*

This view is obviously a radically different account of fictional history in the United States from that which obtained less than two decades ago. Such divergent accounts remain deeply embedded in critical terminology and historical categories. For example, the terms "regionalist" or "local colorist" continues to be applied to Jewett,[20] Freeman, Chopin, Paul Laurence Dunbar, and Charles W. Chesnutt. I think the terms mark them as peripheral to the development of a "national" culture, supposedly one of the major accomplishments of nineteenth-century American letters. But a critical category like "regionalist" is about as useful—and as accurate—in describing these writers as a phrase like "escapist fiction" would be applied to Poe, Melville, and Twain.[21] Categories like "regionalist"—and, I suspect, "ethnic" or even "minority"—encapsulate particular accounts of literary development; they also embody judgments of the value of writers and works. Such evaluations are based on assumptions about the importance of particular subjects as well as of certain forms, and on differing conceptions of the functions of art and the role of artists.

A similar set of problems arises when we examine the use of a category like "realism." In our culture, the term and its cognates (e.g., "realistic") imply positive, perhaps even weighty, judgments. The older account of white male fictional history that I sketched above suggested that realism somehow arose as a later nineteenth-century dialectical corrective to the romance or fantasy tradition self-consciously developed by Poe, Hawthorne, and Melville. In fact, however, literary historians have demonstrated that the roots of fictional realism can be found in earlier nineteenth-century women writers such as Caroline Kirkland, Alice Cary, and Susan Warner.[22] Kirkland described her book, *A New Home—Who'll Follow* (1839) as a "rough picture ...pentagraphed from the life," dealing with "common-place occurrences— mere gossip about every-day people." Judith Fetterley points out that Kirkland specifically dissociated herself from the dominantly male tradition of adventure, mystery, and romance because she chose to tell the story of the frontier from the diurnal perspective of a woman plunged into its not very glamorous woods and fields—or rather, its mudholes and hovels. Similarly, Alfred Habegger has traced some of the ways in which a dominantly female practice of realism in mid-nineteenth-century America shaped the fictional strategy of the later male writers that critics have traditionally described as "realists."[23]

What is at stake here is not simply a revisionist claim to prior occupation of valued turf—however significant that might be. The stakes are evident if we begin from Toni Morrison's proposition that narrative is "the principle way in which human knowledge is made accessible."[24] The issue is, then, what of human knowledge a particular set of narratives, a canon, or an historical construct, encodes, makes accessible—or obscures.[25] In a certain sense, the effect if not the design of literary history is to make it seem self-evident that the kinds of problems literary historians work out constitute the universe of significant issues. The "territory ahead" (at least as it came to be defined as the grounds for the encounter of lone individuals with nature) was far more of a presence in white male imagination for clear material reasons during the middle and late nineteenth century, and for ideological reasons again in the 1920s. Before the Civil War, Horace Greeley's injunction to "Go west, young *man*" simply voiced what had become a commonplace action among many men. With the decline of farming, fishing, and trade in much of New England after the war; the increased mobility and entrepreneurial opportunities stimulated by the war and the growth of the railroads; and that "westering ideology," many Yankee men struck out for new frontiers or imagined what it meant to do so. Therefore it would not be surprising if images encoding the theme of "the territory ahead" characterized the work of white male writers such as Poe, Melville, Twain, Harte, Crane, Norris, London, and Richard Harding Davis, or if that theme reengaged the interests of male intellectuals, professors, and critics after the First World War, when a definition of the United States's "masculine" role on the world stage was being developed.

American Indians, such as William Apes, Elias Boudinot, and Black Hawk shared a vision of the importance of the "frontier," but in their experience, it was often represented as the intrusion of the boots of a giant into the grounds of their hunt or into the land within which the life and culture of their people were rooted. For antebellum black writers, the "frontier" was located as much at the Mason-Dixon line as anywhere else, and the perilous journey from slavery to selfhood was the major concern. In time, to be sure, it became clear that the psychological boundaries presented by color prejudice were more difficult to surmount than the geographical divide between North and South. In such contexts, individual confrontations with whales or wars were never central, for the issue was neither metaphysics nor nature, but the social constructions called "prejudice," and the problem was not soluble by or for individuals (except the very few who could and wished to "pass"), but only through a process of social change.

For women, the "great question" of life might be that addressed by Sarah Orne Jewett in "Aunt Cynthy Dallett" or in "The Foreigner": that is, how to build and sustain a female-centered community in the face of poverty, narrowness, and even pride. Or it might be the problem of how the weak achieve a modicum of power through (civil) disobedience—addressed by Mary Wilkins Freeman in "A Church Mouse" and in "The Revolt of 'Mother,' " or, very differently, by Harriet Jacobs in her *Incidents in the Life of a Slave Girl.* Such concerns have returned to prominence (as I need hardly say) after a half-century in which were taken to be trivial, along with works that encode and intepret them. A canon is, to put it simply, a construct, like a history text, expressing what a society reads back into the past as important to its future.

My intent is not to deny the significance of defining an isolated, heroic self against the forces of nature—a theme, as we all know, that is peculiarly persistent in the romantic fictions of American white males that have constituted the received canon.[26] This theme was, no doubt, of both real and symbolic consequence to American entrepreneurs well into the twentieth century. And ideological manifestations of Romantic individualism remain popular today in the work of many writers and film-makers. But equally substantial and interesting are the social issues: the prices paid, often by women, for men's upward, or outward, mobility; the sacrifices of community to self; and the difficulties of sustaining community. Moreover, the conceptions of self and the processes of definition as they emerge for Deerslayer, Ishmael, Huckleberry Finn, Nick Adams, and Ike McCaslin differ sharply from those of characters we encounter in the work of many minority writers, where the construction of self involves its emergence within conflicting definitions of community and continuity, as is the case in *Their Eyes Were Watching God, The Woman Warrior, Bless Me, Ultima,* or John Joseph Mathews' *Sundown.*

What is at stake here can, I think, be apprehended in two related passages, the first from the introductory material of Leslie Marmon Silko's *Ceremony,* the second from Meridel LeSueur's *The Girl:*

You don't have anything
if you don't have the stories.

Their evil is mighty
but it can't stand up to our stories.
So they try to destroy the stories
let the stories be confused or forgotten.
They would like that
They would be happy
Because we would be defenseless then.

And from *The Girl:*

> Memory is all we got, I cried, we got to remember. We got to remember
> everything. It is the glory, Amelia said, the glory. We got to remember to
> be able to fight. Got to write down the names. Make a list. Nobody can be
> forgotten. They know if we don't remember we can't point them out. They
> got their guilt wiped out. The last thing they take is memory.[27]

Seen thus, what is involved in literary history is survival.[28] If that seems an
aggrandizement of what writers, much less critics, do, consider at the simplest
level the history in this century of works like Frederick Douglass' *Narrative,*
Rebecca Harding Davis' *Life in the Iron Mills,* or Charlotte Perkins Gilman's
"The Yellow Wallpaper." Two decades ago they were virtually extinct as
literary works; they addressed concerns remote from those at the core of the
cultural "mainstream." That they are now enshrined in American literature
anthologies testifies, in fact, to the force exerted on literary history by political
movements. Indeed, when I speak of "survival" here, I refer not so much to
these works in themselves, but to the knowledge they make accessible and
the experiences to which they give expression and shape—experiences which
better enable new generations to comprehend themselves and their world.

The thematic patterns and the relationships among texts that I have been
tracing constitute a more traditional form of *literary* history. The question of
literary *history* intensities, in fact, when we look at how texts invoke specific
historical contexts and at the particular roles texts play in culture. In some
measure, the revived interest in history among literary scholars derives from
the fact that the marginalized texts which they are choosing to study embody,
often depend upon, historical contexts about which critics know little. For
example, the narrators in Louise Erdrich's *Love Medicine* refer only obliquely
to the American Indian Movement and in passing to the Pine Ridge reser-
vation and to the events that took place there in the early 1970s.[29] Yet, I
think, the changes in consciousness such organizations and events produced
explain why the younger generation in that book, Lipsha and Albertine, do
not suffer the same fates as the previous generation, June and Gordie. Lipsha's
power as a healer can be restored and Albertine's study of medicine completed
because specific events have changed their world, or at least the way they
can look at it. Altogether ignorant of that history, my 1989 Anglo students
could not comprehend the movement of the book. In a way, it was easier for
them to understand, at least in the abstract, Leslie Marmon Silko's explicit
use of traditional Indian ceremonies than Erdrich's implicit use of history.

I am not disparaging my students; I suspect they typify Erdrich's non-
Indian readers. Indeed, they represent most of us, brought up as we were on
the kinds of "mainstream" details that make up much of E. D. Hirsch's
cultural dictionary. But that historical ignorance peculiarly disables us from
reading marginalized work adequately or from responding to a marginalized
culture.[30] Frank Barnes, the highly sympathetic Anglo organizer in the film
"Salt of the Earth," mistakes a picture on the living room wall of one of the
Mexican strikers, Ramón Quintero, for the man's grandfather. Quintero com-

ments: "That's Júarez—the father of Mexico. If I didn't know a picture of George Washington, you'd say I was an awful dumb Mexican." Similarly, the cultural meaning of the Mexican war to its veterans, who constitute the center of value of Rolando Hinojosa's *The Valley,* may very likely escape Anglo readers, together with the ambiguities of border life, so critical to that and many of Hinojosa's other books.[31] Eric Sundquist's reconstruction of the fabric of allusion, reference, and echo from which Melville's story "Benito Cereno" is made brilliantly demonstrates how useful is a vastly enriched historical sensibility to the reading of even an eminently canonical text.[32] My argument here is that many marginalized writers deploy distinct historic sensibilities which interested "outside" readers must work at constructing if we are to have access to such texts.

Furthermore, the particular material conditions that have shaped marginalized writing in this country are even less well known than the similar circumstances influencing canonical writing. Literary historians may be familiar, for example, with publishing houses like Ticknor and Fields and its successors, Osgood and (later) Houghton Mifflin, but they are likely to know little about the religious house of Robert Carter, and much less of the Colored Co-operative Publishing Company. Yet to understand the work a text performed in its time, the historically specific circumstances of its creation, publication (or oral narration), and distribution need to be studied.[33] Working-class poetry is often quite specific to the changing forms of labor in which people were engaged, from the chain-gang to the tipple. Yet much of working-class experience, its organization and struggles, its migrations and divisions—even its defeats and victories—is hidden from history. Similarly, significant changes in the telling of a tale or in the text of a song may mark important historical transitions in the life of a community—for example, the need to face new deprivations or opportunities. Thus historical study takes on a new importance in the reading of marginalized works.

That observation brings me to my last point about history: the specific roles literary works play *within* their worlds. Critics have recently focused on the concrete cultural tasks of literary texts in particular historical situations, why they are read by given audiences, and what "work" they perform in the cultural lives of that readership.[34] This project seems particularly important in reading marginalized literatures for reasons I will examine in more detail in the next section, but that have primarily to do with the need for marginalized communities to mobilize whatever resources are available, including artwork, to ensure continuity—or even survival. Neither slave narratives nor early black American fiction can be seen clearly outside the roles they played in abolitionist and anti-racist struggles, nor, as Hazel Carby has shown, can the work of writers like Frances Harper, Pauline Hopkins, and Ida B. Wells be significantly apprehended without seeing how it functioned in relation to particular black and white audiences and the women's campaigns for social and political authority.[35] Similarly, the Mexican Californios (e.g., Mariano Vallejo) who responded to the request of Hubert Howe Bancroft that they write about or report to him on their lives and history, did so with specific audiences and particular objectives: defending their own roles and preserving a culture whose passing, or at least transformation, they directly experienced and mourned. In seeking to speak what she regarded as hard but educational truths to a young female audience emerging from the constraints of domesticity, Elizabeth Stuart Phelps took upon herself specifically didactic roles that unify her fictions and the essays in her periodical *The Independent.* The historical demands upon marginalized writers and the opportunities that specific historical contexts open are often distinct from those to which canonical writers have responded. Our responsibility as critics of marginalized cultures is to reconstruct those particular historical imperatives.

One might argue, for example, that in the past two decades, minority and ethnic writers have increasingly and consciously invoked details—of history, geography, language, and ceremony, for example—likely to fall outside the cultural pale of much of their readership. Thus readers are forced into a process of active encounter, not just with a specific text, but with the cultural contexts from which it derives. That, I suspect, is part of the point. In the 1960s and 1970s, the movements for social change challenged artists to discover how they might themselves be agents of change rather than, at best, chroniclers of it. Writers have addressed that challenge in many ways: Alice Walker's *Meridian,* Leslie Marmon Silko's *Ceremony,* Adrienne Rich's *The Dream of a Common Language* are, among other things, quite different approaches to the problem of creating texts that are actors for change. Another response has been to turn the minority work into what amounts to a cultural challenge to its nonminority readership. That is, such texts tax readers to place intellectual resources where their sentiments ostensibly lie. Such sentiments are addressed at one level by work like that represented by a *New York Times* Sunday supplement entitled "A World of Difference" (April 16, 1989). The problem, and the opportunity, for the minority writer is to move the contemporary reader beyond the easy responses of liberal curiosity and tolerance such supplements evoke toward a broadening of historical knowledge—toward, for example, the reassessment insisted upon by Hinojosa of the Anglo's heroic image of the Texas Rangers, or of the Indian "criminal" in Erdrich's *Love Medicine.* This is by no means a new project, as I shall suggest in the next section; here I wish only to underline the importance of perceiving its specific historical roles to reading marginalized literature.

What I have said thus far suggests a view of the function of art, indeed, a functional perspective *on* art that perhaps is uncongenial to those of us brought up on formalist paradigms. I wish to turn directly now to that concern, for it is indeed true that conceiving American literature as a comparative discipline implies some differing perspectives on what it is literary works attempt to do in our world.

III

Like many minority writers, Charles Chesnutt was extraordinarily sensitive to questions of the functions of art as well as to the status of artists from marginalized groups. For many years, he was regarded as a local colorist, a writer of humorous dialect tales, and, because of the focus on the "tragic mulatto" in his supposedly more serious work, a writer central neither to black nor white fictional concerns. In *The Conjure Woman* Chesnutt compares versions of the roles of a literary artist, and proposes a distinctive function for the African-American writer. The narrator of that book is a liberal white Northerner, John, who has moved to North Carolina in part for the sake of his wife's health and in part to try his hand at making money through grape cultivation. Resident upon the land John buys, and deeply knowledgeable about it, is Uncle Julius, an elderly black man, former slave, teller of tales, and sometime coachman for John and his wife, Annie. John views Julius with something of the well-meaning condescension of a turn-of-the-century white literary critic toward a black artist. On the one hand, Julius' stories serve to while away the long southern hours, and in particular to distract Annie from the meaninglessness of her life. On the other hand, as John sees it, Julius' stories are also a means by which the old man, generally by winning Annie's response, is able to extract a living or some kind of concession from John for himself and his relatives. To John, Julius' art is a kind of minstrelsy, an amusement for his hearers and a source of income, or at least livelihood, for the former slave. Serious art is the kind of novel John reads to Annie—in the vain hope of rousing her from the depression into which she increasingly and fearfully sinks as the book progresses.

In certain respects, the key story in the structure of *The Conjure Woman* is "Sis' Becky's Pickaninny," a tale in which the conjurer uses a hummingbird and a hornet, among other creatures, to reunite Sis' Becky with her child and thus restore her to health. In the course of the narration, Annie—like Sis' Becky in Julius' tale—is moved from a threatening illness toward recovery. The vital ingredient in that cure is the magic *of* Julius' story, clearly presented by Chesnutt as parallel to the conjurer's magic *in* Julius' story, and symbolized by the rabbit's foot Julius carries. To John, the rabbit's foot represents merely the superstition of a race barely emerging from primitive backwardness:

> "Julius," I observed, half to him and half to my wife, "your people will never rise in the world until they throw off these childish superstitions and learn to live by the light of reason and common sense. How absurd to imagine that the forefoot of a poor dead rabbit, with which he timorously felt his way along through a life surrounded by snares and pitfalls, beset by enemies on every hand, can promote happiness or success, or ward off failure or misfortune!"[36]

Julius' response wonderfully illustrates the tactics of the black artist in slipping the yoke: " 'Dat's w'at I tells dese niggers roun' heah,' said Julius. 'De fo'-foot ain' got no power. It has ter be de hin'-foot, suh,—de lef' hin'-foot er a grabeya'd rabbit, killt by a cross-eyed nigger on a da'k night in de full er de moon.' "

Julius' comment also suggests to Annie, and the reader, an alternative way of hearing and therefore of responding to John—as if to say that the terms of John's discourse are not necessarily determinative of how one listens to a narrative.[37] The lesson is not lost on Annie. But John, while he perceives the invigorating impact of Julius' tale upon Annie, cannot understand the source of its power for her, much less the significance of the rabbit's foot itself:

> My wife had listened to this story with greater interest than she had manifested in any subject for several days. I had watched her furtively from time to time during the recital, and had observed the play of her countenance. It had expressed in turn sympathy, indignation, pity, and at the end lively satisfaction.
>
> "That is a very ingenious fairy tale, Julius," I said, "and we are much obliged to you."
>
> "Why, John!" said my wife severely, "the story bears the stamp of truth, if ever a story did."
>
> "Yes," I replied, "especially the humming-bird episode, and the mocking-bird digression, to say nothing of the doings of the hornet and the sparrow."
>
> "Oh, well, I don't care," she rejoined, with delightful animation; "those are mere ornamental details and not at all essential. The story is true to nature, and might have happened half a hundred times, and no doubt did happen, in those horrid days before the war."
>
> "By the way, Julius," I remarked, "your story doesn't establish what you started out to prove,—that a rabbit's foot brings good luck."
>
> "Hit's plain 'nuff ter me, suh," replied Julius. "I bet young missis dere kin 'splain it herse'f."
>
> "I rather suspect," replied my wife promptly, "that Sis' Becky had no rabbit's foot."
>
> "You is hit de bull's eye de fus' fire, ma'm," assented Julius.
>
> (pp. 158–160)

Annie responds to the sentiments communicated by the tale, rather than to its "mere ornamental details"; in the same spirit, she accepts the rabbit's foot from Julius and proceeds in the book's final story to make common cause with him—thus establishing, as it were, a community of feeling to which John is largely marginal. It seems clear to me that Chesnutt is proposing the conjurer/Uncle Julius as a model for the work of the African-American creative artist.[38] Yes, an entertainer, yes, a consummate verbal artist, and yes, of necessity concerned with survival, he trades the commodity he can create, the tale, for the commodities, including recognition, controlled by white entrepreneurs. Still, he (or she) is most fundamentally committed to creating health, and especially "right feeling" (to use Harriet Beecher Stowe's phrase) about race and history, in the audience through the magic of art. "Right feeling" lies at the root of "right actions," and it is right actions in the world to which those who emphasize the social functions of art are committed. The careers, as well as the writings of Chesnutt's contemporaries Frances E. W. Harper and W.E.B. DuBois[39] embody similar conceptions of prose driven by the engine of social reform—though they were, of course, more activists than Chesnutt was. This basic understanding of artistic function has, I think, been asserted, contested, and transformed throughout the history of African-

American letters—and of other minority communities as well. Such ideas played a critical role in the Black Arts movement and in the emergence of Chicano and Puertoriqueño literature in the 1960s. They reemerge in Alice Walker's "faith in the power of the written word to reach, to teach, to empower and encourage—to change and save lives."[40]

My point here is less to argue the validity of such conceptions of the social or political functions of the writer—for they are surely problematic—than to pose them against the more academically accepted view of artistic achievement, and to suggest the implications of this distinction for the development of aesthetic theory and artistic practice among marginalized writers in the United States. In "The Art of Fiction," published just as Chesnutt began to reach his stride as a writer, Henry James states as succinctly as anyone has a contrasting mimetic view of art—especially of fiction, but of painting and history quite as well. James' fundamental assertion is that fiction, like history, is an attempt "to represent and illustrate the past, the actions of men. . . ." He has little patience with a moral view of the purpose of fiction. "What is the meaning," he asks,

> of your morality and your conscious moral purpose? Will you not define your terms and explain how (a novel being a picture) a picture can be either moral or immoral? You wish to paint a moral picture or carve a moral statue: Will you not tell us how you would set about it? We are discussing the Art of Fiction; questions of art are questions (in the widest sense) of execution; questions of morality are quite another affair, and will you not let us see how it is that you find it so easy to mix them up?[41]

Chesnutt had some answers to James' questions. In an often-cited passage in his journal, he posed the aspirations he had set for himself as a literary artist.

> The object of my writings would not be so much the elevation of the colored people as the elevation of the whites—for I consider the unjust spirit of caste which is so insidious as to pervade a whole nation, and so powerful as to subject a whole race and all connected with it to scorn and social ostracism— I consider this a barrier to the moral progress of the American people; and I would be one of the first to head a determined, organized crusade against it. Not a fierce indiscriminate onset, not an appeal to force, for this is something that force can but slightly affect, but a moral revolution which must be brought about in a different manner. . . .
> This work is of a two-fold character. The negro's part is to prepare himself for recognition and equality, and it is the province of literature to open the way for him to get it—to accustom the public mind to the idea; to lead people on, imperceptibly, unconsciously, step by step, to the desired state of feeling. If I can do anything to further this work, and can see any likelihood of obtaining success in it, I would gladly devote my life to it.[42]

Chesnutt sustained this sense of vocation—together with the desire to become rich and famous by writing—throughout his career, even as he perforce observed the failure of prose to contain the rising tide of turn-of-the-century racism.[43]

It should come as no surprise that from the perspective of minority or marginalized groups, art should have a more clearly social, perhaps utilitarian, function. In one of his letters Bartolomeo Vanzetti writes, "our friends must speak loudly to be heard by our murderers, our enemies have only to whisper or even be silent to be understood."[44] Vanzetti is explaining how the imbalance of social and political power requires demonstrative behavior if a group of Italian anarchists is ever to be noticed, much less responded to, in Yankee New England, but what he says is suggestive about marginality more generally. The struggle for survival, for space and hope, commands all the limited resources available to a marginalized people. Art cannot stand outside that struggle; on the contrary, it must play an important role in it,[45] though the precise nature of that role will vary enormously.

It will thus be essential in elaborating a comparative study of American literary cultures to examine how art has functioned in historically specific situations to develop and sustain marginalized communities. For example, the work of creation has definable, if also changing relationships to other kinds of work. Dan Tannacito has examined the role of poetry and song in the organization of western miners during the early years of this century,[46] and Martha Vicinus has surveyed the varied functions of working-class art, primarily in nineteenth-century Britain.[47] Their pioneering studies, and more recent work (especially in England) suggests, first, that working-class art (to focus on that for the moment) often is produced in group situations, rather than in the privacy of a study—or garret—and it is similarly experienced in the hall, the church, the work-site, the quilting bee, the picket line. It thus emerges from the experiences of a particular group of people facing particular problems in a particular time. Much of it is therefore not conceived as timeless and transcendent; rather, it might be called "instrumental." As Tannacito puts it, "the value of the Colorado miners' poetry derived exclusively from the use made of the poems by their audience. The audience was an immediate one. The objective [in writing] was inseparable from those goals" toward which the workers' lives directed them. Vicinus points out that working-class artists, themselves persuaded of the power of literature to "influence people's behavior," aimed to "persuade readers to adopt particular beliefs." Some recommended the bourgeois values embodied in the culture of what they thought of as their "betters." Others, despairing of social and political change, devoted their work to reassuring readers that their lives, debased as they might have become, still had value, and to providing at least some entertainment and consolation in an oppressive world. Many wrote to help change the status quo. Their work, Vicinus says, aimed "to arouse and focus social tension in order to channel it toward specific political actions." By "clarifying" or making vivid economic, social, and political relationships between working people and those who held power, they helped to "shape individual and class consciousness" and to "imbue a sense of class solidarity that encouraged working people to fight for social and political equality."

Tannacito provides a number of instances of the ways in which the miner poets tried to accomplish such goals. Poems of "praise," for example, explicitly tried to link heroic deeds of the past with the contemporary workers' community. Other poems sought to inspire specific forms of struggle, job actions, voting, boycotts. Miner poets, like working-class artists generally, wrote about the world they and their readers shared: the job, oppression by bosses, the militia and the scabs, a heritage of common struggle. They saw art not as a means for removing people from the world in which they lived— however desirable that might seem—nor as a device for producing "catharsis" or "stasis," whatever these terms mean precisely. Rather, art aimed to inspire consciousness about and actions within the world, to make living in that world more bearable, to extend experiences of that world, indeed to enlarge the world working people could experience. Thus, even as sophisticated an example of working-class fiction as Tillie Olsen's "Tell Me a Riddle" centrally concerns the problem of inspiring a new generation with the values, hopes, and images that directed the actions and aspirations of an earlier revolutionary generation and that lie buried under the grit produced by forty years of daily life. Or consider how Morris Rosenfeld renders the experience of time-discipline in his work as a pants presser:

> The Clock in the workshop,—it rests not a moment;
> It points on, and ticks on: eternity—time;
> Once someone told me the clock had a meaning,—
> In pointing and ticking had reason and rhyme. . . .
> At times, when I listen, I hear the clock plainly;—
> The reason of old—the old meaning—is gone!
> The maddening pendulum urges me forward
> To labor and still labor on.
> The tick of the clock is the boss in his anger.
> The face of the clock has the eyes of the foe.
> The clock—I shudder—Dost hear how it draws me?
> It calls me "Machine" and it cries [to] me "Sew"![48]

Rosenfeld is concerned to capture, and to mourn, the passing in a particular historical moment of an older, less time-disciplined order of work, as well as the degradation of the worker to the status of machine. The poem gives names and pictures to the experiences that Rosenfeld and his fellow-workers encountered in moving from the Shtetl to the sweatshops of the new world; it proposes to incorporate the sweatshop, including its time-clock rhythms, into an ideological form that offers its readers a certain power in relationship to, if not over, their working environment.

Working-class art thus functions to focus consciousness and to develop ideology, but it can also play a variety of other roles. Songs were used, especially by black slaves and nominally free laborers, to set the pace of work in a group and, at the same time, to relieve the tension and pent-up feelings born of oppressive labor. Leaders lined out a rhythm for hoeing, chopping, lifting bales, for rowing boats. At the same time, the songs spoke realistically about the shared labor, and more covertly, perhaps, about those exacting it.[49] Similarly, sorrow songs or spirituals served not only to express grief and to sustain hope in slavery, but they were also used as signals to prepare for escapes from it.[50] Again, during the civil rights movement of the 1950s and 1960s, what were originally church hymns underwent conversion to marching songs and sometimes were a means for triumphing over one's jailers, who often threatened singers with punishment.

A different set of instances is provided by the development in the 1960s of newspapers like *El Malcriado* and *El Grito del Norte,* of El Teatro Campesino, and of a variety of other community-based institutions of Chicano culture. Commenting on the poetry published in *El Malcriado,* Tomas Ybarra-Frausto has written that its primary "function was to sustain the spirit of struggle while simultaneously evoking aesthetic response."[51] Similarly, Luis Valdez, the founder of El Teatro Campesino, saw specifically social functions for the work of the troupe. The Actos, he wrote

> (1) inspire the audience to social action, (2) illuminate specific points about social problems, (3) show or hint at a solution, and (4) express what people are thinking.[52]

Cultural activity thus becomes part of a process for transforming people from passive sufferers into activists in struggle.

This is, however, only one of the roles art may play in a community, but those functions will change as a society or a community within it changes. One need only lay side by side Wigglesworth's "The Day of Doom" (or, perhaps more interestingly, Edward Taylor's "Preliminary Meditations"), Whitman's "Song of Myself," and Eliot's "The Wasteland" to observe profound alterations in poetic function—as well, of course, as in form. One cannot, then, simply say that "art functions in thus and such a fashion for minority communities." One needs, rather, to say that in certain periods art may help unify and stir a people; in others it may shape and express sustaining beliefs; in still others it may help arouse the awareness of those outside a group; in yet others, it may become an arena within which differing values and ideologies contest for power; in others it may come to be a mode primarily of individual expression and self-actualization. It may perform all these functions. My point, then, is the need to be aware not only of the varieties of artistic function but of their changing character over time.

Another way of thinking about differing conceptions of artistic function may be provided by the distinction (or relationship), nicely embodied in Uncle Julius' approach to telling tales, between the "exchange value" and the "use value" of art. An especially moving example of "use value" is offered by the Kentucky mountain songs sung at the funeral of "Jock" Yablonski and recorded with great majesty in the film "Harlan County, U.S.A." In a larger sense, all marginalized art (all art[53]) must be explored precisely in terms of its *use.* Partly that is a function of marginality itself: as I have said, the struggle for existence and dignity necessarily involves all available resources, including art. But partly, I think, this phenomenon is explained by the fundamental character of marginalized (in this instance specifically of working-class) culture, what Raymond Williams called "solidarity." Solidarity is not simply a slogan or an abstraction that happens to appeal to many people who work. It is, rather, a way of describing the culture of people who have been pushed together into workplaces and communities where survival and growth enforce interdependence. In this context, the work of the artist—while it may in some respects be expressive and private—remains overwhelmingly functional in his or her community.[54] And an approach to it cannot strip it of this context without ripping away its substance.

In a certain sense, the issue posed between Chesnutt and Valdez or the singers in "Harlan County, U.S.A.," on the one hand, and James, on the other, is less a conflict over hostile theories of art than a difference over what one looks at in the process of creating and experiencing art. James focuses attention on the polishing of technique, the shaping of the forms by which a work achieves the "solidity of specification" he regards as the truest measure of artistic achievement. Lying behind his point of view are the assumptions that artists are people much like himself and that they address people much like himself, that art emerges from fineness of sensibility and intelligence and helps hone a like refinement in its audience. The poets and painters of the ethnic cultural movements of the 1960s and 1970s, like their predecessors, were by no means indifferent to form; on the contrary, in meetings and in print they discussed formal issues, the elaboration of technique, and the need to balance both the demands of social activism and those, perhaps different, of aesthetic excellence. But the primary concern was, in the first instance, how the *creation* of art helps its creators emerge from passivity and indifference before the world. And then, on the other side of the creative work, so to speak, the concern was the *impact* of the work on the consciousness of those who experience it. Creator and audience—James speaks little of them except to urge the young novelist to "catch the color of life," and to state, regarding the reader, that there's no disputing taste. But for most people, and especially those from poor and minority communities, art cannot be contemplated, as it were, only from within.[55]

From another point of view, however, we are facing quite distinct artistic theories. That becomes clear when we realize that the usual standards of aesthetic merit are, as James proposes, the form and language of a text. "Truth of detail," James says, "the air of reality (solidity of specification)" constitute "the supreme virtue of a novel—the merit on which all its other merits (including that conscious moral purpose of which Mr. Besant speaks) helplessly and submissively depend . . . The cultivation of this success, the study of this exquisite process, form, to my taste, the beginning and the end of the art of the novelist" ("The Art of Fiction," p. 85).[56]

"To what end," Chesnutt might have responded, "should a writer 'catch the color . . . the substance of the human spectacle'? Is not merit determined by the capacity of a work to engage genuine feelings and thus to open us to others' lives, and worlds, and needs? Even to prod us to action *in* the world?"

With that idea, James would show little patience. Speaking in what emerges as his own voice, he writes,

> "I needn't remind you that there are all sorts of tastes: who can know it better? Some people, for excellent reasons, don't like to read about carpenters; others, for reasons even better, don't like to read about courtesans. Many object to Americans. Others (I believe they are mainly editors and publishers) won't look at Italians.... [Readers] choose their novels accordingly, and if they don't care about your idea they won't, a fortiori, care about your treatment."
>
> So that it comes back very quickly, as I have said, to the liking: in spite of M. Zola...who will not reconcile himself to this absoluteness of taste, thinking that there are certain things that people ought to like, and that they can be made to like...Selection will be sure to take care of itself, for it has a constant motive behind it. That motive is simply experience. As people feel life, so they will feel the art that is most closely related to it.
>
> ("The Art of Fiction," pp. 89–90)

James speaks with the ease of one whose subjects, at least many of them, will suit the interest and taste, will register the experience of his audience. But that presumption is not universally shared. The artist from a marginalized group can by no means rely on readers feeling the life which throbs in the world of the carpenter or the Italian. Indeed, the very first battle this artist must fight is precisely that defined by Zola: making readers like, or, more to the point, find interest in matters and people quite outside their experience.[57]

There are different ways in which you can respond to the perception that your audience may find your subject not to its taste: you can try to persuade your readers, by novelty, expostulation, or seduction, to take an interest in the case; you can set fresh banners snapping in the wind; you can extend a calming hand, leading quietly down the unfamiliar, rutted path. It may all come to nothing. Your choice may be to settle upon a circle of devotees, running the risk of becoming merely precious to them—and yourself. Or you may lapse, in Tillie Olsen's apt word, into "silences."

The question of function is thus critically related, on the one hand, to subject and, on the other, to audience. These connections force us to shift our gaze from the aspirations writers or political communities hold for their art to its material consequences. For intentions, however good, do not define what a work actually accomplishes, as William Wimsatt pointed out long ago. Rather, we have to look at the material functions creative works perform in a world defined by commodity transactions, productive labor, and ideological contests. Whatever else they may be, art works in a capitalist society are commodities, as Chesnutt's John and Uncle Julius both clearly understand. In this respect art works cannot be understood outside of the context of the culture industry, which is where (if they are read) they are produced and marketed. Unlike in Chesnutt's story, where the relationship between artist and audience is virtually unmediated, in everyday life that relationship is in fact shaped by the complex processes of publication and distribution. The interaction between Julius, John, and Annie offers, in a sense, an idealized picture of the artist at work; the relationships are clearly different from those that exist between Chesnutt the artist and his audience. For those *were* mediated, not only by important white critics like William Dean Howells and by the strong emphasis in magazines of the 1890s on using literary works to sell other commodities advertised in their pages, but also by the ways in which other pieces of writing on the race question—most of them decidedly retrogressive—shaped how an audience could receive Chesnutt's text. Within his texts, the conjurer/artist can create healthy change; outside—or, rather, in the world wherein his stories were bought and sold—that seldom happened. This contradiction marks out the gap between functional aspirations and material consequences, and it is out of this widening abyss that, as one might say, Silence emerged to enfold Chesnutt.

Given the manifold difficulties of identifying the historically specific functions of artworks, not to speak of the problems of differentiating aspiration from consequence, it is not surprising that an emphasis on form has dominated criticism and teaching since the 1920s, and has been revalidated in current debates over appropriate methods for criticizing marginalized work. Formalist critics concentrate on tracing the lineaments of a book's structure, its modes of figuration, its turns of language, perhaps its interactions with other texts; and they judge a work as a more or less fully realized aesthetic object, whether as a picture that "renders the look of things" or as a world in itself. The alternative we have been tracing asks how the work acts *in* the world, of which it and we constitute parts, by touching human feeling, shaping consciousness, simply offering lessons, and providing purchasable commodities. Recent reader response criticism has, once again, begun to examine the experience of literature in terms of its power to influence consciousness and shape concepts of self and community.[58] It seems likely to me that such a trend will be enhanced by the need to reconstruct the role of criticism implicit in a comparative approach to the literatures of the United States. Further, we might then get past what seems to me the quite mistaken notion that coming to understand the social functions of marginalized art somehow demeans it, reducing Richard Wright's *Native Son* to a sociological study and Robert Hayden's "Middle Passage" to a historical tract. To be sure, viewing any work of art *only* in its functional dimensions will produce a limiting criticism, rendering the work itself, as Henry Louis Gates, Jr. has commented, "as if it were invisible, or literal, or a one-dimensional document."[59] My argument is that failing to see the functionality of marginalized art simply misses one of its major values and often opens it, as well, to inappropriately applied formal paradigms.

At the same time, in thus balancing the emphasis on form and structure with a concern for subject, feeling, audience, and impact, I would not wish to be taken as suggesting an indifference to form on the part of marginalized writers. On the contrary, as I wish now to propose, formal questions are critical to a comparative study. At issue are the kinds of forms and structures central to work by marginalized writers, and how these may differ from those working in the tradition represented by Henry James and his successors.

IV

Few elements of human creativity are as hierarchically organized as presentational language. We have, implicitly or explicitly, a Received Standard form of speech, and "dialects," which mark one as lower class or provincial. Certain languages (e.g., French) have carried more status for English speakers than others (e.g., Spanish). In prosody, academic critics value complexity, ambiguity, irony over simplicity, directness, transparency; written, fixed forms over oral, improvisational; the formal genres we call "fine arts" over the "practical" we call "crafts" or "fragmentary genres," like letters. Thus we once learned to place epic poetry at the apogee of forms. Below it, ranging down a great chain of types, we found dramatic and lyric poetry, the novel, short fiction; and then, as if crossing into suspect territory, genres like autobiography, journals, letters, transcriptions. The status of genres in some degree informs the status of their professors. In the study of marginalized literatures, however, we need to reexamine—even suspend—our assumptions about formal hierarchy and concentrate on discovering the formal conventions that emerge from those literatures themselves, rather than from our training as literary practitioners.

Conventions of composition and language are, after all, largely culture specific as well as hierarchic. One of the most persistent and dominant patterns in English poetry, for example, is the iambic pentameter line, which may be rooted in stress patterns in the declarative sentence characteristic of Received Standard English. Poetic structures built on this iambic line, such as blank verse and the sonnet, exercise a compelling influence on writers, perhaps because they simply learn to use patterns they hear, read and study. By contrast, West African-based cultures, including those of black Americans, reflect the importance of a call and response pattern of verse construction— as in work songs, the blues, and many hymns. Similarly, code switching (shifting within a line or sentence from English to Spanish, or the reverse) is important in some Chicano and Puerto Rican poetry—as it can be in street corner conversation, verbal play, and the creole called Spanglish. Likewise, repetitive forms are vital in Native American narratives, chants, and in many poems. Further, the rhythms of black "folk" English differ from those of Received Standard; obviously, the cadences of non-English primary speakers differ still more.

This is by no means to say that African-American writers invariably display the influence of call and response patterns, that bilingual poets inevitably switch codes,[60] and that Native American writers must use repetitive forms. No more do they necessarily use folk speech or remain free of the influence of forms like the sonnet. On the contrary, the pulls of traditional English

forms and upper-class white standards of speech have been very strong on
minority writers, perhaps because such forms implicitly embody the English
tradition they often wish to possess. Indeed, the history of each minority
culture in the United States shows a period in which the artists are influenced
deeply by the practice of earlier generations of British or British-actuated
authors. Thus, most Native American and African-American poetry of the
nineteenth and early twentieth centuries imitates Scott, Byron and Longfellow
to excess, and the early black novel sometimes shows the stifling hand of
sentimental fictional conventions.

Differences in formal conventions come into particular prominence when
we contrast those derived from oral and from written traditions. Written
literary traditions tend to impose a sacredness on texts which, in turn, produces two primary techniques of literary study: historical and textual analysis,
designed initially to establish "true" texts, and *explication de texte,* designed
to tease out its many potential meanings. Underlying this view of the sanctity
of the written text is a romantic understanding of a literary work as the artist's
private product, emerging from the power of "his" genius to express in a
distinctive voice responses to a uniquely experienced world. The function of
literary study, from this perspective, is to focus the reader's attention on the
literary work itself because of its inherent value as an aesthetic structure.
Further, change within the frameworks of a written literary culture is often
wrenching and violent, as if the new poet had to explode out of the gravity
pull of established conventions. Pound's injunction to "make it new" was
only, as it were, a codification of what American predecessors like Whitman
and Dickinson had practiced, but their difficulties in establishing the value
of what they created illustrate my point. Further, the "anxiety of influence"
about which Harold Bloom has written may well be a distinctive feature only
of dominant written traditions.

By contrast, oral traditions are less obssessed with the sacredness *of* a
text, and more concerned with its *functions,* sometimes including its sacred
functions, sometimes its functions in sustaining popular resistance to ideological domination. The *precise* reproduction of a song, poem, or story is
probably of less moment than, on the one hand, the maintenance of its basic
qualities and, on the other, its vivid recreation in a new context for a new
time and need. Improvisation is a major virtue of oral tradition, but it is
important to recognize that improvisation is based on known and shared
materials. New songs are often based upon old ones, and there is less concern
with the unique qualities of art than with building variations upon tunes,
themes, and texts well-known in the community. For example, songs like
"Hold the Fort" and "We Are Building a Strong Union," which began as
gospel hymns, went through a series of metamorphoses in order to serve the
needs of a diverse sequence of workers' organizations—in the case of the
former, including the British transport workers, the Knights of Labor, and
the Industrial Workers of the World. The Wobbly poet, Joe Hill, constructed
some of his best-known songs as takeoffs on Salvation Army hymns. The
spiritual "Oh, Freedom" became one of the most popular songs of the Civil

Rights movement; as the movement's militance increased, many singers changed the song's refrain from "Before I be a slave/ I be buried in my grave/ And go home to my Lord/ And be free" to "Before . . . grave/ And I'll fight for my right/ To be free."[61]

Pound's sense of "make it new"—that is, dispensing with what exists and evoking wholly different texts from differing materials—would probably be regarded with suspicion by people whose culture is distinctly oral. In *Mules and Men* a woman in one of Zora Neale Hurston's "lieing" contests tells a story to explain why Negroes are black. One of the men, offended by her success, accuses her of inventing the "lie": "'Tain't no such story nowhere. She jus' made dat one up herself." Her friend responds, "Naw, she didn't. I been knowin' dat ole tale"—that is, the story is well-established, traditional, and therefore worthy of repeating and staking a claim to.[62] Oral forms also depend upon *apparent* simplicity of structure; upon oral-formulaic devices, including refrains as well as repetition of words, phrases and lines; often upon certain stock characters, situations, phrases, and poetic or song sources well-known to the original audience. Larry Penn's teamster ballad "Been Rollin' So Long," for example, clearly echoes "Lord Randall" in form. These qualities obviously reflect the needs of performance and of reception by a listening audience, but they are at least in some respects carried over into written genres that continue to reflect oral traditions.

It would be a mistake, however, to suppose that the problem with which we are dealing concerns simply the difference between established written and oral cultures. In the first place, virtually all ethnic, minority and working-class literatures in the United States are by now in written form. But more to the point: *all* written cultures represent the transformation and codification of earlier oral cultures; once writing is developed among a people, oral cultures gradually unfold themselves into written form. That is as true of the traditions of British literature as it is of Navajo. Thus, as Ann Fitzgerald has suggested to me, what we are comparing are cultures at different stages in the process of transformation from oral to written. Part of the difference is simply chronological: writing came to Britain twelve or fifteen hundred years ago, but to Native American tribes as well as to most African-Americans within the last century. But perhaps more important, the processes through which oral forms pass into written forms differ substantially from culture to culture. They invariably involve performance, but the concept of performance that informs Shakespearean drama—still close to British oral traditions—is far different from that which underlies Hurston's *Their Eyes Were Watching God* or N. Scott Momaday's *The Way to Rainy Mountain*. The medieval trope and the Elizabethan stage may be cousins, but distant ones, of the AME testimony and preaching and the street corner theatrics Hurston displays in *Mules and Men*. And these, in turn, only remotely resemble the ceremonies and myths that inform Momaday's narrative, or the Chicano texts that derive from folk poetry, such as the Corridos.[63]

Still, it is instructive to remember that Shakespeare composed at the nether end of a process of transformation from an oral to a written tradition. In their

brawling, topical quality, their changeableness from performance to performance, their dependence upon traditional subjects and themes, their function
in reenforcing recently-established social and political norms, and in the manner their language forever plays against the edges of meaning, his dramas
reflect how open they were to the still generative orality of British common
culture.[64] These are, many of them, qualities we might expect—indeed, will
find—in work with which we are concerned here, like that of Hurston, for
example, or that of Toni Morrison and John Wideman. Of course, such writers
use today's most popular genre, the novel, which offers a different set of
opportunities and constraints from Elizabethan drama. Within that genre,
however, they self-consciously strive to sustain a *voice,* at once elevated and
commonplace, serious and linguistically playful. As in oral cultures, success
in verbal play confirms artistic power, serves to provide a certain breathing
space within the dense and often dark fabric of plot, and registers a kind of
ascendancy in the continuing struggle by marginalized cultures to emerge
from the shadows. But there is a cost to what Wideman calls "bi-lingual
fluency"; he writes:

> Afro-Americans must communicate in a written language which in vary-
> ing degrees is foreign to our oral traditions. You learn the language of power,
> learn it well enough to read and write but its forms and logic cut you off,
> separate you from the primal authenticity of your experience, experience
> whose meaning resides in the first language you speak, the language not only
> of words but gestures, movements, rules of silence and expressive possibil-
> ities, of facial and tactile understanding, a language of immediate, sensual,
> intimate reciprocity, of communal and self-definition.[65]

In studying texts still tuned to oral cadences, we need to bring back into
question some generally unexamined critical assumptions and touchstones.
One of these is the idea that a literary work should so far as possible be
complete in itself and should not have to depend for fulfillment of its intentions
on knowledge, ideas, and images that the text does not provide. The best
fiction, Henry James proposes, "renders" the world it pictures; it is not up
to the reader to supply what the text omits. But in many traditional cultures,
those of Native Americans for example, the audience for a tale or ritual
presentation would a priori be familiar with characters or situations. It would
be superfluous, indeed meaningless, for the artists to introduce, describe, and
elaborate upon what is known and shared, like Coyote and his machinations,
the role of the storyteller, or the recent experiences of the tribe. Indeed,
works like Leslie Marmon Silko's "Storyteller" or "Yellow Woman" vibrate
with echoes of those traditional figures. Thus a tale may not be "complete"
precisely because the expectation is that the audience will bring to it whatever
is left unstated. In fact, when we look closely, we find that the notion of a
work of art as self-contained, complete in itself, is a chimera. Any art work
plays upon, or sometimes against, the expectations, the patterns of knowledge, and the assumptions about form and content—not to speak of the
conventions of language—an audience brings to it. Thus, whether we are

talking about a Henry James novel or a Harlequin romance, the issue is not in this respect whether a work is "fully realized" or not, but what it anticipates an audience will bring to it, and what purposes are served by thus depending upon what the reader furnishes for the book. That leads to a new set of questions, like, for example, whether in *Invisible Man* Ellison draws upon certain folk traditions of the trickster to differentiate the responses of black and white readers to scenes like those involving Clifton, whether there are in effect "inside" and "outside" readings of his book.

A second set of issues involves how we evaluate texture. As critics of written literature, we have largely ascribed value to organic complexity in structure, ambiguity, and tension in language—each line crafted new, each situation fresh. T. S. Eliot argues that "poets in our civilization, as it exists at present, must be *difficult*. . . . The poet must become more and more comprehensive, more allusive, more indirect, in order to force, to dislocate if necessary, language into his meaning."[66] Reading such preferences back into the past, Eliot and his successors extolled the virtues of the metaphysical poets, and suiting practice to theory (or, perhaps, vice versa), they developed the complex modernist style exemplified by *The Four Quartets,* Pound's *Cantos,* or Hart Crane's "The Bridge."

A few years after Eliot published his most influential essays, Langston Hughes was traveling across the country reading his poetry at black schools and colleges—both to make a living in Depression America and because, as Mary McLeod Bethune had told him, "People need poetry."[67] In his autobiographical *I Wonder As I Wander* Hughes describes part of what became an expert performance in the following way:

> By the time I reached this point in the program my non-literary listeners would be ready to think in terms of their own problems. Then I read poems about women domestics, workers on the Florida roads, poor black students wanting to shatter the darkness of ignorance and prejudice, and one about the sharecroppers of Mississippi:
>> Just a herd of Negroes
>> Driven to the field,
>> Plowing, planting, hoeing,
>> To make the cotton yield. . . .
>
> Many of my verses were documentary, journalistic and topical. All across the South that winter I read my poems about the plight of the Scottsboro boys. . . .
>
> (p. 58)

Now I would not deny the virtues of complex poetic structures, of ironic distance, or of the dense, allusive modernist line . . . in their place, so to speak. But these are not the only virtues in poetry. Nor are they the only means for representing the modern world, much less "our civilization." Prufrock's is not the only love song, and it tells us no more about "our civilization" than "Same in Blues":

> I said to my baby,
> Baby, take it slow.

> I can't she said, I can't!
> I got to go!
> *There's a certain*
> *amount of traveling*
> *in a dream deferred.*

Indeed, the phrase "our civilization" is itself problematic. Obviously, not all inhabitants of a given space participate in what power defines as "civilization" (or "culture"), much less have real access to its privileges. "Complexity" in language can be, in fact, a mask for privilege, a screen behind which power sustains itself—in criticism as in poetry.[68] What image better catches our "civilization" than Langston Hughes' ordinary "raisin in the sun"? Gwendolyn Brooks had no need for obscurity of language when she sent her poetic journalist to observe the ordinariness of hate in Little Rock. Indirection is not at a premium when Judy Grahn writes of the "common woman," or Susan Griffin thinks of Harriet Tubman and the problem of feeding children, or Denise Levertov writes of what the Vietnamese were like. To what extent is the manner in which one uses language dependent upon where one is placed in "our" civilization, or upon one's audience and one's conception of the functions of art?

An artist's outlook on the culture underlies the conventions he or she adopts. Eliot saw his civilization in decline and from its shards and fragments erected a Great Allusive Wall against the impending ruin. In a sense his poems, like Pound's, constitute a form of humanities curriculum, "The Rise, Decline and (perhaps) Resurrection of Christian Civilization." That may help to explain the great popularity of their poetry with an earlier generation of academics, as well as the faintly musty quality some of today's critics detect. But there are other assumptions about American culture and thus other ways even of "assembling fragments of experience" from the past—indeed, other conceptions of the fragments suitable for preservation, which is at the center of the argument over "cultural literacy." If Hughes's audiences became restless, he would pull out his poem "Cross":

> The first line—intended to awaken all sleepers—I would read in a loud voice:
> > My old man's a white old man. . . .
> And this would usually arouse any who dozed. Then I would pause before
> continuing in a more subdued tone:
> > My old mother's black . . .
> > I wonder when I'm gonna die,
> > Being neither white nor black?

And then he would conclude, "after a resumé of the racial situation in our country, with an optimistic listing of past achievements on the part of Negroes, and future possibilities" by reciting "I, too, sing America" (*I Wonder as I Wander*, p. 59). "De-dop!" is, to be sure, a different fragment from "Shantih," but which expresses "our civilization"?

Similarly, in studying "women's work" like quilts and blankets, Sheila de Brettville has proposed that their "assemblage of fragments pieced together whenever there is time" has often been organized into a "complex matrix [that] suggests depth and intensity as an alternative to progress."[69] Vera Norwood has examined the efforts of a number of southwestern women artists to utilize in their contemporary work fragments of the ordinary lives of their foremothers, such as stitching, pieces of lace, botanical drawings, and snatches of letters, diaries, and conversations.[70] Judith Slomin pointed out some years ago that in diaries and other fragmentary forms favored by women writers "abundant details reproduce the effects of chaos, disorder, and overcrowding. . . . The emphasis on the factual underlines the challenge to or the pressures on creativity that exist when the artist cannot escape from life."[71] Rolando Hinojosa's Klail City Death Trip series assembles fragments of imagined South Texas experience, often widely separated in time—newspaper reports, diary entries, narrative accounts—precisely to contest the definition of what constitutes "our civilization" and who will have power within it. Hinojosa's fragments may be contrasted fruitfully with those arranged in *U.S.A.* by John Dos Passos in what was, for its time, a significant departure in form and subject. Similarly, books as diverse as Momaday's *The Way to Rainy Mountain,* Rudolfo Anaya's *Bless Me, Ultima,* and Maxine Hong Kingston's *The Woman Warrior* are, among other things, efforts to preserve as well as to utilize anew elements, sometimes as fragmentary as in Kingston's tale of "No Name Woman," of their diverse cultural traditions.

Works by marginalized writers are by no means necessarily simple in language or in structure, nor do they inevitably ignore Euro-American traditions. On the contrary, books like *Beloved, Meridian,* and *Ceremony,* not to mention *Invisible Man,* are structurally rich and there are dozens of minority poets whose language and imagery operate fully within modernist or postmodernist modes. Still, one needs to account for certain artifacts of critical response: for example, Thomas Pynchon has published three novels, and there are at least a dozen books and untold articles out explaining them. About the group of black women novelists—Paule Marshall, Toni Morrison, Toni Cade Bambara, Alice Walker, Gayl Jones, Gloria Naylor—writing perhaps the most compelling fiction today, there are relatively few works.[72] To be sure, some of the work of these writers is more recent, and the disproportion will no doubt change over time. But in some degree as readers of literature we have been taught and have learned to valorize the pleasures of the epistemological games constructed by writers like Pynchon, Nabokov, and Barth. Let us leave apart the question of whether promoting the virtues of complexity, denseness, and even obscurity, and maintaining an outlook of genteel pessimism, are in some degree functions of sustaining the roles—and jobs—of literary interpreters. We still need to ask whether the expectation, the demand for denseness and speculative play in a work does not disable critics from apprehending other virtues, of transparency in structure, of immediacy in language, and of feelings deeply engaged by symbol.

Further, few minority writers can evade the tension (and opportunity) imposed by the implicit demand that they appeal to quite differing language and cultural communities. A writer for the *New York Review of Books* can, perhaps, sneer at oral traditions in literature, but minority writers do so, or otherwise detach themselves from the linguistic contexts of their own communities, at peril of drying up the sources of creativity and of validation—evoking from their audience a devastatingly tired "well, so what?" Artworks can be ranged along a wide spectrum, from those that are most dense, elaborated, to those that are most transparent, straightforward. It seems to me that writers from marginalized groups make use of more bands on this spectrum than those whose reference group is in significant measure academic intellectuals. In reading work produced by writers from marginalized groups, in developing a comparative approach to American literature, we must ourselves widen our perception and appreciation of formal features that are often different from those we have been trained to acknowledge as appropriately literary.

We are only at the beginning of understanding and explaining the distinctive forms and conventions, the images and language styles developed by marginalized writers. Gloria Anzaldúa and José Saldívar have focused on the historically-rooted trope of the border as central to Mexican-American writing.[73] Robert Stepto has focused on the pervasiveness of the act of reading as a central trope in African-American narratives and on the tension between the traditional forms of Anglo-American literary discourse and the content with which African-American writers fill them.[74] A number of critics, most notably Sherley Anne Williams, Amiri Baraka, Houston Baker, and Steven C. Tracy have examined the interaction of vernacular and song styles like the blues with the written productions of black writers.[75] Henry Louis Gates, Jr. has presented what he calls the African-American "trope of tropes," Signifyin(g), as the dominant formal feature of black literary (and vernacular) traditions.[76] The understanding of the impact of African call and response patterns has also been extended to fiction. Barbara E. Bowen convincingly analyzed the structure and development of Jean Toomer's *Cane* in such terms, arguing that the book is most successful "when Toomer opens up for us what it means to turn the call-and-response pattern into a literary form."[77] In general, a number of critics have invoked the call-and-response form as a mode for thinking about and framing a range of African-American texts.

Similarly, the subject and aims of Leslie Silko's novel *Ceremony* emerge from patterns of repetition with variation. The story of its hero, Tayo, reproduces, albeit with the differences necessary to new times and the remixing of cultures, the "mythic" purification ceremony carried forward by Hummingbird and Fly on behalf of the people, who have strayed after strange and dangerous magic. The language of the mythic/traditional, and of post-Second World War ceremonies interpenetrates, especially in seemingly casual phrases—like "it wasn't easy," "it won't be easy," "it isn't easy"—that migrate from the mythic passages of the novel into descriptions of the experiences of Tayo and his aunt. What we discover with Tayo is the commonality of that experience, through time.

The anticipation of what he might find was strung tight in his belly; suddenly the tension snapped and hurled him into the empty room where the ticking of the clock behind the curtains had ceased. He stopped the mare. The silence was inside, in his belly; there was no longer any hurry. The ride into the mountain had branched into all directions of time. He knew then why the oldtimers could only speak of yesterday and tomorrow in terms of the present moment: the only certainty; and this present sense of being was qualified with bare hints of yesterday or tomorrow, by saying, "I go up to the mountain tomorrow." The ck'o'yo Kaup'a'ta somewhere is stacking his gambling sticks and waiting for a visitor; Rocky and I are walking across the ridge in the moon-light; Josiah and Robert are waiting for us. This night is a single night; and there has never been any other.

(p. 201)

The book's heuristic objective repeats that of the traditional story teller: "to fight off/ illness and death" by regenerating awareness of pattern and order through the language of ceremonies.[78] What Tayo discovers may serve as a metaphor for the perceptions of marginalized critics: "He was not crazy; he had never been crazy. He had only seen and heard the world as it always was: no boundaries, only transitions through all distances and time (p. 258). Repetition, to say it another way, is not merely a convention of composition here, but the fundamental principle of psychological and social order, and the book takes on ever-deeper echoes as one is familiar with the repetitive patterns of traditional Indian narratives. In this sense, traditional forms become in more than a metaphorical sense the lifeblood of a minority artist.

The problem of identifying and validating differing forms and conventions extends to the work of white women as well. Elizabeth Ammons, for example, has contrasted the organizing principles of Sarah Orne Jewett's *The Country of the Pointed Firs* with the "hierarchical mode" of conventional narrative as created by men. Jewett does not use a linear structure, with its built-toward climax coming near the end, but rather what Ammons describes as a "webbed, net-worked" organization, in which the "most highly charged experience of the book . . . comes at the center."[79] Further, Ammons argues, "psychically, the aggregative structure of Jewett's narrative reproduces female relational reality" in the process of constructing a female-centered community. I do not wish here to enter the vexed and problematic issue of the existence of a distinctly female structure or style. What might help illuminate Jewett could obscure her contemporary, Mary Wilkins Freeman, for she organizes her stories along much more traditional patterns of slowly building and quickly resolving conflict, even though the concerns of women, mostly poor, are at the center of almost all of their stories. My point is narrower: Critics have often asked of Jewett's stories questions drawn from other literary contexts and have thus missed the distinctive organizational strategy with which Jewett was working. Thus she was portrayed as engaging *despite* her presumed formal shortcomings, rather than seen as important because of her formal innovations.

Another instance is provided by Elizabeth Stuart Phelps. She begins both *The Silent Partner* and *The Story of Avis* inside the head of an essentially ignorant young woman, who may be taken to represent her primary audience. Phelps's problem in these novels is to bring such women to consciousness concerning matters about which they know little, for instance industrial work, or even a professionally-defined creative life for women. For that goal, the chatty narrative tactics of Stowe (for example, in *The Minister's Wooing*) do not seem particularly productive. In fact, in *The Silent Partner* Phelps experiments with a number of narrative devices to bring her readers inside the heads of people very much unlike themselves—the factory worker, Sip, for example. An analysis of Phelps's narrative tactics suggests how they are quite consciously devised, on the one hand, to engage a specific audience and, on the other, to pursue the goals of her writing, her desire that her readers "weigh and consider" the particular social issues she dramatizes for them.

The issue here is, then, not only the differences in the forms and conventions marginalized writers use, but the uses to which they put such forms and conventions. "Point of view" is a technical device often employed, by Henry James for example, to produce psychological verisimilitude and intimacy of narrative; Charles Chesnutt uses it in "The Passing of Grandison," however, to raise political consciousness. The story is told from the point of view of a white character *in* it, which necessarily places the predominantly white readership *of* the story outside the head and experiences of the black slave, Grandison. The story seems to be constructed to produce an O. Henry-style surprise ending, in which the slavemasters initially celebrate Grandison's unexpected return from Canada. But the ending is less a surprise than a political lesson, for, like the whites in the tale, readers tend to impose their versions of reality on events. Grandison has his own, which emerges only at the story's conclusion, when we find that he had returned to slavery only long enough to spirit his whole family off to freedom. If that ending is a surprise— and in the classroom I have found that it almost always is, even for black students—it confirms that the audience knows as little of Grandison as his slave master, a matter for some embarrassed reflections. "The Passing of Grandison" uses the device of point of view and the conventions of the "puttin' on ol' massa" tale to pursue certain social objectives. Alice Walker's *Meridian* offers a more complex instance of how point of view and sliding time frames are used to move readers from detached amusement to informed malaise, and thus to point outward from the fiction to the world it encourages us to transform. Thus a reconception of forms entails a comparable rethinking of function.

Formal analysis is, and is likely to remain, the meat and potatoes of the literary profession, at least in the classroom. A comparativist strategy compels us to appreciate a broader range of conventions, to set form more fully into historical and functional contexts, and to comprehend better how audience expectation and assumption mandate formal priorities. It may be useful to imagine two pictures: in one, Eliot is conversing with Pound in the courtyard of 70 *bis,* rue Notre-Dame-des Champs, about the latter's proposed revisions of *The Waste Land;* in the second, Hughes is reading "Christ in Alabama" to a packed audience at the (white) University of North Carolina at Chapel Hill. In any case, it is to this last problem, audience, that I now wish to turn.

V

Twenty-five years ago, audience was seldom a concern in literary study. To be sure, it was important for historians of the drama and for Medievalists to establish what kinds of people saw or participated in a performance. And the starting point for work like Ian Watt's on the development of the novel was the recognition of its primarily bourgeois readership. But on the whole, and certainly in the classroom, the responding reader was conceived to be as universal as the work itself. The wide differences in background, assumption, and perception among readers are now a commonplace of literary instruc-tion—or at least of comment about literature, for it is not at all clear how the commonplace translates into changed classroom practice. However that might be, a new style of literary criticism emerged in the 1980s, focused on the implications of reader response to texts, including the idea that "literary texts become visible only from within a particular framework of beliefs."[80] While this kind of criticism may have had its origins in psycholinguistic and epistemological concerns, it seems to me to have emerged and grown precisely because it registers a central reality which is also vital to the comparative study of American literatures: that is, the diversity of audience response to literature in late twentieth-century America.

That diversity, as I have suggested elsewhere in this chapter, arises from the disparity in cultural histories and needs of the heterogeneous population of this country. Increasingly during the past two decades, that heterogeneity has been reflected in college and university classrooms, and in some degree in changing American literature curricula.[81] Most instructors, however, con-tinue to regard the classroom as a neutral ground for literary study, within which differing works can, whatever the contexts of their original articulation, be studied with equal success, and without a great deal of attention to dif-ferences among students apart from the levels of their literacy. In fact, how-ever, the classroom is hardly neutral territory for literary study, since its character privileges certain kinds of texts—particularly those that offer rich and ambiguous possibilities for interpretation—and strips others of their func-tional qualities, such as those that are parts of rituals and performances, or those with heavily-defined historical missions and contexts. Equally to our point here: While it would be foolish to deny the literacy handicaps many of our students face, it would be equally dangerous not to see that they also come to classrooms with substantially different cultural outlooks and diverse expectations—however unarticulated—about art. To say it another way: The recognition of how audiences for art differ in assumptions and desires has been pressed upon many literary practitioners by the fact of classroom diversity.

In confronting audience diversity, teachers and critics of literature are in a sense departing down a road long traveled by marginalized writers. Both for practical and for ideological reasons, minority writers—and white women, differently—have, since the earliest colonies, had to contend with, even if they finally chose to ignore, disparities between readers from the majority culture and those from their own cultures. Until the turn of the twentieth century, and probably into the 1920s, few minority writers—mainly journalists and pamphleteers like David Walker—could afford to confine themselves to readers from their own group. Black readership, for example, was too limited to provide practical vocations for artists such as Chesnutt, Paul Laurence Dunbar (who turned to musical theater), Frances Harper (who earned a living as a lecturer/ performer[82] and as an organizer and educator), or even Pauline Hopkins, though she published with a black-run press. Only in the 1920s, with the increasing concentration in northern urban centers of blacks who were at least modestly affluent, and with the self-conscious efforts of men like Charles S. Johnson to interest white publishers in black writers, was it possible for a significant number of black writers to begin to depend upon— and thus be able to speak primarily to—a black constituency. Further, earlier black writers—as we have seen in the case of Chesnutt—*wished* to address a white audience as part of a campaign to establish the personhood of blacks in white consciousness. Thus, in some sense like slang or other forms of verbal play, writing both revealed to and hid from the majority audience qualities of the minority writer's society and experience. As a spiritual might signal "happy darkies" to whites and "prepare for flight" to blacks, so a poem or play could figure both play and rage, parroting and parodying white texts.

Such generalizations do not, of course, hold for Native American *tribal* art forms, whose audiences were groups within the tribe, and that, indeed, varied in performance depending upon audience factors—like the age and sex of listeners. To this art, Anglos were, and have largely remained, irrelevant—except, to be sure, to the extent that it was federal policy to obliterate the languages and the very culture in which such forms were expressed. But many of the same dualities faced by black writers also confronted those who began to establish a Native American literature, written in English, during the late eighteenth and through the nineteenth centuries: Though their predominant readership was white, their imperatives were established largely by Native American concerns. Thus the constant tension displayed, for example, in Zitkala-Sa's fiction or in her essay "Why I am a Pagan," between seeking and confronting her audience.

Many authors writing in Spanish within the southwestern United States had their work printed in Spanish-language newspapers whose constituencies identified themselves as Mexican, or at least as Spanish-speaking "borderers." For these authors, of course, the tensions of addressing a dual audience did not exist; or, rather, duality emerged as a function of subject, for many nineteenth-century Spanish-language texts written in the United States, such as the autobiography of Mariano Guadalupe Vallejo,[83] addressed the problem of justifying a culture and a life overrun by Anglo settlement and military power. Other writers of autobiographical or historical narratives, for example, Juan Seguin, felt constrained to write in English, precisely to justify American identity, denied by some Anglos.

It is thus clearly the case that, in regard to audience, the evolutions of minority literatures are even more different from one another than in other respects, and that generalizations are even more fragile here than elsewhere. Still, it does seem that for minority writers, audience becomes problematic— at least after some degree of literacy obtains *within* the group—whenever they choose to speak to those outside the group. But at what point historically that choice appears important—and, indeed, at what point it seems again to be irrelevant—has differed from group to group.

These considerations also apply to the history of white women and white men writers in the United States, though the problems that emerge are clearly distinct. For men like Hawthorne and Melville, as is well known, the "difficulty" was that so many of their potential readers were female, and thus, in certain ways like minority writers, they had to address an audience whose culture and expectations partly differed from their own. The resulting tensions seem to have been the source of considerable rage and perhaps a certain duplicity, especially in Melville's stories. For white women there have been other anxieties. In the 1850s and 1860s, writers like Stowe and Alice Cary could converse quite comfortably in their prose with their dominantly female audience. But after the early twentieth-century attacks on the "genteel tradition" in general and women writers in particular, writing to a definitively female audience, as "lady novelists" were "expected" to do, might also ensure the trivialization of one's work, especially in the hands of male critics. Cather, for example, seems to have invoked a significantly male audience, partly by utilizing male consciousness, however qualified, to tell stories like that of "My Antonia." But at least some of the women modernists may have tried self-consciously to speak in voices heard differently by women and by men, offering themselves ironically, for example, as Amy Lowell's "queer lot/ We women who write poetry," or ambiguously as H. D.'s Helen, so hated by the triumphing Greeks.

But after all, the existence of a dual audience cannot be seen simply as a problem; it is also an opportunity, in at least two respects. First, in ideological terms, it allows an important community role to the marginalized writer, as interpreter of (even apologist for) his or her community to the "outside"— the "straight," the "vanilla"—world, even while becoming a source of instruction, delight, and power within—as is surely the case with Lowell's "The Sisters." One thinks of writers like Langston Hughes, celebrating blackness, or Adrienne Rich; indeed, this duality of audience may help explain some basic features of, and shifts in, her poetry and prose.

The second opportunity is perhaps best suggested by a comment made by Maxine Hong Kingston apropos many of the misguided reviews of her first novel.

> The audience of *The Woman Warrior* is also very specific. For example, I address Chinese Americans twice, once at the beginning of the book and once at the end. I ask some questions about what life is like for you, and, happily, you answer. Chinese Americans have written that I explain customs they had not understood. . . . There are puns for Chinese speakers only, and I do not point them out for non-Chinese speakers. There are some visual puns best appreciated by those who write Chinese. I've written jokes in that book so private, only I can get them; I hope I sneaked them in unobtrusively so nobody feels left out. I hope my writing has many layers, as human beings have layers.[84]

The writer, thus addressing multiple audiences, emerges as trickster and clown, deferential and sweet even as she spins away with a grotesque gesture of . . . is it triumph? defiance? invitation? Survival is serious business that, it may be, cannot be taken—or is it *offered?*—all too seriously; slipping the yoke may always involve turning the joke, and thus the trickster becomes a moving center of marginalized discourse.

In a certain sense, citing Hughes and Kingston in the same paragraph suggests something about the related masks—of simplicity, invisibility, incapacity—minority writers often have chosen to present to at least part of their audience. But the two raise a profoundly contrasting question about audience as well. Hughes wrote regularly in the *Chicago Defender,* in books like *Simple Speaks His Mind,* and generally in his poetry for an extensive black audience. It is not clear, as yet, how widely a writer like Kingston is heard within the Chinese-American community. To be sure, the issue of who reads, who listens is not peculiar to marginalized writers. What is distinctive is the question of how, indeed whether, one can aspire to speak, at once, to generalized "human" or even "American" concerns and for the particular experiences of a people defined in the world by caste and class and gender. At what, if any, historical moment is Invisible Man's assertion that perhaps "on the lower frequencies, I speak for you" true, or does Adrienne Rich's "dream of a common language" become a reality? Can marginalized writers in practical ways speak both to the communities that nurtured them and to the majority audience that is part of the social and cultural fabric of oppression? When does aspiring toward the latter audience cut one off from the former? In what ways does that majority audience itself choose the supposed representatives of minority discourse?

The word *audience* itself involves a second problem, for it assumes a sharp line of demarcation between creator and consumer. That distinction is, in some circumstances, far more fluid than it might appear. One old former slave describes the creation of a "spiritual" in a pre-Civil War religious meeting in these words:

> I'd jump up dar and den and hollar and shout and sing and pat, and dey would all cotch de words and I'd sing it to some old shout song I'd heard 'em sing from Africa, and dey'd all take it up and keep at it, and keep a-addin' to it, and den it would be a spiritual.[85]

In such situations, the individual creator is generally less significant than the group; or, rather, to the extent that individuals are creators, they shape a common stock to new group purposes without diminishing or expropriating that common stock. The song leader in church is not asked to provide new hymns (much less copyright old ones) and would be looked at with suspicion if she did so. She is asked to reinvigorate a hymn that is known, perhaps to add something especially appropriate for the occasion.[86] The jazz or blues musician may be admired for a new melody, but probably more important— at least until recently—is the ability to ring variations on melodies the listeners know and follow. I am emphasizing here the "folk," communal elements of certain art forms, in some degree at the expense of art produced by self-conscious individual artists. I do so because an approach through people's culture helps to focus certain distinctive qualities of marginalized art, certain "centers of gravity," that are not so easily seen if one concentrates on the productions of separate artists. Yet, obviously, a continuum exists between songs, poems, and tales that are, so to speak, common property, and works created primarily by individual imaginations.

But what is critical here is precisely the relationship between individual and community. Lawrence Levine, for example, directly connects the *form* of the spiritual with the underlying social reality of black slave life.

> Just as the process by which the spirituals were created allowed for simultaneous individual and communal creativity, so their very structure provided simultaneous outlets for individual and communal expression. The overriding antiphonal structure of the spirituals—the call and response pattern which Negroes brought with them from Africa and which was reinforced in America by the practice of lining out hymns—placed the individual in continual dialogue with his community, allowing him at one and the same time to preserve his voice as a distinct entity and to blend it with those of his fellows.[87]

I would carry the argument in a slightly different direction by suggesting that one center of gravity in much marginalized art is its high level of integration of creator and audience. Works often have their origin, as well as their being, in situations—like performances of El Teatro Campesino—that do not absolutely distinguish active performer/artist from passive audience. Again, critical concentration on artworks distinctive in their isolation is, in part, an artifact of our professional specialization, which sharply distinguishes the study of fixed and participatory forms. It may also be, in part, a hangover of that romantic sensibility that accounted for art simply as the individual product of isolated genius.

In its effort to move away from such romanticism, contemporary critical theory has foregrounded what has always, in my view, been a crucial component of the marginalized writer's consciousness: namely, the reading (or listening) communities for his or her work. As I have suggested, available reading communities have not always shared a writer's discourse; that is no new thing. What is new, I think, are the kinds of questions to which one might now be led by that perception. If I am not the "right" reader for a text, who is? What is the discourse, the assumptions, the ways of talking, shared by the text and the readership it tries to define for itself?[88] In what ways do the needs and interests of particular audiences themselves define not merely the extent to which a particular work is read, but what is discovered in it? These are by no means questions relevant primarily to marginalized literatures. Indeed, the construction of a particular version of Melville in the 1920s bears witness to how the ideological and professional priorities of critics determine how a writer is viewed. But the shift in critical focus represented by such questions is, I think, enabling for reading the marginalized. For it helps free such literatures from the unexamined reading "center" that has, in fact, been crucial to the very construction of marginality.

I recall the argument at a small discussion group at the Modern Language Association convention in San Francisco a decade ago. One of the male scholars was criticizing Zora Neale Hurston: *Their Eyes Were Watching God* concerns the process by which Janie finds her voice, he insisted, but she fails to use it—or, rather, Hurston fails to show her using it—in the trial scene. It was, I think, Alice Walker who responded that while *many* of us find our voice, *some* of us learn when it's better not to use it. In retrospect, it seems to me there was virtue in both positions. Within the book Janie chooses her specific audience, Pheoby, and through her, if it suits, others in the black community. But it is not a life, not a story, intended for white judgment and therefore the courtroom may be an inappropriate forum. Hurston thus builds into her novel what amounts to an idealized parable about the black woman writer and her audience. But Hurston herself did not, as a writer, share that luxury, for her income depended upon white patronage or readership. At the end of the trial scene, Janie is surrounded by a protective cordon of *white* women and emphatically separated from the black community, a separation eased only by Pheoby when Janie returns home. Furthermore, as Mary Helen Washington has suggested, the discourse Janie creates is not so much her own as still that of the men who, out of possessiveness or passion, largely define—or even silence—her.[89] The parable thus emerges as a paradox. It concerns the tension between a marginalized writer's desire to speak in her own voice and the ways in which social power continues to shape that voice; her voice, her expression may be limited, indeed silenced, even by her very internalization of ideas about power, self-definition, and, of course, audience. This ambiguous parable may serve as a coda for this section on audience.

VI

A comparative approach to the literatures of the United States imposes serious scholarly and pedagogical responsibilities upon us. We need to learn about, study, be sensitive to a far broader range of audiences, conventions, functions, histories, and subjects than has in general been the case in literary analysis.[90] In pursuing such tasks, I think we must acknowledge the limitations of our own training. For example, relatively few students of

American literature are familiar with how oral cultures have influenced writing. But rare indeed are those thoroughly familiar with more than one of the differing oral traditions of the United States, like those of Native Americans and African-Americans. Some scholars of Emerson, Thoreau and Whitman have shown how their work rings of platform and pulpit; but few are also knowledgeable about working-class or minority oral traditions, or the platform practices of black women like Frances Harper or Ida B. Wells. In fact, a comparative approach could not have been proposed twenty years ago, because the detailed study of minority, ethnic, or even female cultures had not then sufficiently advanced: Too many texts were unavailable or unexamined; little had been done to pose comprehensive theories about African-American literary traditions, the "female imagination," the evolution of Chicano literature, the vivid distinctions among cultures grouped as "Asian-American," and like subjects.

But such work has moved forward rapidly, and while it is not yet adequately reflected in undergraduate, much less in graduate school, curricula, the changes are notable. Further, we can learn from our colleagues in other fields. For example, in approaching literary works still moving partly within the orbit of one or another oral tradition, we can benefit from the modes of studying early English texts. They remind us of how much work in linguistics, cultural and social history we must do in order to engage the literary works. Beyond that, many feminist and minority critics have perforce trained themselves as comparativists; their work exists as both challenge to and lesson for the profession at large. Among the assumptions that such scholarship implicitly questions is the idea that the study of British literature necessarily constitutes the core of an English department. The argument that a course in Milton or in the Eighteenth century is necessary whereas a course in African-American or in Chicano literature is not seems to me unpersuasive. The issue is not literary nationalism, but whether an English major shall be dominantly antiquarian or designed to provide students access to the living cultures of twenty-first century America. When English departments consider, as I think they must, constructing meaningful tracks focused on American as well as on British literature, they rapidly will face the changing critical issues to which this chapter is devoted.

I do not wish to exaggerate the difficulties of this task: if we are, as I suggested at the beginning, not very far advanced in the processes of collective exploration, with commitment we may more rapidly than has seemed possible fill in the map and provide richer understandings of *all* the literatures of the United States.[91]

Notes

1. See, for example, Sacvan Bercovitch, ed., *Reconstructing American Literary History* (Cambridge: Harvard University Press, 1986).

2. A striking case in point is provided by Frances E. W. Harper, probably the best known American black woman writer of the nineteenth century. As I have pointed out in the chapter on teaching nineteenth-century American women writers, Harper has begun to be "rediscovered" in the last few years, but she is essentially missing from most reference texts, not to mention library catalogues, critical discussions, and classrooms.

3. Gilles Deleuze and Felix Guattari make a related point in contending that "the second characteristic of minor literatures is that everything in them is political" (*Kafka: Toward a Minor Literature,* Dana Polan, trans. [Minneapolis: University of Minnesota Press, 1986], p. 17). Minor literatures are thus inevitably concerned with the relationships of language and power. Implicitly, Deleuze and Guattari seem to suggest that not *everything* in "major literatures" is thus "political." It is certainly the case that it is harder, perhaps impossible, for artists from marginalized groups to check their politics at the door of what is designated as "culture." The problem here is defining the limits of "not everything," for surely major literatures—Sophocles, Shakespeare?—are deeply political as well. Indeed, a central problem for the critic of marginalized literatures remains revealing the political content of cultural categories.

It also seems to me that the polarity "major/ minor," like all such dualisms, slides inevitably from description into valuation, even if one wishes to validate "minor" as much as "Protestant." "Marginalized" is not immune to that complaint, especially when it is reduced to "marginal." The value of "marginalized" is that it foregrounds the political *process* rather than (as in "minor" or "marginal") implicitly accepting its cultural consequences.

4. I want to foreclose a certain line of thought here, and also to note one theoretical danger in this strategy. I am not proposing that those I have defined as marginalized share any common "essence." I am not in any case attributing any essential qualities to women—whatever their race—or to people of color—whatever their gender—but focusing on a social process to which social theorists have given the name "marginalization." It seems to me that the essentialist search for an inherently common core of culture has been sufficiently criticized by others to need no additional discussion here. (See, for example, Linda Alcoff, "Cultural Feminism Versus Post-Structuralism: The Identity Crisis in Feminist Theory," *Signs: Journal of Women in Culture and Society* 13 [1988]: 405–436.)

At the same time, by suggesting certain commonalities in *differing* forms of marginalized cultures, I realize that I run the risk of reproducing precisely that power-laden dichotomy between what Nancy Hartsock has described as "the universalizing and totalizing voice postmodernists denounce as the voice of Theory" and the "devalued," silenced, "opaque" Other. (See Nancy Hartsock, "False Universalities and Real Differences: Reconstituting Marxism for the Eighties," *New Politics* 1 [Winter 1987]: 83–96.) This problem will, I think, be somewhat diminished if we recognize that a comparative account involves looking at differences *among* marginalized cultures as well as between them and what has previously been accounted as "center." Hartsock's is a useful formulation: "We know that we are not the universal man who can assume our experience of the world is the experience of all. But . . . we still have to name and describe our diverse experiences. What are our commonalities? What are our differences? How can we transform our imposed Otherness into a self-defined specificity?" (p. 94).

5. An amusing but not, perhaps, so very unusual instance was provided for me by a student response to a Zuni creation narrative, with which I begin a survey of

American literature. The student wrote: "Furthermore, the whole story was difficult to get involved with because there was absolutely no character development (in fact, the two main characters never talk to each other) and the plot is too far-fetched. Most importantly, though, there is no excitement, suspense or entertainment." Another student, however, queried her own cultural assumptions thus:

> . . . the repetition obscures the action and the significant facts of the tale. This also shows the cultural bias that I bring to my reading of this narrative. I want action and facts; the Zuni would undoubtedly find this attitude to be missing the essential meanings and significance of the emergence story. I'm sure they would say that the significance is in the repetition itself.

6. Does the conception of a marginalized discourse in its construction necessarily entail the positing of a "center?" Is it thus constituted by that center, the terms of its existence already defined and limited? These are, perhaps, interesting theoretical questions, which have been addressed in suggestive ways by a number of writers (e.g., R. Radhakrishnan, "Theory of Ethnicity and the Ethnicity of Theory," typescript c. 1985). But the issues seem to me tangential to what is at stake here. Whether a writer is from a marginalized group (like Yezierska) or from a group with economic, political, and social power (like Hawthorne), he or she is subject to fundamental historical contingencies: for example, access to publishing outlets and to audiences, the influence of established formal patterns of art and language—in short, the kinds of concerns this chapter addresses. No one creates "outside" such contingencies for there is no "outside." What a comparative strategy usefully enables us to do is to perceive the similarities and differences between those contingencies for authors differently situated, as well as how those differences do and do not change over time. It may also help in tracing the flows of creative influence to and from writers at differing places in the structure of a culture.

7. Marge Piercy, *Braided Lives* (New York: Fawcett, 1982), pp. 274–75.

8. See, for example, Richard H. Brodhead, "Sparing the Rod: Discipline and Fiction in Antebellum America," *Representations* 21 (Winter 1988): 67–96.

9. Cf. Haki R. Madhubuti, "Black Writers and Critics: Developing a Critical Process Without Readers," *The Black Scholar* 10 (Nov.–Dec., 1978): 35–40.

10. Raymond Williams, *Culture and Society, 1780–1950* (New York: Harper Torchbooks, 1966), pp. 325–26.

11. *Ibid.*, p. 327.

12. On the critical role of publishers in providing access to particular audiences and sustaining writers' reputations see Jane Tompkins on Hawthorne and Warner, *Sensational Designs: The Cultural Work of American Fiction, 1790–1860* (New York: Oxford University Press, 1985), esp. pp. 23–34.

13. Cf. Joseph Sommers, "Critical Approaches to Chicano Literature," in *Modern Chicano Writers: A Collection of Critical Essays,* Joseph Sommers and Tomas Yberra-Frausto, eds. (Englewood Cliffs, N.J.: Prentice-Hall, 1979), pp. 37–38; for example, "Logically, then, the trajectory of Chicano literature differs crucially from the mainstream models both of Mexico and the United States."

14. Some of the criticisms of the *Columbia Literary History of the United States* (ed. Emory Elliott) suggest just how near the beginning of that process we remain. Critics complained precisely that the *Columbia History* did not provide a clearly identifiable single line of development in American culture, but rather covered the same time periods from differing—that is, minority or feminist—perspectives. This "repetition" and overlapping was taken as a fault rather than, as its editor intended,

a fair representation of the "diversity of the literature and the variety of current critical opinion." See Emory Elliott, "The Politics of Literary History," *American Literature* 59 (May, 1987): 268–276.

15. Nancy C. M. Hartsock, "False Universalities and Real Differences," *op. cit.*, p. 94. Hartsock continues: "When the variety of 'minority' experiences have been described, and when the significance of these experiences as a ground for a critique of the dominant institutions and ideologies of society is better recognized, we will at least have the tools to begin to construct an account of the world sensitive to the realities of race, and gender as well as class" (p. 95).

16. Geoffrey Hartman, *Criticism in the Wilderness* (New Haven: Yale University Press, 1980), p. 299.

17. Thus the objection to most of the narrow graduate and undergraduate reading lists that have characterized the academic study of literature, and to the overemphasis on a limited set of paradigmatic critical texts—for example, those of Derrida or Barthes. To sharpen the point of this objection, compare the indexes in books of almost any male theoretical critic—structuralist or poststructuralist—with those of any of the recent collections of feminist and African-American critics. The worlds of experience represented by these sets of references differ profoundly, and in some cases absolutely.

18. Richard Yarborough, "Violence and Black Heroism: The Wilmington Riots in Two Turn-of-the-Century Afro-American Novels," paper presented at the Modern Language Association convention, Washington, D.C., December, 1984.

19. For example: "My thesis throughout is that Stowe's manipulation of maternal ideology is adapted and remodeled in illuminating ways in the work of American women writing before the 1920s and that, taken together, this body of fiction from Stowe forward constitutes a rich female tradition in American literature that challenges the dominant, twentieth-century, academic construction of the canon in terms of the adventure tale and the antisocial, which is to say antifeminine, escape narrative." Elizabeth Ammons, "Stowe's Dream of the Mother Savior: *Uncle Tom's Cabin* and American Women Writers Through the Turn of the Twentieth Century," in *New Essays on "Uncle Tom's Cabin"* Eric J. Sundquist, ed. (Cambridge: Cambridge University Press, 1986), p. 156.

20. Or "minor" as in Louis Renza's oddly ahistorical *"A White Heron" and the Question of Minor Literature* (Milwaukee: University of Wisconsin Press, 1984).

21. Josephine Donovan has taken a somewhat different tack, attempting to rehabilitate such terms, as the title of one of her books illustrates: *New England Local Color Literature: A Women's Tradition* (New York: Frederick Ungar, 1983).

22. Judith Fetterley, *Provisions: A Reader from 19th-Century American Women* (Bloomington: Indiana University Press, 1985); Jane Tompkins, *Sensational Designs: The Cultural Work of American Fiction, 1790–1860* (New York: Oxford University Press, 1985); Josephine Donovan, *New England Local Color Literature: A Women's Tradition, op. cit.*

23. Alfred Habegger, *Gender, Fantasy and Realism* (New York: Columbia University Press, 1982).

24. Toni Morrison, Speech at Modern Language Association convention, Washington, D.C., December, 1984.

25. Cf. Richard Yarborough, " 'In the Realm of the Imagination': Afro-American Literature and the American Canon," *ADE Bulletin* 78 (Summer, 1984): 36–37.

26. Nina Baym's is, I think, the most useful analysis of the power of this theme

in canon formation; see "Melodramas of Beset Manhood: How Theories of American Fiction Exclude Women Authors," *American Quarterly* 33 (1981): 123–139.

27. Leslie Marmon Silko, *Ceremony* (New York: New American Library, 1978), p. 2; Meridel LeSueur, *The Girl* (Minneapolis: West End Press, 1978), p. 142. Gary Soto touches the same issue in his poem "History" (*The Elements of San Joaquin* [Pittsburgh: University of Pittsburgh Press, 1977], p. 41):

> And yet I do not know
> The sorrows
> That sent her praying
> In the dark of a closet,
> The tear that fell
> At night
> When she touched
> Loose skin
> Of belly and breasts.
> I do not know why
> Her face shines
> Or what goes beyond this shine
> Only the stories
> That pulled her
> From Taxco to San Joaquin,
> Delano to Westside
> The places
> In which we all begin.

28. Cf. Barre Toelken and Tacheeni Scott, "Poetic Translation and the 'Pretty Languages,' " in *Traditional Literatures of the American Indian,* Karl Kroeber, ed. (Lincoln, Nebr.: University of Nebraska Press, 1981), p. 80. Toelken asks the storyteller, Yellowman, why he tells the stories. " 'If my children hear the stories, they will grow up to be good people; if they don't hear them, they will turn out to be bad.' Why tell them to adults? 'Through the stories everything is made possible.' " Later Toelken and Scott examine the role of ritual (the stories) in establishing health through ordering "an otherwise chaotic scene" (p. 88).

29. See, for example, *Voices From Wounded Knee, 1973* (Mohawk Nation, via Rooseveltown, NY: Akwesasne Notes, 1974).

30. Cf. Michael Dorris, "Native American Literature in an Ethnohistorical Context," *College English* 41 (1979): 147–162.

31. Teresa McKenna has pointed out the key role of immigration, as historical fact and central metaphor, in twentieth-century Chicano writing. See " 'Immigrants in Our Own Land': A Chicano Literature Review and Pedagogical Assessment," *ADE Bulletin* 91 (1988): 30–38.

32. Eric Sundquist, "*Benito Cereno* and New World Slavery," in *Reconstructing American Literary History,* Sacvan Bercovitch, ed. (Cambridge: Harvard University Press, 1986), pp. 93–122.

33. See, for example, Hazel V. Carby, " 'Of What Use is Fiction?': Pauline Elizabeth Hopkins," in *Reconstructing Womanhood: The Emergence of the Afro-American Woman Novelist* (New York: Oxford University Press, 1987), pp. 121–27. It is interesting to speculate on the effect of Edith Wharton's switch from Scribner's to Appleton on her reputation in post-World War I America.

34. Richard Ohmann has, for example, examined the roles of 1950s and 1960s novels focused on what he calls the "illness story" in rationalizing for its middle-class readership the malaise they encountered in the conflict between their growing material

and social comfort and their sense that the times were, nevertheless, "out of joint." See his "The Shaping of a Canon: U.S. Fiction, 1960–1975," in *Canons,* Robert von Hallberg, ed. (Chicago: University of Chicago Press, 1984), pp. 377–401. And Richard Brodhead has shown how many popular fictions of the antebellum period functioned to forward a new ideology of loving discipline and to attack both the reality and the ideological implications of whipping. See his "Sparing the Rod: Discipline and Fiction in Antebellum America," *Representations* 21 (Winter, 1988): 67–96.

35. Hazel V. Carby, *Reconstructing Womanhood: The Emergence of the Afro-American Woman Novelist,* op. cit. See also the section on Harper's poem "Aunt Chloe's Politics" in my chapter on teaching American women writers.

36. Charles W. Chesnutt, *The Conjure Woman* (Ann Arbor: University of Michigan Press, 1969), p. 135. All references are to this text.

37. The work of Herman Beavers on African-American aurality has suggested this reading to me.

38. It may be interesting to compare this view of the African-American creative artist with Houston Baker's appropriation of Trueblood, in Ellison's *Invisible Man,* to that role. Houston Baker, "To Move Without Moving: Creativity and Commerce in Ralph Ellison's Trueblood Episode," in *Black Literature and Literary Theory,* Henry Louis Gates, Jr., ed. (London and New York: Methuen, 1984), pp. 222–248.

39. W. E. B. DuBois, for example, wrote that

> all Art is propaganda and ever must be, despite the wailing of the purists. I stand in utter shamelessness and say that whatever art I have for writing has been used always for propaganda for gaining the right of black folk to love and enjoy. I do not care a damn for any art that is not used for propaganda. But I do care when propaganda is confined to one side while the other is stripped and silent.

The Crisis 32 (October 1926): 296.

40. Alice Walker, New York Times Book Review (May 13, 1984), 28.

41. Henry James, "The Art of Fiction" (1888), in *Representative Selections,* Lyon N. Richardson, ed. (New York: American Book Company, 1941), pp. 94–95. All references are to this text.

42. Charles W. Chesnutt, Journal, May 8, 1880, quoted in *The Short Fiction of Charles W. Chesnutt,* Sylvia Lyons Render, ed. (Washington: Howard University Press, 1974), p. 8.

43. Cf. William L. Andrews, *The Literary Career of Charles W. Chesnutt* (Baton Rouge and London: Louisiana State University Press, 1980), passim. Andrews also emphasizes the role Chesnutt took on in relation to the elevation of the black community (e.g., p. 76).

44. Bartolomeo Vanzetti, in *Letters of Sacco and Vanzetti,* Marion D. Frankfurter and Gardner Jackson, eds. (New York: Dutton, 1960), p. 277.

45. One can observe this phenomenon even in the most pastoral paintings produced by the peasant artists of Solentiname in Nicaragua. The *subjects* are seldom even remotely political, but the *process* of creating the paintings was a major factor in energizing and mobilizing the people to emerge from their sense of "marginalization" (the term is one they use) and enter the struggle against the Somoza dictatorship. That they could create art said that they could create change.

46. Dan Tannacito, "Poetry of the Colorado Miners: 1903–1906," *Radical Teacher* 15 (March, 1980): 1–15.

47. Martha Vicinus, *The Industrial Muse* (New York: Barnes and Noble, 1974); see especially pp. 1–3. Cf. my own primarily bibliographical essay "Working-Class

Women's Literature—An Introduction to Study," *Women in Print I,* Ellen Messer-Davidow and Joan Hartman, eds. (New York: Modern Language Association, 1982), pp. 109–134.

48. Morris Rosenfeld, quoted by Herbert G. Gutman in *Work, Culture, and Society in Industrializing America* (New York: Knopf, 1976), pp. 23–24, from Melech Epstein, *Jewish Labor in the United States* (New York: Trade Union Sponsoring Committee, 1950), pp. 290–91.

49. See John W. Blassingame, *The Slave Community* (New York: Oxford University Press, 1972), pp. 49–59.

50. See, for example, Lawrence Levine, *Black Culture and Black Consciousness* (New York: Oxford University Press, 1977), pp. 30–31.

51. Tomas Ybarra-Frausto, "The Chicano Movement and the Emergence of a Chicano Poetic Consciousness," *New Scholar* 5 (1972), 85.

52. Luis Valdez, quoted from *Actos* (San Juan Bautista, Ca.: Menyah Productions, 1971) by Ybarra-Frausto, p. 87.

53. The usual distinctions between "poetry" and "propaganda," or between "fine arts" and "crafts" hinge on the issue of function. Modern critics have, in one form or another, generally assumed that "poetry is its own excuse for being" and that a poem should "not mean, but be." This is not the place to argue such claims. I don't find them particularly convincing, though it is obvious enough that art can have differing functions in different cultures. Let it suffice to assert here that viewing marginalized cultures from the standpoint of such assumptions will fatally mislead the critic.

54. Meridel LeSueur's narrative "I Was Marching" usefully illustrates this outlook on art.

55. Cf. Tomas Ybarra-Frausto, p. 94: "Although the artist was free to experiment with form and content, the 'Plan de Aztlan' called for an art that was functional in extending the political consciousness of its audience. . . . The function of art is to extend and heighten our cognition of the world, its limitations and its potentialities for action. It is not an autonomous, internal mode of individual realization."

56. A loving but critical comment by Edith Wharton helps underline certain of the limitations of James's outlook:

> I sent the book [Proust's *Du Coté de chez Swann*] immediately to James, and his letter to me shows how deeply it impressed him. James, at that time, was already an old man and, as I have said, his literary judgments had long been hampered by his increasing preoccupation with the structure of the novel, and his unwillingness to concede that the vital centre (when there was any) could lie elsewhere. Even when I first knew him he read contemporary novels (except Wells's and a few of Conrad's) rarely, and with ill-concealed impatience; and as time passed, and intricate problems of form and structure engrossed him more deeply, it became almost impossible to persuade him that there might be merit in the work of writers apparently insensible to these sterner demands of the art.
>
> Edith Wharton, *A Backward Glance* (New York: Charles Scribner's Sons, 1933), p. 323.

Cf. her comment on James's own late fiction on p. 190.

57. In general, many readers are willing enough to become engaged with people of higher status, with more money and power, than they. The problem Zola identifies is, we may say, engaging readers without condescension in a "downward" view.

58. See, for example, Marshall W. Alcorn, Jr. and Mark Bracher, "Literature, Psychoanalysis, and the Re-Formation of the Self: A New Direction for Reader-Response Theory," *PMLA* 100 (May 1985): 342–354.

59. Henry Louis Gates, Jr., "Criticism in the Jungle," *Black Literature and Literary Theory* (New York and London: Methuen, 1984), p. 6. The core of Gates's polemic is contained, I think, in his assertion that "The black literary tradition now demands, for sustenance and for growth, the sorts of reading which it is the especial province of the literary critic to render; and these sorts of reading all share a fundamental concern with the nature and functions of figurative language as manifested in specific texts" (*Ibid.,* p. 5). This is not the place to argue whether what the black literary tradition—or any previously marginalized culture—most needs in the era of Reagan and Bush are the reading faculties of literary professionals. Gates is surely right in asserting the need to look intensively at texts themselves, " . . . their internal structures as acts of language or their formal status as works of art" (p. 5). On the other hand, the dichotomy he erects between such formal analysis and "social and polemical" readings of black literature seems to me to express a *narrowed* conception of the work of criticism, in fact an understanding of criticism rooted in an unexpressed acceptance of conventional academic ideas about professional specialization: the "true" critic's province is X (tropes) but not Y (sociology). More important, it strikes me as unnecessarily limiting our understanding of how texts function: There is no inherent need for positing "functional" or "anthropological fallacies" to justify the need to read marginalized texts *in*tensively. Happily, Gates's own practice provides something of a bridge over this divide.

60. In fact, the Chicana poet Lorna Dee Cervantes has suggested that code-switching and other forms of verbal play are rather more characteristic of male Latino poetry than that of female.

61. A recent documentary film traces in specific historical detail the transformation of a Sea-Island hymn, "I Shall Overcome," via the Highlander Folk School, into the unifying anthem of the Civil Rights movement, "We Shall Overcome."

62. Cf. Barre Toelken and Tacheeni Scott, "Poetic Retranslation and the 'Pretty Languages,' " pp. 79–80:

> When I asked him if he told the tale exactly the same way each time, he at first answered yes; but when evidence from compared tapes was brought into the discussion, it became clear that he had understood me to be asking him if he changed the nature of the prototype tale of his own volition; the wording was different each time because he recomposes with each performance, simply working from his knowledge of what ought to happen in the story and from his facility with traditional words and phrases connected, in his view, with the business of narrating Ma'i stories. He did not mention it, but it is quite obvious from the tapes made of his stories when no children were present that the audience plays a central role in the narrative style. . . .

63. See Américo Paredes, *With His Pistol in His Hand: A Border Ballad and Its Hero* (Austin: University of Texas Press, 1958).

64. A theater-piece like "The Gospel at Colonus" illustrates that many of these qualities continue to obtain in the *performance* of some black-defined drama. The work sets Sophocles' drama as if it were being presented at a black Pentecostal church service. While much of the text consists of the Fitzgerald translation of Sophocles, not only delivery, but actual phrases change somewhat from performance to performance. And the choir/chorus continues in some degree to improvise its responses to the more set speeches and preaching.

65. John Wideman, "The Black Writer and the Magic of the Word," New York Times *Book Review,* January 24, 1988, p. 28.

66. T. S. Eliot, "The Metaphysical Poets," *Selected Essays* (New York: Harcourt, 1950), p. 248.

67. Langston Hughes, "Poetry to the People," *I Wonder as I Wander* (New York: Hill and Wang, 1964), p. 41.

68. Cf. Peter J. Rabinowitz, "Our Evaluation of Literature Has Been Distorted by Academe's Bias Toward Close Reading of Texts," *Chronicle of Higher Education,* April 6, 1988, A40:

> The schools in vogue may change, but we still assign value to what fits our prior conceptions of reading, and the academically sanctioned canon consequently consists largely of texts that respond well to close reading. Once you give priority to close reading, you implicitly favor figurative writing over realistic writing, indirect expression over direct expression, deep meaning over surface meaning, form over content, and the elite over the popular.

69. Sheila de Brettville, "A Re-Examination of Some Aspects of the Design Arts from the Perspective of a Woman Designer," *Women and the Arts: Arts in Society* I (Spring–Summer 1984): 117–18.

70. Vera Norwood, "Thank you for My Bones: Connections Between Contemporary Women Artists and the Traditional Arts of Their Foremothers," *New Mexico Historical Review* (1983).

71. Judith Slomin, Untitled ms., reprinted in *The Canadian Newsletter of Research on Women* (1976).

72. For example, Barbara Christian, *Black Woman Novelists* (Westport, Conn.: Greenwood, 1984); Mari Evans, ed., *Black Women Writers (1950–1980)* (Garden City, N.Y.: Doubleday, 1984); Marjorie Pryse and Hortense J. Spillers, eds., *Conjuring: Black Women, Fiction, and Literary Tradition* (Bloomington, Ind.: Indiana University Press, 1985). Fortunately, the number has increased even since this note was initially written.

73. Gloria Anzaldúa, *Borderlands/La Frontera: The New Mestiza* (San Francisco: Spinsters/Aunt Lute, 1987); José Saldívar, "Chicano Border Narratives as Cultural Critique," in *The Dialectics of Our America: Genealogy, Cultural Critique, and Literary History,* ms.

74. Robert Stepto, *From Behind the Veil: A Study of Afro-American Narrative* (Urbana, Ill.: University of Illinois Press, 1979).

75. Sherley Anne Williams, "The Blues Roots of Contemporary Afro-American Poetry," in *Afro-American Literature: The Reconstruction of Instruction,* Dexter Fisher and Robert B. Stepto, eds. (New York: Modern Language Association, 1979), pp. 72–87; Amiri Baraka (LeRoi Jones), *Blues People: Negro Music in White America* (New York: William Morrow, 1963); Houston Baker, *Blues, Ideology, and Afro-American Literature—A Vernacular Theory* (Chicago: University of Chicago Press, 1984); Steven C. Tracy, "To the Tune of Those Weary Blues: The Influence of the Blues Tradition on Langston Hughes' Blues Poems," *MELUS* 8 (Fall 1981): 73–98.

76. Most extensively in Henry Louis Gates, Jr., *The Signifying Monkey: A Theory of Afro-American Criticism* (New York: Oxford University Press, 1987).

77. Barbara E. Bowen, "Untroubled Voice: Call and Response in *Cane,*" in *Black Literary Theory,* Henry Louis Gates, Jr., ed. (New York and London: Methuen, 1984), pp. 187–203. "For Toomer," Bowen writes, "the way to burst asunder the forms of the Anglo-American novel was to turn to the form he discovered in the black south: the spiritual. If *Cane* is an elegy, it is an elegy for a form," the spirituals or folk-songs which, he felt, were doomed to die in the desert of "industry and commerce and machines."

78. Cf. Barre Toelken and Tacheeni Scott, "Poetic Retranslation and the 'Pretty Languages,' " p. 88.

79. Elizabeth Ammons, "Going in Circles: The Female Geography of Jewett's *Country of the Pointed Firs*," *Studies in the Literary Imagination* 16 (Fall 1983): 85, 89. The web is also an important organizing principle of certain Native American works, as is the image of the spider as creator.

80. Jane Tompkins, *Sensational Designs: The Cultural Work of American Fiction, 1790–1860,* (New York: Oxford, 1985) p. 16.

81. See Paul Lauter, ed., *Reconstructing American Literature* (Old Westbury, N.Y.: Feminist Press, 1983), as well as the next chapter.

82. In fact, many of Harper's poems, as well as her lectures obviously, seem to have been created primarily as platform pieces that she performed for audiences, rather than strictly as book verse for private consumption. Nikki Giovanni is, in many respects, a contemporary platform artist in this sense.

83. The whole, among many other such works, is part of the Bancroft collection at the University of California, Berkeley. Two excerpts from Vallejo's narrative, among many other of the works discussed in this essay, are included in *The Heath Anthology of American Literature,* 2 vols. (Lexington, Mass. 1990), for which I served as coordinating editor.

84. Maxine Hong Kingston, "Cultural Mis-readings by American Reviewers," in Guy Amirthanayagam, ed., *Asian and Western Writers in Dialogue* (London: Macmillan, 1982), p. 65.

85. Jeanette R. Murphy, "The Survival of African Music in America," *Popular Science Monthly* LV (Sept. 1899): 662; quoted by Blassingame, *op. cit.,* pp. 27–28.

86. See "The Burning Struggle: The Civil Righs Movement," an interview with Bernice Johnson Reagon, *Radical America* 12 (November 12, 1978): 18–20.

87. Lawrence Levine, *Black Culture and Black Consciousness* (New York: Oxford University Press, 1977), p. 33; cf. p. 207.

88. I discuss this issue at somewhat more length in examing *Walden* in the chapter on "Teaching Nineteenth-Century American Women Writers." In thinking through this problem I have found the comments of my colleague Tucker Farley particularly helpful.

89. Mary Helen Washington, " 'I Love the Way Janie Crawford Left Her Husbands': Zora Neale Hurston's Emergent Female Hero," in *Invented Lives: Narratives of Black Women, 1860–1960* (Garden City, N.Y.: Anchor Books, 1987), pp. 237–254.

90. "In constructing hypothetical relations between their texture, text, and context, we can only *improve* and *extend* our appreciation of the art of the writers and enrich our understanding of the cultures from which their works emerged. Exactly the same exploring processes are appropriate and rewarding for Indian literatures, although often we must start from more basic elements because Indian literatures lack the wealth of earlier studies with which Western works are surrounded. It is our scholarship, not Indian literature, which is 'primitive' or undeveloped." Karl Kroeber, "An Introduction to the Art of Traditional American Indian Narration," *Traditional American Indian Literatures, op. cit.,* p. 9.

91. I wish to express particular appreciation to the Soviet and American participants in the Symposium on Literatures of American Ethnic Groups, to Joel Conarroe, President of the Guggenheim Foundation, and to Ann Fitzgerald; this chapter would not exist without their support and encouragement.

Reconstructing American Literature: Curricular Issues

Next to where I type, I have tacked up the syllabi for two American literature courses taught in the 1980s at well-known, indeed prestigious, institutions in the United States—one in California, the other in Ohio. Both are survey courses, one called "The American Literary Imagination," the other "Life and Thought in American Literature." One covers, in a single semester, thirty-two writers, including Philip Freneau, William Cullen Bryant, Washington Irving, John Greenleaf Whittier, John Crowe Ransom, and Ezra Pound; *all* are white and male, except for one assignment on Emily Dickinson and one poem by Marianne Moore. The other, a two-term course, includes twenty-three white male writers and Emily Dickinson. I do not want to argue that today such courses have no right to exist, for that kind of statement would engage the significant issue of academic freedom. But such courses are simply not truthful, nor professionally current. The pictures they present to students of the American literary imagination or of American life and thought are woefully incomplete and inaccurate. In the profession of literary study they represent what, in Psychology, was represented by generalizations about moral development based on interviews with a sample of white, male, college sophomores and juniors; or in History, was represented by conclusions about the "expansion" of opportunity under Jacksonian democracy when, in fact, white women's opportunities and those of black people were largely contracting. Were such courses titled "American Literature from the Perspective of 'Diner'" (a film set in 1958), they might have accurately represented themselves. But now, over a quarter of a century later, a large new body of scholarship has transformed the intellectual base of our profession. To be responsive to this scholarship and to present an accurate picture of the development of the literary cultures of the United States, teaching has begun to change. A number of recent volumes record such change and offer means for encouraging its systematic development.[1]

The changes in our profession I am describing are rooted in the movements

In its initial form this article served as the Introduction to *Reconstructing American Literature: Courses, Syllabi, Issues* (Old Westbury: Feminist Press, 1983). It has been substantially revised here.

for racial justice and sex equity. Those who worked in the movements came to see that to sustain hope for a future, people needed to grasp a meaningful past. In the 1960s programs were created, often in the form of courses in "freedom schools" or "free universities," to explore areas like black history and culture. Soon after, courses were developed that examined the lives and achievements of women; and still others focused on ethnic and racial minorities. In time, often accompanied by well-publicized conflict, such courses began to be incorporated into the curricula of existing colleges and universities, and in some secondary schools as well. The initial set of questions thus brought by the social movements into academe really involved efforts to understand the present: How did things get to be this way? What have been the historical experiences that led to where we are? How have people like us responded to racism and sexism in the past? What are our courses of study really saying to people like us—and to people whose experiences, whose race, whose gender, whose sexual preferences are different from ours? Such questions directed intense attention to existing curricula.

Once they had been asked, it was only a short step—at least for some— to begin designing courses that attempted to answer such questions. And so at the first stage of curricular reform in the late 1960s and early 1970s we began to see courses on Black Writers and Women Writers, and others that explored "images" of women in literature. Such courses were important in establishing that, indeed, such writers existed, were interesting to students, and were valuable to study. They were, in curricular terms, the equivalent of the first steps of the rich new developments in minority and feminist scholarship. But they remained essentially peripheral in the academy. The students who enrolled for them were often extraordinarily enthusiastic and motivated to unusual feats of reading and research; but they were relatively few in number. Meanwhile, in the "mainstream" introductory and major courses, the majority of students—a dwindling band they were in literature—encountered little change.[2]

To be sure, some courses and the major anthologies added a few women and blacks (mostly male) and expectantly stirred. Kate Chopin's *The Awakening* and a bit of Frederick Douglass' *Narrative* of his life became standard fare; safe enough, even for the recalcitrant, since the excerpts from the latter preached literacy and the former "resolved" a woman's role conflicts through suicide. In fact, however, such works and the many others soon crowding to the barriers of our attention remained marginal to the structures of academic knowledge. Our accounts of cultural history and our understanding of aesthetic value had not changed. Even into the 1980s, for example, no portrait of the development of the American novel reflected at all adequately the fact that many if not most of the major fiction writers during the fifty years after 1870 were women: Elizabeth Stuart Phelps, Harriet Spofford, Sarah Orne Jewett, Mary Wilkins Freeman, Pauline Hopkins, Edith Wharton, Willa Cather, Ellen Glasgow, Mary Austin, among others. Literary commentators continued to assert that the dominant mode of American fiction was the romance, and that the literature of the United States was peculiarly devoid of social novels—as if those women and others like Stowe and Susan Warner never wrote.[3] Similarly, critics and instructors maintained that complexity, irony, and ambiguity were the only significant virtues for a poem; and thus they stood mute before the repetitive, deceptively simple text of a Native American chant. Of course, the new scholarship has begun to say goodbye to all that, but courses have been remarkably slow to change.

In 1981, I conducted a survey of the content of introductory American literature courses at selected colleges and universities in this country. I later followed up that survey by collecting American literature syllabi of more than 500 courses. Analysis of the broader sample simply bore out the findings of the original study. I found that of the sixty-one authors taught in three or more of the initial fifty courses surveyed, only eight were women, five were black men, and none were black women; other minority or ethnic writers did not appear in as many as three of the courses. Emily Dickinson, who was taught in twenty of the courses, appeared twelfth on the list of most-often taught writers. She was preceded by Twain, Whitman, Henry James, Hawthorne, Melville, Poe, Faulkner, Emerson, Fitzgerald, Hemingway, and Thoreau. Edith Wharton, the next woman writer to appear, was taught in but eight courses, and was twenty-seventh on the list; she was followed by Kate Chopin, twenty-ninth, and Ralph Ellison, the first black writer, thirtieth. Before them appear, among other authors, Franklin, Dreiser, Pound, Edward Taylor, W. D. Howells, and Washington Irving. The next women, in order of frequency, were Sarah Orne Jewett (thirty-eighth) and Anne Bradstreet (fortieth); they were preceded by writers like e. e. cummings, William Cullen Bryant, and Saul Bellow. The next black writer, Richard Wright, appeared in but four courses.

This situation represented little significant improvement over 1948, when the National Council of Teachers of English reviewed American literature in the college curriculum. Had I limited my summary to the first thirty-seven writers to appear, as did the NCTE, there would still in 1983 have been only three women among them, though Chopin would have replaced Cather, and Dickinson moved up from seventeenth to twelfth.

Perhaps the slowness of change is not that remarkable. For there are major barriers to change that instructors continue to encounter much more than scholars or critics. The most practical of these has simply been the availability of texts. As a scholar, I could locate in one or another library a copy of, for example, Phelps's *The Silent Partner;* thus I could read and think about the implications of that book for the history of working-class and women's literature. While there was money for photocopying, I could even reproduce the novel for a small class on the Literature of Industrialism and Work. But that money ran out during the 1970s, a class of thirteen was too large for handouts, and I had to give up the book until it was finally reprinted.

If I chose to use an anthology—and financial pressures on students have pushed strongly in that direction—the situation was until very recently even worse. For even the most "enlightened" anthologies provided me with one—and only one—predictable story by Charles Chesnutt, Freeman, or Cather—

and absolutely nothing by Charlotte Perkins Gilman, Zora Neale Hurston, Leslie Marmon Silko or Alice Walker, among others. Existing anthologies displayed the same dramatic limitations I found in teaching practice; indeed, they remain a major cause of them. A 1982 study by Peggy McIntosh and Elizabeth Janick of the Wellesley Center for Research on Women of the seven leading anthologies then in use suggested that they had changed little since 1952, when Ben Fuson had examined twenty-seven American literature texts. The 1982 study found that, of pages devoted to nineteenth-century writers, only 2 to 8 percent were occupied by the work of women. The writers in this study included some of the most successful and widely read in American literary history, among them Harriet Beecher Stowe and Edith Wharton. In the three best-selling anthologies of 1982, women were 8 of 41 nineteenth-century writers in the Norton text and 6 of 40 in both the Macmillan and Random House volumes. While the proportion of women writers had increased slightly over 1948, space devoted to them had not. To say it another way, women and minority writers of both sexes were represented in these anthologies thinly—largely by one story or a few poems.

During the decade of the 1980s, a number of interesting changes took place. The new Norton collection stated with some pride in its advertising and its preface that it reflected a "major responsibility . . . to redress the long neglect of women writers in America" and "to do justice to the contributions of black writers to American literature and culture."[4] In fact, in its 1985 second edition, it included the work of thirty-five women and sixteen black authors. Ironically, in percentage terms, this represented little change from the 1979 edition; women are here 22 percent of the authors included, and occupy 15 percent of the page space; blacks are 10 percent of the authors and occupy 4.5 percent of the pages. Still, the Norton text is, in terms of inclusion, far ahead of the equally popular Macmillan volumes. In them, the twenty women authors (15.3 percent of the total) occupy only 322 pages (8.2 percent), while the eleven black writers (8.4 percent) take up a mere 3.2 percent (127) of the pages. The disparity in both these texts between number of authors and the relatively smaller proportion of pages derives from the fact that both concentrate on presenting the work of eleven white men: they take up nearly 41 percent of the total pages in the Norton text and, in the Macmillan volumes, a whopping 49.2 percent.

Counting pages can be misleading and is never a substitute for analyzing real content; still, some numbers can be revealing. In the Macmillan volumes, for example, Norman Mailer occupies more pages (thirty-eight) than any black or female author except for Chopin; indeed, his "The White Negro" takes up more space than all but three of the entries for black writers. Franklin, James, and Emerson each have about as many pages devoted to them as all the black writers combined; both Cooper and Twain are allotted more space than all the women writers (apart from Chopin) taken together. Even in the Norton text, Hawthorne, Melville and Twain together have substantially more pages than all the women writers combined. The trend however, is away from such anomalies. The more recent (1987) Harper text contains work by forty-three women and twenty black writers, as well as twenty-three Native American texts, four from Spanish originals, and work by one Asian-American and one contemporary Chicano writer. In percentage terms, these texts occupy about the same relative space that women and minority writers do in the Norton text, although the eleven white male worthies are down to 35 percent of the space. The new *Heath Anthology of American Literature*[5] carries this trend a good deal further; it includes work by 109 women writers of all races, twenty-five individual Native American authors (as well as seventeen texts from tribal origins), fifty-three African-Americans, thirteen Hispanics (as well as twelve texts from earlier Spanish originals and two from French), and nine Asian-Americans. While this text has done remarkably well in commercial terms, going into a second printing within six months of publication, needless to say it has not taken over the market. Thus the problems presented by most anthologies are by no means at an end.

Nor does sharing syllabi, useful as that is, resolve the practical difficulty of texts; indeed, in certain respects, it underlines that problem. Since syllabi outline real courses taught in real institutions, their instructors were forced to use texts that were available. In some cases, one can practically feel the instructor pushing up against the edges of what could be ordered or even reproduced for students.

Instructors may face an even more difficult practical barrier in the reluctance of departmental colleagues and deans to accept differences in curricular priorities—let alone to change their own ideas of them. That reluctance is not at all hard to understand—even, moderately, to sympathize with. At one level it derives from the same kind of psychological process that motivates women to seek out women's texts and Chicanos to seek out Chicano works. Many of us white male professors were taught that writers like Hemingway, Bellow, or—God save the mark!—Mailer expressed our own values, if not our experiences. If such gods of our literary pantheon are to be displaced to make room for a Zora ("Zora who?"), were our values, *all* values, to be displaced? Were *we* to be displaced? In a profession of displaced persons, were we to join the roaming ranks? To be sure, that progression of thought will stand neither the test of logic nor that of academic power realities. But it is a factor for all that, just as is the reluctance to take on works from different cultures about which we feel ignorant. Such ignorance can, of course, be overcome through study and experience, to which more and more of our colleagues have committed themselves in faculty development seminars, in institutes, and in their own changing research. But differences in theory persist: at more fundamental levels, the reluctance to change involves questions of aesthetics and pedagogy. It is to these that I wish to turn now.

II

How do we decide what to include in a course or in an anthology? Once we recognize that the answer to that question is not foreordained by God, the curriculum committee, or even the Norton anthology, a spectacular and dangerous world of choice opens before us. In a practical way, as I have indicated, the real possibilities of choice have been less brilliant than they at first appeared, but in the end we will not be satisfied with selections dictated by a base pragmatism. We want them to conform to some set of standards, aesthetic principles, pedagogical theories. Let us, then, imagine ourselves walking freely—as in fact we are—in a world of many hundreds of authors and thousands of pages of texts. We recognize some old friends, we nod familiarly here and there, we are startled by a few unforeseen apparitions, and we are always asking, "Of these many—appealing, strange, unsettling, ordinary— what few do we take back with us into a fifteen-week class?"

This is a serious enterprise. And perhaps the beginning of wisdom here is to recognize the peculiar way in which our profession has trivialized our own work. We have made ourselves largely guides to the forms of language in texts—no mean task, but not, especially in classrooms, the heart of the enterprise. For as teachers of literature, we are mediators between fictions in language and people we call students. If our profession draws us to the formal aspects of literary art, the core for most of our students remains the experiences they encounter in the books and poems we bring them to.

Take, for example, the following comment by Tomás Borge, a poet and also one of the leaders of the successful guerilla struggle to liberate Nicaragua from dictatorship:

> But as to my personal formation, my vocation, my dedication to just causes, to politics, was due greatly to reading a German author who wrote about the west of the United States. His name was Karl May. He might not be very well known, but he wrote some novels; and the people in those novels had some definite qualities: loyalty, courage, honesty. And I made the effort, not always successful, to imitate them. Writers thus contribute to the formation of men. Another such writer, whose individual history does not interest me, was John Steinbeck.[6]

Borge's comment illustrates one way in which books—the experiences and people in them—influence consciousness and thus actions in the world.[7] This may indeed be their main value. Thus, we must begin by considering seriously the nature of the experiences we select for the classroom.

This is an argument neither for "relevance" nor for "morality." We must be aware that no culture values all experiences equally and that our curricula— as I point out elsewhere—have validated certain experiences at the expense of others. Some of the most popular texts in American literature present hunting—a whale or a bear—as paradigms for "human" exploration and coming of age, whereas menstruation, pregnancy, and birthing somehow do not serve as such prototypes. We need to consider whether texts of quality which explore such crucial female experiences—like Edith Summers Kelley's *Weeds,* Meridel LeSueur's "Annunciation," Paule Marshall's *Brown Girl, Brownstones*—do not have important places in our curriculum. To take another example, do we define heroism or even courage as qualities exclusive to the battlefield and perhaps the bullring? Or do we extend the definition to include the New England spinster struggling for a place to live and grow old with dignity, or the fugitive slave's quest for freedom in the North? Again, a significant portion of canonical literature presents men pushing toward frontiers, exploring, conquering, exploiting the resources of sea and land. But for many immigrant and female writers, removal to the frontier represents a tearing up of roots; their concern is less self-discovery or conquest of new territory than the reestablishment of family, community, and a socially productive way of life. To the extent that we concentrate primarily on work from the antisocial, escapist tradition in United States letters, we keep our students from learning of that more socially-focused tradition concerned with how to make life work in the here and now.

My point is not to argue for the importance of any one set of experiences or values. Rather, it is to bring to the surface the fact that an element in curricular choice is subject matter, or perhaps more accurately, the paradigms of human experience embodied in a work, and also to propose a wider set of experiences for our curricula. That would be desirable, I think, even if collegiate student bodies consisted as they once did predominantly of white young men. But broadening curricula becomes even more imperative when we perceive not only the heterogeneity of our students, but of the world into which they are growing. Literary study can become central once more to the academic enterprise precisely because it provides students imagined opportunities to learn of experiences and cultures not their own and to encounter and to begin to judge differing values.[8]

At this point we engage significant objections; I would summarize them as follows: "Accepting that your argument is not directed to a curriculum determined by the 'relevance' of its subject matter, are you not, nevertheless, using as standards of choice criteria external to the world of literary art? Are we not obligated to teach "the best" of what has been written, rather than works that are representative, either of experience or of history? Would you have us include *inferior* work because it is by or about women, or minority people, or the working class? Or because it "illustrates" some set of historical circumstances or contemporary issues? Do we not, if we use any but aesthetic standards for choice, make literature and its study into a handmaiden of history or sociology, or the servant of someone's politics?"

These issues are fundamental and therefore not to be disposed of by short answers, however valid. It is important to realize that most curricula—like those I described above—and all anthologies include works on bases other than absolute aesthetic quality. It would be hard to maintain on purely aesthetic grounds that Mather, Bryant, Cooper, Irving, Holmes, Norris, cummings, and Mailer—all of whom are regularly anthologized and often taught—are more important than Rowson, Douglass, Freeman, Wharton, H. D., Hurston, and Alice Walker, who appear far less frequently, if at all, in anthologies or courses. It is, in fact, perfectly reasonable to include a work because it is historically representative or influential. Further, it is naive to assume that *nothing* but aesthetic quality goes into making even such fine

works as Crane's *The Red Badge of Courage* or Faulkner's *Absalom, Absalom*
part of our literary canon while excluding Gilman's "The Yellow Wallpaper"
or Hurston's *Their Eyes Were Watching God*. Surely, the political system
called "patriarchy" is at some level involved in choosing works that focus on
male experience and perspectives.

Nevertheless, the problem of aesthetic standards needs to be encountered
on its own ground. Unfortunately, however, such standards were not delivered
on tablets of bronze into the hands of T. S. Eliot or Ezra Pound. They derive
from social practice and they change over time. Fifty years ago, Wyndham
Lewis and Joseph Hergesheimer were all the rage; *ubi sunt?* And then there
was that *serious* 1950s novelist from Maryland—Lord, what was his name?
Few are the artists whose names persist through time, and—dare one say
it?—no North American is as yet indisputably among them. One must ask,
then, not how to apply a given and persisting set of standards, but where
standards come from, whose values they embed, and whose interests they
serve.

III

Common academic experience exaggerates the degree to which aesthetic standards appear to be "universal." Place a group of literature professors in a
room, give us ten unidentified texts, and more than likely we will agree on
the value of half of them, perhaps more. Not surprising. After all, we have
very similar training and congeneric lives, whose profound impact on our
consciousness is pervasive if difficult to discern. We have all been taught the
formalist virtues: economy, irony, well-articulated structure, and the like. We
know the modernist catechism: Literature is a form of discourse that "has no
designs on the world," that represents (or creates) things without trying to
change them, and that speaks in a language whose claim is originality, not
clarity or simplicity. We also know that for many of the works we have learned
to value, standards like complexity and detachment are, indeed, appropriate.
This does not make them universal in literary study.

In this context it may help to recall that our views of literary excellence
derive largely from criticism of recent vintage, for only in the 1920s and 1930s
was the professional focus on texts and structure developed. Such formalist
criticism emphasized as the poetic virtues complexity, irony, emotional restraint, and verbal sophistication. Allen Tate, for example, argued that "tension—the full organized body of all the extension and intension we can find
in it"—determines greatness in poetry.[9] Such a standard responded to the
modernist poetry then being written—Eliot, Pound, Hart Crane—and it provided a basis for combatting the moralistic and "subjective" writing of "genteel" critics. It brought back into vogue the metaphysical poets and tended
to disparage writers like Percy Bysshe Shelley, Walt Whitman, and Edna St.
Vincent Millay—one of Tate's favorite targets. But while formalist *explication*

de texte was effective both as a classroom tactic and for exploring a great many powerful texts, it provided no useful basis for approaching that great body of literature that placed a premium on *apparent* simplicity, transparency, and emotional directness—from Native American chants and spirituals to Langston Hughes's "Montage of a Dream Deferred" and Judy Grahn's "Common Woman" poems, from *Uncle Tom's Cabin* to *Daughter of Earth.*

This is not the place to explore in detail where Tate's standards, so sophisticated and powerful yet so exclusive and limiting, came from. Their origins are complex, as I have suggested in the chapter on "Race and Gender in the Shaping of the American Literary Canon: A Case Study from the Twenties," but one source involves the social position of the "man of letters in the modern world." In a mass society, as Tate characterized twentieth-century America, the social and cultural power of the critic was in decline. In the sphere of language and literature, however, he (the pronoun is apt) could retain a degree of authority as part of a priesthood of the word. But that could be true only in interpreting works amenable to complex analysis by the enlightened. This is not the whole story, of course, nor is it meant to disparage formalism as a strategy for appropriate texts. But I do wish to underline the fact that when the demands of a critical style become fundamentally determinative over *curricular* choice, they become barriers to apprehending other kinds of literary merit, and they limit what we do in our classrooms.

In general when we talk about "literary" or "aesthetic" merit we are speaking of the interest the form and language of a text hold for us—even if its values are alien, even if we have to ask our students to make believe that they can willingly "suspend disbelief." What if one were to argue that merit resides as importantly in the capacity of a work to move us, to evoke authentic feelings, even to prod us into action? It seems to me that literary training—perhaps on the medical model—practices us in dissociating what a work is about and how it affects us from the ways in which it is put together. Thus we teach the shape and sinew and texture of a hand, not whether it offers us peace or a sword. It is, after all, far easier to talk of form than of feelings—especially in a classroom. And yet, the question persists: In what ways does aesthetic merit reside in the production of affect and in what ways in the details of structure?

Probably no American writer raises that question more vividly for us than Harriet Beecher Stowe. In his "Afterword" to the Signet edition of *Uncle Tom's Cabin,* John William Ward describes the novel as the "despair of literary critics and a puzzle for social historians." He continues:

> Its immense, incredible popularity puts a problem to both literary and historical understanding. For the literary critic, the problem is simply how a book so seemingly artless, so lacking in apparent literary talent, was not only an immediate success but has endured. More importantly, if one of the tests of the power of fiction is the way in which a novel provides images that order the confusing reality of life, then *Uncle Tom's Cabin* ranks high. Uncle Tom,

Little Eva, Simon Legree, Topsy who just growed—these are characters who
now form part of the collective experience of the American people.

(p. 480)

But the puzzle may lie more in the questions the critic asks and the terms
the critic uses than in the novel itself. Stowe is reasonable clear in the
matter.

> The writer has given only a faint shadow, a dim picture, of the anguish
> and despair that are, at this very moment, riving thousands of hearts, shat-
> tering thousands of families, and driving a helpless and sensitive race to
> frenzy and despair.... Nothing of tragedy can be written, can be spoken,
> can be conceived, that equals the frightful reality of scenes daily and hourly
> acting on our shores, beneath the shadow of American law, and the shadow
> of the cross of Christ.
>
> And now, men and women of America, is this a thing to be trifled with,
> apologized for, and passed over in silence? Farmers of Massachusetts, of
> New Hampshire, of Vermont, of Connecticut, who read this book by the
> blaze of your winter-evening fire,—strong-hearted, generous sailors and ship-
> owners of Maine—is this a thing for you to countenance and encourage?...
> And say, mothers of America, is this a thing to be defended, sympathized
> with, passed over in silence?
>
> ... But, what can any individual do? Of that, every individual can judge.
> There is one thing every individual can do,—they can see to it that *they feel
> right*. ... See, then, to your sympathies in this matter!

(pp. 471, 472)

The book is meant to produce the "right feelings" of sympathy and outrage
which lie at the root of "right action." Clearly, there is nothing in the least
"artless" about Stowe's capacity to generate such feelings. Indeed, she is as
artful in achieving her goals as Henry James—who patronized the book as a
"wonderful 'leaping' fish" flying about outside "the medium in which books
breathe"—was in achieving his.

Yet for years, few critics apart from Leslie Fiedler treated *Uncle Tom's
Cabin* and Stowe's many other works with anything like the seriousness they
deserve. And even fewer teachers presented her as anything but a marginal
figure in nineteenth-century literature; indeed, no anthology offered more
than a single story by Stowe, or at most a couple of chapters from *Uncle
Tom's Cabin*.[10] It may well be that she was the victim precisely of her success
in generating, not so much sales, as Fiedler proposes, as emotion. The dominant view, certainly since the modernist revolution against nineteenth-century
gentility and emotionalism, has been suspicion of literary sentiment; indeed,
among the most damning terms in a critic's arsenal has been "sentimental."
We have much preferred the detachment and aesthetic distance of irony, the
tight, masculine lip. If an affection for a pleasing sentimentality was the curse
of Victorian literati—and it was—surely our own has been to clamp feeling
at a distance, to teach that big boys don't cry, and to busy ourselves in cerebral
linguistic enterprises. We are familiar enough with the dangers of sentiment,
the slippery slope that leads downward past the death of Little Eva to *Stella*

Dallas, "All My Children," and the Harlequin romances. What is problematic about irony has been less obvious, though one can track the path down the slope opposite to that of emotionalism past "Icarus in Flight" and "Is There An American Cinema?" to the cocktail party chatter of the junior English major: "She did her dissertation on Elinor Wylie, you say. I see. Elinor Wylie."

Beneath the questions of curriculum and what we choose to emphasize in class are political issues. The allegation of "sentimentality" does not, finally, explain the "puzzle" of Harriet Beecher Stowe. Of course Stowe can be dreadfully sentimental—as can Hawthorne—but the curve of her reputation has little to do with this, or indeed with any other purely aesthetic consideration. It does, however, coincide remarkably with the fall and rise of interest in the rights of black people and of women of all races. The restoration of *Uncle Tom's Cabin*—even despite its racial stereotypes—to a degree of literary grace in the last decades testifies more to the impact of the civil rights movement than, as yet, to a shift in our literary aesthetic. Similarly, the more recent interest in Stowe's later fiction, like *The Minister's Wooing,* developed initially from concerns given new weight by the women's movement.

What I am suggesting is that standards of literary merit are not absolute but contingent. They depend, among other considerations, upon the relative value we place on form and feeling in literary expression as well as on culturally different conceptions of form and function. Thus, in seeking to teach "the best"—as we should—of the various literatures that constitute our national culture, we need constantly to reexamine our cultural yardstick. Otherwise, we shall confine ourselves to works that happen simply to conform to standards with which we have been familiar or that will suit our professional roles as traditionally defined in academe.

I do not want to be misleading here: I do not believe that somewhere out there is, say, a working-class poet, ignored through bourgeois prejudice, who actually wrote better metaphysical poems than Donne or more singular ones than Pound. No more do I think that a factory organized along truly socialist lines will be more "efficient" and "productive" than a capitalist factory; capitalists often find means to do rather well what it is they want to do—in this case to squeeze as much profit from workers as they can. But that does not necessarily make for a humane, safe, creative, or socially responsible workplace—as many "socialist" advocates of the "free market" economy seem to have forgotten. The goals are different; the values and thus the priorities different. To be sure, it has been demonstrated that there were forgotten black and white women authors who wrote fictions as good in traditional terms as that of many of the canonical stalwarts. My main point, however, is that if there are probably no working-class "Cantos," neither did Pound write verses for "Which Side Are You On?" And if Florence Reece's song does not demonstrate the fine elaboration of exceedingly complex languages to be found in the "Cantos," it is also the fact that none of Pound's poems—not all of them

together, I dare say—has served to sustain and inspire so many thousands
of oppressed people. What, finally, is art about?

IV

Changing the curriculum is more than a matter of abstract theory. Too many
faculty have come to me after workshops and asked, "How can you teach
that? What is there to say in class?" These questions, painful and real, suggest
the connection of curricular revision not only to aesthetic but to pedagogical
strategy.

The classroom is only one of the many contexts in which we and our
students engage literature. We assume that the classroom is in some sense
neutral, that the forms of literary encounter it implies do not do violence to
a given work. But is that in fact the case? A Native American tale, for
example, can be read in ethnographical publications, it can be recited aloud
by a student or instructor, it can even be heard and its recitation by an Indian
teller can be seen on a video tape. But all of these forms of literary encounter
lift the tale from the tribal context in which it takes its living shape. The
actual audience for the tale would have received its ritualized clues as to the
kind of tale about to be told and would thus have its expectations defined.
Further, such an audience would generally be familiar with the central characters and thus need not be introduced to them. Often, beyond all that, the
tale fulfills definable, perhaps sacred, functions within the life of a tribe. All
these elements are missing or badly distorted in the classroom, where the tale
becomes an artifact of study. The instructor's task thus begins to shift from
interpretation of the text itself to recreation of the cultural, social, and performance contexts that shape it. But even the most successful *re*creation
cannot reproduce the real function of such a tale *within* the tribe and thus its
real impact on the people by and for whom it was created. This might appear
to present a discouraging prospect for an instructor. But in fact, it provides
us with an opportunity to explore the important problem of how responses
to a work differ according to the circumstances in which it is encountered
and depending, also, upon the reader's or listener's own position in the world.

Although the problem is, perhaps, somewhat more extreme with Native
American literature than with other cultural traditions, the difference is in
degree only, not in kind. The circumstances in which culture is produced and
encountered, the functions of culture, the specific historical and formal traditions that shape and validate culture—these all differ somewhat from social
group to social group and among classes. In this respect, the problem of
changing curriculum has primarily to do with learning to understand, appreciate, and teach about many varied cultural traditions.

A few examples may be helpful here. In teaching the Zuni origin story
called "Talk Concerning the First Beginning," it is useful to have students
read passages aloud and then critique each other's reading. It rapidly becomes
clear that the repetitive, stylized dialogue implicitly requires distinct voicings

and a degree of acting out nowhere made explicit in the text. That perception in turn, leads to a set of questions about the extent to which we, in that classroom, share in the text's discourse, are situated outside its frameworks, approach it as ethnographic "evidence" rather than from within its belief system (as distinct, for example, from how a believer might read the western Bible). It may then become more possible to talk about the functions of such a story in Zuni life, as well as the often buried "Western" origin tales in our own.

From the beginning, African-American artists have drawn on two differing cultures: the variety of European-American traditions available to and often thrust upon them, and the indigenous and equally varied cultures of black Americans and, to some extent, black African and Caribbean people. The latter, largely an oral and to some degree a "folk" tradition, includes forms as different as the slave narrative, "spirituals" or sorrow songs, and work songs, the blues, dialect tales, the verbal play—signifying—common in black communities. But form is not the only thing that has separated black American culture. Phyllis Wheatley, while she uses customary British forms in beginning to express a distinctly American poetic voice (e.g., in "To His Excellency General Washington"), also draws upon her own persona as an "Ethiope" to construct a still-different African-American literary presence (e.g., in "To the University of Cambridge in New England"). In other cases, the circumstances in which forms were created and enacted and the functions they served *within* the black community and in relation to whites were significantly distinct.[11] A spiritual might be a mode of solace—or a signal hidden from the white listener. The teller of tales might provide amusement and distraction, but also a means of sustaining sources of power within the black community.

The debate about the extent to which black artists do or should draw on popular tradition has long raged among African-American critics. For our purposes it is necessary only to point out that many black artists did so. It thus becomes necessary to establish that African-American context in order to work fully with Charles Chesnutt's stories, Jean Toomer's *Cane*, Claude McKay's poems and novels, Ralph Ellison's *Invisible Man,* poems by Langston Hughes and Gwendolyn Brooks, precisely as it is necessary to familiarize students with the Western history and traditions upon which T. S. Eliot, Ezra Pound, and William Faulkner drew. It is even more necessary, since fewer of our students are likely to be at all familiar with even the popular, daily ground of African-American culture, much less its artistic forms. The point here is not, however, to provide "background," but to understand the narrative strategies both of Uncle Julius as a character and Chesnutt as an author in the conjure tales; the construction of poetic lines based formally though quite differently both on traditional African-American genres and on Anglo-American forms in work from Dunbar through McKay and Hughes to Michael Harper; the ways in which Zora Neale Hurston applies ideas about African-American oral discourse she develops in *Mules and Men* to structure Janie's narrative in *Their Eyes Were Watching God.*

A decade ago, it would have been virtually impossible to undertake the pedagogical tasks upon which I have touched here. Many of the key texts were not in print, or were available only in research libraries. More to the point, perhaps, very little analysis of the distinctive qualities of minority and white female literary traditions had been published. Now, however, we have entered a phase in teaching, as in research, in which we can look at the received tradition of American letters alongside those newly recovered and have at our disposal serious, and increasingly comparative, analyses of both. That process, I am suggesting, not only allows us to review the subject matter of texts, the standards of literary value we use to make curricular choices, and some of the pedagogical changes implied by altered choices; it also forces us to examine the way in which revised courses should, or inevitably do, respond to the imperatives of historical study. It is to that final subject I wish to turn now.

V

To some degree, every text inscribes the social ground against which it was created. Indeed, one can argue that literary works arise in the intersection of historical reality with cultural tradition. It follows that if we are interested in a more comprehensive view of the past, we will select historically and culturally diverse texts. As I pointed out above, we do that now when we include the New England schoolroom poets or James Fenimore Cooper in a survey course. Along such lines, there is no logical bar to broadening selection to include Suzannah Rowson, Lydia Maria Child, John Rollin Ridge, and Harriet Wilson. For the historical and cultural grounds they encode are surely as valid and interesting as those of the white and male writers with whom we are more familiar. My point here, however, is not to reify the previous discussion of content, nor to preach a sermon about the responsibility of literature courses to clarify the history and past culture of this nation for students who are too ignorant of these subjects.

I want, rather, to consider the transformation of perception that, I believe, occurs when a traditional literary category is shattered by adding a range of different works to prior accounts of it. Begin with F. O. Matthiessen's definition of the "American Renaissance": Emerson, Thoreau, Poe, Melville, Hawthorne. Add to it, now, Margaret Fuller, including her *Woman in the Nineteenth Century* and her late reports from revolutionary Italy; and now, Frederick Douglass' 1845 *Narrative;* and again, Harriet Jacobs' *Incidents in the Life of a Slave Girl,* and some of the other slave narratives and the domestic fictions that she evokes—some of Alice Cary's early stories, like "Uncle William's" and "Uncle Christopher's", say, or Susan Warner's *The Wide, Wide World.* A curriculum that includes this variety will, of course, provide us with a more comprehensive view of cultural crosscurrents in the period leading up to the Civil War. My argument, however, is as much directed to how our perceptions of the traditional Renaissance texts alter both in terms of private reading and of classroom presentation.

I am suggesting that familiar works change when we read them alongside others, less familiar, but that grew from the same historical soil. One can, for example, consider *The Scarlet Letter* (1850) with *Incidents in the Life of a Slave Girl* (1861); Douglass' *Narrative* (1845) with Emerson's "Self-Reliance" (1841) and "Politics" (1844). Or, to touch on other periods and categories, one might examine the "realism" of Crane's "The Bride Comes to Yellow Sky" (1898) and *Maggie* (1893) with that of Freeman's "Louisa" (1891) and "Old Woman Magoun" (1909), or even Caroline Kirkland's *A New Home—Who'll Follow?* (1839), or the captivities of Mary Rowlandson, the Keres' "Yellow Woman" story, and Olaudah Equiano. Nor have we yet wandered far from the received curriculum—we might want to proceed a step further, setting beside Thoreau's evocations of Native American experience their visions of their own lives and those of the whites, such as William Apes's "An Indian Looking-Glass for the White Man" (1833), George Copway's *The Life of Kah-Ge-Ga-Gah-Bowh* (1850), or John Rollin Ridge's "The Stolen White Girl" (1868). In putting together differently a broader set of texts, the creators of many recent courses are not only engaged in historical clarification, but are providing renewed access to familiar works alongside fresh perceptions of a range of newly-valued literatures. And, of course, they are reshaping the very terms—"American Renaissance," "realism," for example—that we have used to organize literary study.

This historical approach to the study of culture implicitly brings into question the hierarchy of forms as well. Many of today's courses regularly use more diaries, letters, and other "discontinuous" forms that traditional curricula might, and they probably make greater use of autobiographical writing, at least by minority writers and white women. In part, such curricular broadening is a consequence of new feminist and minority scholarship. Not only have such scholars uncovered what once might have been surprising riches in, for example, women's journals and letters, but they have shown why many women sought self-expression in discontinuous, nonfictive forms, and how the tendency to disparage these forms was both consequence and cause of the devaluation of women's writing. In part, too, this kind of curricular shift reflects a heightened concern for "private" as well as "public" worlds, and the intersection of the two in autobiographical texts like that of Julia Foote (*A Brand Plucked From the Fire*, 1879), Zitkala-Sa ("The School Days of an Indian Girl," 1900), or Mary Antin (*The Promised Land,* 1912). Autobiographical writing by successful public men, such as Benjamin Franklin and Henry Adams, has always been part of the American literature curriculum. It has been a relatively short step through the remnants of racism from their work to that of Douglass, Booker T. Washington, and perhaps even W.E.B. DuBois. Narrators like Linda Brent (in Jacobs' *Incidents*) and Mamie Pinzer (in the letters of *The Mamie Papers*) represent a more substantial departure because they are not people of public importance, not, indeed, "people" speaking in their own names at all, and their concerns are the more "mundane" problems of sexuality, family, poverty, housing, clothing—"love and money"—to adapt Jane Austen's formulation of the subject matter of the novel. The renewed interest in such works in literary study parallels the shift in history from an overwhelming emphasis on political, diplomatic, and military study to a new regard for social history, and especially history "from the bottom."

This more historical approach has one further significant virtue. Literary works are often presented as the production of individual genius, isolated from the social world in which all human beings live. That mystifies writing, for authors, like other people, are part of, not separated from, the world they inhabit. And they compose in response not only to their literary predecessors, however influential, but also to their social circumstances—as well as, of course, to their personal qualities. To say it another way, works of literary art express—in different balance—both the distinctive subjectivity of individual writers *and* the social dynamics of the world in which they lived. Again, Stowe is helpful here. It was not she, Stowe said, who wrote *Uncle Tom's Cabin,* but God, writing through her. As a metaphor, the statement has a certain validity, for the book does indeed inscribe the all-but transcendent social and cultural forces shaping antebellum American politics—the imperatives of evangelical Christianity, the reshaping of family life and child rearing. And her metaphor compels us as readers to engage those forces emotionally and not simply as objects of study. For in a certain sense, we do not read simply as private individuals, any more than writers write that way. We are people in a world, not merely students of an art form. As books speak out of social as well as private realities, so they speak to and help form us as social beings. They affect what we value, how we see, and perhaps even how we act.

To examine and reflect upon a set of reasonably well-scrutinized texts can be intellectually rewarding, but it seems to me to hold us looking backward at fragments of the past. Implicit in the curricular changes I and others wish to advance is, I believe, an aspiration to shape an equitable future in this most diverse of nations. I read that as a healthy and cheering development in our profession. For it means we are endowing what we do with the energy of our values, that we have revived the seriousness with which we once regarded the work of "The American Scholar." The job of reconstructing American literature is thus part of a broader movement for equal and fulfilling education. And its importance lies precisely in placing the study of our national cultures (plural) at the heart of educational renewal.

Notes

1. See, for example, *ADE Bulletin* 91 (Winter 1988); Paula Gunn Allen, ed., *Studies in American Indian Literature: Critical Essays and Course Designs* (New York: Modern Language Association, 1983); *Black Studies/Women's Studies: An Overdue Partnership—Courses Addressing Issues of Race, Gender, and Culture* (Amherst, Mass:

[Five College] Black Studies/Women's Studies Faculty Development Project, n.d.); Dexter Fisher and Robert B. Stepto, eds., *Afro-American Literature: The Reconstruction of Instruction* (New York: Modern Language Association, 1978); *Initiating Curriculum Transformation in the Humanities: Integrating Women and Issues of Race and Gender* (Wayne, N.J.: William Patterson College Humanities faculty, c. 1987); Paul Lauter, ed., *Reconstructing American Literature—Courses, Syllabi, Issues* (Old Westbury, N.Y.: Feminist Press, 1983).

2. See, for example, Florence Howe and Paul Lauter, *The Impact of Women's Studies on the Campus and the Disciplines* (Washington: National Institute of Education, 1980).

3. One of the few histories of fiction that seriously integrates works by black writers and white women is Linda Wagner-Martin, *The Modern American Novel, 1914–1945* (Boston: Twayne, 1989).

4. The language is that of the first edition of the current Norton text (p. xxv). Those volumes printed work by twenty-nine women writers, including two black women, and that of fourteen black authors overall. These represented 22 percent and 10.6 percent, respectively, of the total number of authors included; in terms of space, however, works by (and introductions about) women occupied 13.9 percent, and works by blacks occupied a mere 3.9 percent of the 4,953 pages. Even these very modest figures then represented something of a break-through in coverage, though further change has come about since.

5. Paul Lauter, et al., eds., *The Heath Anthology of American Literature*, 2 vols. (Lexington, Mass.: D.C. Heath, 1990).

6. Tomás Borge, Interview, Managua, Nicaragua, August 1983.

7. In *Gender, Fantasy and Realism,* Alfred Habegger points out how certain novels provided the Victorian reader with the opportunity "to try on a certain role— to think out with the help of a book-length narrative the potential life-consequences of being a given kind of woman" (New York: Columbia University Press, 1982), p. ix.

8. Diana Hume George wrote concerning this issue:

> Those exploring/conquering/aggressive texts, made the centers of literature and humanities curricula, turn our classrooms into the 'educational' equivalents of the prime-time TV world, where program after program captures and keeps its audience by feeding it myths about danger and excitement—as if such experiences were at the heart of being human. In an era that is seeing the demise of the word and the rise of the video image, we might offer something different, not only generically; I mean that the issue of balance is not just internal to the classroom—there are new reasons in the hyper-TV generation to offer gentler, more humanistic, more complex versions of human experience; otherwise we give students only a more cerebral version of tube ethics.

9. Allen Tate, "Tension in Poetry," *The Man of Letters in the Modern World* (New York: Meridian Books, 1955), p. 71.

10. The new Harper anthology offers three separate selections, though they total but twenty pages—as compared with the 279 devoted to Hawthorne, the 182 to Melville, and the 64 to Saul Bellow. The new Heath anthology includes eight chapters from *Uncle Tom's Cabin* as well as five other selections, in total some 93 pages.

11. See, for example, Lawrence Levine, *Black Culture and Black Consciousness: Afro-American Folk Thought from Slavery to Freedom* (New York: Oxford University Press, 1977).

Teaching Nineteenth-Century Women Writers

During the last twenty years the opportunities and challenges to teach nine-teenth-century American women writers have widened almost beyond the comprehension of those trained in previous decades. When I was in graduate school in the 1950s at Indiana and Yale, we read Emily Dickinson. Period. Today, that would be considered a scandal. The changes have been great, and good, but they have not been without problems. In this chapter I address a number of what I perceive as significant issues in *teaching* nineteenth-century American women writers. These I have named the problem of texts, the problem of history, the problem of context, the problem of subject, the problem of form, the problem of difference, and the problem of standards. As will be plain, the names are occasionally arbitrary and the categories somewhat overlap, but they may provide frameworks useful not only for those of us who were expected to know no more than Dickinson, but for those expecting to teach no less than Frances Ellen Watkins Harper and Lydia Maria Child.

As recently as five years ago, a comprehensive course on nineteenth-century American women writers could only be taught by copious use of the copying machine. For if you wanted your students to know anything by Harper or Child—or even anything *about* them—you had no choice. That is, beyond the brief anthology selections of seventeen writers (including Harper) one finds in Gilbert and Gubar's *Literature by Women*,[1] the nine (spread over two volumes) in the *Norton Anthology of American Literature*,[2] or the twelve in the recent *Harper American Literature*,[3] few texts were available.

The only piece of Child's writing then in print was an excerpt from *Ho-bomok* (1824) in Lucy Freibert and Barbara White's useful volume called *Hidden Hands*.[4] Apart from that book, only Judith Fetterley's pioneering 1985 collection, *Provisions: A Reader from 19th-Century American Women*,[5] had resurrected such women, and others like Caroline Kirkland, Fanny Fern and Alice Cary, from oblivion. Now, however, full works by writers such as Child are becoming available, together with books by E.D.E.N. Southworth,

Parts of this paper, on Frances E.W. Harper, appeared in different form in *Legacy* V (Spring 1988): 27–34. Other parts of it were first presented on a panel at the National Council of Teachers of English convention, Philadelphia, 1985.

Rose Terry Cooke, Catharine Maria Sedgwick and others, as part of Rutgers University Press's excellent American Women Writers Series.[6] Jane Tompkins has edited a reissue of what was America's first real best seller, Susan Warner's *The Wide, Wide World* (1850).[7] Additionally, Oxford University Press has issued the remarkable Schomburg collection of the writings of nineteenth-century black women, including the work of Anna Julia Cooper, Pauline Hopkins, and Mrs. N.F. Mossell, among others. Many of these white and black women are also included in the new *Heath Anthology of American Literature* (1990), the final product of the Reconstructing American Literature project.

As for Harper, 1987 was a good year. After making the 1986 edition of *Granger's Index to Poetry* and the *Cambridge Handbook to American Literature,* she was prominently represented in Mary Helen Washington's important new collection, *Invented Lives.*[8] As part of another new series reprinting fiction by black women, Beacon Press has recently reissued her 1892 novel, *Iola Leroy,* with a fine introduction by Hazel Carby;[9] her collected poems constitute one of the Schomburg volumes; and Carby's book, *Reconstructing Womanhood,*[10] devotes a full chapter to Harper as well as two to Pauline Hopkins. She has even twice made the pages of the New York Times *Book Review,* in Henry Louis Gates's review essay on the Washington book and on the tradition of black women's writing, and in the Sunday *Times* review of the Schomburg series.

Now one might reasonably ask why I invoke Southworth and Harper, Child and Cary when we have accessible lots of the work of the "main" nineteenth-century American women writers: Fuller, Stowe, Dickinson, Jewett, Freeman, Chopin, and Gilman. Is this not an inversion of those older forms of pedantry that insisted upon studying John Pendleton Kennedy's *Swallow Barn,* and authors like Johnson Jones Hooper, Jones Very, and Frederick Goddard Tuckerman? Those last three are, in fact, included in one or more of the older American literature anthologies, unlike Southworth, Harper, Child, and Cary. But the point isn't to match every Johnson Jones Hooper with an E.D.E.N. Southworth or every excerpt from Cooper with one from Child. The problem is that we are only at the beginning of the process of reevaluating literary works of the past in the light provided by today's feminist and minority criticism. Those of us who have grown up in the United States are all products of its capitalist economic and social relations, even if we call ourselves "socialists." Thus we are likely in practice to share with our unabashedly entrepreneurial sisters and brothers much of America's individualistic, competitive, materialistic culture—however much we might theoretically deplore these. So too, as literary people we have been acculturated by the work of those we have been taught are significant—Hawthorne and Melville, Emerson and James. We become what Judith Fetterley has called "resistant readers" to presumptively "classic" texts only through a slow process which involves decentering them from our structures of valuation. In practice, I think, that process necessarily involves reading many alternative texts and talking about them with others—what one best does in the classroom. That we cannot do without the texts. Indeed, we need more than the usual single story by Stowe or Jewett or Freeman offered by most anthologies. We need to sift a richness of possibility in order to cook up a new American canon—that our students or "grandstudents" may in their turn set on the shelf.

When the academic wing of feminism first generated a publishing component in the early 1970s, we searched for works whose literary qualities were substantially similar to those of the dominantly male and white texts which had formed our tastes. Thus we published and promoted works like Gilman's "The Yellow Wallpaper" and Davis's "Life in the Iron Mills," both now enshrined in American literature anthologies. Writers like Harper and Child seemed "propagandistic" or "sentimental." Furthermore, we assumed that even a text like Elizabeth Stuart Phelps's *The Story of Avis,* whose politics continue to be relevant, was unlikely to be used in classes and thus was economically not feasible to publish—much less *Hobomok* or *Ruth Hall.* That presses like Rutgers, Oxford, and Beacon are now successfully distributing works by Child, Harper, Fanny Fern and Southworth tells something of the broadening of the base of a revisionist study of American literature.

It also marks a step in the process I was describing. It says that the decentering and reconstructing of what we call "American literature" has been carried forward to new ground. Critics and historians such as Elizabeth Ammons, Nina Baym, Hazel Carby, Barbara Christian, Josephine Donovan, Annette Kolodny, Jane Tompkins, and Mary Helen Washington, among others.[11] have provided purchases in the rugged terrain of literary history from which we can get fresh looks at its peaks and valleys . . . and, it may be, come to revise our views of what we thought were its more prominent features. But again, criticism without text is an exercise in abstraction. For it is not merely literary concepts and historical configurations that are undergoing reconstruction; it is our *consciousness,* that set of internal assumptions and outlooks that forms what we see, or even what we look at. The experience of fictions and the encounter with writers of another time are part of what shape consciousness, as Frederick Douglass points out in an important section of his *Narrative.*[12] Consciousness, to speak crudely, shapes standards of value, the bases on which we determine texts to be sufficiently significant to include in curricula and reading lists. Thus the very availability of texts helps, in a certain paradoxical way by shaping consciousness, to determine their availability. But that is only one problem.

Equally important is the need to revise historical understanding, our second problem. We have largely been taught to think in terms of unitary—or at least of what are called "mainstream"—traditions in American literature; *The American Tradition in Literature,* as one anthology is titled. But in fact, American culture is deeply heterogeneous. The history of fiction constructed around the canonical writers—Poe, Hawthorne, Melville, James, Twain, Hemingway, Faulkner, and Fitzgerald—is altogether a different history from that which emerges from a study of key white women or black writers of fiction. At the beginnings of the feminist reconstruction of the canon, it was argued that novelists like Chopin or Wharton succeeded in creating formally complex works of timeless excellence—that is, succeeded in precisely the terms critics had used to valorize canonical male writers. The women's exclusion from the canon was thus demonstrably an exercise in prejudice, that, we optimistically assumed, would be corrected as it was perceived. But simply placing women into a dominantly male tradition is clearly a first, and inadequate, step—however much it remains our primary mode. In time, therefore, critics began to construct a separate history of women's (as well as of black) narratives, focusing on writers like Stowe, Harper, Jewett, Freeman, Hopkins, Cather, Glasgow, and Hurston, as well as on Chopin and Wharton. That history continues to emerge as, for example, the origins of realism get pushed earlier and earlier into the nineteenth-century, to women writers like Caroline Kirkland, Alice Cary, and Susan Warner. Kirkland, in turn, leads us to the English village sketches of Mary Russell Mitford. Nor are these earlier women interesting only as the inadequate predecessors of Crane and Howells; indeed, pairing them with such later male realists offers a very useful pedagogical technique for perceiving the overlapping and distinctive features of each.

The issue I want to raise here, however, is not that of the derivation of literary styles but the question of how literary texts are perceived as encoding and transmitting powerful ideas, how they are historical agents. For example, in introducing Thoreau one anthology says in a manner characteristic of writing about him, that in 1849, three years after refusing to pay his poll tax, "he formalized his theory of social action in the essay 'Civil Disobedience,' the origin of the modern concept of pacific resistance as the final instrument of minority opinion, which found its spectacular demonstration in the lives of Mahatma Gandhi and Martin Luther King."[13] Ten years before Thoreau spent his night in the Concord lockup, in her "Appeal to the Christian Women of the South" (1836) Angelina Grimké wrote in the cadences of a biblical prophet:

> Can you not, my friends, understand the signs of the times; do you not see the sword of retributive justice hanging over the South, or are you still slumbering at your posts?—Are there no Shíphrahs, no Puahs among you who will dare in Christian firmness and Christian meekness, to refuse to obey the *wicked laws* which require *women to enslave, to degrade and to brutalize women?* . . . Is there no Esther among you who will plead for the poor devoted slave? . . . Listen, too, to her magnanimous reply to this powerful appeal; "I *will go in unto the king, which is not according to law, and if I perish, I perish.*"[14]

In fact, of course, the idea of nonviolent resistance, indeed of nonviolent positive action, was a commonplace of evangelical Christianity during the early nineteenth century, especially among abolitionists like the Grimkés and William Lloyd Garrison. No one would deny that Thoreau gave powerful expression to the idea, or that in certain important respects he helped secularize the mode of prophetic testimony, though perhaps in his time, the example of not paying a small tax was less persuasive than the nonviolent conduct of the members of the Ladies' Anti-Slavery Society when they were attacked in 1835 by a mob of "gentlemen of property and standing" in Boston.[15]

My objective here in no sense is to debunk Thoreau. But I do think it important to help students (and ourselves) see through two commonplace canards of intellectual history. One concerns the notion that "great ideas" (like civil disobedience) spring, like Athene, from the foreheads of great, and generally male, geniuses ("*his* theory of social action"). The other fallacy is that such ideas are transmitted, as it were, from mountaintop to mountaintop, like smoke signals: Thoreau to Gandhi to King. In fact, as this instance suggests, ideas frequently develop in a complex interaction between the practice of many, often nameless, individuals caught up in the power of a cause—abolition, the rights of workers or of women—and the formalizing power of what the nineteenth century called a "Poet." The Poet names—no small power—what she and others had learned to do. Those of us devoted to cultural study tend, it seems, to assimilate to naming all the power of this process, but that is to falsify reality as well as to aggrandize the work of commentator and critic—as if texts alone determined history and academic theorists in New Haven were the engines of change.

An equivalent pedagogical problem is posed by tracing the idea of "civil disobedience" from Thoreau only through men of great public standing, like Gandhi and King. Nonviolent direct action is, in fact, a primary weapon of the weak and dispossessed, and therefore of women, as is brilliantly demonstrated by Mary Wilkins Freeman in her story "A Church Mouse." In this story, the heroine, Hetty, an elderly woman alone in the world, is driven from her dwelling by its sale following the death of the woman with whom she has lived. By standing in the way of the main church deacon as he rakes hay, "clogging" his farming with her "full weight," however slight, she manages to obtain the keys to the meeting house, and, despite the opposition of the minister and deacons, even to set up her quilt and cookstove in order to live there. As Freeman says

> When one is hard pressed, one, however simple, gets wisdom as to vantage-points. Hetty comprehended hers perfectly. She was the propounder of a problem; as long as it was unguessed, she was sure of her foothold as propounder.

Ultimately, Hetty's passive resistance—she locks the church door against the deacons when they attempt to move her out—mobilizes the support of the women of the community, who speak up on her behalf and against the men's attempts to remove her by violence. Thus she is enabled to stay in what has become her "home." It is a small triumph, but perhaps closer to the political experience of most of our students—especially nowadays—than the wonderful but remote demonstrations of soul-power of Gandhi and King, or even the dominating assertiveness of Thoreau himself.

A problem related to the tracking of ideas is provided by the need for historical *contexts* not often available to us, given the compartmentalized organization of the American academy. Take, for example, Frances Ellen Watkins Harper's poem, "Aunt Chloe's Politics," published in her 1872 book, *Sketches of Southern Life.*

Aunt Chloe's Politics

Of course, I don't know very much
   About these politics,
But I think that some who run 'em,
   Do mighty ugly tricks.

I've seen 'em honey-fugle round,
   And talk so awful sweet,
That you'd think them full of kindness,
   As an egg is full of meat.

Now I don't believe in looking
   Honest people in the face,
And saying when you're doing wrong,
   That "I haven't sold my race."

When we want to school our children,
   If the money isn't there,
Whether black or white have took it,
   The loss we all must share.

And this buying up each other
   Is something worse than mean,
Though I thinks a heap of voting,
   I go for voting clean.

At one level, a poem like this may be taken to explain the existence of American Studies as a discipline. For it comes to full life when one illuminates it with the insights of both literary and historical analysis. Harper is remarkably successful in suggesting the speech patterns, syntax, and vocabulary of an unschooled southern black woman without, on the whole, presenting her in dialect. This is clearly a conscious and I would say political choice, for in *Iola Leroy* Harper does portray a number of dialect-speaking characters. Here, however, she wishes to draw a shrewd and upright woman of the people who is not, like Stowe's Aunt Chloe, distanced from her audience, white or middle-class black, by the "color," so to speak, of her language. Like most Americans, this Aunt Chloe uses some slang—like "honey-fugle round," to cajole or wheedle, and "a heap"—some nonstandard grammar—"have took it"—and the mock ignorance of the savvy: . . . "I don't know very much/About these politics." Harper carefully establishes in the third line—"But I think that some who run 'em"—Aunt Chloe's control of standard, informal English before, in the next to last line—"Though I thinks a heap of voting"—she presents her using a specifically southern black locution.

Aunt Chloe's language is, I believe, designed to legitimate her keen political commentary for an audience unused to the idea of women, much less *black* women, voting. In these five stanzas she touches on many of the most sensitive political issues of the Reconstruction period, especially in the south:

for example, whether or not public funds should be appropriated for the education of children, white or black; and the conduct of some black male politicians who used race loyalty to excuse corruption. She also touches on the general level of political morality at a time that saw the exposure of Boss Tweed in 1871 and the Credit Mobilier scandal in 1872.

All of this is, I think, an implicit argument for Aunt Chloe's right to vote, which emerges only in the last line. This was not, if we will recall, a distant and unlikely possibility in 1872. After all, women had gone to the polls in Wyoming and Utah in 1870 and 1871, and neither the territories nor the Republic had tottered. It was in 1872, after women had previously attempted to vote in ten states and in the District of Columbia, that Susan B. Anthony tried to cast her ballot in the presidential election. While Harper, like Frederick Douglass, had broken with Anthony and Elizabeth Cady Stanton over the issue of the Fifteenth Amendment, like them she worked to support a federal women's suffrage amendment, first introduced in the Congress in 1868, and given considerable visibility by Victoria Woodhull's congressional testimony in January of 1871. The fundamental point Harper articulates here both in and through Aunt Chloe is consistent with what she presented in her 1894 address to the World's Congress of Representative Women on "Woman's Political Future." There she said:

> Political life in our country has plowed in muddy channels, and needs the infusion of clearer and cleaner waters. I am not sure that women are naturally so much better than men that they will clear the stream by virtue of their womanhood; it is not through sex but through character that the best influence of women upon the life of the nation must be exerted.
>
> I do not believe in unrestricted and universal suffrage for either men or women. I believe in moral and educational tests. I do not believe that the most ignorant and brutal man is better prepared to add value to the strength and durability of the government than the most cultured, upright, and intelligent woman.

Two decades before, Harper had presented such strength of character in the persona of Aunt Chloe. The only point in the 1894 speech implicitly absent from "Aunt Chloe's Politics" is Harper's insistence that "The hands of lynchers are too red with blood to determine the political character of the government for even four short years." It has taken 80 years and more to fulfill this objective.

The problem, of course, is that few English majors, let alone American literature specialists in graduate school, really learn much about American history. Even the minimal details on which I touched above will be found in no basic American history texts and in relatively few introductory courses, and these details are essential to reading "Aunt Chloe." Ordinarily, this line of reasoning leads to a defense of American Studies, but that is not my point. My contention here is that writing by marginalized groups—women or "minorities"—is for a number of reasons more directly implicated in the immediate problems of historical change. Then any arrangement which systematically separates the texts from the historical contexts in which they are embedded arrests our capacity to read them. The point is *not* that, say, black texts need to be read as social documents rather than as formal structures of language; nor that "majority" texts "transcend" their historical moments, and therefore have no politics. All literary works perform functions within their times, though the functions, and thus the politics, of texts that emerge from a dominant culture may be more deeply buried under what have become widely-shared assumptions. To miss the politically stabilizing force of Shakespeare's histories and tragedies, for example, is to miss precisely what allowed his wide popularity. The presumed transcendence of such works, like their canonical status, measures the social power of the values they promoted.

If one pursues this line of argument, one is inevitably drawn to the contention that academic structures in America promote what turns out in practice to be a racist and sexist division of knowledge. Thus the problem of context involves considerably more than providing "background" that marginally extends the reading of a text. Rather, it raises the fundamental problem of how the organization of knowledge (and study) promotes particular social and political interests. These issues cannot, it seems to me, remain submerged in a classroom dealing seriously with women's writing. To ignore them suggests that the political functions of a poem like "Aunt Chloe's Politics" are, at best, secondary concerns, that the proper study of literary texts is their form, and that works that insist upon their contexts are inevitably of lesser value than those that transcend context. Rather than calling into question the value of Harper's work, I would want, rather, to question the legitimacy of academic structures that have left it in an intellectual limbo.

What is at stake here, as I have suggested earlier, is the question of what one considers important. Harper offers another painful case in point. Apart from the two 1986 books I mentioned before, she does not appear in any of the usual guides to American literature: not the 1962 *Reader's Encyclopedia of American Literature,* the still-standard 1968 *American Authors, 1600–1900,* nor even the 1983 *Oxford Companion to American Literature.* All three, I should say, contain entries for Edward (Ted) Harrigan, author of *The Mulligan Guard Chowder,* among other plays, and two of them for Henry Harland, author of *The Cardinal's Snuff Box.* Frances E. W. Harper does not appear in *Webster's American Biographies* (1974), nor even in Webster's 1980 *Biographical Dictionary,* which does include George McLean Harper, who was professor of literature at Princeton in the early part of this century and author of *The Legend of the Holy Grail* and *Literary Appreciations,* and also includes Robert Francis Harper, who was an Assyriologist at Yale and at the University of Chicago, where his brother (George McLean Harper) was president. Nor had she made the *Encyclopedia Britannica,* at least into 1989, though that work includes entries for Robert Almer Harper, who did research on the cytology of reproduction among fungi, and on Jesse Harper, who coached football at Notre Dame both before and after Knute Rockne.

Our historian colleagues offer no more encouraging record. There is no entry for Frances Harper in the 1982 *Encyclopedia of American History,* edited by Richard B. Morris and (perhaps ironically) published by Harper and Row (whose American literature anthology ignores Harper). The history encyclopedia does contain entries for Fletcher Harper, the originator of *Harper's Bazaar,* an important women's magazine; Robert Goodloe Harper, who named the country of Liberia; and William Harper, who, responding to *Uncle Tom's Cabin* in 1852, published a collection of essays called *The Pro-Slavery Argument.* Indeed, I've found no reference to Frances Harper in any of the standard history texts, not even in James MacGregor Burns' 1985 *The Workshop of Democracy,* which advertises itself as chronicling "America from the Emancipation Proclamation to the eve of the New Deal. . . . "

We are engaged here, I think, not with the particular problem of Harper's significance as a literary or historical figure—she was, after all, the most widely-read black woman writer of the nineteenth century—but with the issue of *what* is significant and how it gets to be so in the academic world. It is what I like to call the problem of subject matter: What we consider important—the Notre Dame football coach, for example, or racist responses to *Uncle Tom's Cabin*—depends on who "we" are and the assumptions about gender and race to which we have been trained. One way of bringing this problem of subject into focus is to choose in teaching passages and themes that bring differences into relief.

For example, we might begin with the theme stated in the title of the second chapter of *Walden:* "Where I Lived and What I Lived For." The problem of a place to live is central to many nineteenth-century women's texts, including "A Church Mouse." We find it in works as diverse as Kirkland's *A New Home—Who'll Follow,* Warner's *The Wide, Wide World,* a number of Child's *Letters from New York,* Harriet Jacobs' (Linda Brent) *Incidents in the Life of a Slave Girl,* and Jewett's story "A New Year's Visit." The home provides the central locus of values in *Uncle Tom's Cabin,* especially as it is incarnated in the Quaker settlement; indeed, for Stowe, the breaking up of home and family is the primary symbol for the sinfulness of slavery. Likewise, the restoration of family provides Stowe with her primary symbols of order. Furthermore, being deprived of, and searching to establish, a stable home is a central subject in what Baym calls the "woman's novel."

The issue in these books may be clarified by contrasting them with how Thoreau addressed the question of where and how he lived. The opening of that chapter, often skipped for the better-known passages about his house, living deliberately, simplifying, and fishing in the stream of time, establishes a context in which power over one's world is assumed rather than achieved through struggle:

> At a certain season of our life we are accustomed to consider every spot as the possible site of a house. I have thus surveyed the country on every side within a dozen miles of where I live. In imagination I have bought all the farms in succession, for all were to be bought, and I knew their price. I walked over each farmer's premises, tasted his wild apples, discoursed on husbandry with him, took his farm at his price, at any price, mortgaging it to him in my mind; even put a higher price on it,—took everything but a

deed of it,—took his word for his deed, for I dearly love to talk,—cultivated it, and him too to some extent, I trust, and withdrew when I had enjoyed it long enough, leaving him to carry it on. . . . Wherever I sat, there I might live, and the landscape radiated from me accordingly. What is a house but a *sedes,* a seat?—better if a country seat. . . . Well, there I might live, I said; and there I did live, for an hour, a summer and a winter life; saw how I could let the years run off, buffet the winter through, and see the spring come in.

How wonderful this passage is; yet how absurd it would sound in the mouths of Hetty the "Church Mouse," or of Linda Brent, hiding from her slavemaster for seven years in the attic of her grandmother's house; of Stowe's Eliza or even George Harris, or of Ellen Montgomery, the heroine of *The Wide, Wide World*—or, perhaps, in the minds of our students. What Thoreau confidently takes for granted is precisely, for the characters I've mentioned, the problem. Heard, as it were, from their ears, this passage perfectly demonstrates the assumptions as well as the rhetoric of privilege.

Thoreau's initial move here is contained in the universalizing "our" and "we," which at once attempt to incorporate the reader into his experience and effectively demand that "we" share in its qualities. What are these? Leisure and mobility: "I have thus surveyed the country . . . " A degree of financial resource: "In imagination I have bought. . . . " Privileged information: " . . . I knew their price." An almost mythic egocentrism: " . . . the landscape radiated from me. . . . " And a relationship to farm and farmer partly presented in the metaphors of male dominative sexuality, which takes, enjoys, and withdraws. All of this constructs an assumption of power over environment—" . . . I could let the years run off"—likewise projected by the verbs: "surveyed," "bought," "knew," "buffet." And it establishes the terms upon which we may visit Thoreau in his personal castle.[16]

We might contrast this passage with what Caroline Kirkland writes about her connection to the establishment of the village of Montacute on the banks of the Turnip in the Michigan frontier:

> When my husband purchased two hundred acres of wild land on the banks of this to-be-celebrated stream, and drew with a piece of chalk on the bar-room table at Danforth's the plan of a village, I little thought I was destined to make myself famous by handing down to posterity a faithful record of the advancing fortunes of that favored spot.
>
> "The madness of the people" in those days of golden dreams took more commonly the form of city-building; but there were a few who contented themselves with planning villages, on the banks of streams which certainly could never be expected to bear navies, but which might yet be turned to account in the more homely way of grinding or sawing—operations which must necessarily be performed somewhere for the well-being of those very cities. It is of one of these humble attempts that it is my lot to speak, and I make my confession at the outset, warning any fashionable reader who may have taken up my book, that I intend to be "decidedly low."

In contrast to the position of power from which Thoreau surveys the coun-
tryside, Kirkland's is a view from below: a village, not a city; the commonplaces of grinding and sawing, not the "golden dreams" of city building; a
"decidedly low" chronicle, not a fashionable tale. If her husband's aspirations
are modest indeed—"chalk" on a "bar-room table," a village on the Turnip—
hers are even more so, as the mock-heroics and the alliteration of "f" toward
the end of the first paragraph suggest. Kirkland's self-deprecating irony not
only anticipates her reader's derision at the trivia of frontier life, but it also
effectively grounds her freedom as observer and chronicler in a realistic ap-
praisal of the situation into which she has been placed by her husband's
purchase. Her problem is to construct a home and a book from the "meagre
materials" handed to her—materials "valuable only for [their] truth"—and
from the ill-assorted cultural furnishings she has brought from the east. Simplifying her household by, for example, turning a "tall cup-board" into a
corn-crib, is not a matter of choice but of making the most of the little one
has—which is also her stance as a writer.[17]

In certain respects, of course, the focus of women writers on a home
reflects ideas about women's "sphere," the notion that a woman's creativity
could be expressed, and her moral authority developed, through her organization of home and family as the alternative to the corrupt world of business.
But writers did not need to share the ideology developed by Catharine
Beecher and Harriet Beecher Stowe to focus on this subject. The problem
of a place to live, of establishing and maintaining a home arose realistically
from the repeated experience of being displaced because, as in Kirkland, a
man decided to pull up stakes and move west or, as in Fanny Fern's *Ruth
Hall,* he suffered business reversals or died leaving wife and children without
resources, or abandoning slaves to be sold off. In real life, such problems
confronted Sara Willis Parton (Fanny Fern), Warner, Southworth, and Louisa
May Alcott; it was because husbands died or were financially unstable, or
because fathers were improvident that they took up writing. Making a place
to live in the woods or the city is thus not so much a metaphor for the
construction of an autonomous self but a straightforward matter of day to
day survival.

Further, the problem of home and family is deeply connected in many of
the writings, as in many of the lives of nineteenth-century women, with the
problem of creativity. Mid-century ideology fixed women's primary duty as
maintaining home and family. To discharge that duty, women like Warner
and Southworth, and in a sense Stowe, had to earn sufficient money as authors;
their work as writers was, first, a means for ensuring family stability. In her
story "Psyche's Art," Louisa May Alcott presents a heroine who achieves
artistic substance only by first devoting herself to family duty. But later in a
work like Elizabeth Stuart Phelp's *The Story of Avis,* and of course in Chopin's
The Awakening and Mary Austin's *A Woman of Genius,* art or a version of
self-creation is posed against the tenacious and draining obligations of home
and family—as had been the case originally in fact for Stowe. I am not

suggesting that this complex of themes fails to appear in the work of men, but seldom, if ever, is it so central. It is, of course, only as we take a woman artist seriously that books which focus on that subject become important to us.

Just as the writing of women coheres around distinguishing themes, so may it utilize certain genres differently, and here we encounter the problem of form. Judith Fetterley has pointed out, in explaining the structure of *A New Home—Who'll Follow* (1839), that Kirkland tried to solve what was at once an artistic and social problem by posing her narrative as an adaptation of a series of letters. Writing for publication was an activity still viewed in many quarters as inappropriate to women, precisely because it was public. Letter writing, however, sustained the quality of private communication, often between women. In a sense, the letter form offered the possibility of being at once public and private. That may explain the popularity of the form with many women writers of the antebellum period. Sarah Grimke's major work was *Letters on the Equality of the Sexes* (1838), among Lydia Maria Child's most successful books were the two series of *Letters From New York,* and Jane Swisshelm again adopted the form in her *Letters to Country Girls* (1853). One might argue that the letter form of Margaret Fuller's late dispatches to the New York *Tribune* allowed her a peculiarly successful balance of personal and political observation.

But perhaps the most fascinating adaptation of the letter form to the needs of a kind of publication was made by Emily Dickinson. We are all familiar with Dickinson's characterization of her poems:

> This is my letter to the World
> That never wrote to Me—

A number of Dickinson's letters *are* poems; others, while not written in verse formally, can still be scanned.[18] But perhaps more to the point: It is within the context of letters that Dickinson undertook her major form of "publication," that is, making her work known to a "public." In her characteristic way, to be sure, Dickinson redefined that "public" as the largely individual recipients of the letters. But it remains the case that by far the largest number of her poems to find readers during her lifetime—fully a third of them, in fact—did so within the context provided by letters.

Thus, when we speak of the importance of the "discontinuous" forms—letters, journals, diaries—to the canon of women's writing, we need, I think, to be aware of how these forms served a number of compatible functions. They are, of course, modes of private expression of self. They also can be forms of publication for a selected audience. And, as I have suggested, they can be generic means for bridging private and public worlds. Since students are more likely to have written in these forms than in any others, they provide, as well, an important point of entry into the often unnecessarily distanced world of the creative artist. One can generate assignments in which students use the conventions of their own letter writing to accomplish certain of a writer's goals; or, in reverse, apply the conventions of a writer's "letters" to their own purposes.

Form can also be shaped by a writer's sense of her or his marginality. Consider four books published within approximately a quarter century of one another: Two of these, Jewett's *The Country of the Pointed Firs* (1896) and Charles W. Chesnutt's *The Conjure Woman* (1899), were composed by marginalized authors, two, Sherwood Anderson's *Winesburg, Ohio* (1919) and Ernest Hemingway's *In Our Time* (1925), by white men of core, if somewhat ambiguous, status. In structure, they consist of apparently separable stories, but all are in fact unified narratives. In Jewett and Chesnutt, the stories themselves are told by rural, sometime magical, dialect speakers, primarily Mrs. Todd and Uncle Julius. However, their tales are set in frame plots and are narrated to readers by intermediaries, an urban woman and a Northern white man, respectively. In Anderson and Hemingway, the frame, narrative voices have atrophied, though traces remain. It seems to me that Jewett and Chesnutt must provide their audience with surrogates to interpret, guide, suggest responses, precisely because of the appreciable distance between, on the one side, the world of matriarchs—the country of the pointed firs—and the slave world of violence and conjure, and, on the other side, the increasingly urbanized culture of the turn-of-the-century buyer of books. By contrast, Anderson and Hemingway, like Thoreau, can assume a certain identity among themselves, their white, male heroes, and a substantial segment of their readership. Further, the central theme of Jewett and Chesnutt concerns success and failure in establishing a community of feeling among people in their tales, in their frame plots, and between authors and readers as well. This process depends upon the narrative structure; indeed that structure of incorporation provides a paradigm for the process of establishing community. Anderson and Hemingway, on the other hand, write versions of male *bildungsroman*, largely defined in American bourgeois culture as *isolated* experiences within society or nature. Narrative form thus embodies and tries to implement social and compositional objectives.

This discussion seems to me to suggest how far afield is the common wisdom about Jewett, to the effect "that her principal artistic skills are in style and characterization rather than in plot...."[19] Elizabeth Ammons has suggested that in a book like *The Country of the Pointed Firs* her organizing principles are simply different from the "hierarchical mode" of conventional narrative, and are designed rather in a "webbed, net-worked" design which may be identified with female patterns of development and socialization.[20] Ammons' suggestive argument about the form of Jewett's narrative can be extended into other of her works, like "The Foreigner." What these observations about Jewett suggest is that in examining the formal qualities of nineteenth-century white women and black writers we will often have to set aside assumptions about structural norms and ask, rather, why a story or a volume assumes its particular design. That question may lead us to reconstruct

The Country of the Pointed Firs and *The Conjure Woman* not as defective precursors of the modernist classics of Anderson and Hemingway, but as distinctive classics in their own modes.

These comments about *difference* lead directly to my sixth problem. A pedagogical strategy of pairing works seems to me the most useful way of getting at difference. For example, in courses at San Jose State University and at Trinity I have linked Hawthorne's *House of the Seven Gables* and Stowe's *The Minister's Wooing;* Twain's *Pudd'nhead Wilson* and Chesnutt's *The Marrow of Tradition;* Jewett's *Country of the Pointed Firs* and Anderson's *Winesburg, Ohio;* and Hemingway's *A Farewell to Arms* and Hurston's *Their Eyes Were Watching God.* I have taken up together Emerson and Fuller, Child or Jacobs and Thoreau, Poe and Alice Cary, F. Scott Fitzgerald's *The Great Gatsby* and Meridel LeSueur's *The Girl,* and considered pairing Dreiser's *Sister Carrie* and Mary Austin's *A Woman of Genius,* Henry Adams and W.E.B. DuBois, Jean Toomer's *Cane* and Stein's *Three Lives,* Eliot's *The Wasteland* and H.D.'s *Trilogy* or Langston Hughes' "Montage of a Dream Deferred," just to mention what might be a few suggestive examples. Many of us know how effective such pairings can be, simply at the level of generating classroom response.

But something more fundamental is at stake. Placing the Hawthorne and Stowe works side by side allows us to see how radically similar their literary origins were, how they work with closely related assumptions, materials, and sentiments. Both frame examinations of the significance of America's Puritan heritage within conventional romance plots. In these, the wise purity of an American princess redeems the straying, never evil, though unconventional boy. Neither Phoebe nor Mary possess sufficient power to win over the evil geniuses—Judge Pyncheon and Burr—who cross their paths. But each combines the intense practicality and naturally inspired values necessary to establishing domestic tranquility, marriage, and home, for themselves and those around them. In this respect they are much like the heroines of many other women's novels of the 1850's.

The very "relatedness" of these books in these and many other ways forces our students to reexamine what it was, and is, that has defined Hawthorne as a "classic" and Stowe as, at best, an imposing figure in the *popular* tradition. In fact, their differences as well as their similarities raise this issue, for they offer very distinct centers of value, narrative strategies, and understandings about the force of history. In a certain sense, history does not exist for Hawthorne, as for many of his Romantic contemporaries; it simply reflects, generation by generation, the repeated operation of Pyncheon greed and Maule's curse, inheritances of domination and blood. His interest lies in the impact of such persisting forces on the aesthetic temperament, embodied in Clifford. Thus Hawthorne's characters can emerge from the closed circle of essentially repeated events only by the unconvincing *dei ex machina* that kill off Judge Pyncheon and his son, hitch Phoebe and Holgrave, and thus permit the happy ending commanded by sentimental tradition. The often-noted awkwardness of Hawthorne's plot derives from his failure to find credible measures within its domestic conventions to overcome Maule's curse.

For Stowe, the legacy of Puritanism is more complex than repeated instances of "sin and sorrow": rather, it invested everyday life with millenial significance, and therefore the diurnal activities of her people with ultimate power. Thus, the "faculty" Mary derives from her mother's upbringing and the moral urgencies she inherits from her abolitionist father provide a basis for order beyond the creation even of the best of Puritan divines, like the Rev. Mr. Hopkins. Hopkins sustains the moral intensity of Puritan forbearers like Jonathan Edwards, especially in his condemnation of the sin of slaveholding, but he is also blinkered by his devotion to a heartless metaphysical system. That system fails to embrace the real-life needs for love and comfort of ordinary people facing the contingencies not of a mysterious curse, but of the common lot of separation, loss, and failure. The historical issue for Stowe, which bears directly upon the conduct of life in mid-nineteenth-century America, is how to sustain the moral seriousness and fervor of Puritanism without its terrorizing theology. The marriage which celebrates the ending of her book presents her symbolic solution to this problem as well as satisfying the period's conventions.

Hawthorne's work is a sustained, I would suggest an enclosed, meditation upon aestheticism outside history (which may be part of its attraction to aesthetically-minded literary critics). Stowe's is, I think, an effort to translate the values of a previous era into actions comprehensible to a contemporary audience. One might say that Hawthorne's aim is to create a "timeless" fable, a transcendent allegory whose particular details are illustrative rather than defining. Stowe's book lives and breathes much more particularly in mid-nineteenth-century America—a fact which recollects the problem of context I examined above.

But these differences also raise the question of value: is Hawthorne's a "better" book for evading (transcending) the particular moment of its birth? Obviously, the answer to that question depends on what we mean by "better." If we accept the definitions of literary excellence constructed in significant measure from the canonical works and used to perpetuate their status, we will inevitably place most of the fiction by nineteenth-century white women and black writers at a discount, and view them as at best elegiac local colorists, at worst, domestic sentimentalists. Indeed, we will not see what these writers are attempting to accomplish, much less how well or poorly they do what Jane Tompkins calls their "cultural work."

Alfred Habegger illustrates this problem in his otherwise excellent book, *Gender, Fantasy and Realism in American Literature.* Habegger contends that Elizabeth Stuart Phelps' *The Story of Avis* is not a "classic," but "an important document for nineteenth-century literary and social history." *Avis,* he says, was too feminine. That is to say, it was written for women, in defense of women's interests and in support of women's myths and values, and was therefore a highly partisan book. . . . It was not an exploration of the bitter antagonism between men and women [as, Habegger suggests, we find in Howells and James]; it was itself bitterly antagonistic.[21]

I think it is true that *Avis* is partisan; the issue is whether the nonpartisan appearance of canonical writers is an "objective" fact or an artifact of the status critics attribute to them. The obvious case is, of course, Henry James's *The Bostonians.* As Habegger points out, those who attempted to canonize *The Bostonians* as one of James' supreme achievements, notably Philip Rahv and Lionel Trilling, really recreated it as an argument for their own politics, which had begun to feature a retreat from social activism. Pairing *The Bostonians* and *Avis,* or perhaps Twain's *Pudd'nhead Wilson* and Chesnutt's *The Marrow of Tradition,* suggests that in dealing with highly charged social issues writers from marginalized groups may *appear* partisan whereas those from the dominant culture can take on the coloration (white?) of "objectivity" or "universality."

But a more interesting case emerges by contrasting *The Portait of a Lady,* generally accepted as one of James's best, with *Avis.* For here one encounters not the issue of attributed status and politics (as with *The Bostonians*), but the problem of a novel's *function* in the cultures in which it is read. One might well accept Habegger's account of *Portrait* as an enormously rich literary exploration of American masculinity and still dispute the value—to whom? for what?—of *Avis.* The question here is why people read novels, today or an hundred years ago. The extension of a work into the world indeed compromises its objectivity, makes it party to a cause, an incitement, a weapon, or proof. We are accustomed to view such partiality as necessarily a defect, but that judgment depends upon how we define the "cultural work" fiction is designed to perform. After all, "objectivity" and detachment are hardly independent standards; on the contrary, they are generally banners in the human parade carried by those wishing to translate worldly power into cultural terms. The self-containment of a literary work generally extolled by critics in our culture then appears as no unassailable virtue, but as one problematic for classroom analysis.

Pairing works like those of Stowe and Hawthorne, James and Phelps, and Chesnutt and Twain allows us and our students to clarify alternative assumptions about literary value rather than to assume the absolute validity of canonical literary standards. This is perhaps the most central problem of all. For so much of nineteenth-century women's writing has long been set at a discount, indeed the whole corpus has been construed in such trivializing ways—even in pointing to Dickinson as the notable exception—that no course of serious study can avoid the most thoroughgoing reexamination of settled standards. That is at once, I think, a directive for and an argument in favor of teaching nineteenth-century American women writers. The debate over "cultural literacy" and the foreclosing of American intellect is at heart a debate over standards of value. My own experience suggests that few enterprises bring these issues more sharply into focus than turning our attention, and that of our students, to writers like Child, Harper, Jacobs, Kirkland, Fern and Phelps—as well as to Fuller, Stowe, Dickinson, Davis, Jewett, and Freeman. Their concerns, their ideas, their styles, and the lives and cultures their work encodes place today's debates into the American history of which they form only the latest paragraphs.

Notes

1. Sandra M. Gilbert and Susan Gubar, *The Norton Anthology of Literature by Women* (New York: W.W. Norton, 1985).

2. Nina Baym, et al., *The Norton Anthology of American Literature,* 2 vols. Second Edition, (New York: W.W. Norton, 1985).

3. Donald McQuade, et al., *The Harper American Literature,* 2 vols. (New York: Harper, 1987).

4. Lucy Freibert, and Barbara White, eds., *Hidden Hands: An Anthology of American Women Writers, 1790–1870* (New Brunswick, N.J.: Rutgers University Press, 1985), pp. 68–83.

5. Judith Fetterley, *Provisions: A Reader From 19th-Century American Women* (Bloomington: Indiana University Press, 1985).

6. Lydia Maria Child, *Hobomok and Other Writings on Indians,* Carolyn L. Karcher, ed. (1986); Rose Terry Cooke, *"How Celia Changed Her Mind" and Other Stories,* Elizabeth Ammons, ed. (1986); Fanny Fern, *Ruth Hall and Other Writings,* Joyce W. Warren, ed. (1986); Louisa May Alcott, *Alternative Alcott,* Elaine Showalter, ed. (1987); Alice Cary, *Clovernook Sketches and Other Stories,* Judith Fetterley, ed. (1987); Harriet Beecher Stowe, *Oldtown Folks,* Dorothy Berkson, ed. (1987); Catharine Maria Sedgwick, *Hope Leslie,* Mary Kelley, ed. (1987); Caroline Kirkland, *A New Home—Who'll Follow?* (1988); E.D.E.N. Southworth, *The Hidden Hand,* Joanne Dobson, ed. (1988); Harriet Prescott Spofford, *Selected Stories,* Alfred Bendixen, ed. (1988); Constance Fenimore Woolson, *Women Artists and Exiles: Stories,* Joan Weimer, ed. (1988). The series also includes Mary Austin, *Stories from the Country of Lost Borders,* Marjorie Pryse, ed. (1987); and Nella Larsen, *Quicksand and Passing,* Deborah E. McDowell, ed. (1986). Rutgers University Press also published Elizabeth Stuart Phelps' *The Story of Avis,* Carol Kessler, ed. (1985).

7. Susan Warner, *The Wide, Wide World,* Jane Tompkins, ed. (New York: Feminist Press, 1987).

8. Mary Helen Washington, ed., *Invented Lives: Narratives of Black Women 1860–1960.* Garden City, N.Y.: Doubleday Anchor Books, 1987. Earlier articles about Harper are listed in Ann Allen Shockley, *Afro-American Women Writers 1746–1933: An Anthology and Critical Guide* (Boston: G. K. Hall, 1988). In addition, her story, "The Two Offers," was earlier reprinted with critical comment in *Old Maids,* Susan Koppelman, ed. (Boston: Pandora Press, 1984).

9. Other twentieth-century authors included in this series are Gayle Jones, Ann Petry, Coleen Polite, Octavia Butler, Alice Childress, and Marita Bonner.

10. Hazel V. Carby, *Reconstructing Womanhood,* (New York: Oxford University Press, 1987).

11. I am thinking, for example, of Elizabeth Ammons, "Stowe's Dream of the Mother-Savior: *Uncle Tom's Cabin* and American Women Writers Before the 1920s," *New Essays on Uncle Tom's Cabin,* Eric J. Sundquist, ed. (Cambridge: Cambridge

University Press, 1986) and "Crossing the Color Line: White Feminist Criticism and Black Women Writers," in *Reading Black, Reading Feminist,* Henry Louis Gates, Jr., ed. (London: Methuen, 1988); Nina Baym, *Woman's Fiction: A Guide to Novels by and about Women in America, 1820–1870* (Ithaca, N.Y.: Cornell University Press, 1978); Hazel Carby, *op. cit.;* Barbara Christian, *Black Women Novelists: The Development of a Tradition, 1892–1986* (Westport, Conn.: Greenwood, 1980), and *Black Feminist Criticism* (New York: Pergamon Press, 1985); Josephine Donovan, *New England Local Color Literature: A Woman's Tradition* (New York: Frederick Ungar, 1983); Annette Kolodny, *The Land Before Her: Fantasy and Experience of the American Frontiers, 1630–1860* (Chapel Hill: University of North Carolina Press, 1984); Jane Tompkins, *Sensational Designs: The Cultural Work of American Fiction, 1790–1860* (New York: Oxford University Press, 1985); Mary Helen Washington, *Invented Lives, op. cit.*

12.

> The reading of these documents enabled me to utter my thoughts, and to meet the arguments brought forward to sustain slavery. . . . As I read and contemplated the subject, behold! that very discontentment which Master Hugh had predicted would follow my learning to read had already come, to torment and sting my soul to unutterable anguish. As I writhed under it, I would at times feel that learning to read had been a curse rather than a blessing. It had given me a view of my wretched condition, without the remedy. It opened my eyes to the horrible pit, but to no ladder upon which to get out.

Frederick Douglass, *Narrative of the Life of Frederick Douglass, An American Slave, Written by Himself* (New York: New American Library, 1968), p. 55. Douglass' is also a particularly striking account of the limits of consciousness, absent the possibility of action.

13. Sculley Bradley, et. al., *The American Tradition in Literature,* Volume I (New York: Random House, 1981), p. 1444.

14. Angelina Grimké, "Appeal to the Christian Women of the South," *The Anti-Slavery Examiner* I, 2 (September 1836): 25.

In 1893, writing about his twenty-fifth birthday, W.E.B. DuBois considers the relationship of his self-development to the needs of his people:

> The general proposition of working for the world's good becomes too soon sickly and sentimentality. I therefore take the world that the Unknown lay in my hands & work for the rise of the Negro people, taking for granted that their best development means the best development of the world. . . .
>
> These are my plans: to make a name in science, to make a name in literature and thus to raise my race. . . .
>
> I wonder what will be the outcome? Who knows?
>
> I will go unto the King—which is not according to the law & if I perish—*I perish.*
>
> (Ms. in DuBois papers)

15. See Grimké, "Appeal," pp. 23–24.

16. As in Emerson, a house becomes a metaphor for the self. Emerson wrote to Margaret Fuller that he would "open all my doors to your sunshine and morning air." But, Fuller later responded, her friend "keeps his study windows shut." Quoted by Joyce Warren, "The Gender of American Individualism," *The American Narcissus,* from *Letters of Ralph Waldo Emerson,* Volume II, 337.

17. One might pursue an analogous set of contrasts between Thoreau and Lydia Maria Child's lament for the lost garden of Jane Plato in her account of a city fire (*Letters from New York* XVI, August 7, 1842).

18. A number of these details were pointed out to me by Ellen Louise Hart of the University of California, Santa Cruz, and Katie King of the University of Maryland; this passage owes a great deal to conversations with them.

19. Gwen L. Nagel and James Nagel, "Introduction," *Sarah Orne Jewett: A Reference Guide* (Boston: G. K. Hall, 1978), p. ix.

20. Elizabeth Ammons, "Going in Circles: The Female Geography of Jewett's *Country of the Pointed Firs,*" *Studies in the Literary Imagination* 16 (Fall 1983), esp. 85, 89.

21. Alfred Habegger, *Gender, Fantasy and Realism in American Literature* (New York: Columbia University Press, 1982), p. 46.

The Two Criticisms—or, Structure, Lingo, and Power in the Discourse of Academic Humanists

In October of 1966 the Johns Hopkins Humanities Center was the site of an international symposium on "The Languages of Criticism and the Sciences of Man." The name of the symposium expresses part of its ambition: to model literary criticism on certain "scientific" paradigms. In particular, the meeting was designed to explore the implications of structuralist thinking—and especially that of continental scholars—on "critical methods in humanistic and social sciences." Whatever the organizers may have meant by "humanistic . . . sciences," and whatever the value of the conference in examining structuralist thought, as it turned out the symposium will be remembered historically, if at all, as a beginning of *post*structuralist analysis in the United States. For at the conference Jacques Derrida made his American debut, delivering a critique of structuralism whose title, "Structure, Sign, and Play in the Discourse of the Human Sciences," embodied many of the terms and concepts that have since characterized academic criticism in this country.[1] In the two decades after that Baltimore conference, some version of Derridean analysis—call it deconstructionist, speculative, formalist, or, my preference, "ludic"—has come to be increasingly central to the practice of literary study . . . at least as it is carried out in the influential academic towers of New Haven and its suburbs across the land.

A few months before this event in 1966, and I dare say unnoted at that conference, Stokely Carmichael had posed a new slogan for what had been thought about up to that time as the "civil rights movement." Carmichael had been arrested by Greenwood, Mississippi police when, on June 16, participants in the march named after James Meredith had attempted to erect their tents at a local black school. During that evening's rally, Carmichael

This article was, in rather different form, first presented as the keynote address to the College English Association, Philadelphia, 1985. Somewhat revised, it was published in Betty Jean Craige, ed., *Literature, Language and Politics* (Athens, Ga.: University of Georgia Press, 1988), pp. 1–19.

angrily asserted that blacks had obtained nothing in years of asking for freedom; "what we gonna start saying now," he insisted, is " 'black power.' "
The crowd responded immediately to those words, chanting its "black power"
response to Carmichael's call. In the months that followed, Carmichael and
other leaders of the movement enunciated their conception of black power:
In one moment of rhetorical fervor Carmichael asserted "when you talk of
black power, you talk of building a movement that will smash everything
Western civilization has created."[2]

One other 1966 event brought questions of power and politics directly into
sanctified academic halls: At the University of Chicago Naomi Weisstein, a
psychologist, taught an undergraduate course on women.[3] It was probably
not the first, for others had been developed at free universities and similar
"movement" institutions. But Weisstein's course may have represented the
initial effort at converting the as-yet unformed ideas of the women's liberation
movement into curricular terms.

Now it may seem "ludic" indeed to speak within two pages of structuralism
and Black Power, of a Johns Hopkins symposium and an undergraduate
course on women, of Jacques Derrida, Stokely Carmichael, and Naomi Weisstein. But I want to suggest that the Johns Hopkins symposium on the one
hand, and, the Black Power march and the course on women on the other,
may serve well as symbols of two alternative movements in contemporary
literary study. I want to sketch out these significantly distinct forms of critical
and teaching activity. And because I speak as a partisan, from within one, I
want to say candidly from the start that my intention is to promote a particular
outlook on the work English teachers and scholars do. It is my view that,
especially at this historic moment of reform in American higher education,
the power exercised by formalist, ludic modes of criticism in American academic circles is peculiarly pernicious and needs consciously to be contested.
I will ask that readers join in the contest, but in citing the Meredith march,
Carmichael, and Black Power at the outset, I wish to suggest that the contest
is at its heart political as well as cultural, social as well as literary, and that
the choices involved are as conflicted today—if not as brutally explicit—as
they were on that steaming Greenwood night twenty-five years ago.

The two forms of literary study I wish to distinguish here are, first, the
various formalist or speculative criticisms, heavily indebted to Continental
philosophy, deeply concerned with questions of epistemology, and practiced
primarily at a set of graduate institutions in the United States, France, and
elsewhere on the European continent; and, second, what I shall term "canonical" criticism, focused on how we construct our syllabi and anthologies, on
the roots of our systems of valuation, and on how we decide what is important
for us to teach and for our students to learn, or at least to read.

I am not proposing that the existence of two such alternative forms of
criticism distinguishes our time, or that this distinction is especially original.
Barbara Herrnstein Smith, for example, draws an analogous distinction between the primarily interpretive criticism of the past half century and the
evaluative modes of writing it has largely displaced—especially in the Amer-

ican academy.[4] Or, somewhat differently, Laurence Lerner argues that "the division between those who see literature as a more or less self-contained system, and those who see it as interacting with real, extra-literary experience ... is a profoundly important one—perhaps as important as any other. . . . "[5] But he goes on to dismiss the difference as not useful to critical practice. I think that this distinction—however philosophically naive Lerner's statement of it may be—is the most recent version of an old contention between what might be called aesthetic (formalist, interpretive) and moral and thus evaluative or what I will call "canonical" approaches to texts. Unlike Lerner, I believe that understanding the history of these differing forms of literary study in the past three decades is crucial to perceiving where literary study is now and where one might want it to go. Consequently, I want to begin with some admittedly crude distinctions and then refine them by placing my two critical paradigms in the specific historical contexts represented by the Johns Hopkins symposium, on the one hand, and the Black Power march and women's studies course, on the other.

I

What I am calling aesthetic or formalist criticism began in our time by viewing literature as in some sense a special kind of discourse,[6] composed by specially talented individuals called poets (and, more recently, theorists), and offering unique forms of knowledge or experience, interpreted by specially-sensitized individuals called critics, whose job it was, among other things, to distinguish poetic discourse from that of science or journalism or rhetoric (propaganda). It has ended by absorbing into this segregated aesthetic domain every kind of text.[7] The other, moral or canonical criticism, has seen literature as one among many forms of discourse whose objective is to move, enlighten or, perhaps, to mystify human beings. The first maintains that while we might, in Emerson's language, be "the richer" for the poet's knowledge, poetic expression involves no necessary extension into the world, that indeed, literature has no designs on our conduct, that a poem, to take this position to its familiar New Critical extreme, "should not mean but be." The other, the moral view, emphasizes the impact of literary works on how we conduct our lives, how we live within, extend or restrict, and develop the communities that give our lives meaning. Literary commentators, in the aesthetic vision, have constituted a kind of priesthood of the craft, performing a task of formal analysis given sanction by the special importance of poetry itself or by the notion that texts alone are in some sense "real." The moral practitioner emerges rather more as a teacher, the value of her or his pedagogy affirmed, if at all, by its social consequences. The universe of aesthetic discourse, at least as it largely has come to be defined by academic critics and by poets like Wallace Stevens as well, is thus distinct, removed, even self-enclosed— a singular place where initiates speak mainly to one another in special languages and discuss texts in hermeneutical modes whose authenticity seems measured by their density. In the universe of moralist discourse persons as diverse as Stokely Carmichael, Naomi Weisstein, and Michel Foucault speak—indeed, often shout—in what appears at first as a babel of expedient tongues joined in a contest for priority.

The division I am charting may be illustrated by an anecdote—one which, incidentally, suggests that the sides cannot easily be ranged along the usual Left/Right political spectrum. In about 1970, a group of scholars approached the Modern Language Association with the proposal to hold a "Marxist Forum" at the annual convention in New York. Having been refused, they turned to the Radical Caucus of the MLA, an officially recognized "allied organization," which agreed to sponsor the event. Plans for the forum eventually generated considerable conflict between Radical Caucus members and Marxist scholars, largely because the latter's plans called for all the presenters to be white and male. Still, when the event began, the crowd was so large that the walls of the ballroom in which it took place had to be opened to accommodate the press of people. By the second highly theoretical paper, however, fully half those who had come were out in the hall, noisily renewing old acquaintances, discovering what others were doing, hatching plans for political actions during the convention—to the intense disgust of those within the hall. And while the Radical Caucus continued to sponsor the forum for a year or two more—until a separate Marxist Literary Group was established—conflict between the groups became, if anything, even more intense than their quarrels with the MLA. "Academic Marxologists," one side sneered; "mindless activists," the other retorted. To be sure, it was a contentious, sectarian time on the Left, and personalities as always played a role in exaggerating this division, but at heart, I think, the groups had significantly differing agendas. One sought primarily to legitimate Marxist theory as a framework for interpreting texts; the other, to open the profession and thus the culture to what it saw as fundamental change. One wished to expand the kinds of critical production which would be seen as professionally valid; the other to mobilize the people within a professional organization (or a collegiate institution) to act as concerned citizens—or even as revolutionaries!

Of course, there is no necessary connection between what I have here termed aestheticism as an approach to literature and the institutionalization of this form of criticism in the academy. Nor has aestheticism always faced inward. Indeed, more than once historically—in Shelley, for example, or in Wilde—aestheticism emerged as a revolutionary thrust against prior moralizing styles. But in *our* time aesthetic or formalist criticism seems to me to have embodied not only many of the virtues of speculative thought first demonstrated by Plato but all the limiting features of Plato's Academy as well: its symbolic location in an Athenian suburb; its emphasis upon abstraction and its contempt for the rhetoricians of Isocrates' school for politics; and, of course, its master's devotion to publishing.

His master, as we know, perished. Plato was out of town at the time. No surprise, as one of my colleagues at San Jose State commented, since Western civilization has been notoriously hard on its teachers. I will return to that observation shortly, but first I want to follow rather more carefully the emergence of formalism as the most privileged form of literary discourse in the American academy.

Book titles provide us with something of a superficial but still useful set of guideposts to the history of American literary criticism over the past half century. Cleanth Brooks's *The Well-Wrought Urn*[8] may be taken to represent New Critical practice at its best. Brooks focuses, as the title suggests, on the work itself: its character ("urn" rather than beaker or crock), its quality ("well-wrought"), and on his metaphysical sources of poetic value (Donne's "The Canonization"). He makes little reference to the social or cultural circumstances that determined the potter's clay, available glazes, and decorative modes. Or, indeed, who might a potter be. While we are all indebted to, or at least influenced by, the habits of mind established by Brooks and his colleagues—close reading of texts, sensitivity to qualities like ambiguity, irony, paradox—New Criticism represented an elitist, if unsystematic, mode of critical dissection and worked with a narrow set of texts amenable to its analytic methods. Indeed, to the extent that such critics addressed the question of which texts were worthy of study, they did so—at least explicitly—in formalist terms. "Good poetry," Allen Tate wrote, "is a unity of all the meanings from the furthest extremes of intension and extension. . . . the meaning of poetry is its 'tension,' the full organized body of all the extension and intension that we can find in it." Tate uses this standard of linguistic tension to attack Edna St. Vincent Millay's poem about the execution of Sacco and Vanzetti, "Justice Denied in Massachusetts," as "mass language."[9] Some years later, John Crowe Ransom characterized Millay's as a lesser "vein of poetry," "spontaneous, straightforward in diction," with "transparently simple" structures and "immediate" effects.[10] As New Critical methodology became academic orthodoxy, the question of which texts were worthy of interpretation—that is, the question of the canon—receded ever further toward the margins of legitimacy and the virtues of irony, complexity and tension emerged as gospel.

Northrop Frye, whose work at once looks back to the practical criticism of Brooks and Ransom and forward to the more systematic efforts of structuralism, borrows his central, taxonomic metaphor from biology: *Anatomy of Criticism.*[11] The metaphor proposes a closed, if organic and growing, domain for criticism, in which the critic's role is to identify the distinctive features and underlying functions of each part of the literary body and to discern how they may be related both to one another and to the underlying mythoi that Frye sees, like genetic determinants, at the center of all literary texts. But Frye, even more than the New Critics, lays aside canonical questions as matters merely of speculation.

Beginning in the late 1960s, and with increasing rapidity, various forms of structuralism—those, for example, associated with Roland Barthes[12] and with Marxists like Fredric Jameson[13]—emerged as the dominant critical paradigms, only to be contested in short order by bewildering varieties of poststructuralist theorizing. The title of Harold Bloom's early work, for example,

The Anxiety of Influence,[14] emphasizes a psychological category as key to a viable theory of poetry and collapses history into the set of pressures imposed by strong poetic predecessors upon every individual practitioner. One can go on in this mode: Paul de Man's *Blindness and Insight* suggests something of the ludic, paradoxical quality of much recent theoretical writing, whereas Geoffrey Hartman's *Criticism in the Wilderness*[15] mirrors its somewhat pessimistic tone and its claims to social marginality. But my intention is not to impose such reductive characterizations on these works; rather, I want to suggest something of their variety in order to ask whether such disparate projects have anything in common, apart, that is, from the quite narrow set of texts that provide the basis for their analyses.

There seem to be two ways of answering that question. One, via philosophy, is to ask whether these modes of critical writing share certain characteristics or concerns or assumptions, whether they have any common essence, to use an altogether slippery word. I will speak briefly to that in a moment. But my major interest is to see whether these varied critical styles are radically alike in terms of the roles they have played, and the practical effects they have had, on the literary profession and on the institutions, English departments, colleges and universities, in which English teachers and critics work. As for the first, Frank Lentricchia has tracked the "repeated and often extremely subtle denial of history" in the work especially of American theorists who came, to use the title of his book, *After the New Criticism.*[16] In using the words "formalist" and "aesthetic" to name these varied styles of criticism, I wish to point to their pervasive effort to separate literary texts (whatever might be meant by "literary") as well as critical acts from history, to their tendency to ignore the particular roles their work is playing in educational institutions and in society, and to their consequent tendency to turn the domain of literature, again in Lentricchia's words, into a "vast, enclosed textual and semantic preserve." "Formalist" suggests that the whole enterprise of literary theorizing subsists behind dense academic walls, where de Man speaks only to Heidegger, and Heidegger speaks only to God. While theoretical criticism can be challenged on its own philosophical grounds, as indeed Lentricchia partly does,[17] that seems to offer no exit from the "Wilderness" where Geoffrey Hartman has most recently located criticism. And worse, it seems to me to accelerate the centrifugal force that moved literary study to the very fringe of college education. We need, rather, to understand why speculative criticism developed such an enormous vogue in the late 1960s and 1970s, why its practitioners have come to be dominant figures in the American literary establishment, why its terminology slips so trippingly from the tongues of serious graduate students, why job lists multiply calls for practitioners of "theory," and, finally, why so much of it has spun increasingly into irrelevance to the concerns we face every day as teachers and as intellectuals.

I want then to ask whether the rise of formalist theory—whatever precisely one means by that term[18]—as the dominant mode of literary discourse in American academic circles can be understood in the specific historical context of the last twenty-five years, and whether formalist criticism taken as a whole has played an identifiable institutional role and had specific impact upon university education. Here my initial symbols—the Johns Hopkins symposium, the Black Power march, and the women's studies course—again become helpful. The New Criticism emerged in the 1920s and 1930s precisely as the social authority of those who came to practice it was being undermined. Similarly, the cultural and social authority of those of us whose job it presumably was to sustain and transmit the heritage of Western civilization was sharply being challenged at the end of the 1960s, as Stokely Carmichael's comments about Black Power illustrate, and as the subsequent disruptions of normal academic life on most campuses were shortly to dramatize. Not only were we accused of irrelevance in our provincial pursuit of ironies, myths, and publication, but we were charged with leading humane study up academic labyrinths at the very moment its insights were needed to negotiate the multiplying crises of civil rights, the Vietnam War, continued domestic and colonial poverty, not to mention "the Bomb." In the 1968 charge on the Modern Language Association convention,[19] one could all but hear echoing from the marbled halls of the old Hotel Americana a version of Wordsworth's cry to Milton: "England has need of thee,/ She is a fen of stagnant waters" ("London").

The responses to the charges of irrelevance or of complicity in racism and the war machine varied across the political spectrum. Within the academy, self-defined conservatives were—and remain—largely unheard. Most of our colleagues, identifying themselves less by ideology than by professional field, tried to sustain academic business as usual. Frye's work, like that of many writers after him, had represented a seemingly reasonable effort to impose theoretical coherence on the exceedingly miscellaneous practices displayed by literary criticism as it, like academic America generally, dilated wildly through the 1960s. Furthermore, new models being created in other disciplines (for example, the structuralism of Levi-Strauss) proved readily adaptable to literary analysis. As the centrality of humane, and especially of literary, study eroded through the 1960s and into a decade focused on "career" preparation, some theorists attempted at first to reprivilege cultural work by attaching it to these supposedly more scientific paradigms. Thus literary structuralists adapted to their criticism anthropological accounts of social organization and of underlying historical and linguistic patterns. Later, deconstructionist critics attempted to link—or perhaps it might be more accurate to say "transform"—literary study to the presumably more rigorous philosophical styles represented by Derrida and Foucault.

In every discipline, academic activists tried to respond to the charges of the 1960s by seeking out ways to unify our intellectual and pedagogical practice with our social and political values. That proved more difficult than it first seemed. Not only did academic training seem to drive a wedge between inquiry and political action, but American politics, left-wing or otherwise, produced no consistently sustained relationship between theory and practice. Indeed, the division between advocates of "theory" and of "action" played

a central role in the demise of political organizations such as SDS (Students
for a Democratic Society) and its more academic counterpart NUC (New
University Conference). Many of the sects which lived within these organizations insisted upon trying to apply European intellectual models to intran-
sigent American social issues. "Study theory," they commanded. "Less talk,
more action," was the responding shout from the "action faction." Those
shouts came to sound ever shriller and more empty, particularly after the real
defeats suffered by the Left, and by liberalism generally, in 1968 and 1969.
It perhaps aggrandizes the events of the late 1960s to compare them with
1848, but the subsequent triumph of reaction cannot be ignored. Historically,
it has not been unusual for intellectuals, retreating from a lost social battlefield, to attempt to sustain a movement for change in their writing and teaching. Better, at least, to challenge traditional cultural norms than to acquiesce
altogether in the old order. To view it positively, *some* of the theoretical
moves that with the decline of the social movements came into vogue in the
early 1970s offered at least the sense of joining an effort to carry out political
dissent on an academic battlefield.[20]

Described differently, however, the practice of theory—as its connections
to a social movement withered and dropped off—offered, in the face of
political defeat and the disintegration or cooptation of many movement initiatives, the consoling *appearance* that "la lucha continua."

For some younger members of the profession in the early 1970s, familiarity
with Maitre Jacques, *S/Z*, or the Frankfurt school provided a powerful tool.
At worst, one could deploy modes of analysis, a "text milieu," and a discourse
altogether unfamiliar to an older generation of empirical critics; in that approach was power. At best, certain theoretical moves seem to have been as
intellectually freeing for some entering graduate work during the Nixon years
as participation in the movements for social change of the prior decade was
for me and my activist comrades. They undercut the claims to objectivity and
disinterested interpretation of texts—or of events—made by those in power.
Certain forms of theory demanded the rehistoricizing not only of literary
works but of the work of literary people—even as they called into question
the relationship between textual depictions and the "realities" of which they
were presumed to be accounts. What Lyndon Johnson's "construction" of
Vietnam forced some of us to understand, Derrida's historical construction
of *différance* appears to have opened to others. Further, certain theorists
began to break down idealist distinctions between "literary" and assertedly
"nonliterary" texts, thus opening to study an ever-broadening range of noncanonical works. Indeed, the tactics of deconstructive analysis could well serve
to analyze presidential addresses or medical textbooks; thus its practitioners
could experience their trade as contributing meaningfully to political debate
rather than merely elucidating putatively literary works.

What theoretical study at its best provided, or at least claimed the ability
to provide, was a more self-conscious account of the underlying assumptions
used in situating works critics read and commented upon; the theorists, and
especially the poststructuralists, said "before we look at the pattern we see

on the page, let us examine the glasses through which we necessarily perceive it, and which may, in fact, have given a coherent shape to an otherwise undifferentiated blob of ink." And thus a new generation of critics has come to study the lenses of perception, the contingencies of textual production, together with (often in place of) the texts perceived.

For all that, theory as a mode of literary discourse (or, as I would describe it, largely a maneuver in academic political rhetoric) has primarily succeeded in reestablishing academic privilege—ironically, not for the study of literature in the academy, but for those who practice theory within the literary profession. In fact, as English departments lost ground through the 1970s and early 1980s, the practical effect of the privileging of theorists has been to deepen the abyss—and also to widen the pay differential—between those who dwell in the towers of academe and those who inhabit its trenches. All one needs to see are the salaries paid the new specialist in theory at Texas and the often older (and very likely female) teacher of freshman English at San Jose State. *Différance* indeed! In retrospect it should not be surprising that yesterday's theoretical *enfant terrible* so rapidly becomes today's MLA president, or that yesterday's gauntlet becomes today's protector of the most traditional anthologies and curricula. American literary theory has proven remarkably easy to assimilate to the structure of American university life; indeed, it has become a strong reenforcement of existing academic norms. The practice of literary theory in no sense challenges the individualistic, production-oriented forms of the American academy, much less the marketplace ideology and the organizational structures into which the colleges largely guide their students.[21] Indeed, a certain marriage of convenience emerged in Western academies during the 1970s. A thrust by some academic leaders to incorporate Marxist and other intellectually radical ideologies within the domains of bourgeois culture was matched by the desire of academic Marxists and practitioners of Left discourses to legitimate their intellectual activity in the terms defined by the professional marketplace. Like any other form of critical production, the work of theorists can easily be measured (so many articles, books, or citations in other works), and displayed to appropriate authorities. Further, it offers the illusion—at least in rhetoric—of deeply contested debate within the "marketplace of ideas." And it helps maintain a hierarchical relationship between the privileged discourse of the academy and practical criticism, mainly carried out in the classroom.

In that regard, the obscurity of language that has come to characterize most theoretical writing is no unfortunate accident but rather an essential element. To be sure, as theory has developed over the last two decades, its practitioners have with increasing self-consciousness sought above all else originality, at least of expression if not always of idea. But the real function of linguistic opacity is little different from that of the Latin scrawls of physicians to pharmacists: Keep the unwashed out of the game. If you don't know the values of chips like "extradiscursive formations," "neo-Gramscian framework," "hegemonic discourses," "monologic ideologization," "representational algorithm," you're likely to lose your shirt in the play of discourse.

And if a critic wants to "call into question both the economy of identity and the axiology of binarity that underwrites the nomology of identity," who are most of us to ask "does it matter"? Discussion of complex ideas can, of course, be complicated, and the Derridean play of language and ideas can occasionally be as entertaining as a few moments in a Ping Chong performance. But finally we need to ask about the functions of particular language practices in the American academy. The ostensible political objectives of the essays from which the above examples are chosen are quite progressive, but the linguistic style is exclusionary, elitist, and what Raymond Williams has called "dominative"; that is its purpose.

Suiting practice to theory, moreover, formalism in any of its modes has sustained a fifty-year tradition of privileging in literary study "major" works by "major" authors. If you apply what I like to call the "index test" to the work of the leading theoretical critics, you obtain figures like the following: Paul de Man's *Blindness and Insight* refers to 139 men and, passingly, to two women. Hartman's relatively more popular essays in *The Fate of Reading*[22] mention 232 men (many frequently) and eleven women. The notion that the universe of academic discourse is a male (and not so incidentally white and European) world is thus strongly reenforced. One looks through such pages almost in vain for any account of W.E.B. DuBois, of Virginia Woolf, of C.L.R. James, much less of Lu Hsun. It is then no long step to the position taken up by Howard Felperin in his 1985 defense of theoretical criticism, disingenuously titled *Beyond Deconstruction*. Felperin acknowledges that "the question of the canon goes to the heart of the institution's peculiar existence." He continues,

> Just as a certain kind of writing, the kind that has come to be known as "literature," is inconceivable without authorship, so the institutional study of that writing is inconceivable without a canon. Without a canon, a corpus or cynosure of exemplary texts, there can be no interpretive community. . . . The argument for a canon derives, that is, not from the importance of our reading the *right* texts, whatever our criteria of rectitude (moral, political, historical, rhetorical), but from the necessity of our reading the *same* texts, or enough of the same texts, to enable the discourse of the interpretive community to go on.[23]

Thus Felperin, asserting the primacy of maintaining theoretical discourse, argues for a "conservative approach" to canon formation. "Let us," he quotes Keats, "have the old poets and Robin Hood," and he comments

> While "Robin Hood" may assume the guise of popular, women's, or ethnic literature in response to special historical interests, it seems unlikely that a fully institutional canon could ever be formed out of them, simply because the interests they represent are special or sectarian, and hence, exclusive.
>
> (p. 48)

It amazes me how a critic trained in the tactics of deconstructive textualism can so blithely imply the supposedly universal character of the rather special interests represented by the traditional canon, and embodied in the indices upon which I reported above.

These comments dramatize one of the reasons that theoretical criticism has often, in the American academy, given aid and comfort to defenders of the institutional status quo: Values are here subordinated to the need for sustaining "the interpretive community." That is, the priorities of professional life overwhelm all others. That should come as no surprise, for the glue binding literary practitioners is not ideology but their membership and participation in certain professional organizations like the Modern Language Association, or an English department. In 1968, the one vote lost at the MLA convention by the coalition of radicals, leftists, and liberals concerned the Association's continuing participation in the Center for Editions of American Authors (the CEAA). It was one thing to come out against the Vietnam War, racism or Mayor Daley, or even to elect a socialist as vice-president; it was quite something else to tamper with the professional interests that helped keep subsidies flowing and provided members with a sense of their social legitimacy. Felperin's remarks suggest one reason criticism and teaching that coheres around the issue of the canon leads in directions radically different from the cul-de-sac in which theory has left literary study.

But there seems to me to be a more fundamental reason much poststructuralist theorizing has often turned out to be politically paralyzing, and that is its tendency to promote a radical Pyrrhonism. Here I must trot out the single quotation from the work of Jacques Derrida that readers will find in this book. He is discussing a fragment from (perhaps) Nietzsche's unpublished manuscripts: " 'I have forgotten my umbrella' ".

> Nevertheless, by dint of diligence and good fortune, the internal and external context of the "I have forgotten my umbrella" could even one day be reconstructed. Such a factual possibility, however, does not alter the fact of that other possibility which is marked in the fragment's very structure. (The concept of fragment, however, since its fracturedness is itself an appeal to some totalizing complement, is no longer sufficient here.) For it is always possible that "I have forgotten my umbrella," detached as it is, not only from the milieu that produced it, but also from any intention or meaning on Nietzsche's part, should remain so, whole and intact, once and for all, without any other context. The meaning and the signature that appropriates it remain in principle inaccessible.
>
> That inaccessibility though is not necessarily one of some hidden secret. It might just as easily be an inconsistency, or of no significance at all. What if Nietzsche himself meant to say nothing, or a[t] least not much of anything, or anything whatever? Then again, what if Nietzsche was only pretending to say something? In fact, it is even possible that it is not Nietzsche's sentence, and this notwithstanding any confident certainty that it is indeed written in his hand. What, after all, is handwriting?[24]

Or a book, for that matter—*Mein Kampf*, say? Indeed, what is an umbrella? A truncheon? Or, perhaps, a spur (*éperon*) or prod? A cattle prod, say? Who do they prod? Whence? And who forgets them? In San Salvador, Gaza, or Soweto?

To be sure, analyses that depart from such passages may, apart from enchanting by their display, help fortify resistance to naive assertions, such as "workers of the world unite," or "we hold these truths to be self-evident," or "the history of mankind is a history of repeated injuries and usurpations on the part of man toward woman," or "the problem of the twentieth century is the problem of the color line." But do they arm—or disarm—intellectuals for combat in an increasingly dangerous world? It is not my observation that the spread of poststructuralist theory has spurred academics into progressive activity, on campus or off. On the contrary, it seems to have provided them with a textual umbrella to keep them wet in these dry times.[25] Skepticism about political claims is, of course, a reasonable response to the defeat of progressive social aspirations, like those of the 1960s, but at some point the schematizing of agnosticism comes to sound suspiciously like a rationalization of paralysis.

I do not wish to be misread here as supporting the uninformed and generally naive theory-bashing of those who claim simply to be pursuing empirical research. The issue to me is not theory versus nontheory, for every form of research utilizes, whether consciously or not, some kind of theoretical models on the basis of which scholars decide what they believe to be questions worth examining and the legitimacy of methods for answering them. Rather, I am concerned that the *institutional* roles played by American advocates of what has been called "theory" have been largely retrogressive and have helped deepen the crisis of the humanities to which the former Secretary of Education, William Bennett, and his successor at the National Endowment for the Humanities, Lynne Cheney, have, however wrongheadedly, given notoriety.[26] The pejorative use of "theory," and especially "deconstruction," by liberals as well as right-wing officials may primarily bespeak fear and misapprehension on the part of critics, a perceived threat to the stability of their academic identities. Yet, one cannot so easily dismiss these criticisms, or their ready reception both within and outside the academic world, as so much false consciousness. It may be, as I have tried to suggest, that contradictions between the project of theory and its institutional role make it peculiarly vulnerable to such attacks.

II

The distinctive qualities of canonical criticism may come sharply into relief if we contrast it with the kind of formalism I have been describing. I want to outline the project of canonical criticism and suggest three stages in its development. As my signposts—the Meredith march and the Weisstein course—suggest, the roots of this form of literary activity reach deeply into the movements for social change of the 1960s and 1970s. Indeed, it would not be too much to say that canonical criticism constitutes a part of a broader effort to reconstruct our society, and particularly our educational institutions, on a more democratic and equitable basis. It emerges from a fundamental perception: that curricula, reading lists, degree requirements, standardized tests, and anthologies institutionalize ideas about what is important, *whose* experiences and artistic expressions are to be valued. As affirmative action in personnel procedures reflected the efforts of minorities and white women to penetrate and reshape American institutional life, so canonical criticism as it emerged two decades ago was at heart an effort to open up literary study and to reconstruct it on new, more inclusive bases.

For example, if we strip away from Carmichael's exposition of "black power" some of its rhetorical vehemence, we will quickly see that the slogan significantly represented for him an effort "to reclaim our [black] history and our [black] identity . . . ," that it named a "struggle for the right to create our own terms to define ourselves and our relationship to society, and to have these terms recognized."[27] In such a struggle, education and culture necessarily played critical roles in overturning the old saying, embodied in most 1950s curricula, "out of sight, out of mind." To place the work and life of women and minority men into the curriculum *was* in important ways to make them a presence in educational institutions. To be sure, if curricula and other forms of institutional life were so conceived and so structured as to exclude the history, identity, and achievements—not to speak of the physical presence—of minorities or of white women, then indeed academic practice and organization would have to be reconstructed. And since privilege and power are not lightly surrendered, since what we understand as norms are not quickly transformed, Carmichael's operative verb might indeed emerge as "smash," as in "smash everything Western civilization has created," that is, the exclusive construction of culture—or of philosophy—expressed in most Western civilization courses and similar curricula before the late 1960s.

I am not proposing that Carmichael's rhetoric or the intellectual processes it implies were comforting or even compatible with North American academic norms. But I do want to make two things clear: First, the issue of the canon— what we study, what we conceive as significant, not just in literature but in almost every discipline—has always arisen from efforts to redress social wrongs. And second, debate over canonical issues—as was the case when biblical canons were argued and established—deeply affects the ways people conceive, regulate, and change their lives. In other words, the problem of the canon will persist so long as we see education, and more particularly, cultural practice and study, as fundamentally related to social justice, or even to the evolution of human communities. Indeed, the progress of canonical criticism cannot be understood separately from the personnel practices designated as "affirmative action."

These points may be clarified by considering some of the significant texts of early canonical criticism. I would cite first the series called Female Studies, published in the late 1960s and early 1970s by KNOW, Inc. and The Feminist Press. These volumes collected syllabi and course materials from the first practitioners of women's studies in many disciplines and in a variety of academic settings. They were by nature collective rather than individualistic, since they displayed the scholarship and pedagogical practices of many teachers. They emerged, of course, from the experience of teachers and spoke to practical classroom problems: what texts to use, how to organize them, how such choices were related both to changing student populations and to traditionally-defined academic structures, such as departments and course requirements. Whereas such volumes were enormously important "contributions to knowledge," that phrase was not conceived by contributors to the books in traditional terms: That is, while a new syllabus, as we all know, often reflects an intense scholarly enterprise, and generally new research as well, it is neither posed nor presented as a permanent cultural monument, but rather as an educational tool that will, in time, be superseded. We write our most precious conceptions onto the ditto-master for distribution, and next year we use the surplus copies for scrap. We are like the Japanese fisherman who inscribed his poems on scrolls, which he then necessarily used to wrap the fish he sold.

Among those concerned primarily with African-American literature, canonical criticism in the late 1960s and early 1970s often emerged in the form of anthologies and collections of essays by different hands. To be sure, the appearance of such books revealed primarily publishers' judgments that black literature was being taught and might also sell in the general literary market. But these volumes also represented a means by which black artists and critics expressed ideas about what constitutes the distinctive canon of African-American literary art. Most of the 1968 anthologies—for example, Abraham Chapman's *Black Voices,* James A. Emanuel and Theodore L. Gross's *Dark Symphony,* and Amiri Baraka and Larry Neal's *Black Fire*—contain both belles lettres and social and political criticism (the distinction is not emphasized) in proportions markedly different from those that characterize traditional, dominantly white anthologies. Similarly, Paul Bremen's *You Better Believe It* (1973) includes poetry from Africa, the West Indies and the United States, emphasizing the relationships among these, and Stephen Henderson's *Understanding the New Black Poetry: Black Speech and Black Music as Poetic References* (1973) includes Georgia Sea Island and other songs, and black folk rhymes, as well as formal poetry, to represent the range of black poetic forms that need to be taught and studied by critics. Addison Gayle's widely read *The Black Aesthetic* (1971) and his *Black Expression* (1969) also include essays on music, art, and on folk culture, as well as on formal literature, thus offering what might be termed an interdisciplinary perspective on African-American art—and incidentally suggesting one reason American academic structures present barriers to its integrated study. That five of my seven titles use the word *black* (and one *dark*) also suggests a central concern that these books share with Carmichael: to define what it means to be black in late twentieth-century America.

As it emerged in the late 1960s and early 1970s, then, canonical criticism focused first on practical matters such as organizing syllabi and making otherwise buried and forgotten texts and authors available, especially for classrooms. These pedagogical and archaeological tasks continue, as is illustrated by the ongoing process of reprinting nineteenth-century women's texts in the Rutgers University Press American Women Writers series, the recent success of the Schomburg Library of Nineteenth-Century Black Women Writers (Oxford University Press, 1988), the efforts of Daniel Littlefield and others to locate and reprint nineteenth-century Native American works in English, the wealth of unpublished Spanish-language texts in the Bancroft collection at Berkeley, and the fact that most of Frances E. W. Harper's novels have yet to be reprinted—or, indeed, fully located in the nineteenth-century black periodicals where they first appeared. But alongside this work, often in fact as a part of it, have developed certain other strands of critical practice that I wish to identify and trace.

Beginning around 1966, texts previously ignored in syllabi and anthologies began to be read in (and sometimes out of) the classroom. I refer to works like Zora Neale Hurston's *Their Eyes Were Watching God,* Rebecca Harding Davis' "Life in the Iron Mills," Frederick Douglass' *Narrative* of his life, and Margaret Fuller's *Woman in the Nineteenth Century.* At the same time, significant contemporary works that drew on ethnic traditions began to achieve a wide audience—works such as Rudolfo Anaya's *Bless Me, Ultima,* Leslie Marmon Silko's *Ceremony,* and Maxine Hong Kingston's *The Woman Warrior.* More recently, too, critics have begun to reexamine whole bodies of distinctive works—for example, the poetry of female modernists or the 1850s fiction of American women. In many ways, all these works fell outside the existing accounts of American or British literary traditions, and so there began to develop a second, *synthetic* stage of canonical criticism. Rather early, black critics, such as Stephen Henderson, Addison Gayle, and Houston Baker,[28] mounted a project to define the particular qualities that constitute an African-American tradition in American writing. Similarly, feminist critics such as Ellen Moers, Elaine Showalter, Sandra Gilbert, Susan Gubar, and Barbara Christian began to describe dominantly female (and, except in Christian's work, largely white) traditions in literature[29] as well as woman-centered cultural networks, such as the late-nineteenth-century group that cohered around Sarah Orne Jewett and Annie Fields.[30] The efforts of African-Americans to define a peculiarly "black" content in their writing and to trace its impact in the historical worlds inhabited by black people have recently been criticized by more formalist commentators.[31] But such complaints really miss the point of what these early canonical critics were about: Their problem was less to define the underlying structural principles of writing by black Americans and by women, than to seek out the ways in which such writing played roles in the "struggle for the right to create our own terms to define ourselves . . . and to have these terms recognized," to return to Carmichael's formulation. The major cultural task of canonical criticism in the late 1960s and 1970s, its second stage, was, first, to "define ourselves," and then to force into literary consciousness ("have these terms recognized") texts like those I noted above that were previously conceived as peripheral—

or, rather, texts that illustrated a whole cultural tradition and thus the life of a marginalized group or people. Establishing such traditions not only demonstrated the extent and range of African-American or female cultures but also showed the critical difference inherent in such cultures, indeed, that they *were* different. That presented a direct challenge to the ideology of academic formalism, which rejected the idea that literature might legitimately play such social roles, and which at some level continued to assert universality, not difference, as fundamental to literary value. It may be that the earliest black critics can be reproved for their limited accounts of how literature plays roles in the world and about the character of African-American tradition; if we recall, however, how fully formalist criticism and McCarthyite politics had buried ideas about the social functions of writing, we will regard the work of these early black critics as a heroic effort to reconstruct a lost critical tradition.

These canonical critics recognized that underlying the questions of what is taught and to whom, what is anthologized, published, and written about, are ideas about what a culture values and why. Standards of value tend to be self-perpetuating: We are taught to seek the works that illustrate the qualities we value; we learn to value the qualities that characterize such works. Responding to the social movements of the 1960s, and to the first stage of discovery of "new" texts, these critics ironically enacted the process of canonical change described by T. S. Eliot in "Tradition and the Individual Talent," the "modification" of the "ideal order" of the "existing monuments" of culture. In that process, we began to recognize that touchstones of literary value are not, in fact, inscribed on tablets at all, but are mutable constructs devised at particular times by particular people with particular aspirations and constraints. We saw that such standards change, that they are differently held by distinct communities; indeed, by virtue of our participation in such diverse communities—of nationality, race, sex, class, profession, institution— we ourselves may maintain conflicting sets of values and thus of literary standards.

When we begin to acknowledge how distinct value systems are embodied in diverse cultural assumptions and forms (the third stage of canonical criticism, where we find ourselves today), we begin to deconstruct the underlying assumptions of received systems of evaluation. It seems to me that works like Smith's "Contingencies of Value" and Jane Tompkins' 1985 book, *Sensational Designs*,[32] represent this kind of cultural work. On the one hand, Tompkins cuts through the mystifications that have been used to certify particular writers, like Hawthorne, as "classics"; on the other, she illuminates the social and literary values that define the importance of marginalized writers, such as Stowe and Susan Warner. I take Tompkins' project (which must stand here for others' work) in two ways. It involves a kind of reconciliation of insights provided by theoretical study and the practice of canon revision and reformation—or, perhaps more accurately, it offers certain theoretical frameworks to help explain the practice in which canonical criticism has been engaged since the late 1960s. In so doing, it underlines the need for a radical reassessment of literary standards—if we take that phrase to mean the professional determinants of what gets taught, read, and valued. In bringing such "standards of value" into question, canonical criticism plays what I think will be an increasing role in the determination of American social and political values as well.

III

If I have correctly mapped these alternative parabolas of recent critical history, what do the curves imply for teaching, as well as for professional and institutional practice? I wish to focus on two issues: What model of learning is implied by current critical activity? And to whom do critics speak?

I suggested earlier that the tendency of theoretical criticism has been to reinforce institutional norms, whereas the tendency of canonical criticism has been to bring them into question. I do not want to overstate the distinction, for writing *about* canons does not by itself guarantee a challenge to regressive institutional practices, much less to racism or patriarchy. And yet, efforts to *change* a canon necessarily engage one in struggles to reshape local syllabi, course requirements, reading lists, national examinations, requisites for graduate school admissions, and the like. Canons do not, after all, exist in the sky; rather, they are made manifest in particular social and educational practices. Canons and curricula are by no means identical; curricula (whatever one might have meant by that word) were probably irrelevant to the establishment of biblical canons. But today, given the power of academic institutions to shape cultural priorities, institutional forms like curricula are central to the maintenance or modification of canons, not only in literary study but throughout the educational system.

Canonical criticism has been directed less at simply examining canons than at changing them by altering educational practices. In that process, canon critics engage power. For it is precisely in the effort to effect change that one discovers how power is organized, and how it is expressed in particular institutional forms and social priorities. Critics did not come to understand canons, or even the processes by which they are established, reproduced, or altered, until some of us set about efforts to change them. The efforts to bring writers of color and white women authors into curricula brought to the surface—in fact, allowed many to discover—the deeply racist, patriarchal, heterosexist assumptions that actually shaped such seemingly innocent documents as reading lists, book order forms, and literary histories. Similarly, practical efforts to change institutional hiring procedures and priorities revealed the power equation implicit in seemingly neutral, meritocratic criteria. Theoretical models, however sophisticated, do not explain the concrete operations of power in particular institutions at historically specific junctures—which is how we experience them. If you want to understand the world as it is actually working, you must try to alter it. "If you would know the taste of a pear, you must change it by eating it."

Central to the project of canonical criticism is thus a theory of learning that emphasizes individual action to achieve change as the key to understanding culture. And this question of epistemology, more perhaps than anything else, differentiates where it is that theoretical and canonical criticisms lead.

If, as I have been suggesting, the bearings of these two forms of criticism differ sharply, the arena within which they have been played out has remained largely the academy. Certainly, the world of theory has been circumscribed by a scholasticism not only of language but of intent: Critics, we are frequently told, write to other critics. But canonical criticism, too, whose energy was initially generated by the social movements of the 1960s and early 1970s, has been focused *within* educational institutions. Indeed, even as the movement to open up the canon has been succeeding within academic literary study, the defenders of traditional canons, the Bennetts and Blooms, have dominated public discourse. The 1990 annual program for the Modern Language Association convention bears little resemblance to that of 1969, and virtually every major university and college is busily competing for faculty members in African-American literature and in ethnic studies. Yet it is not at all clear that this revolution in literary sensibility reaches far beyond the college's gates. Certainly, it does not extend into the legislative halls, where public budgets are determined, or into most newspaper editorial rooms and TV studios, where public opinions are shaped. These are sources of power that cultural workers cannot ignore. Furthermore, the idea that the responsibility of critics is fundamentally to other critics—or even to our profession—seems to me an expression of academic elitism. In naming her audience as the "common reader," Virginia Woolf posed an ideal toward which, I think, intellectuals must aspire. She carried on a tradition, and redefined a word, which in our time works like Adrienne Rich's *The Dream of a Common Language* and Judy Grahn's "The Common Woman" poems may be taken to represent. It is worth naming some others of Woolf's contemporaries in that tradition, changers of canons in their time, rediscovered in ours: José Martí, Charlotte Perkins Gilman, W.E.B. DuBois, Meridel LeSueur. We will not, of course, always succeed in "the drive to connect," as Rich phrases it. But certainly we will not if our aspirations lie elsewhere, in the kinds of specialized goals toward which the practice of "theory" has, I think, been leading.

In one respect, at least, Bennett and Bloom are right: The ideal of humane study ought, above all, to be citizenship, not specialization. As I argue elsewhere, I think their definition of citizenship is painfully antediluvian. It is not that the work of the specialist has no validity; on the contrary, it helps establish a relatively stable ground upon which intellectuals contest public issues. Theory has done much in that regard. But it is time to move on to define in public forums, as well as in academic curricula, the widening world of writers and books vital to citizenship in a future more diverse and challenging than any that human beings have lived in up to now.

Notes

1. For an account of this symposium see Frank Lentricchia, *After the New Criticism* (Chicago: University of Chicago Press, 1980), pp. 157–162.

2. For an account of the Meredith march and the origins of the "Black Power" slogan see Clayborn Carson, *In Struggle: SNCC and the Black Awakening of the 1960s* (Cambridge: Harvard University Press, 1981), pp. 209–210.

3. See Sara Evans, *Personal Politics: The Roots of Women's Liberation in the Civil Rights Movement and the New Left* (New York: Vintage, 1980), pp. 185–86.

4. Barbara Herrnstein Smith, "Contingencies of Value," in Robert von Hallberg, ed., *Canons* (Chicago: University of Chicago Press, 1984), pp. 5–39.

5. Laurence Lerner, "Introduction," *Reconstructing Literature* (Totowa, N.J.: Barnes and Noble, 1983), p. 6.

6. Howard Felperin argues that "all of the dominant schools of contemporary criticism—marxism, structuralism, and deconstruction—have converged upon" the "myth" of a "privileged literary language," "dismantling it of its idealist and metaphysical yearnings and trappings, its Arnoldian inheritance of displaced religion. . . . " *Beyond Deconstruction* (Oxford: Clarendon Press, 1985), p. 11. Yet the concept continually, perversely, reemerges. For example, Paul de Man argues that "Literature, unlike everyday language, begins on the far side of this knowledge [that "sign and meaning can never coincide"]; it is the only form of language free from the fallacy of unmediated expression. All of us know this, although we know it in the misleading way of a wishful assertion of the opposite. Yet the truth emerges in the foreknowledge we possess of the true nature of literature when we refer to it as *fiction.*" *Blindness and Insight* (New York: Oxford University Press, 1981), p. 17. The obvious problem in de Man's formulation is in his dichotomizing "literature," on the one hand, and "everyday language," on the other, and in his privileging "literature" as "the only form of language. . . ." In truth, literary and everyday language are radically alike, both involve—more and less—the construction and recommendation of "fictions," the use of images, the mobilization of rhetorics, and the like. In fact, a major cause for failure in the teaching of literature is our habit of erecting linguistic and formal walls between it and our students' use of language.

7. Cf. Robert Scholes, "Some Problems in Current Graduate Programs in English," *Profession 87,* 40:

> This second reduction in our field left behind only poetics (and its handmaiden, philology, which has since been dismissed or relegated to the basement). Free to concentrate exclusively on the poetic or literary side of English textuality, we were led, inevitably, to a greater and greater degree of formalism in literary studies; to New Criticism, to the Chicago school of generic criticism, later on to structuralism, and finally to deconstruction—which is the aestheticizing of all discourse, the denial that any really persuasive, or informational, or speculative discourse can exist.

8. Cleanth Brooks, *The Well Wrought Urn* (New York: Harcourt, Brace and World, 1947).

9. Allen Tate, "Tension in Poetry," *Essays of Four Decades* (Chicago: The Swallow Press, 1968), pp. 64, 58.

10. John Crowe Ransom, "The Poet as Woman," in *The World's Body* (New York: Scribner's, 1938), pp. 103–105. In *Stealing the Language: The Emergence of Women's Poetry in America,* Alicia Ostriker has analyzed how the ideology shared by Tate and Ransom operated to marginalize women poets.

11. Northrop Frye, *Anatomy of Criticism: Four Essays* (New York: Atheneum, 1967).

12. See, for example, Roland Barthes, *Mythologies,* Annette Lavers, trans. (New York: Hill and Wang, 1972) and *S/Z,* Richard Howard, trans. (New York: Hill and Wang, 1974).

13. See Fredric Jameson, *The Prison-House of Language: A Critical Account of Structuralism and Russian Formalism* (Princeton, N.J.: Princeton University Press, 1972).

14. Harold Bloom, *The Anxiety of Influence: A Theory of Poetry* (New York: Oxford University Press, 1973).

15. Geoffrey Hartman, *Criticism in the Wilderness: The Study of Literature Today* (New Haven, Conn.: Yale University Press, 1980).

16. Frank Lentricchia, *After the New Criticism* (Chicago: University of Chicago Press, 1980), p. xiii.

17. Ironically, in *After the New Criticism* Lentricchia himself falls into an often ahistorical mode, citing much more the epiphenomena of professional conflicts than the larger processes of social change in his explanations of critical development.

18. "Theory" is, as Jonathan Culler points out, virtually a nickname for a variety of writings that, in the American academy, fall outside the prior domains of "English" or "philosophy" or the empirical "social sciences" as they are generally practiced. See Jonathan Culler, *On Deconstruction: Theory and Criticism after Structuralism* (Ithaca: Cornell University Press, 1982), pp. 8–10. In a strict sense, theoretical writing simply concerns the assumption—for example, about language, the relationships of "signifier" and "signified," the "binary" structure of most Western thought, the relations of culture to class-conflict—that we all use in thinking and writing about literature—or anything else that provides us with a "text" or subject. In practice, however, the looser sense of the term prevails.

19. For an account of these events see Louis Kampf and Paul Lauter, "Introduction" to *The Politics of Literature* (New York: Pantheon, 1972).

20. I suspect that the relatively late appearance of "theory" in academic feminist circles reflects the fact that the activism of the women's movement continued apace when organizations such as SDS, SNCC, NUC, and the Black Panther Party, and what they quite variously represented, were long buried.

21. Edward Said makes a similar point in "American 'Left' Literary Criticism," *The World, the Text, and the Critic* (Cambridge: Harvard University Press, 1983):

> . . . it is our technical skill as critics and intellectuals that the culture has wanted to neutralize, and if we have cooperated in this project, perhaps unconsciously, it is because that is where the money has been. . . . The result so far as critical practice is concerned is that rhetorical individualism in criticism and in the texts studied by the critic is cultivated for its own sake, with the further result that writing is seen as deliberately aiming for alienation—the critic from other critics, from readers, from the work studied. . . . The irony is, however, that literary critics, by virtue of their studious indifference to the world they live in and to the values by which their work engages history, do not see themselves as a threat to anything, except possibly to each other. Certainly they are as governable as they have always been since state worship became fashionable, and certainly their passive devotion to masterpieces, culture, texts and structures posited simply in their own 'texts' as functioning yet finished enterprises, poses no threat to authority or to values kept in circulation and managed by the technocratic managers

(pp. 173, 174).

22. Geoffrey Hartman, *The Fate of Reading* (Chicago: University of Chicago Press, 1975).

23. Howard Felperin, *Beyond Deconstruction,* pp. 46–47.

24. Jacques Derrida, *Spurs: Nietzsche's Styles,* Barbara Harlow, trans. (Chicago: University of Chicago Press, 1978), pp. 125, 127.

25. In a certain way, advocates of "theory" can, perhaps by virtue of analytic blinders, end up sounding peculiarly naive. Joan Scott, for example, criticized Alice Kessler-Harris' testimony in the Sears case as insufficiently informed by the kinds of insights into the difference/equality dichotomy that might be provided by a deconstructive analysis. See Joan Scott, *Gender and the Politics of History* (New York: Columbia University Press, 1988). Underlying Scott's criticism, however, is the assumption that courts, in the current political climate, are looking for philosophical sophistication rather than for rationales for supporting corporate power. Can anyone suppose that a deconstructionist approach to testifying would have brought the court to support the female complainants?

26. See William Bennett, "To Reclaim a Legacy: A Report on the Humanities in Higher Education," National Endowment for the Humanities, November 1984; and my critique of Bennett's ideas in "Looking a Gift Horse in the Mouth" elsewhere in this volume.

27. Cited in Clayborn Carson, *In Struggle: SNCC and the Black Awakening of the 1960s* (Cambridge: Harvard University Press, 1981), p. 216.

28. Stephen Henderson, *Understanding the New Black Poetry* (New York: Morrow, 1972); Addison Gayle, ed., *The Black Aesthetic* (Garden City, N.Y.: Anchor, 1972); Houston Baker, *Long Black Song: Essays in Black American Literature and Culture* (Charlottesville, Va.: University of Virginia, 1972).

29. Ellen Moers, *Literary Women: The Great Writers* (Garden City, N.Y.: Doubleday, 1976); Elaine Showalter, *A Literature of Their Own: British Women Novelists from Bronte to Lessing* (Princeton, N.J.: Princeton University Press, 1978); Sandra M. Gilbert and Susan Gubar, *The Madwoman in the Attic: The Woman Writer and the Nineteenth-Century Literary Imagination* (New Haven, Conn.: Yale University Press, 1979); Barbara Christian, *Black Women Novelists: The Development of a Tradition, 1892–1976* (Westport, Conn.: Greenwood, 1980).

More recent works have begun further to define a parallel, largely separate, but sometimes related tradition among black women writers. Among these works are Mary Helen Washington, *Invented Lives* (Garden City, N.Y.: Anchor, 1987), Hazel V. Carby, *Reconstructing Womanhood* (New York: Oxford *University Press,* 1987), and Elizabeth Ammons, "New Literary History: Edith Wharton and Jessie Redmon Fauset," *College Literature* 14 (1987): 207–218.

30. See Josephine Donovan, "Annie Adams Fields and Her Network of Influence," *New England Local Color Literature: A Woman's Tradition* (New York: Frederick Ungar, 1983), pp. 38–49.

31. See, for example, Henry Louis Gates, Jr., "Preface to Blackness: Text and Pretext," in Dexter Fisher and Robert B. Stepto, eds., *Afro-American Literature: The Reconstruction of Instruction* (New York: Modern Language Association, 1979), pp. 44–69.

32. Jane Tompkins, *Sensational Designs: The Cultural Work of American Fiction, 1790–1860* (New York: Oxford University Press, 1985). See note 4.

Canon Theory and Emergent Practice

I want to begin with what some might cite as a characteristic move of the socialist intellectual in capitalist society: namely, biting the hand that feeds you. In the course of explaining to me the rejection by the National Endowment for the Humanities board of a highly-rated proposal for a Seminar for College Teachers, the NEH program officer wrote that "some reviewers were concerned that the focus on the canon, while doubtless an important issue for teachers of American literature, lacked the kind of scholarly significance generally expected of Summer Seminars. . . . " Pursuing this theme, he later wrote that my "application was rather more thesis-driven than most of our seminar proposals."

I discover everywhere signs of this division. On the one side, we find the supposedly pedagogical or professional problems raised by the question of the canon, and on the other side, what is lauded as "of scholarly significance" or, more simply, criticism or theory. In a recent "Newsletter for Graduate Alumnae and Alumni" issued by the Yale English Department, for example, Cyrus Hamlin ruminates "precisely how this procedure of hermeneutical recuperation" he is proposing "should affect the canon and the curriculum of our institution is difficult to say. . . . " and he proceeds to ignore the question (p. 2). In the same document, Margaret Homans suggests why he does so. "At Yale," she writes

> while post-structuralism has proven to be intellectually more unsettling than liberal humanism, the feminist versions of post-structuralism are institutionally more easily accommodated than some of the projects of liberal feminism, such as challenging the content of the canon we teach, with its vast preponderance of white, male authors

(p. 4).

Interestingly, Homans here appropriates the project of canon revision solely to the domain of "liberal feminism," a common enough way of trying to limit

Parts of this chapter have appeared in different form in *Left Politics and the Literary Profession,* Lennard Davis and M. Bella Mirabella, eds. (New York: Columbia University Press, 1990). Sections were initially prepared for presentation at a Modern Language Association convention panel in 1987.

the scope of this intellectual movement to a supposed clique of uppity, middle-class women. Like the characterization of canon revision as dominantly a "pedagogical" issue, and thus a matter only slightly removed from teachers' college trivialities, defining it as a project of "liberal feminism" must be seen simply as one more move in the academic political struggle that I shall try to characterize here.

This division between the concerns of what I have come to call "canonical criticism" and those of what is called "theory" is, I think, one fact of current literary practice in the United States. In another chapter I have attempted to trace the very differing histories of canonical and academic criticism since the late 1960s; I do not wish to pursue that story here, except to underline the fact that canon criticism was initially an effort to carry the politics of the 1960s social movements into the work socially-engaged academics actually did, especially into our classrooms. Consequently, canon criticism first influenced curriculum and thus gradually the margins of publishing and scholarship. Somewhat later, it came to affect the selection of texts about which graduate students and critics write; more slowly still, which works became sufficiently revered to find their way into footnotes, indices or other measures of academic weight. More recently, it has begun altering the "mainstream" of publishing as well as generating wide public debate. Such has been the history of books like Frederick Douglass' *Narrative,* Charlotte Perkins Gilman's "The Yellow Wallpaper," or, more recently, Harriet Jacobs' *Incidents in the Life of a Slave Girl.* In the most recent stages of this process, as I shall point out below, some of the concerns of canonical criticism have converged with those arising from academic "theory." Even so, this division is only one of those that need to be explored. If one were at a convention of educators, one might be struck by the conflict between those advocating and those denouncing the canonical proposals of William Bennett, Allan Bloom, and Lynne Cheney. If one were at the National Women's Studies Association conference, one would probably notice the differences *among* those committed to changing the existing canon. Here, I want to chart the multiple conflicts that have arisen as the question of the canon has come to play a larger role on the intellectual stage.

An issue of *Salmagundi* concentrating on "Cultural Literacy: Canon, Class, Curriculum" (#72, Fall, 1986) provides a useful starting point. The issue contains an essay by Robert Scholes called "Aiming a Canon at the Curriculum" and a set of responses to Scholes's article. For Scholes, the problem is to resist efforts by the Bennetts to impose upon educational institutions a particular canon of great books or a recipe for "cultural literacy" like E. D. Hirsch's. Scholes's essay can be taken as representative of the general reaction of the academic community to the cultural prescriptions of Reaganism. "What I am opposing," he writes, "is the learning of a set of pious clichés about a set of sacred texts" (p. 116). Most readers are sufficiently familiar (one might even say bored) with the ideas of Bennett and Cheney on this subject so I need not restate Scholes's well-drawn critique except to say that he brings into the open the right-wing politics that fuel Bennett's analysis as well as his solution. Scholes approvingly quotes T. S. Eliot's formulation of the matter: " 'to know what we want in education we must know what we want in general, we must derive our theory of education from our philosophy of life. The problem turns out to be a religious problem' " (p. 107; the Eliot quote is from "Modern Education and the Classics"). Seen in this light, the question of the canon becomes a conflict of values, and therefore, translated into public policy, of politics.

Of course, the issue is seldom joined in these terms; neither side in this debate puts forward explicitly political criteria for choosing texts they think worth studying. Bennett claims that the "great books" simply emerge over time through some kind of consensus among the properly educated. The opposition is formulated in terms of resisting the imposition of an essentially narrow vision of "Western Culture as a single coherent object, constructed of masterpieces built by geniuses," which is how Scholes characterizes the Bennett doctrine (p. 114). Bennett would not explicitly claim that Twain, Faulkner, and Martin Luther King, Jr., whose work he includes on his list, among them sufficiently "cover" the issue of racism in America; but in practice, adoption of that list as a basis of curriculum effectively marginalizes, if it does not altogether silence, the oppositional voices of writers such as David Walker, Harriet Jacobs, William Lloyd Garrison, Frances E. W. Harper, W.E.B. DuBois, or Malcolm X. Against this effort effectively to narrow the limits of significant debate, all the commentators on Scholes's piece stand united on what amounts to a platform of liberal pluralism. Even E. D. Hirsch, whose idea of "cultural literacy" is embodied in a dictionary of words and phrases that "every American should know," essentially joins Scholes on this score. Indeed, a broad consensus exists among literary practitioners to oppose efforts like those of Bennett's successor in the National Endowment for the Humanities, Lynne Cheney, to "politicize" criteria for selecting panels and projects or to project a single, federally-approved core curriculum.[1]

But this consensus soon unravels. In her criticism of Scholes's position, Marjorie Perloff correctly points out that he assumes against this implied effort by federal conservatives to impose curriculum an existing "genuine freedom of choice as to what texts shall be read . . ." ("An Intellectual Impasse," p. 124). On the contrary, Perloff argues, there is "a canon operative in our current humanities programs, however reluctant professors and educators are to admit it" (p. 126). Perloff examines the subjects of articles in recent issues of *PMLA* to illustrate the content of that canon; she also demonstrates how pervasive are certain intellectual touchstones in these articles, notably Derrida, Freud, Barthes, Plato and Foucault, among others one could quickly name. Thus she concludes—no surprise—that today's "professors themselves carry on the traditions they themselves learned not so long ago in graduate school" with respect both to the imaginative texts worth studying and to the language and procedures by which they ought to be studied. Perloff's comment invokes a second, equally familiar front of the canon controversy: the effort within the academic community to *extend* the range of texts—and the modes for encountering them—about which we think, write, and teach.

On this front, those who were united in opposition to the Bennett or Cheney prescriptions may well part company. For it is precisely at this point that those dominantly concerned with what is called "theory" turn with a shrug back to "hermeneutical recuperation." While it might not seem to matter precisely which texts one subjects to psychoanalytic, semiotic, or deconstructive analysis—and thus even the most hardened poststructuralist might in theory join the effort to broaden the canon—it turns out in practice that few "theorists" have participated in the effort to reconstruct literary canons—at least when one looks beyond the work of some feminist and black critics. Barbara Herrnstein Smith has effectively argued in her essay "Contingencies of Value"[2] that the positivistic stance and universalizing tendencies of academic criticism make it largely irrelevant to, and its practitioners finally uninterested in, the issues of valuation that are central to the question of the canon.

Furthermore, it is sometimes argued by enthusiasts of "theory" that deconstruction, in particular the work of Foucault, introduced the issue of power into literary discourse and thus raised the problem of canon formation. But the idea that cultural structures, such as a reading list or a set of criteria for admission to higher education, embody and sustain power relationships was quite clear long before poststructuralist theory emerged on the French, much less the American, scene. It was no accident that Mao Tse-tung's final effort to overcome the institutions of class in China was called the "cultural revolution"; the core of his ideas on that subject are contained in his 1942 "Talks at the Yenan Forum on Art and Literature." Further, demands for "open admissions" and "black studies" shook American universities long before Foucault had become a household word. The notion that debate over the canon derives from poststructuralist theory expresses something of the insulation of the academy. The general lack of contribution until quite recently of most American practitioners of "theory" to the debates about the canon also suggests something of the profound conservatism of the academy, in which the citation of precedent and authority ("as Derrida proposes in *Épirons*...") have weighed far more heavily in the scales of tenure than the presentation of an "unknown" like Frances E. W. Harper. Such qualities exemplify the problem Mao tried to address, badly or well: how to bring into the open, and thus into question, the power relationships embedded in the consciousness of academics as well as in the cultural institutions we inhabit. And these qualities suggest that part of the importance of the effort to widen the canon is precisely the need to counter the tendency of academics to absorb social conflict into debates, over language and form, for example, that they can more easily control.[3] But revolution is not a linguistic phenomenon.

A useful illustration of the problem is offered by an anonymous comment on an earlier version of this essay provided to the Columbia University Press. The reviewer complained that Lauter "offers up the thoroughly critiqued (and dismissed) view that the institution of literature and literary studies change simply by adding more texts by third world and minority writers. . . . Thus Lauter completely ignores the more important question of how one reads, what contexts one reads in, who the reader is and other problems that have been brought to critical attention through the debate over the canon." Anyone who has been engaged in adding minority and white women's texts to syllabi, reading lists and anthologies, and in the closely related problem of adding women and minority men to faculties and enrollments, will know there is nothing "simple" in these processes. In fact, they have entailed meaningful changes in literary, and other, forms of study, as the numerous books tracing significant alterations in academic paradigms and priorities indicate.[4] But such changes are generally dismissed by literary academics for whom problems of epistemology ("how one reads") are self-evidently "more important" than what one reads. They miss the dialectical relationship between on the one hand, the subjects and authors of texts, and, on the other, who teaches and reads them in the educational systems of American capitalism. Or, indeed, who makes it into, or in, those systems.

If the second front of the debate is about *extending* rather than constricting the canon, the third front involves the substantial conflicts among those of us who work to change the existing canon; once again, I think, different political agendas translate into differing cultural priorities. One position is that taken up by cultural pluralists: We are many in these United States and any canon, any curriculum, ought to be "representative." I do not wish to disparage this answer for in many respects I agree with it; indeed, I think that the currently fashionable attacks on cultural pluralism, exemplified by Werner Sollors' "A Critique of Pure Pluralism," are badly misplaced. I shall return to Sollors' essay and to the book in which it is found shortly, but first I want to clarify differences among those committed to changing the canon.

Formulating the case for pluralism simply by asserting the value of representation obscures what is in question. For how can any canon be fully representative? Even if one ignores the problem of room at the inn—and I would be the last to deny that in anthologies, curricula, and literary histories this *is* a problem, though not always insuperable—do not the very processes of canonization necessarily reflect the structures of social and political power and thus embed in their product an unrepresentative, if widened, set of texts organized even at best along hierarchical lines? Does it not follow, then, that the goal must be to abolish canons altogether and to substitute, rather, the authority of various individual or ethnic group experiences freed from the constraints of any official discipline? It is to this issue that the most interesting essay in *Salmagundi*, that by Elizabeth Fox-Genovese, is addressed.

Fox-Genovese is altogether uninterested in my first front; she refers to

Bennett only in her concluding paragraph. As for the second front, she has little patience with the moves of elite white academic theorists, of whom she writes (and I cannot resist quoting):

> They share an explicit distaste for "bourgeois humanism" and for the personal subject or author. They are offering us society as text and text as society and both as process or system. They are contributing to the disillusionment with values that had been tailored to the measure of man. Yet they have done little or nothing to reestablish the accountability of the Humanities to a pluralistic society. . . . From the perspective of those previously excluded from the cultural elite, the death of the subject or the death of the author seems somewhat premature. Surely it is no coincidence that the Western white male elite proclaimed the death of the subject at precisely the moment at which it might have had to share that status with the women and peoples of other races and classes who were beginning to challenge its supremacy.
>
> ("The Claims of a Common Culture:
> Gender, Race, Class and the Canon," p. 134)

But her primary argument is with those who wish to abolish all canons. While our students, she contends, may feel "colonized in relation to that elite western culture that has constituted the backbone of our humanistic education," throwing out the canon "does not solve their problem any more than expurgating all traces of western technology solves the problem of colonial peoples." Transforming "the canon and the surveys in response to changing constituencies has less to do with rewriting the story than with reinterpreting it," she concludes (pp. 135–36).

How to accomplish this goal? Fox-Genovese's proposal is to reread canonical texts as much for what they do *not* say as for what they make explicit. The work of Hobbes and Locke, for example, can be read from a gendered perspective: "We can teach elite culture from the perspective of gender, race, and class if we are prepared to accept attention to issues of gender, race, and class as proxies for the subjective testimony of those excluded from the most exalted cultural roles" (p. 140).[5] While this strategy is important, a problem with it inheres in the word "we," and in Fox-Genovese's implicit methodology. Again: "we can transform the entire focus of conventional courses by the themes we select" (p. 141); or, shifting pronoun, but retaining the teacher-dominant tactic, "one can *present* the individual as the problem rather than the solution" (p. 141; my italics). In effect, Fox-Genovese is shifting the ground of the debate from *what* is taught to *how* it is presented.[6] Her questions (though not her objectives) are similar to those asked by certain critics sceptical of the whole project of revising the canon. They ask: Does it really matter whether students read Harriet Jacobs or Nathaniel Hawthorne, Fitzgerald or LeSueur in class, since it is not at all clear what they do and do not learn by studying any of them? Or, more generally, does the reading of canonical stalwarts necessarily imply the transmission of elitist values, or the study of working-class texts dependably yield working-class consciousness? These are interesting empirical questions, perhaps mainly for educational sociologists.

They evoke the studies of the late 1950s which suggested that collegiate learning affects the values, at least of the students examined, marginally, if at all.⁷ Such scepticism extends the critique poststructuralists have mounted against the too-easily presumed value of revolutions, or even of revolutionary movements, organizations, and goals.

One problem with these questions is that they invite broad generalizations about *all* students in *any* circumstances. In fact, a good deal of evidence, mainly anecdotal, suggests that students of diverse class and racial backgrounds respond quite differently to books such as *The Girl, Daughter of Earth,* and *Their Eyes Were Watching God,* and that the character of such responses changes in response to different political conditions. It can be extremely important for students from marginalized backgrounds to know that the domain named "literature" belongs to them as well as to others. But the main problem with sceptical social critiques, reasonable as they may seem, is that they too easily lead to political paralysis, and they play into reactionary ideologies that, for example, deny *any* value to radical change, whether retrospectively in Cuba or prospectively in South Africa. In the context of canon debate such scepticism over the value of altering canons can hardly help but provide fuel for those indifferent or hostile to such change. The argument then becomes: "Let us await persuasive evidence that it makes a difference before we disrupt the rooted norms of academic study." It is important to call into question exaggerated claims for the effects of canon change. Still, the assumption that such change matters to what readers experience, envision, and believe seems to me a useful intellectual and pedagogical hypothesis on the basis of which to act. Only through such action do we find in social practice whether or to what extent and under what conditions that hypothesis is valid.

Fox-Genovese does *not* seem to me to share this sceptical conservatism. Rather, her assumption seems to be that certain teachers can approach texts with a degree of consciousness about gender, race, class, sexuality, nationality—marginality generally—sufficient to enable them to "present" the texts from these angles of vision. That seems to me rather more complicated than her essay allows, which may emerge more clearly by looking at the results of curriculum "integration" projects, as they are called. In these projects, faculty members, usually white and male, whose specialities are *not* women's studies or minority or ethnic studies, develop new courses or units that "integrate" the findings of scholars in those areas with more traditional disciplinary materials. Such projects, which have largely been initiated by women's studies programs, have produced a good deal of interesting curricular work, particularly within the California State University system, at the University of Arizona, Wheaton College, and at Towson State University, and as I suggest in another chapter, they offer one of the most significant strategies for changing curricula. But they have also regularly encountered two difficulties. First, because the traditional faculty members engaged in such projects are in general marginally familiar with the shifts in disciplinary paradigms insisted upon by women's and minority studies, they seldom alter their course frameworks, and thus their presentations of conventional materials. They might, for example begin to include works like Jean Toomer's *Cane* and H. D.'s *Trilogy,* Meridel Le Sueur's *The Girl* or Zora Neale Hurston's *Their Eyes Were Watching God* in a course on the 1920s and 1930s, but that seldom affects their approach to Eliot, Pound, and Hemingway. At the same time, incorporating noncanonical works has not necessarily guaranteed that these "new," much less traditional texts, are presented from a gender- and/or race-conscious perspective. The question of the canon can thus end up being narrowed to the problem of what one has time to add to an otherwise unaltered course. Further, as a range of critiques have indicated, consciousness about gender does not guarantee consciousness about race, and vice versa. The problem, then, is how "we" can develop that social consciousness, that historical perspective necessary to carry out Fox-Genovese's approach.

To be sure, the process of engaging in curricular change does help to alter consciousness. One learns something about marginality and about what is really at stake in academic structures through efforts to change them. And classroom discussions can act like consciousness-raising groups, particularly when they are dealing with texts with which instructors are relatively unfamiliar and about which, therefore, student responses may be more vigorous. But Western schooling assumes that we learn primarily by reading. In his 1845 *Narrative,* for example, Frederick Douglass writes:

> In the same book, I met with one of Sheridan's mighty speeches on and in behalf of Catholic emancipation. These were choice documents to me. I read them over and over again with unabated interest. They gave tongue to interesting thoughts of my own soul, which had frequently flashed through my mind, and died away for want of utterance.... The reading of these documents enabled me to utter my thoughts, and to meet the arguments brought forward to sustain slavery....[8]

I suspect that the central reason it is necessary to read noncanonical texts is that they *teach us* how to view experience through the prisms of gender, race, nationality, and other forms of marginalization. From what other source would, for example, Anglo teachers in New England begin to comprehend Southwestern Latino experience than the work of writers like Américo Paredes, Rolando Hinojosa, or Gloria Anzaldúa? Reading, I want to reiterate, is not the only way we learn about how power is structured, and how those at the margins define their own relationships to such structures; there is not substitute finally for eating the pear of social change. Still, reading is a vital way to gain power in a literate society. That is why marginalized groups have always had to struggle against usage or law to obtain access to the power of literacy—or, having obtained it, to get a hearing for their literary productions, which returns us to the question of the canon.

While I think Fox-Genovese is right about the importance of rereading the traditional canon, it also seems to me that the best lens for that rereading is provided by noncanonical works themselves. For their outlook is likely to be less constrained by the deep conservatism of academe than that of professors, however progressive. In a sense, what seems to be involved is a reversal of the usual process by which noncanonical texts are appraised from

the perspective and in the terms of those long established; rather, we are
learning to reread—and thus to decenter—canonical texts, such as *The Great
Gatsby* and *A Farewell to Arms,* from the perspectives provided by noncanonical works, like *The Girl* and *Their Eyes Were Watching God.* I have used
as the slogan of the Reconstructing American Literature project the statement
"so that the work of Frederick Douglass, Mary Wilkins Freeman, Agnes
Smedley, Zora Neale Hurston and others is read with the work of Nathaniel
Hawthorne, Henry James, William Faulkner, Ernest Hemingway and others."
I offer that not as an article of pluralist faith, but as, in the first instance, an
epistemological proposition. And, in the second instance, a challenge to theory and to history: What are the theoretical conceptions, the critical practices,
the historical designs, the ideas about function and audience, that must be
reconstructed *so that* these works can, indeed, be read?

Materials with which to answer those questions—at least with respect to
American culture—are being provided in a number of ways. One answer, I
think, is through the republication of lost or abandoned works, such as those
so notably recovered to us in Judith Fetterley's *Provisions* (Bloomington:
Indiana University Press, 1985), in Mary Helen Washington's *Invented Lives*
(Garden City: Anchor, 1987), in the Rutgers University Press American
Women Writers series, in the volumes Cathy Davidson has edited (and written) for Oxford University Press (like Susanna Rowson's *Charlotte Temple*),
and in the two black women writers series being issued by Beacon and Oxford
University Presses, respectively. The new *Heath Anthology of American Literature* (Lexington, Mass., 1990) represents a broad platform in this process
of canon change, a kind of still point in the changing cultural world, from
which future departures will undoubtedly be made. Such volumes force on
us very different conceptions of American literary and cultural history, simply
in order to account for the existence, much less the characteristics, of such
texts. They ask us to think not about the narrow group of works previously
categorized as "literature," but about that "broader, more humane [category]
of writing."[9] They also insist on a revised, broadened understanding of the
formal features of writing, as well as of the functions of and audiences for
such varied works. In addition, many new voices from outside the academic
literary circuit are being provided opportunities to be heard by specialized
presses, such as Arte Publico of Houston, Thunder's Mouth of New York,
or The Crossing Press of Trumansburg, New York.

The republication of a range of noncanonical writings and the wider distribution of a variety of new voices make possible, indeed demand, a different
range of historical and theoretical studies focused on the question of the
canon. Indeed, the failure to focus on this issue seriously limits what might
otherwise be a more vital critical practice. The collection *Reconstructing
American Literary History* edited by Sacvan Bercovitch (Cambridge: Harvard
University Press, 1986) offers a case in point. While the volume contains a
number of interesting essays, read in terms of the question of the canon it
produces more problems than it resolves. To begin with, there is the title.
"Reconstructing American Literature" is a phrase that has been defined by

a movement for change within the literary profession to mean an effort to revise the canon—as in the Northeast Modern Language Association section called Reconstructing American Literature. The use of this title for Bercovitch's volume illustrates how what is effectively a defense of the traditional canon can screen that fact by appropriating a sign invested with a certain power by a movement for change. A sign, but *not* what it has come to signify. For almost all of the essays in this collection, brilliant as some of them are, focus upon the canonical stalwarts—Emerson, Melville, Whitman, James, Eliot, and the like.

In the main the essays consist of *explication de textes,* elaborated by detailed analyses of the contemporary implications of key words and images and of the historical interrelationships between canonical figures like Emerson and the Jameses. Almost all the analysis of noncanonical work, apart from that assigned to the category "popular," is found in Robert Stepto's important essay on African-American ambivalence about literacy. To justify the title of the book, or even, in fact, to realize their potential as essays, most contributors needed to step outside the canon. A truly reconstructed view of the "ideologies of poetic modernism," to use, for example, Frank Lentricchia's title, might more clearly emerge by using the work of Charlotte Perkins Gilman, W.E.B. DuBois, and José Martí as lenses to understand aspects of modernist ideologies, male and female. Lentricchia interestingly claims that the works of Santayana, James, and Royce "are themselves collaborative modernist texts, the original metapoetic idiom of the youth of Eliot, Frost, and Stevens," in fact, "more expansive, detailed, and precise expressions of theory than anything written in prose by any of the important modern American poets" (p. 223). But the thrust of Santayana's attack on the genteel tradition that I discuss elsewhere must be understood as critical to the construction *not* of modernism but of *male* "high-modernist" sensibility. Surely it is essential to explicate the gendered character of such writing, especially in light of the most recent reconstructions of American poetic modernism by critics like Marianne DeKoven and Alicia Ostriker.[10] They make problematic what Lentricchia here seems to take for granted, that is, the identities—"Eliot, Frost and Stevens"—of the "important modern American poets," as well as the character of their work. Furthermore, the racial exclusivity of "mainstream" modernism, not to mention the deeply disturbing connections between modernist and colonialist sensibilities, can and should be illuminated by noncanonical writers like DuBois and Martí.[11] Finally, the now-traditional definition of poetic modernism as formally experimental but politically conservative depends, Cary Nelson has argued, upon sharply limiting the modernist canon, continuing to eliminate from literary history exponents of radicalism in function and subject as well as in form. Taking into account noncanonical writers such as Mina Loy, Mike Quin, Genevieve Taggard, and Sol Funeroff, as well as Claude McKay and Langston Hughes, Nelson suggests, forces us to rewrite modernist history in terms of a cultural struggle over conflicting definitions of poetry itself.[12] The work of critics like DeKoven, Ostriker, Nelson, and Elizabeth Ammons[13] on American modernism may stand here as instances of a much broader process, compelled by the question of the canon, of re-writing literary history. The new emergent portraits offer views not of settled traditions, being slightly augmented by the "really new," as Eliot conceived in "Tradition and the Individual Talent." Rather, cultural history emerges as a series of struggles over competing definitions not only of "tradition," but of culture itself.

Canonical issues appear by virtue of what Lentricchia does *not* say; Werner Sollors' essay, however, engages more directly the institutional implications of a changing canon. The bulk of Sollors' piece is, unfortunately, an assault on a straw man, Horace Kallen, an early advocate of cultural pluralism. To be sure, Kallen shared most of the racialist attitudes of his early twentieth-century contemporaries but his resemblance to any living intellectual really eludes me. Furthermore, by focusing on Kallen's racist ideas, Sollors largely misses the progressive impact of early pluralists, especially given the reactionary boosterism of post-World War I America.

Apart from the dubious issue of the paternity of cultural pluralism or the significance of such paternity, Sollors does touch upon some central issues. First, he correctly argues against the notion that you have to be Jewish to bake or evaluate Levy's rye bread, and also against the theory that ethnic (and one can read, as well, minority or female) writing can be defined entirely *within* a specific ethnic culture—as if one's marginalized status were an insulation against the power of "mainstream" culture to shape (but not determine) consciousness and art. Indeed, marginalized writing responds both to "internal" and "external" cultural influences and the impact of those influences changes over time. That should be clear by now. What is murky, however, are the implications of these realities for curriculum, academic programs, literary histories, and anthologies. Sollors complains that "literary pluralists" display a "dislike of mixings" and "would like to construct a mosaic of ethnic stories that relies on the supposed permanence, individuality, and homogeneity of each ancestral tradition. . . . " (p. 274). He also doubts that "the very same categories on which previous exclusivism was based" should "really be used as organizing concepts" (p. 255). I take it from these and other of his comments in this article that Sollors would be sceptical of the value of separate black studies or women's studies departments, of volumes devoted exclusively to the work of Chicanas, of surveys of or entries in literary histories on the writings of American women, of American literature anthologies that, for instance, present as a separate unit the work of the Harlem Renaissance writers. These seem to me to be the potentially dangerous conclusions implicit in Sollors' position.

The fact is that neither separation nor integration provide wholly satisfactory methods for presenting or studying marginalized cultures. On the one hand, simply to integrate the writing of Jean Toomer, Zora Neale Hurston, Langston Hughes and Nella Larsen—to speak of the most likely—with Pound, Hemingway, and Eliot misrepresents the milieu from which and in which black writers created; on the other hand, to place them solely within the context of the Harlem Renaissance underplays their qualities and influence as "modernist" authors. A separate women's studies, African-American or Chicano studies department runs the risk of falsifying by homogenizing the diverse experience of all black women and men in America; and that also may contribute to the ghettoization of female and minority studies as well as to the indifference of academics in other departments to such concerns. On the other hand, without such centers of intellectual work and hubs for political struggle, the culture and experiences of the marginalized will be marginalized even more systematically, or so the experiences of curriculum "integration" projects and American history strongly suggest. Few in this country are very comfortable with the notion of assigning jobs or housing on the basis of race or ethnicity, but without specific numerical goals and timetables, the effects of racism persist even unto a generation cured—as this is not—of racism. So it is, as I argue elsewhere, with respect to culture: The distinctive qualities of the arts of marginalized groups need to be determined and celebrated by viewing each group collectively even as we acknowledge how much male and female, as well as black, Latino, white, Indian, and Asian cultural traditions in the United States overlap. That requires processes *both* of separation and of integration. Sollors' critique of pluralism in the Bercovitch book seems to be an obstacle to this dual process.

It is not, I should say, that an emphasis on or celebration of difference is, in all circumstances, socially cohesive let alone demonstrably progressive. No one usefully could argue such a generalized position in view of the re-emergence of what can only be called tribalism in parts of Eastern Europe and the Middle East. The meaning and thus the value of cultural difference depends fundamentally on how it functions in particular societies at specific historical moments. Similarly, to be sure, with respect to a canon: Its establishment can and often does serve dominantly hegemonic functions, but it can also be, at least in theory, part of a process by which a society generates and maintains a necessary level of unity, and in certain circumstances, offers the opportunity for democratic participation to its members. Part of the current debate over cultural canons in the United States concerns the question of whether what is now necessary in this country is, above all, a unity of tradition (and if so, whose) or a fuller, indeed for the first time a meaningful, recognition of the character and importance of its diversity.

Sollors' contribution to this debate, as expressed in his own book, is by no means one-dimensional. But the choice of this essay to represent the approach of the Bercovitch volume to ethnicity and literature illustrates how the book appropriates from the universe of discourse on ethnicity an element that casts a narrowing political shadow. It also, perhaps, rationalizes an approach to writing literary history which differs sharply from that of the new *Columbia History of American Literature* edited by Emory Elliott. Elliott's book has been mocked (in the New York *Times Book Review,* for example) for taking multiple approaches, especially to noncanonical authors. But that seems to me to be one of its strengths. For while some of Sollors' strictures against the oversimplifications of cultural pluralism are well taken, the thrust of his argument is finally disabling to the effort to change existing power relationships within the literary community as well as outside it.

I have tried to suggest that the effort to reconstruct the canon involves a set of complex struggles: against the reactionary effort to impose a narrowed view of Western traditions on all; against the practice of academic formalism, which habitually avoids such canonical issues as "pedagogical"; with the parochialism of those who would simply substitute a local or individual set of texts for any canon; with the process—illustrated by the very names in the Reconstructing American Literature slogan quoted earlier—by which reconstructions harden into new canons; and even with sometimes allies, when their work seems to reenforce existing definitions of significance and thus of power. Those, I believe, have been the issues, and it is important to emphasize that they continue to be sharply contested. The competitive demands of academic life, like those of other markets under consumer capitalism, forever impel practitioners (like the Columbia University Press reader) to foreclose "old" debates in order to offer new products: corn toasters, orange corn toasters, cranberry-orange corn toasters; studies of minority texts, studies of the conditions of study of minority texts, studies of the studier studying the conditions of study of minority texts. . . . Further, looking at the canon-challenging *Heath Anthology of American Literature* (2 vols., Lexington, MA, 1990) and a document like the annual program issue of PMLA might lead one to conclude, given their enormous diversity, that the effort to expand the canon has triumphed and the issues I have charted can safely be laid to rest as we frantically try to make criticism new. That would be a mistake, for in the on-going contests for cultural authority it would be as foolish to assume that these questions are permanently decided as it would have been to suppose that Reconstruction or perhaps the Civil Rights Movement had settled the issues of race relations in the United States. Furthermore, in a number of important areas the question of the canon seems to me to be generating increasingly important scholarship.

One challenging direction is offered by cultural critics who question the privileging of "literary" texts implicit in many debates over a canon. If presumed aesthetic value no longer determines our choice between reading Henry James and Elizabeth Stuart Phelps, why read novels at all rather than, say, nineteenth-century medical or legal texts? They are, after all, often as interesting, and surely as reflective and probably more determinative of cultural assumptions about gender as fictions. Some of the most interesting syllabi I have recently seen do, in fact, combine traditionally-defined "literary" texts with those of mid-nineteenth-century physicians and social commentators (for example, Mayhew). Still, it would be shortsighted to slight the emotional power of "literary" narratives and of poetic language, or the prestige with which such forms have been invested in our culture. It is, I think, precisely to the socially constructed differences between, say, the authority of legal texts and the differing prestige of fiction, the power of "Roe v. Wade" to affect lives and the capacity of *The Color Purple* to invoke conflicted feelings, that cultural study most usefully can lead us.

For my own part, the most interesting frontiers of canon study have to do, in theoretical terms, with the implications of the material and institutional conditions of authorship and literary study, and with the functions of canons in establishing and maintaining boundaries (as well, in pedagogical terms, with the comparative study of canonical and marginalized texts about which I comment in another chapter). In her well-known article "Why Are There No Great Women Artists?" Linda Nochlin offered an institutional analysis of the processes by which art is created and valued. "The question 'Why are there no great women artists?' " she wrote, leads

> to the conclusion that art is not a free, autonomous activity of a superendowed individual, "influenced" by previous artists, and, more vaguely and superficially, by "social forces," but rather, that art making, both in terms of the development of the art maker and the nature and quality of the work of art itself, occurs in a social situation, is an integral element of the social structure, and is mediated and determined by specific and definable social institutions, be they art academies, systems of patronage, mythologies of the divine creator and artists as he-man or social outcast. . . . By stressing the *institutional*—that is, the public—rather than the *individual* or private preconditions for achievement in the arts, we have provided a model for the investigation of other areas in the field.[14]

Literary practitioners have, on the whole, been slow to take up this analytic challenge. Nina Baym has examined the "Melodramas of Beset Manhood" that provide a kind of exclusionary mythology. Jane Tompkins and Cathy Davidson have investigated the impact of particular publishing houses and practices, as well as the effect of peer networks, on the establishment and maintenance of reputations and thus of canons in the nineteenth century. Hazel Carby has explored the relationship of specific audience and educational objective to the texts of black women writers. More recently, Richard Brodhead has looked at how specific opportunities to enter the profession of authorship carried with them certain restrictions as to audience, subject, and convention—and thus implicitly, restrictions as to access to forms of composition, including those generally defined as significant or major. I have examined the effect of the post-World War I decline of women's literary clubs, and the enormous network they informed, on the radical reshaping of an American literary canon.[15] Such works are notable for a number of reasons. They demystify the processes by which reputations and canons are constructed; they offer fundamentally altered accounts of literary history and cultural relations; they define the origins and changing characteristics of the literary practices engaged in by noncanonical writers; they bring into focus contrasting readings of American history and culture provided for us by canonical and noncanonical works; and they reveal the material supports—or their lack—that prove critical not only to literary production but also to the survival of works of art—a point to which I shall return later. In short, the work of these critics helps us to understand canon formation and change in terms of concrete institutional developments at particular historical junctures.

Perhaps the most politically explosive example of such study is that contained in Martin Bernal's *Black Athena*.[16] Bernal argues that the generally accepted understanding of the origins and nature of classical Greek civilization was, in fact, constructed in Northern Europe during the mid-nineteenth century—constructed in such a way as to deny the rich Phoenician (Semitic) and Egyptian (African) influences that profoundly shaped Hellenic culture. A narrow canon of classical study was thus shaped within a definable institutional framework by identifiable intellectuals to serve particular political ends—having to do with a racist struggle to assert the dominance of Northern European, Aryan, cultures over those of Africa and Asia. Bernal's account of classical culture—indeed, of the origin of the Greek language—if sustained by further study undermines the politically-laden but ahistorical and simplistic image of Athens as the one true "cradle" of "our" civilization. But it also offers a particularly vivid instance of a more general point: that canons are not handed down from Mount Olympus, nor yet from Mount Horeb, but are the products of historically specific conflicts over culture and values.

Work like Bernal's also underlines the function of canons in defining and maintaining borders. A particular ethnic cast was given to "Western Civilization" by excluding from its definition, and from the study of its "monuments," other Asian and African texts and cultures. Similarly, academic discourse in the United States has traditionally defined "American literature" as the study of what is, finally, a part of *North* American culture. Recent work by critics like Gloria Anzaldúa and José Saldívar gives a significantly different cast to terms like "American" and also holds important implications for the classroom.[17] Beginning from Martí's concept of "our America," with its deliberately problematic possessive, and developing Roberto Fernández Retamar's reconceptualization of Caliban as cultural critic, Saldívar constructs a conception of American culture not limited by the borders, or even the power, of the United States. In so doing, he and Anzaldúa bring into question the very function of "American literature" as a field of study. It emerged and grew in its dominant form, as I document elsewhere, at particularly intense moments of North American nationalism. One might argue that, for example, the virtual exclusion of early Spanish and French exploration texts, or of black and Indian sermons and autobiographies from received definitions of "American literature" served the important ideological role of maintaining boundaries between what was truly "American," "ours," and what was "other," marginal. From this viewpoint, it is not surprising that debate over the canon has taken the forms I have outlined here. For when accepted borders are, from the perspective of those interested in maintaining them, "violated," a struggle will likely ensue to reconfirm boundaries—even if they are somewhat differently shaped. The efforts to desegregate schools, neighborhoods, and places of work, which developed in intensity during the 1950s and 1960s, were as we know closely followed by the canon debates in which we are engaged today. The question before us is who may inhabit the "neighborhoods" called "American literature," "western civilization," or "cultural literacy," how are the boundaries of these intellectual subdivisions to be redrawn *not* to keep "them" out but to reconstitute social and educational institutions in this country as truly equal.

Thus, I think, the canon debate leads out of a narrowly construed set of professional concerns and back into the broader social and political world. The efforts to keep noncanonical work in print and to provide for its wider distribution, the controversies over literary prizes, like that recently involving Toni Morrison, the debates over whether, or to what, the "American mind" is closed make it clear that canonical issues are not simply matters of academic dispute. Like any meaningful cultural concern, the question of the canon directly affects lives. There is a vital dialectic between the recognition of a writer like Morrison and the need to understand her predecessors, like Frances E. W. Harper, Nella Larsen, Ann Petry, and Gwendolyn Brooks; but more, between the creative aspirations of such writers and the lived experience of black women in American society. Likewise, a dialectic functions between accounts of the origin of "our" civilization and who shares power within it. What is at stake, after all—to return to the initial problem with the cultural maven of Reaganism, William Bennett—is what a society sees as important from its past to the construction of its future, who decides that, and on what basis.

To be sure, the ways to reunite canon study and political action in practice are not always self-evident. At one point, the demand to take up and to take seriously Frederick Douglass, W.E.B. DuBois, Charlotte Perkins Gilman, and Agnes Smedley could, and often did, precipitate sharp conflicts, not only in curriculum committees but in the wider communities concerned with education. Today, canon study is perhaps as popular a subject for academic disquisitions as poststructuralist theory, and the issues are publication and promotion, not black power and sexual politics. It should be no surprise that an institution like the academy could thus largely absorb a serious challenge to its assumptions and structures. After all, the *New York Review of Books* found the diagram of a molotov cocktail useful to selling magazines. But if the ideas that canons are socially constructed *by* people and *in* history, that they have always changed and can be changed, that they are deeply shaped by institutions and the material conditions under which writing is produced and consumed—if these and related ideas have essentially triumphed within the academy, they remain deeply conflicted outside scholastic walls. It is all but impossible, I am told, to convince a Congressperson of the importance of studying Zora together with—God forbid in place of—Ernest. That is no defeat; it says to me, in fact, that while the advocates of a broad, multicultural canon have consolidated our position within most educational institutions, the Bennetts and Blooms have been hard at work in the public arenas. To me the next challenge is to shift the locus of struggle precisely to such public forums, even now as the academic right-wing bemoans the triumph of het-

erogeneity in the university. For all the academic fascination with herme-
neutics and epistemology, it is in the realms of ethics and politics that the
question of the canon must now be contested.

Notes

1. As in Lynne Cheney, *50 Hours: A Core Curriculum for College Students*
(Washington, D.C.: National Endowment for the Humanities, 1989).
2. Barbara Herrnstein Smith, *Contingencies of Value: Alternative Perspectives for
Critical Theory* (Cambridge: Harvard University Press, 1988).
3. Many of these issues of the social functions of criticism and the political
character of what was not then called the "canon" were being discussed in the late
1960s among those who contributed to the volume called *The Politics of Literature*,
Louis Kampf and Paul Lauter, eds. (New York: Pantheon, 1970).
Moreover, the use of the term "theory" to designate the various structuralist and
poststructuralist forms of criticism currently being ground out by literary intellectuals
amounts to an effort to appropriate to such writing alone what has become an academic
honorific. It suggests that those of us who wrote in the 1960s or before had no "theory";
that we were, as critics both of the right and the left have suggested, mindless activists,
chirruping onto our not so innocent pages our "native woodnotes wild."
4. For example, Susan Hardy Aiken et al., *Changing Our Minds: Feminist Transformations of Knowledge* (Albany, N.Y.: State University of New York Press, 1988);
Patricia Hill Collins and Margaret L. Andersen, *An Inclusive Curriculum: Race, Class,
and Gender in Sociological Instruction* (Washington, D.C.: American Sociological
Association, 1987); Adelaida R. Del Castillo, *Women's History in Transition: Theory,
Methods and Content in Mexican/Chicana History* (Los Angeles: University of California Chicano Studies Research Center, 1985); Ellen DuBois et al., *Feminist Scholarship: Kindling in the Groves of Academe* (Urbana, Ill.: University of Illinois, 1985);
Diane Fowlkes and Charlotte McClure, eds., *Feminist Visions: Towards a Transformation of the Liberal Arts Curriculum* (Tuscaloosa, Ala.: University of Alabama Press,
1984); Elizabeth Minnich, Jean O'Barr and Rachel Rosenfeld, eds., *Reconstructing
the Academy* (Chicago: University of Chicago Press, 1988); Bonnie Spanier, Alexander
Bloom, and Darlene Boroviak, eds., *Towards a Balanced Curriculum* (Cambridge,
Mass.: Schenkman, 1984); Dale Spender, ed., *Men's Studies Modified: The Impact of
Feminism on the Academic Disciplines* (New York: Pergamon Press, 1981).
5. An excellent illustration of this approach is provided in a reading of Aristotle's
Politics provided by Elizabeth Victoria Spelman in *Inessential Woman: Problems of
Exclusion in Feminist Thought* (Boston: Beacon, 1988).
6. Myra Jehlen raises a similar set of concerns in "How the Curriculum is the
Least of Our Problems," *ADE Bulletin* 93 (Fall 1989): 5–7.
7. See, for example, Philip E. Jacobs, *Changing Values in College: An Exploratory
Study of the Impact of College Teaching* (New York: Harper, 1957), and Kenneth A.
Feldman and Theodore M. Newcomb, *The Impact of College on Students*, 2 vols. (San
Francisco: Jossey-Bass, 1969).
8. Frederick Douglass, *Narrative of the Life of Frederick Douglass, An American
Slave, Written by Himself* (New York: Signet, 1968), pp. 54–55.
9. The distinction is that drawn by Wayne Franklin in "The 'Library of America'
and the Welter of American Books," *Iowa Review* 15 (Spring/Summer, 1985): 190.

10. Marianne DeKoven, *A Different Language: Gertrude Stein's Experimental Writing* (Madison, Wis.: University of Wisconsin Press, 1983); Alicia Ostriker, *Stealing the Language: The Emergence of Women's Poetry in America* (Boston: Beacon, 1986).

11. Apart from the well-known essays on education and art in *The Souls of Black Folk* (1903) and *Darkwater* (1920), see, for example, DuBois' "The Negro in Literature and Art," *Annals of the American Academy of Political and Social Sciences* XLIX (September 1913): 233–37 and the chapter on "African Culture" in *The Negro* (1915). See also José Martí, *On Art and Literature: Critical Writings,* Elinor Randall and Luis A. Baralt, trans. (New York: Monthly Review Press, 1982); *Our America: Writings on Latin America and the Struggle for Cuban Independence,* Elinor Randall, trans., with additional translations by Juan de Onis and Roslyn Held Foner, Philip S. Foner, ed. (New York: Monthly Review Press, 1977).

12. Cary Nelson, *Repression and Recovery: Modern American Poetry and the Politics of Cultural Memory, 1910–1945* (Madison, Wis.: University of Wisconsin Press, 1989).

13. See particularly in this regard Elizabeth Ammon's important comparison of Edith Wharton and Jessie Redmon Fauset in *College Literature* 14 (1987): 207–218.

14. Linda Nochlin, *Women, Art, and Power and Other Essays* (New York: Harper and Row, 1988), pp. 158, 176.

15. Nina Baym, "Melodramas of Beset Manhood: How Theories of American Fiction Exclude Women Authors," in *The New Feminist Criticism: Essays on Women, Literature and Theory,* Elaine Showalter, ed. (New York: Pantheon, 1985), pp. 63–80; Jane Tompkins, *Sensational Designs* (New York: Oxford University Press, 1985); Cathy Davidson, *Revolution and the Word: The Rise of the Novel in America* (New York: Oxford University Press, 1986); Hazel V. Carby, *Reconstructing Womanhood* (New York: Oxford University Press, 1987); Richard Brodhead, in a paper delivered at the 1988 convention of the Modern Language Association, New Orleans, La.; Paul Lauter in an unpublished paper, "Clubs and Canons: Nineteenth-Century Women's Study Groups and 'American Literature' " (1989). Other notable instances are provided in Hortense Spillers' and Marjorie Pryse's *Conjuring* (Bloomington, Ind.: Indiana University Press, 1985) and Carolyn Karcher's splendid introduction to Lydia Maria Child's *Hobomok and Other Writings on Indians* (New Brunswick, N.J.: Rutgers University Press, 1986).

16. Martin Bernal, *Black Athena* (New Brunswick, N.J.: Rutgers University Press, 1987).

17. See, for example, Gloria Anzaldúa, *Borderlands/La Frontera: The New Mestiza* (San Francisco: Spinsters/Aunt Lute, 1987); and José David Saldívar, "The School of Caliban: Pan-American Autobiography," in *Essays in Multicultural American Autobiography,* James Payne, ed. (forthcoming), and "The Dialectics of Our America: Genealogy, Cultural Critique and Literary History," book ms.

Part II

"I'd better consider my national resources"

The University and the Republic

Retrenchment—What the Managers Are Doing

When part of this article was first written in 1974, large-scale retrenchment of college faculty was a relatively new phenomenon. To be sure, there had been occasional layoffs when an institution threatened to go broke, and the 1940 AAUP statement on tenure provided that it could be nullified for reasons of "financial exigency." But such cutbacks were infrequent and unusual, the exceptions that proved the solidity of college job security. What was new in the early 1970s was the invocation of retrenchment processes *not* necessarily because a college was edging toward bankruptcy but because it wanted to change its programs, its "product." That seemed to many of us an outrageous violation of collegiate norms. Many faculty had been led into teaching precisely because of its stability and its insulation from market forces. Now the market in all its worst forms was invading the campus. Furthermore, we believed, decisions about what could be taught were being removed from the hands of their proper judges, the faculty, and appropriated by a fleet of increasingly remote administrators. No one's work was safe! The essential quality of the academic community was at stake! Thus, when colleagues in History or English or Education received pink slips, we bitterly protested.

But it rapidly became clear that protest was not enough, that the new breed of collegiate managers, whose skills had been honed by the student activism of the previous decade, were not going to be impressed with impassioned speeches at faculty Senate meetings or with letters to the student newspaper—or, indeed, to the New York *Times*.[1] Nor were faculty unions— such as they then were—going to be much help; indeed, our union president shrugged that "you can't force Ford to keep making Edsels forever"—a remark which hardly endeared him to laid-off historians. We found that we had to understand this new phenomenon better if we were to have any chance to organize against it. Why was retrenchment coming upon faculties at this historical moment? How valid were the arguments of declining enrollments and needed flexibility being made by college managers? What were our legal

Parts of this chapter were first presented at a Modern Language Association convention panel in 1974 and later published in the first issue of *Radical Teacher*. It has been recast and brought up to date for presentation here.

rights and their legal constraints? What strategies could we develop to counter those being generated in managerial circles, and put into practice against the interests of faculty?

To pursue such issues, the Radical Caucus held a well-attended meeting at the 1974 convention of the Modern Language Association. Part of this chapter initially constituted one of the presentations. The other two focused on the underlying bases of college layoffs, and on practical approaches to fighting cutbacks. In his talk, Cadwell Ray noted a number of causes for retrenchment. The war on Southeast Asia had diverted substantial funds from other "Great Society" programs. Rising costs of colleges had not been met by equivalent rises in income: Inelastic state tax systems, for example, failed to bring in needed revenues, and competition by other social sectors for scarcer dollars left less for education. Colleges were also vulnerable to a backlash against the 1960s activism for which they had provided a base, and were specific targets of the Nixon administration's attack on "effete intellectual snobs" and a generally "overeducated" workforce.

It was in such a political context that administrators first deployed "retrenchment" as an important tool of college management. The context has changed somewhat in a decade and a half: The courts have generally upheld management's power to retrench and the rationales for doing so have been elaborated. Most of all, in the intervening years, the practice of retrenchment has become more systematic and subtle; indeed, the major change since the mid–1970s has been the *institutionalization* of retrenchment in planning and in practice. Books and manuals have multiplied, repeated studies have been developed to determine which programs have priority and which might be slated for discontinuance.[2] Sadly, however, the basic situation has not altered sufficiently to outdate the analysis which follows. Indeed, it appears that higher education is heading into another round of conflict over management-initiated cutbacks, prompted in part by "consumer" resistance to the rapid upward spiral of private institutions' tuition fees[3] and, as this chapter suggests, by the desire of administrators to regain greater control over programs. I have brought the details of this chapter up to date, but I have also tried to retain its original tone and language, for I believe its 1960s-bred outrage is rather a better response to what has proved to be a destructive assault on faculties and the academy generally than the equivocations of postmodernist politics.

I

In the aftermath of 1960s expansion and activism, college managers developed a rationale for retrenchment that, in 1990 as in 1974, runs roughly as follows:

1. College enrollments are down;
2. Costs of educating students are up;
3. Student interests and demands are shifting;
4. Therefore, the fewer available dollars have to be allocated by the

application of cost-benefit techniques and under the guidance of a more business-like management.

Each of these statements was, and remains, inaccurate, half-truths or less; taken together, they present not a reasonable argument but the ideology of a powerful sector of American society. I shall examine each of these statements, suggest alternative explanations of retrenchment, and then turn to the managerial objectives in retrenchment and their tactics for carrying it out, which were first being developed in the early 1970s and are now well-sharpened by use.

First, college enrollments were not then down, though the rate of increase had fallen. In fact, the expansion of enrollments between 1973 and 1974 (621,000) was striking, and the following year's increase (961,000) was the largest in a decade.[4] Since 1974, in fact, collegiate enrollments have risen by over 2.3 million,[5] despite the persistent predictions of serious declines, despite statistics showing reductions in the size of the "normal" college-age population, and despite occasional downturns. To be sure, enrollments in some colleges, in some localities, and in some programs have fluctuated; indeed, nearly one-third of all institutions "underwent enrollment decline" of some size in the 1970s.[6] In a couple of years, primarily in response to the 1974–75 and 1981–82 recessions, total enrollments did decline very modestly. But the fact was that in the early 1970s, state universities in New York, Michigan, North Carolina, Illinois, and Florida, for example, were placing heavily constricting *limits* on enrollment. In 1975, the State University of New York had turned away as many as 50,000 applicants. In short, more people than ever before have been attending American colleges.[7]

Focusing on the supposed decline in enrollments functioned to obscure more fundamental demographic realities: For example, the proportion of eighteen to twenty-four-year olds attending college varied from 24 percent to 59 percent, depending on the state; in the fall of 1973, entering classes contained one million more men than women; of low-income people of the usual college age, no more than about 15 percent were gaining entrance to postsecondary education. Statistics also made clear that substantial numbers of "older" people—i.e., past twenty-four years old—previously bypassed by higher education would return to school *if* opportunities and relevant programs were developed for them.

Two points emerged from such figures: The sweeping "declining enrollments" argument for retrenchment was, and remains, false in most situations, and certainly in terms of the overall picture. Additionally, and critically, who goes to college, and how many people go, are not independent variables, but are directly related to *what* colleges offer, *how much* college costs, and the kind of culture colleges offer potential enrollees. Nothing illustrates that more dramatically than the fact that by 1979 more women than men were enrolled in colleges, and by 1986 the disparity was about 600,000 in favor of women. Most colleges sought actively to recruit more women (as well as more mature and part-time students[8]), provided them with more attention and services,[9] and thus were able to change the projections that had been delusively based upon the continuation of the same predominantly male pattern of student enrollments. To be sure, in some institutions enrollments were maintained by admitting less well-prepared students. But that practice calls, if anything, for hiring *additional* staff to meet the greater needs of such students.

Second, costs were up for education in 1974, and they have continued to climb even more rapidly since. But that is not a natural phenomenon, like the tides. Rising costs reflect a general inflation, of course, but they also register shifts in economic resources from one area to another. If a state or private college must pay exorbitant prices to heat classrooms, it has less money for scholarships or for paying teachers, but the oil companies have more money for investment and profit. Similarly, if the government increases the budget for weapons procurement more rapidly than inflation, but increases educational spending at less than the rate of inflation, obviously it shifts resources away from education and those who provide it, and toward the military and those who provide it. Educational economists argue that colleges were caught in the 1970s in a squeeze between rapidly rising expenditures and increasingly restricted income.[10] Federal spending—which could be based on borrowing—declined relatively under Nixon and his successors and the states, far more limited in their abilities or willingness to raise funds, had to take up more of the burden, which they were largely unwilling to do.[11] While this analysis is true as far as it goes, it utterly misses the political choices—never irreversible—that lay behind these fiscal decisions. In addition, when governments decrease the proportion of educational costs paid from tax levies, and if those costs remain stable or continue to climb, then the burden of payment falls increasingly on private individuals (or their parents) seeking the commodity of education. Private individuals are, of course, far more sensitive to such costs than they are to precisely how the tax dollar is divided; in fact, the greatest single factor discouraging students from attending college is rising costs. Moreover, to the individuals seeing a college degree priced out of their range, it can easily come to seem that the colleges themselves—which impose the tuition hikes—are responsible, not the politicians and corporate leaders determining such fund shifts. Thus the political support for higher education further erodes. And this is critical. For while all of these economic factors have been at work, the central point here is that such shifts of resources reflect social and political decisions made by *people* who have *power,* not the working of some ineluctable economic gods.

The questions we needed to ask—and have continued to ask with perhaps diminished impact—are not simply how to "adjust" to new economic realities, but whose interests are being served, and how, by the movement of money away from all human services, including education, and into other areas of spending? And whose interests are finally served by the increasing privatization of the costs of critical services like education, health care, and housing? It is not that the nation's economic problems are illusory; rather, the issue has been who will bear the burden of such economic problems. The decision to make education more expensive[12] and less available means that, in part, the burden was shifted to those for whom this desirable commodity has become much dearer. And in part, the consequences of such economic shifts also has fallen upon the educational workforce, the faculty faced with retrenchment.

Third, student interests do indeed fluctuate, but such changes do not descend from the sky. Like other consumption patterns—private autos, stereo equipment, deodorants—they are manipulated and used. If businesses announce (as they did in the Nixon years) that they will hire, and help support, students in business programs, it will be no surprise, especially in recessionary periods, that students will seek to enroll in business programs.[13] If one of the remaining sources of financial aid is LEAA, there will be no shortage of corrections officers, guards, or cops. Such shifts in students' interests are not accidental, and they do serve some clear economic interests. An unsettled economy offers corporations the opportunity to push onto the educational system even more responsibility for training the workforce, both to particular specialities and to more docile behavior than the collegiate population demonstrated in the sixties.

In striving for more "career-oriented" programs, college managers have taken advantage of the fact that traditional liberal arts curricula were brought into deep disrepute during the student movement of the sixties. While many faculty have yearned for the dear days prior to the uprisings, and have held tenaciously to antiquated divisions of knowledge or definitions of subject matter, college managers, acting in the name of "student interest," seized the initiative of innovation in the early 1970s and in many respects have retained it. That they have, by espousing a marketplace philosophy, produced a cheapened and standardized brand of education, more amenable to corporate than to student interests, only gradually became clear. In short, the manipulation of shifts in student demand, like the manipulation of who bears the burden of an "economic crunch," is highly political and is therefore another focus for struggle.

Fourth, in such a political context, cost-benefit analysis is by no means a neutral tool; nor, one need hardly say, is collegiate management a disinterested party. In fact, as I shall indicate below, a main objective of retrenchment policies is to center increasing control over resources, personnel, and curriculum in the hands of college managers and those to whom they report: the boards of trustees, generally indistinguishable from industrial or financial boards of directors.

In sum, in the early 1970s funds began to be diverted from higher education, thus making it more difficult for many students, especially those from poor and working-class families, to be able to attend college. Those who made it into the academy were increasingly channelled into supposedly job-related curricula, whose real effect was to narrow their educations and make them less mobile and therefore more pliable to the needs and wishes of their bosses. Meanwhile, those excluded from college were even more tightly locked into their job stratum, or out of jobs altogether.

The management argument can thus be reformulated:

1. The college-going population continues to increase, although the rate of increase varies depending on locale, sex, age, and general economic conditions; how large the increase gets and who goes to college depend on the amount of money available for education and more profoundly on what is taught, both by the curriculum and by a college's culture;
2. All costs are up; how much money is available for education is a question that will be determined not by economic "laws" but in political struggle;[14]
3. Students seek a meaningful education; if more of the vague exposure to "culture" and dissociated facts familiar from high school is the only alternative offered to accounting and business-letter writing, many will choose the latter;
4. What kind of and how much education the available dollars will buy is a fundamental political question not to be decided by technical devices nor by technocrats.

In many ways the key issue is not whether there shall be more or less education, but what kind of education there shall be, who shall get it, whose interests it serves, and who decides. In these matters, teachers and other intellectuals need to hearken to the popular wisdom that doubts the value of more teachers simply doing more of the same things. If support among the people is to be won back for education and if cutbacks are thus to be successfully resisted, it is necessary to reformulate in concrete and meaningful terms what, beyond credentials of less and less value, is important in education. In this effort, many faculty shall be pitted against the definitions imposed by college managers and those they serve. What follows is an effort to understand how the managers work, and toward what; in particular, how they have used retrenchment procedures to attempt to gain greater control over jobs, curriculum, and students.

II

Both the concept and the practice of "retrenchment" expanded rapidly during the Nixon years. The 1940 "Statement of Principle on Academic Freedom and Tenure," endorsed both by the American Association of University Professors (AAUP) and the Association of American Colleges (AAC), limits retrenchment to one cause: "financial exigency." And, in many institutions, by contract, practice, or endorsement of this statement, *bona fide* financial exigency remains the only legitimate cause of retrenchment. AAUP's 1968 document called "Recommended Institutional Regulations on Academic Freedom and Tenure" adds to financial exigency, for reasons I have never been able to fathom, "program or departmental discontinuance." In effect, that addition, however it was meant, opened the gates since it effectively assented to administrative claims to control—annulling even considerations of tenure—over curriculum and therefore of staff. How wide the gates had swung is illustrated by the contract signed in 1974 between the State University of New York (SUNY) and its professional staff union, the United University Professions. The retrenchment clause reads as follows:

> Retrenchment shall be defined as the termination of the employment of any academic or professional employee during any appointment, other than a temporary appointment which may be terminated at any time, as a result of financial exigency, reallocation of resources, reorganization of degree or curriculum offerings or requirements, reorganization of academic or administrative structures, programs or functions or curtailment of one or more programs or functions University-wide or at such level of organization of the University as a campus, department, unit, program or such other level of organization of the University as the Chancellor or his designee deems appropriate.

Not surprisingly, this contract clause was used to define Russian History as an appropriate "unit" for retrenchment in one institution and the graduate teaching of astronomy in another—and thus to fire the "unit" members.

Nor will it surprise anyone that the use of retrenchment provisions likewise grew rapidly. A 1974 study of 163 institutions in fourteen states showed a 291 percent increase in retrenchment between 1971 and 1974. A total of 954 faculty jobs in these institutions had been lost during that period; 74 percent of four-year private and 66 percent of four-year public institutions reported retrenchment activities.[15] During this period, eighty-eight faculty were retrenched out of jobs in the Wisconsin state system. At Bloomfield College in New Jersey, thirteen were fired, eleven of whom were tenured (they won a court decision reinstating them). At Southern Illinois, 104 were retrenched, twenty-eight of whom were tenured and another twenty-eight of whom were on continuing appointment. In the Kansas state system, at least sixty-two met the axe; at Murray State in Kentucky, twenty-one (eleven tenured). The 1975–76 SUNY budget projection called for "elimination" or "abolition" (to use its words) of fifty-eight faculty positions in some colleges, while adding faculty lines in others; in fact, 103 faculty were retrenched by 1976, sixty-two of whom were tenured. And all of that came before the New York City fiscal crisis and the elimination of over 1,000 jobs at the City University.

And even more radical propositions were in the wings. One pair of educational managers proposed what they described as a "Decentralized Market Mechanism" (DMM or Dim). Dim called for providing students with educational "credits," like vouchers, that they could use to purchase educational services—i.e., courses. If your courses don't sell, you're out of work.[16] This market manager's nightmare of educational planning might seem bizarre to teachers, but it is not all that different, except in degree, from the increasingly rigid use of measures like cost per student credit hour to decide whom to fire. And the idea behind Dim has been revived periodically, most recently in connection with proposals for National Youth Service.

In the context of a vastly expanded use of retrenchment processes over the last two decades, what have college managers sought to accomplish, what have been their long-range strategies, and what are the particular tactics they have devised to carry our retrenchment? First, as is usually the case with bureaucrats, they have been concerned to protect their own domains and, at the center of that concern, to keep their own jobs. One rarely hears of administrators being retrenched. In SUNY, for example, the 1975–76 Governor's budget called for eliminating only eight "instructional support" positions along with fifty-eight faculty; not all or even any of those eight were necessarily administrators. In fact, retrenchment itself, like almost any other academic procedure nowadays, seems to spawn *new* administrators: offices of Institutional Research, Budget Planning, and even what one might call ADF—Aid to Decapitated Faculty. There are, if anything, more administrators, not less, as the great shadow of Parkinson's Law falls across the desiccated landscape.

A related concern of administrators is to cover over planning errors, poor management procedures, and similar misfortunes of prior years. Axing employees and programs implicitly carries the implication that poor judgment in planning led to their being aboard in the first place. Wouldn't a perceptive manager have foreseen contraction in the boom time of the 1960s? Weren't contingencies called for before the wolf approached the door? But this isn't Maoist China—we don't invite bureaucrats to criticize themselves and improve, nor have we a convenient Liu Xiao-chi or Deng Xiaoping to blame for official folly, so excuses need to be found: "unforeseeable" shifts in student demand, "irresponsible" faculty pressure, the zeitgeist. And studies related to retrenchment are invariably future-oriented, concerned with where "we" have to go, not with who got us into the soup.

A major strategic objective of management, related to covering itself, is shifting the burden of the problem onto the faculty. It seems particularly difficult for faculty to acknowledge that this is a critical goal of management, since "faculty participation" in retrenchment decisions is often posed as a central objective for faculty organizations to achieve. I shall examine this matter in detail below; suffice it here to point to the obvious: The chestnuts don't burn when it isn't your hand in the fire. The key distinction here is between participation in decisions about *whether* to retrench at all—which management shows no inclination whatever to share—and participation in the implementation of retrenchment—in which management is anxious to ensnare faculty.

One other strategic objective encourages management to seek faculty participation, while two more impel them to limit it. The latter concern control over curricula and over selection of faculty slated for elimination. In their *College Management* review of "Staff Reduction Policies," Joanne M. Sprenger and Raymond E. Schultz posed as a primary recommendation a process of "continuous review" of academic programs by management:

> An institution or system should install a process of continuous program review for planning, establishing priorities and *moving available resources* from low to high priority programs. Existing programs should be reviewed according to pre-determined criteria in order to curtail, phase out or consolidate those judged to be unproductive or unnecessarily duplicative [italics added].
>
> (pp. 22–23)

In other words, with funds short and faculty organizations relatively weak, take advantage of the retrenchment crisis to seize control over curriculum from the faculty and its committees. In management circles this is called "recapturing institutional flexibility."[17] This was precisely the model adopted by Southern Illinois University when it fired 104 faculty, mainly from the liberal arts and social sciences, while *at the same time* hiring new staff in programs like Correctional Services, Secretarial and Office Specialties, and Mortuary Science and Funeral Service. Management tactics in pursuit of this objective, to which I shall turn shortly, will make it clearer that what is involved is an effort to transfer power over what teachers teach from the faculty itself to collegiate managers who need never step through a classroom door.

A different kind of transfer of power—over personnel—is implied in numerous management proposals to take advantage of the retrenchment scare to eliminate faculty "deadwood." Again, tactics will tell us more about this goal. What needs to be underlined here is that college management, like its peers in Texas Air or Consolidation Fuel and Iron, regards periods of economic contraction as opportunities to win greater control over jobs. In the early 1970s this was particularly important since court decisions and growing union strength had begun to limit management's prerogatives in hiring and firing.

Finally, a mainspring of management's action with respect to retrenchment is its imperative to keep the peace. If matters get out of hand on campus, if faculty protest and students march, it doesn't matter whether an administrator is at fault—in the eyes of those who pay him, he is responsible. Thus from the management point of view, even planning for retrenchment is dependent on campus peace and quiet:

> It should be apparent that the successful utilization of operational analysis depends upon a climate of institutional mental health receptive to change. Participants, e.g., faculty members, should be willing to consider and accept change—reassess the objectives of existing programs, make alterations to meet new objectives and annually audit to assess the successful movement toward stated goal objectives.[18]

In the words of Todd Furniss, one of the major spokespersons for management in such matters, "A campus . . . low in anxiety and conflict may be a suitable goal for retrenchment procedures." It is for such reasons that managers have come to prefer cutting entire programs, and doing it quickly, rather than trimming here and there. You don't want centers of angry and unhappy faculty hanging around and stirring up their colleagues.[19]

III

Within the framework of these administrative objectives, management has developed a set of retrenchment tactics. To begin with, there is planning. On most campuses there are now plans for retrenchment and for monitoring programs and departments in anticipation of possible retrenchment. Even on small campuses one increasingly finds bureaus of institutional research, study, or planning, and special funds budgeted for research projects related to possible retrenchment. Why this growing emphasis on planning, even as it becomes increasingly clear that much academic forecasting, and especially that sort based on manpower projections, has been inaccurate or misleading?[20] In the first place, there is what we might call the Herman Kahn tactic: Once you get people talking about the possibility of a set of events—say thermonuclear war or widespread job cutbacks—such events shift, by virtue simply of discussion, from the category of the unlikely, the remote, the obscene, not worth discussion, to the category of the possible—not desirable, to be sure, but necessary to talk about, even to plan for. Once you begin to discuss retrenchment, then to plan for its possibility, even its eventuality, its advent seems less an avoidable catastrophe, more an unfortunate but natural consequence of immutable economic activities, like *the* earthquake, for whose coming every California institution has well-developed plans and instructions. So college administrators are advised in the literature to begin discussions of the possibilities of retrenchment with their divisional directors, chairpersons, and senior faculty. Share with them, it is urged, the literature in the field; establish task forces to examine the options that might, in one or another set of circumstances, become available.

Planning also provides the framework, in fact the excuse, for gathering information. It its statement on retrenchment, the AAC says that "every effort must be made to determine the nature of the fiscal limitations and within those constraints to establish appropriate educational priorities"—a reasonable sounding objective for institutional research. In fact, however, the more realistic college managers phrase it another way: You must, they say, "build the case for staff reduction."[21] You must have ammunition ready for any opposition on campus and, even more important, to establish in court if it comes to that that a *bona fide* fiscal emergency exists. In the Bloomfield College case, for example, the court ruled that the college had failed to prove that such a fiscal emergency existed and that it was prohibited by contract from retrenching for other reasons. Thus, in the name of being prepared, administrators increasingly collect data on every aspect of institutional financing, on student-faculty ratios, on enrollments and their changes, on admissions trends, on personnel, and on statements of program needs and quality. How far this process is being carried out may be inferred from the fact that some institutions are now demanding of faculty transcripts of their undergraduate as well as their graduate records. Should retrenchment have to be carried out, and should some "objective" criteria be sought on which to base the decision about who stays and who goes, matters like one's grade point average or the variety of courses taken might be useful. Your "A" in Chaucer may balance the scale toward you and away from the other Assistant Professor who had "B's" in The Latin Satirists and Restoration Drama! Absurd? No more so, in its way, than hanging decisions on nothing but the cost per student credit hour.

Gathering such information has an additional virtue: It involves widening circles of the faculty in the process that may lead to individuals being retrenched. Chairpeople are asked to collect data, teachers in charge of a program are involved in its evaluation, external teams descend every year or two. Thus responsibility is diffused, the hand that holds the knife that cuts the job is hidden in the crowd of participants.

By emphasizing widespread planning, you also have the great advantage of choosing the terrain on which the issues will be fought. Students of guerilla warfare know that if a guerilla band fights an enemy rich in troops, tanks, big guns, and aircraft on a level plain, where all the enemy's resources will give him the advantage, the guerillas will surely be lost. Victory for the guerilla depends largely on the careful choice of terrain to emphasize the advantages the guerillas have of mobility, surprise, and morale. Administrators will always be in better positions if they can force the issues to be fought on the terrain of cost-benefit ratios, enrollment projections, and elaborate statistical models. In the first place, there is momentum, which makes political decisions into "natural" outgrowths of data.

> Adding to these [numerous] qualitative reports was a management information system that revealed a great deal about admissions demand, enrollment trends, degrees awarded, faculty workload, relative program costs, and other data elements. Against this backdrop, the decisions [about program discontinuance] can be seen as a culminating step in a much longer process of analysis. All that was necessary was for the administration and the faculty committees to develop a system for organizing the voluminous data in an orderly fashion.[22]

Second, management has people with no other jobs than to prepare such information in a way suited to their purposes. The Office of Analytic Studies at the college at which I taught invariably prepared statistical material to conform to the preferences and objectives of the administration; corrections might be made in meetings, but I never saw them reflected in subsequent written documents. We took to preparing our own statistics, on the theory that you can't beat something with nothing, but that involved major commitments of time borrowed from preparing classes, scholarship, or sleep. Third, it is true that student interests are volatile and are subject to manipulation by the pressure of propagandists for, say, "career education." Student enrollments will shift, and if the issue is fought on statistical grounds, the clever administrator can choose which set of shifting statistics to use in order to justify cutbacks. At a Florida university, for example, the dean explained pending cuts in Arts and Sciences as a function of projected declines in student interest. It turned out that Arts and Sciences enrollments grew by 45 percent between 1972 and 1973, and slumped by only 3 percent in 1974. Nevertheless, heads were to roll, regardless of how good a case the Arts and Sciences people might make for the educational integrity of their programs. Objectivity is the claim; manipulation is the game.

How one plans ahead thus is clearly as significant as why. Increasingly, academic planning has taken the form of statistically-based cost-benefit or "operational" analyses. Robert H. Maier and James W. Kolka argue for the virtues of "operational analysis" in their retrenchment "Primer"—and it is important to remember that retrenchment *is* the context for their ideas:

> In order to be externally responsive to requests for accountability and internally responsive to a plan for the allocation of resources, the university community must engender a desire to periodically evaluate and stimulate the goals articulated by the faculty and administration. . . . Departments should utilize operational analysis as a method to justify or expand existing programs. [The corollary, unstated here, is that it can be used to justify cuts as well.] Hopefully, the following types of statements could be expected. "We can demonstrate to the dean that we can accomplish our planned expansion at lower cost." "It is part of our responsibility to recommend changes in policy." "Let's challenge tradition and attempt this on a trial basis for 3 years."[23]

"Operational analysis" is thus presented less as a means for really finding out something—in that regard it is remarkably simpleminded—than as a technique for maneuvering departmental policy-making into a framework acceptable to the dean. The department is modeled as the passive (female?) organism in which "desire" must be "engendered" and responsiveness stimulated so that it can satisfy the accountable, goal-oriented (and male?) dean!

Cost-benefit techniques are applied to education in the following manner: " . . . a program competing for undesignated dollars must be more *beneficial* than all other programs that might be supported by the same undesignated dollars."[24] The questions, of course, are what is to be construed as "beneficial," to whom, and who makes that determination. The article that presents this cost-benefit approach suggests a number of criteria of beneficiality, many of which remain as subjective as the term "beneficial" itself: for example, relative worth of programs; whether sufficient resources are available to do a program well in the first place; complementariness—whether one program supports others; substitutability—whether something else will do; whether a program builds on what already exists at an institution. Experience suggests, however, that in the vast majority of instances—especially of cutbacks as distinct from program expansion—the fundamental criteria are student-faculty ratios, cost per student credit hour, and like measures. The more one views the practical effects of such educational planning—the labored annual studies read by three bureaucrats, the detailed program projections ignored even by them, the endless unopened collections of faculty vitae and yearly accomplishments—the more one concludes that plans constitute elaborate smokescreens behind which the critical decisions about retention or elimination of programs and jobs are made by educational managers.

That is true, even, of the efforts to pose "objective" criteria to determine, in retrenchment, who is fired and who is retained. In certain respects, objective criteria are useful for managers since they are taken off the hook of making decisions about who goes. Rather than having individuals decide, you simply establish a program, install it in your computer, feed it data such as rank, time in service, academic degrees, perhaps grades in graduate school, and similar "objective" materials, and out will come the lowest-ranked name with a black spot next to it and an envelope addressed for mailing. But there are also disadvantages to this procedure from management's point of view, since it limits the moving finger from writing the names of those professors you might on other grounds wish to dispose of. So Todd Furniss suggests that one must add to these "objective" data other factors which must be "weighed": for example, "relative competence"—wonderful phrase—the relation of teaching skills to program needs. And he argues that even "objective criteria" need to be weighted differently in different situations—a neat rationale for cooking the data. Much of this planning is unobjectionable if one once accepts the premise that retrenchment must, or likely will have to, be done. The difficulty is that carrying out such planning has inevitably undermined the capacity of faculty and students to resist cuts, or even to question whether the basketball team or the Art History department is to go.

A second set of tactics for handling retrenchment situations can be expressed by the instruction "attack the most vulnerable first." Obviously, the people who can complain the least are those outside the institution, so the first tactic is not to let them in, which is accomplished by freezing lines and not hiring replacements. They never will be missed. Similarly, part-timers are more vulnerable than full-timers, so while you may save less money by firing part-time staff, you will also get less resistance. Thus part-timers are next on the dean's little list. Then there are the "old folk"—that goes by the name of "encouraging early retirement." Now someone who is 58 or 62 might not wish to retire, nor be able in inflationary times to afford to do so. But if, at that point in one's career, one has become unused to being hassled, and if people one likes and respects such as the department chair and the dean are forever explaining how the bright young man—or woman—of thirty-five has a family to support . . . well, a graceful exit into discard may be easier than continued campus discord. So older faculty are next on the little list.

The cognate of attacking the most vulnerable is offering some of their flesh as a carrot to those who remain.

> The retention [on campus] of freed financial resources was important, but there was a related principle that had a bearing on internal politics. The reallocation of those freed resources was also crucial to the acceptance of the program discontinuances on the campus because it created more "winners" than "losers." The resources from each retrenched program could be shifted to four or five continuing ones; for every department that was shattered and hurt by the decisions, there were four or five who saw themselves able to advance.[25]

In other words, promote academic cannibalism.

Another set of tactics has been devised to soften the blow of retrenchment. These include psychological techniques as well as means for shifting people's jobs to avoid immediate or outright termination. Individuals will take layoffs more philosophically, managers are advised, if they do not see it as a matter of personal failure; therefore, managers should identify "external forces as the source of inevitable termination." Make it clear that the institution really has the interests of the individual being fired at heart. So the University of Wisconsin established a new administrative office—yet another—to help "tenured faculty designated for lay off." Such offices are, presumably, responsible for instituting plans for retraining faculty for new positions—that is, if such plans were ever significantly funded, or instituted within half a dozen years of the time of major layoffs.

With or without retraining, the manuals propose, some job transfers can be accomplished: computer programmers can be shifted to a math department, or vice versa, teachers to administrative work, though seldom the reverse. Positions can be downgraded, professors asked to accept associate rank, full-time faculty to split single positions, tenure-track faculty asked to shift into nontenure-bearing ranks. All in the name of saving jobs, to be sure. An adaptation from industry involves use of the "furlough":

> When staff reduction is necessary, treating it as an unpaid leave or furlough rather than as termination of employment softens the psychological blow to the individuals affected. It affords assurance of re-employment if a position for which an individual is qualified later becomes available. It may also permit continued participation in retirement and insurance plans. If this procedure is followed, however, there should be the likelihood that a person could be reinstated within a reasonable time. Otherwise, furloughing may constitute a cruel hoax.[26]

The primary means for softening the blow appears, ironically, to be provision of mechanisms to assure "academic due process." This may seem like an excessively cynical interpretation of the AAC's statement that faculty should have the opportunity to be heard in regular appeals of termination decisions. The problem, however, is that such "due process," while it may involve fired faculty in endless hearings, appeals and other procedures, seldom if ever leads to a reversal of termination decisions. After all, the ultimate judge in these proceedings is precisely the same person who originated retrenchment. The University of Wisconsin instituted a fairly elaborate procedure[27] that involved appeals hearings before a faculty panel. In most cases, the hearings sustained the layoffs, and in the four cases in which faculty panels recommended against retrenchment, the chancellor simply rejected the findings. When the cases came to court, Judge Doyle upheld the university's firings, ruling that such procedures were necessary, but also sufficient, to guarantee elemental fairness. No wonder, then, that one writer describes "due process" as "needed both for legal reasons and to insure fairness. . . ."[28] But how "fair" is it, really, to involve faculty who have already been fired in appeals, briefs, arguments, and hearings that can hardly be expected to conclude in reversing so serious and fundamental a decision as firing a tenured person? It is not, in my view, cynical to argue that such "due process" serves the interests of "fairness" less than the interests of management. Those interests are twofold: One is to satisfy minimum legal requirements, such as those mandated by Judge Doyle; the other is to divert the anger and energy generated by firings into approved channels, where time and the weight of procedure will dissipate them. In short, the general value of due process should not obscure the fact that in particular situations, familiar to students of the law, it will work against the interests of individuals set into conflict with large institutions.

The problem of due process and its value in retrenchment decisions leads directly into another widely misunderstood tactic of management, and that is to "involve" faculty. At a general policy level, the AAC and the AAUP, for example, seem to agree: Faculty should be involved or consulted at every stage in the retrenchment process. But even a casual reading of management literature on the subject reveals that the objectives of administrators in involving faculty are far different from the objectives of faculty organizations. Here, for example, is John Gillis suggesting how faculty involvement can overcome the problems of personal loyalties and protection of special interests.

> If, however, those who are ultimately responsible for the decision [i.e., managers] will share information and provide appropriate opportunity for others to share in their deliberations, staff reductions may be accomplished with a minimum of adverse consequences.[29]

The objective here is avoiding such "adverse consequences"—i.e., unhappy faculty and efforts to defend "special" relationships or "privileges." The technique is involvement in "deliberations," though—carefully—not in "ultimate" decisions.

Or here is Sandra Warden arguing for using research data not to allocate resources but to promote change.

> A third and very important consequence of shifting the emphasis from defensive justification of what is to constructive analysis of what might be, could be a change in the attitude of Faculty toward accepting reallocated priorities and limited resources as a challenge to their ingenuity rather than to their jobs. If faculty are regarded as important members of a team working together on a problem, their approach is likely to be far more positive.[30]

Once again, the goal is producing "positive" faculty attitudes toward retrenchment, and the technique is involving them as members of a "team."

Finally, and most straightforward of all, there is David C. Brown, former executive vice-president at Miami University. Brown is concerned with the politics of "pruning programs," and how to overcome the faculty's natural resistance to change. "Involve the 'action people' in the pruning decision," he recommends. That makes them more sympathetic. Get deans or chairpeople to project goals for the year ahead and to devise quantitative measures to see if they are achieved. Faced with frivolous statements of goals, such people may save you the trouble by suggesting program terminations themselves. Broaden the decision-making unit, he urges, and facilitate trade-offs:

> The faculty of the Secretarial Sciences department, for example, will not vote itself out of existence, but the faculty of the School of Business, with its broader perspective, may vote Secretarial Sciences out, especially if the

Business School faculty are assured that they will have responsibility for reallocating the resources saved. . . . The key here is the reward for cutting, which is the right to "spend" the saved funds. Without this reward, programmatic cutbacks are unlikely. To facilitate such rewards, the decision-making group needs broad responsibility to increase the alternatives for reallocation of funds.[31]

Brown's should not be taken for an isolated cynicism. For if we substitute, say, Italian Department or Education for Secretarial Sciences, and Arts and Sciences for Business, the scenario will be familiar to many faculty in those traditional areas.

The point here is not that faculty involvement is necessarily a charade, useful only to manipulative managers. The AAUP insists, as have some NEA-affiliate unions, that faculty be involved in at least four levels of decision-making: first, as to whether or not a *bona fide* financial exigency exists; second, where in the academic program retrenchment can occur; third, in establishing criteria for terminating people; fourth, in at least deciding who will finger the individuals to be fired. The problem is that level one is a prerogative that, especially in public institutions, management jealously guards for itself. A glance at the SUNY/UUP contract quoted toward the beginning of this chapter shows how far faculty in SUNY are from a voice—even a whisper—in deciding that primary question. Yet, without a decisive voice in that first determination—are cutbacks really necessary?—the rest does, indeed, become a charade of value primarily to management. For then they decide the dirty work that must be done, and you decide merely how to do it. In this light, most efforts on the part of management to "involve" faculty in retrenchment, however clothed in participatory rhetoric, must be understood as efforts to overcome faculty resistance and to pass on to faculty the burden of wielding the axe against their colleagues. The alacrity with which some faculty seize the axe-handle may, of course, say something equally unpleasant.

Most of the tactics I have touched upon concern particular procedures that administrators on one or another campus have used to ward off trouble. But offense remains the best defense, and a number of such offensive tactics remain to be described. The attacks on tenure must be seen in this context. Tenure, claims Boston University president John Silber, "functions as sinecure" and encourages "academic license and abuse."[32] "At that point when tenure is used to secure and maintain economic privilege" rather than academic freedom, says a midwest provost, "it will be rejected by the public and we will have lost our academic freedom as well."[33] Changing the tenure system comes to be directly related to the goals of retrenchment.

Management's interest is in maintaining flexibility so that changing educational needs can be met. To the extent that tenured faculty cannot meet those needs, they must be re-educated or replaced. Management cannot effectively achieve reform if it is legally bound to retain faculty who cannot or will not effectuate reform.

The faculty's interest is to protect academic freedom, freedom in teaching, research, and learning. The tenure contract protects that freedom and provides economic security to attract and retain people of ability to the teaching profession. The tenure contract must be reformed to accommodate management's need to achieve changing educational goals and the faculty's need to protect academic freedom. The challenge lies in redefining the contract so that the abuses of tenure can be eliminated without diminishing academic freedom.[34]

Such statements, and they have multiplied over the intervening years, serve to create a climate in which the task of retrenching tenured faculty is that much easier. For if tenure becomes in the public mind a questionable guarantee, or a privilege needing to be reformed, abrogating it seems that much less significant. So efforts to eliminate tenure or to impose tenure quotas, while they may not themselves succeed, can help make the task of retrenchment down the road much easier. Furthermore, as Margaret Schmid has pointed out, the enormously expanded use of "nontenure-track" appointments and the increasing denials of tenure on the basis not of cause but of alleged program needs have the effect of undermining the tenure system itself—in effect, carrying out the "reforms" desired by college managers.[35]

The courts can also be an arena for offensive actions by management, like the suit brought by the Southern Illinois administration against faculty they had fired. Again, the legal case might not prevail, but it can serve to harass and intimidate faculty, who do not have access to institutional resources to carry on legal battles.

Finally, there are consultants, outfits like the Academy for Educational Development, which proposed that in order to raise student-faculty ratios, management should agree to "increasing salaries only when faculty agree to teach larger classes." Our friend David C. Brown finds consultants particularly useful for reenforcing the wisdom of decisions already made by management. They can also, he points out, serve as scapegoats for such decisions—"it was not I," the dean says, "but the Academy for Educational Development that decided you were superfluous."

IV

These are the tactics I have found that educational managers have devised to carry out retrenchment. In all these instances, it may be objected, I have assumed the worst of administrators, taken what may be genuine and legitimate efforts to ease suffering as cynical manipulations of victims. In particular cases, no doubt, the intentions of administrators are honorable. But in this context, the good intentions of specific administrators weigh lightly against their institutional functions. One of their main functions, like those of managers in steel or coal, is to push the burdens of economic dislocation onto the shoulders of those who work, teachers in this instance. I am more impressed with the administrator who refuses to go along with retrenchment—like one president of a Pennsylvania state college in the mid–1970s—than with the one who manages it "sensitively." Finally, whatever the intentions, these tactics simply do make the manager's task easier even if, in some instances, they might help the retrenched academic. It is not cynical to point this out, but only a realistic way of looking at the actions of those who choose to administer retrenchment policies.

Underlying the notion that, after all, *someone* must make decisions about shifting resources away from some "products" and into others is an ideological commitment to a marketplace philosophy of education. There are alternatives, followed by most consistently fine colleges. One is to do very well what in the best judgment of a given academic community it can do, rather than shifting with the temporary winds of student fancy. Retrenchment strategies grow out of a marketplace ideology and are a primary means for trying to enforce that political perspective on the academic world.

Furthermore, situations in which alternatives to retrenchment do not exist are in my observation quite rare. Management has, in fact, used a variety of tactics to meet real financial problems. Important, if peripheral, benefits have been cut, sometimes on a temporary basis: for example, released time to develop new courses or to carry out administrative tasks; load reductions for research; sabbaticals. It has not even been necessary to eliminate sabbaticals, for example, though at some institutions what had been a norm has emerged as a privilege that must be elaborately justified case by case. Also utilized are the classic industrial tools of speed-up. At Old Westbury in 1975, for example, management imposed all of the following:

- Regular faculty lines were frozen at about 20 percent below authorized strength.
- "Adjunct," part-time faculty—who were paid about $900–$1,000 per course—were added to make up about half the deficit.
- Twenty-two percent more students were admitted than had been budgeted.
- Classroom contact hours were expanded by one third.

Thus fewer faculty were teaching more students for longer hours and, on average, for less pay—a model for speed-up surely worthy of Henry Ford. Such tactics are by no means desirable in themselves, even as temporary expedients, but their impacts need to be weighed against those produced by retrenchment.

Moreover, positive alternative approaches to cutting or postponing costs can be successful in meeting even extreme fiscal emergencies. The Pennsylvania state college and university system, for example, slated a large number of layoffs in 1975–76 at the expiration of a no-retrenchment contract clause with the faculty union. Some 200 staff, including eighty-two faculty, received notice of retrenchment. Ultimately, however, the eighty-two faculty notices (and many of the others, as well) were rescinded when a variety of methods for saving funds was devised and when the union agreed to limit across-the-board salary increases over two years.[36]

All that apart, a nation which can afford billions to keep petty tyrants like

Thieu (in Vietnam) and Park (in South Korea), or to support the murderous Contras in Nicaragua, can afford the millions needed to maintain teachers in jobs.

But the issue really is not whether constructive alternatives to retrenchment can be found to meet real or fabricated financial problems. In reading twenty years worth of management literature on the subject, I have been overwhelmed by how utterly insensitive administrators can be to the enormously destructive impacts of retrenchment on faculty morale, on a college's educational programs, and on the sustenance of a critical resource like the professoriat—not to mention the devastating impact of layoffs on individual lives.[37] No one has examined in detail what seems to me the unmistakable relationship between the widespread deployment of retrenchment tactics in the last decade and a half and the dangerous decline in faculty morale and status documented by Jack Schuster and Howard Bowen.[38] Yet in the fifteen-year period since part of this article first appeared, retrenchment has increasingly come to be seen among administrators as a primary managerial technique rather than as a last resort. Why?

I do not think the answer is simple. To be sure, American—unlike Swedish or Japanese—managerial culture is singularly indifferent to the fate of employees when management decides to make changes. Nothing better illustrates that than the devastation visited on the people of Youngstown, Ohio, when Youngstown Sheet and Tube closed its factory and moved production elsewhere or the devastation of Flint, Michigan, produced by General Motors' withdrawal. Indeed, that pattern of pushing onto workers the consequences of managerial decisions *not* to renew older plants (but to invest capital in "diversification" or other takeover schemes) produced the severe human dislocations characteristic of what has come to be called the "rust belt." College managers increasingly share the culture—and often the educational backgrounds—of their industrial peers. But more than managerial culture is involved in the spread of retrenchment.

Its underlying agenda is, I believe, concerned not so much with finances but with program and personnel control. Here I need to draw one further industrial analogy. The assembly line as developed by Henry Ford has, over the years, come to seem no more, and in some cases rather less, efficient than other techniques for organizing production. Certain auto manufacturers have, for example, moved toward production-team methods. But the assembly line does offer significant advantages in two respects important to modern scientific management: It allows for a greater transfer of skills from workers to machines, and it offers the most direct and systematic means for controlling the workforce. It seems to me that the imperatives to de-skill and to control the teaching force, which are closely related, underlie the managerial emphasis on retrenchment and, as I suggest in the next chapter, the use of adjuncts and part-timers.

In the first place, if managers take seriously what Caesar Naples calls their authority to "direct and guide the enterprise," then they should—from their own perspective—be able to determine what gets taught and what does not.[39]

Professors, however, have traditionally and notoriously tried to act like entrepreneurs—individualistic, self-determined, powerful in their own domains. Not only have they thus singly and collectively established centers of power resistant to administrative control, but they have presented to students models of behavior quite at variance with those desirable, from a managerial standpoint, in a relatively skilled workforce. In fact, it has been argued that the entrepreneurial liberalism of professors encouraged 1960s student resistance to bureaucratic control, whether exercised by the "multiversity" or by Selective Service boards. It has not been easy for college managers to assert control over the professoriat, even in those large, bureaucratic state and community colleges that the majority of students attend. No more was it simple for steel manufacturers to take power over the industrial process from the hands of skilled steel masters. Such transfers of skill and power take time, and in complex organizations such as colleges and universities, they take a variety of tools. Retrenchment is one,[40] a particularly useful one since it provides both the carrot of participating in managerial initiatives and forwarding one's own project and the stick of worry about one's own job and program.

When retrenchment first appeared on the academic scene in a significant way during the early 1970s, it seemed a threat to prevailing academic norms. That it is taken today as part of the academic landscape seems to me to measure the success this and related strategies have had in blunting or coopting faculty opposition, as well as in pushing the currently prevailing marketplace ideology onto the campus. To be sure, many faculty—especially in the more elite institutions—continue to function along older, individualistic parameters, but for most the distance between that ideal and the realities of teaching have grown apace. Still, there are some signs of change. What has, perhaps, begun to alter the power equation is the perception that the mechanistic organizational models used by administrators do not fit the complex, organic character of colleges and universities. As a manager, you can gain greater control over program and personnel through the threat of retrenchment and other devices, but there turn out to be costs which may make that success Pyrrhic. It may be that, as in the public schools, the price of achieving a more productive, energized workforce will be restoring to faculty precisely those areas of control retrenchment strategies were designed to abrogate.

Notes

1. Speaking in 1981, Caesar J. Naples, who was then General Counsel of the State University system of Florida, put it this way:

> There is, about the land, a myth that retrenchment may only occur as a result of—or in reaction to—external forces such as a shortfall in income, a reduction in the legislative appropriation, a voter revolt leading to a Proposition 13, 2 ½, etc. This is, I emphasize, merely a myth. A university administration exists, among other things, to *manage* the institution; to direct and guide the enterprise; to define its mission, aims, goals, scope,

means and ends. Now, I'm not making these up; and I didn't read this listing in some management manual on 'What to do when a union organizer knocks on your door?' This listing is taken from state laws all over the country. . . . These rights and other similar ones have been constantly reinforced in the courts and PERBs [Public Employee Relations Boards] around the country. These sources define not only the legal authority of management, but also the expectation society in general holds for institutional managers. The authority to mold, shape, aim and direct, redefine, expand and contract the institution—i.e., to define its mission—cannot be abdicated.

Any restrictions on the exercise of management's authority sought by employee organizations at the bargaining table should be resisted. . . . The decision to retrench is management's alone.

"Impact of Retrenchment in Higher Education," in
Proceedings of the Ninth Annual Conference of the National Center for the Study of Collective Bargaining in Higher Education, Joel M. Douglas, ed. (New York: Baruch College, City University of New York, 1981), pp. 29, 30.

2. A number of these are summarized in Kenneth P. Mortimer and Michael L. Tierney, "The Three 'R's' of the Eighties: Reduction, Reallocation and Retrenchment," AAHE-ERIC Higher Education Research Report #4, 1979 (Washington: American Association for Higher Education, 1979), pp. 34–35. Among other elaborations on this theme are the following: F. E. Balderston, *Managing Today's Universities* (San Francisco: Jossey-Bass, 1975); David C. Brown, "Criteria for Pruning Programs," *Educational Record* 51 (Fall 1970): 405–409; Kenneth P. Mortimer, "Procedures and Criteria for Faculty Retrenchment," in *Challenges of Retrenchment,* James R. Mingle and Associates, ed. (San Francisco: Jossey-Bass, 1981), pp. 153–170; R. C. Shirley and J. F. Volkwein, "Establishing Academic Program Priorities," *Journal of Higher Education* 49 (September/October 1978): 472–488.

3. See, for example, Larry Gordon, "Cutting Costs on Campus," Los Angeles *Times,* May 31, 1990, pp. 1, A38–A39.

4. Most of the statistics used here were derived from *Statistical Abstracts of the United States* and rechecked in the 1989 edition. These differ somewhat from the more precise figures compiled by the Carnegie Foundation for the Advancement of Teaching, which I have consulted to supplement the clear general picture offered by *Statistical Abstracts.*

5. The Carnegie Foundation's figure for the increase over the period 1976–1986 is 1,485,471, an expansion of 13.5 percent. "New Strategies Keep Enrollments Growing," *Change* 21 (January–February, 1989): 40.

6. James R. Mingle and Associates, *Challenges of Retrenchment,* p. 4.

7. "Enrollments have not only held up but have increased," says the Carnegie Foundation for the Advancement of Teaching, "New Strategies Keep Enrollments Growing," p. 39.

8. These are related. In 1975, there were about 1.5 million men between the ages of 25 and 34 enrolled in colleges, and about 569,000 ages 35 and over In 1985 the comparable figures were 1.4 million and 561,000, a net loss of 108,000. However, in 1975 947,000 women between ages 25 and 34 were enrolled, and 614,000 ages 35 and over. In 1985, the comparable figures were about 1.6 million and 1.1 million, respectively, a net *gain* of 1,139,000.

The Carnegie Foundation points out that

"part-time enrollment grew by 31.2 percent at the privates and 24.5 percent at the publics between 1976 and 1986." Furthermore, "women made up 50.9 percent of the part-time enrollment in 1976 and 57.5 percent in 1986. The importance of part-time enrollment as a vehicle of access to higher education for women was underscored by

the fact that men remained in the majority among full-time students, though only by a single percentage point."
                                                       "New Strategies Keep Enrollments Growing," pp. 40, 41.

9. "Classes in the evenings and at odd hours, weekend colleges, credit for life experience, child care on campus, career-oriented majors—all grew along with the enrollment of a new kind of student." Carnegie Foundation, "New Strategies . . . " p. 39.

10. " . . . concentration on the projected decline in enrollments diverts attention from the continuing 'cost-income squeeze' faced by most institutions." Mortimer and Tierney, "The Three 'R's' of the Eighties," p. 52.

11.

> The overall trend in state support for higher education, as measured by 21 years of two-year percentage gain figures, is downward from gains of 40 percent or more in the 1960s to the 30 percent range in the early 1970s to the 20 percent range in the late 1970s to the teens in the 1980s. In absolute dollars, states have provided more to higher education each year, but in percentage gains there has been a consistent and significant lessening in support.

Edward R. Hine, "State Support of Higher Education: A 20-Year Contextual Analysis . . . " in *Proceedings of the Sixteenth Annual Conference of the National Center for the Study of Collective Bargaining in Higher Education and the Professions,* Joel M. Douglas, ed. (New York: Baruch College, City University of New York, 1988), p. 18. Corrected for inflation, the "increases" in absolute dollars during the last decade turn out to be real decreases.

12. Average tuition and fees for all public institutions in 1975 were $432; by 1986 they had risen to $1,044, a 242% increase; in private colleges, the rise was from $2,117 to $5,778, a 273% increase.

13. Indeed, one might ask to what extent the current modest surge in enrollments in traditional academic programs such as English, Classics, and History—at least in the more elite colleges—is in part a product of the expressed preference of employers for more broadly educated students, and also, in part, a way of stratifying higher-level employees (English majors, say) from lower-level (Business majors).

14. The 1989 demonstrations against tuition increases by City University of New York students illustrates the point. Essentially, they made it too costly to try shifting more of the economic burden onto them and their families. But they did not significantly succeed in regaining a larger proportion of state dollars for higher education.

15. Joanne M. Sprenger and Raymond E. Schultz, "Staff Reduction Policies," *College Management* IX (May 1974): 22.

16. Stephen A. Hoenack and Alfred L. Norman, "Incentives and Resource Allocations in Universities," *Journal of Higher Education* 45 (January 1974): 21–37.

17. Mortimer and Tierney, "The Three 'R's' of the Eighties," p. 53.

18. Robert H. Maier and James W. Kolka, "Retrenchment—A Primer," *Liberal Education* 59 (December 1973): 435.

19. See, for example, J. Fredericks Volkwein, who was then assistant to the president of the State University of New York at Albany, "Responding to Financial Retrenchment: Lessons from the Albany Experience," *Journal of Higher Education* 55 (May 6, 1984): 395.

20. See, for example, the report on studies of academic planning in *The Chronicle of Higher Education,* February 3, 1975.

21. See, in addition to the articles already cited, John W. Gillis, "Academic Staff Reductions in Response to Financial Exigency," *Liberal Education* 47 (October 1971): 346–377.

22. J. Fredericks Volkwein, "Responding to Financial Retrenchment: Lessons From the Albany Experience," p. 396.

23. Robert H. Maier and James W. Kolka, "Retrenchment—a Primer," p. 436.

24. David C. Brown, "Criteria for Pruning Programs," *Educational Record* 51 (1970): 407.

25. J. Fredericks Volkwein, "Responding to Financial Retrenchment: Lessons From the Albany Experience," p. 398.

26. Joanne M. Sprenger and Raymond E. Schultz, "Staff Reduction Policies," p. 23.

27. Described in a staff paper titled "Development of Tenured Faculty LayOff Procedures in the University of Wisconsin System."

28. See W. Todd Furniss, "Retrenchment, Layoff, and Termination," *Educational Record* 55 (Summer 1974): 159–170.

29. John W. Gillis, "Academic Staff Reductions in Response to Financial Exigency," p. 376.

30. Sandra A. Warden, "Socio-Political Issues of Faculty Activity Data," *Journal of Higher Education* 45 (June 1974): 470–71.

31. David C. Brown, "Criteria for Pruning Programs, p. 408.

32. See John Silber's address to the 1974 meeting of the American Association for the Advancement of Science.

33. John W. Gillis, "Academic Staff Reductions in Response to Financial Exigency," p. 369.

34. Dena Elliott Benson, "Whether Tenure Is An Obstacle to Reform," in *Proceedings of the Twelfth Annual Conference of the National Center for the Study of Collective Bargaining in Higher Education and the Professions,* Joel M. Douglas, ed. (New York: Baruch College, City University of New York, 1984), p. 51.

35. Margaret Schmid, "Is Tenure An Obstacle to Reform," *Ibid.,* pp. 57–58.

36. See Mark D. Johnson and Kenneth P. Mortimer, *Faculty Bargaining and the Politics of Retrenchment in the Pennsylvania State Colleges 1971–1976* (University Park, Pa.: The Center for the Study of Higher Education, 1977), pp. 47–68.

37. Irwin Polishook makes many of these same points in "Impact of Retrenchment," in *Proceedings of the Ninth Annual Conference of the National Center for the Study of Collective Bargaining in Higher Education,* op. cit., pp. 25–26. Polishook's comments were responded to by management's spokesperson, Caesar Naples, in passages such as the one quoted in note 1.

38. Jack H. Schuster and Howard R. Bowen, *American Professors: A National Resource Imperiled* (New York: Oxford University Press, 1986).

39. This process has proceeded a good deal further in the elementary and secondary schools. See, for example, Michael W. Apple, "Curricular Form and the Logic of Technical Control," *Economic and Industrial Democracy* 2 (1981): 293–319.

40. Others include, as I have suggested, the use of a variety of non tenured appointments, as well as the incorporation of certain faculty into managerial ranks, a process accelerated by the Supreme Court's decision in the *Yeshiva* case, which argued that professors in private colleges were by virtue of their positions "managerial employees" with no rights to organize for collective bargaining.

A Scandalous Misuse of Faculty—Adjuncts

While increasing attention began to be focused a decade ago on the scandalous misuse of part-time or "adjunct" faculty in colleges, their use has persistently spread.[1] In fact, new varieties of "temporary" positions continue to be invented by college managers. "Part-time" faculty now include some who teach what amounts to a full load, but who are paid on a credit hour or per course basis, others who scramble for one or two courses each term and are paid flat rates, as well as a few whose salaries and benefits are prorated fractions of those of a full-timer. But there are now many "off-tenure" full-time appointments as well: "lecturers," whose contracts are renewed every year or two but who may remain in their positions, without tenure, indefinitely; "nontenure-track" instructors and assistant professors, who may stay at an institution for four, six or more years but who, at the point of a tenure decision, must move on; "replacement" appointments, who fill lines for a year or two and then migrate to similar positions elsewhere. I shall use the term "adjunct faculty" or "adjuncts" to describe this quite varied group of individuals,[2] for while the word is not precisely appropriate in all cases, its dictionary definition calls attention to the fact that such faculty, while "joined or added" to the institution, are in critical ways "not essentially a part of it."

Handwringing over the plight of adjuncts has brought no relief, and even most union contracts have so far been marginally helpful.[3] That should be no surprise, for the exploitation of adjuncts serves a number of crucial interests of college managers and of those to whom they report. It is important to identify these interests more clearly if the abuse of this large number of our colleagues is ever to be brought under control, much less halted. For the exploitation of adjuncts is not a function of managerial nastiness, nor is it—any more than was the War on Vietnam—an unfortunate product of historical "accidents." Rather, it is rooted in a particular conception of college management designed to serve historically distinctive social and political interests.

College managers play quite specific institutional roles—they are there,

An early version of this article appeared in the December 1978 issue of *Universitas*, the magazine of United University Professions, the State University of New York faculty and professional staff union. In that form it was reprinted a number of times in other union journals and, in another form, in *The Chronicle of Higher Education* on May 14, 1979.

after all, to *manage* and, especially in public or large private colleges, such roles impose on them, however personally beneficent they may be, certain goals and behaviors. First, while management has a good deal of discretion in carrying out day-to-day tasks in an institution, it must ultimately implement policies established by governing boards. No college president or dean who consistently contravenes the wishes of the board of trustees will keep the job. Such governing boards, whether in public or private institutions, reflect in their composition and their outlook an elite—national, statewide or local— of business, finance, law and politics. In aggregate, the policies they adopt represent the interests—occasionally modified through student, public, or organized faculty pressure—of that elite. College managers are there to carry out such policies and to develop educational and fiscal programs that correspond to the priorities defined by these boards.

A fundamental priority since the end of the plush 1960s has been to run institutions very economically. Another, of increasing importance, has been to keep control over programs and also personnel. In addition, like other bureaucrats, college managers have a stake in protecting, indeed in extending, their own domains. The best way to do that is, of course, by expanding what you control, the number of jobs around you, the perquisites of your fiefdom. In view of these major functions of college managers—economic, programmatic, and personnel control—the attractions of employing adjuncts, and especially part-timers, become clear.

I

First, there are major economic incentives. Adjunct salaries are usually based on a flat rate (per course or per contact hour), adjusted minimally, if at all, for experience or education, and seldom raised. Further, few adjuncts receive benefits to which the college contributes, nor do they have sick leave—if they miss a class, they do not get paid. For example: the State University of New York College at Old Westbury is a small institution—in 1977–78 it had about 87 full-time and 53 part-time adjunct faculty. The adjuncts averaged around $1,000 per four-credit course (then about par, though far under a living wage, on Long Island). They taught some 55 courses, at an approximate cost to the institution of $55,000. Had the courses been taught by full-time faculty at comparable appointment levels, the cost to the institution would have been approximately $2,500 per course, or a total of $137,500, just for the base salary. To that one had to add roughly 30 percent (more now) for benefits for full-timers, none of which the adjuncts received. The total cost would then have come to no less than $178,750. In short, by having those 55 courses taught by part-time adjuncts, the College at Old Westbury "saved" about $123,750; it paid less than one-third of what it would have cost to staff the courses with full-time faculty.[4]

Old Westbury is, financially, small potatoes. Comparable figures for a much larger institution were analyzed by Emily Abel in issue #5 of *Radical*

Teacher. In the spring of 1976, Santa Monica (California) College employed 664 part-time faculty and another 91 full-timers teaching overloads at adjunct pay. There were but 170 full-time faculty altogether. The part-timers were paid $900,000, which represented a saving to the institution (from what full-timers would have been paid) of some $1,350,000! In the fall of 1975, the saving was over $1.1 million; in total, then, the saving for the academic year 1975–76 came to about $2.5 million. That is a lot of money in any college, but especially in one with a total budget of only $13 million.

While there are, of course, hidden personnel costs in employing, terminating, and rehiring temporary staff, the margin between adjunct and full-time pay rates has probably widened in most disciplines since the mid–1970s. In the 1986–87 academic year, according to the annual AAUP survey, the average starting salary of an assistant professor was $29,435.[5] Data on that year collected by the Modern Language Association suggest that adjunct pay in English and the modern languages varied from $1,000 to $2,000 per course;[6] other reports place it at about $1,500–$1,800 across all departments.[7] If we use this last (probably high) figure and the AAUP's *starting* salary for assistant professors, the per-course discrepancy—based on a full-time eight course (24 credit units) per year load—is $1,879, with benefits, about $3,056. For Old Westbury's six-course load, the discrepancy for the same 55 courses (of course, by the 1980s, far more were taught by adjuncts) would have come to $4,675 per course, or a total of $257,103 "saved" in that single academic year, more than double what it had been in 1977–78.

Where does such "saved" money go? Abel had some answers: Between September 1974 and 1976 at Santa Monica, six new administrative positions were created, with appropriate support services. In addition to that, a number of faculty were declared "management" and significant salary increases were provided for all management personnel. Administrative costs in that two-year span rose from about $427,000 to $711,000, or some 66 percent. New buildings were also put up, including a library that contains a meeting room for the board of trustees and expanded administrative offices, among other niceties. The action that perhaps most fully characterized the situation, Abel suggests, was the conversion of the lounge previously used by the adjuncts to prepare classes into an expanded office for an administrator.

Santa Monica College is by no means the heaviest user or the worst offender of adjuncts; nor would I want to suggest that most funds "saved" by hiring adjuncts are dissipated in employing managers or putting up buildings. Adjuncts are exploited in every area of the country, and much of the money thus "saved" makes up for the declining levels of governmental and, probably, corporate support. Still, no one has yet added up the "savings" made by college management by means of such exploitation, nor the extent to which it is redistributed into managerial functions. But it takes no computer to tell us that we are dealing with enormous sums, of special concern in a period in which colleges have been faced not only with declining levels of support but with a serious expenditure/income gap. The dollar figures make this a seemingly intractable problem, but to focus on money alone would be altogether misleading.

II

To see why employing adjuncts is desirable to college managers concerned with program control, it is useful to turn briefly to industrial history. One major imperative of the movement called "scientific management," which grew in importance around the turn of the century, was to concentrate production decisions in the hands of managers. That provided management with "flexibility"—a term popular among college administrators today. "Flexibility" is one of those smooth ideological terms masking the intense conflict between management and labor in the industrial workplace. Workers, particularly skilled workers, wished to retain control over their jobs by controlling the work process itself. They could thus help to ensure continued employment, while limiting the pace of work and maintaining some say over the quality of work life. Management, on the other hand, has one goal: to maximize profits. To do so, they have had to overcome the power of skilled workers to control their own jobs. Only if they accomplished that goal could management control and vary in its own interests the pace of work; only then could they introduce mechanical devices that eliminated jobs and that moved critical productive skills from the workers into the machines (and thereby into the hands of management). Scientific management can be seen as a game plan for concentrating all decisions about production—what is produced, how much, how rapidly, by whom, where—in the hands of management, which can then shape its decisions on the basis of profitability without much regard for the rather differing interests of workers in safe, interesting, stable, and well-paying jobs.

Colleges are not, of course, manufacturing concerns, and yet management's own arguments—as I noted in the previous chapter—draw significant parallels. Colleges, they say, are subject to similar "market forces." They cannot continue to produce a "product"—German, say, or Milton or eighteenth-century French history—for which there is insufficient demand. They must therefore be "flexible" and provide what the "consumers" request. Professors of German, English literature, or French history, like skilled nineteenth-century steel workers, try to control output for their own benefit; managers, however, have a broader, "public" interest in view and must therefore be the ones to determine "output"—what in colleges are described as programs or courses of study.

In one sense, the accuracy of this argument is tangential to our concerns: Since large numbers of college managers seem to accept and act upon it, the analysis—however fallacious—undergirds their treatment of adjuncts. It is useful, however, to pause for a moment to consider the substance of what is being argued here. The argument assumes, first, the existence of a "free market," in which students make unconstrained choices among the variety of goods (courses) being offered to them. But students are about as free in such choices as Los Angeles commuters are free to choose economical mass-transit alternatives to choked freeways. Students cannot, of course, be commanded into a given major, but they are subject to intense propaganda, which identifies the possibility of getting a job for which one might qualify after graduation with majoring in a particular field, like marketing or "communications." They are, to use the word made famous by Selective Service Director General Hershey in the 1960s, "channeled" into decisions preferred by those who establish university priorities.[8] When you replace the Miltonist with the teacher of "correctional services," students do not need a weatherman to tell which way the wind blows.

Second, this process of manipulating the market and "channeling" the consumers is by no means an expression of casual trustee preferences. One result of student and community agitation in the 1960s, of the civil rights and women's movements, was the extension of educational opportunities to far broader constituencies. The United States has witnessed similar extensions before. Once won, such opportunities cannot easily be withdrawn, whether the arena of conflict is the City University of New York or Tiananmen Square. Rather, extended educational opportunities must be *converted,* from liberal and political education, for example, into vocational training. So, in the past, as more working-class students were able to get into and remain in high school, educators devised means for tracking them into vocational and other "non-academic" programs, "suitable" for their job prospects. Similarly, while primitives like Spiro Agnew grumbled that too many young people were going to college, more sophisticated policymakers were intent on changing what it was that they studied. The desire of young people and their parents for higher education could not be blocked easily, though it could be dampened by making college more costly to them. But more skillfully, that desire could be used to train and stratify tomorrow's workforce. Thus the greatest growth areas in postsecondary education in the past two decades have been precisely those offering collegiate-level vocational training. And it is in those enrollment-driven institutions that the greatest exploitation of adjuncts has taken place.

Since this is not, as General Hershey reminded us, a totalitarian country, students are not directed into a course of study but urged, pressured, persuaded—"channeled," in short. This is, however, an untidy process: It is difficult to match workers produced by educational institutions with available jobs, more difficult still to correlate the number of educational workers needed in a given field precisely to "consumer" demand. In this context, the virtue of employing adjunct faculty becomes obvious. Using them avoids the "inertia" built into full-time and especially tenured appointments. Full-time faculty are, after all, better positioned to pursue their vested interests in their own subject matter. Adjuncts come and go—they are hired to teach a course that managers decide needs to be taught, but they have nothing to say about what gets taught. And if the course does not gain sufficient enrollment, if it doesn't "make," it can easily be dropped without inconvenience to anyone—

save, of course, the poor adjunct, who has little recourse in any case. New "products" can thus be tested out at minimal cost and without long-term commitments.

In this context, too, senior faculty are drawn increasingly onto management's side with respect to their department's part-time help. As directors of multisectioned courses, some have been converted into "management confidential" personnel, out of union bargaining units, onto the other side of the table. But even if they do not become managers as such, the short-term interests of many full-time faculty can be served by the presence of adjuncts. For it is most often the adjuncts who teach the least desirable service courses—freshman composition, basic math, elementary language study. Full-timers can then be left to focus more on their academic specialties, on which advancement and professional mobility are largely based.

III

All this leads, in turn, to the third of management's major objectives in using adjuncts: personnel control. Increasingly, we see a three-tiered academic workforce at colleges.[9] At the top are tenured professors, relatively secure and stable, with some (often a large) degree of control over their work, and sometimes over that of others. At the bottom are the adjunct faculty. Whether they may be described as the products of "overproduction" by graduate schools, as labor underutilized by the higher education system, or in some other fashion is matter for debate. But the nomenclature really doesn't matter, for they *function* as a classic reserve labor pool: That is, they can be called upon hastily whenever extra hands are needed and they always constitute a threat to the job security of those currently employed ("if you don't like it here, there are plenty of others out there . . . "). In the middle are junior faculty on regular, term appointments—and some "off-tenure" full-time adjuncts. Most are, of course, striving to attain one of the decreasing number of tenured slots; but perhaps more, they are struggling to avoid falling back into the reserve pool of part-time, irregular workers. It is a pattern familiar to us from industrial history.

Such a three-tiered system produces tremendous pressures upon that middle group to behave, not to get organized, to devote themselves to "appropriate" scholarly activities. The longer a person in the middle group is in academe, the more intense those pressures become, since a fall back into the reserve labor pool after six or eight years of full-time teaching practically guarantees a lifetime of sporadic, irregular employment. And, with retrenchment, this system also pressures even those at the top, for they, too, can always be replaced. Further, it is hard for tenured faculty to sustain their economic demands when the number of (and sometimes the same) courses taught by a $50,000 a year professor can be covered by $12,000 worth of adjuncts. This system also maximizes conflict between adjunct and full-time faculty, each group striving for a bigger piece of the pie—adjuncts, indeed, competing to get to the meat rather than the crust alone. And there are significant instances of management playing such groups against each other to hold down salaries and to minimize the gains of organized faculty.

Further, union contracts have tended to promote more stylized and regular processes for evaluating full-time faculty. But overwhelmingly, part-timers and some other adjuncts are hired by means most closely resembling the old hiring hall, and sharing all the abuses of a system in which favoritism is rampant and payoffs are hardly unknown. In brief—again the analogies to industry are telling—the use of adjuncts provides management with a significant instrument for personnel control and manipulation.

If this begins to sound like a cynical interpretation of managerial motives, consider one relatively smaller matter in the treatment of adjuncts: office space. The lack of adjunct office space is often cited as an instance of counterproductive, penny-wise and pound-foolish administrative decision-making. In fact, however, if adjuncts do not have offices, they are far less visible—to each other as well as to their colleagues, as I can testify from having tried to locate them in order to recruit them into the union. The less visible they are, the more easily exploited. Thus, if the lack of an office inhibits adjunct-student as well as adjunct-colleague interaction, it also marginalizes even further the adjunct and makes her more vulnerable to administrative control.

IV

Typically at this point articles about the "problem of adjuncts" turn to "solutions." Underlying this move—almost a convention of the form—is the assumption that if one can mount sufficient evidence and a persuasive argument, college managers, governing boards, and public officials will see the error of their ways and somehow reverse the policies that have produced the scandal of adjuncts. From what I can tell, however, few such people see these employment tactics as "errors." At best, they perceive them to be practices imposed on academe by larger economic and social forces.

> In the face of the enrollment and resource uncertainties of the last decade
> and a half, American colleges and universities have had to seek alternative
> staffing strategies to the full-time regular tenure track faculty appointment.[10]

Almost every phrase in that sentence hides specific political and economic choices, and the alternatives, behind a paper curtain of necessity. But a more precise exploration of where such personnel practices tend to prevail may provide even a more calculated rationale for their continuation.

California's three-tiered system offers a beginning. According to Christine Maitland's figures, 60 percent of the faculty teaching in the community colleges taught part-time; in the California State University system, 49 percent of the faculty were adjuncts; in the University of California, 34 percent (excluding graduate teaching assistants).[11] In general, the further up the ladder of academic elitism one moves, the less likely one is to find substantial numbers of adjunct faculty. And this stands to reason, for what parents would be willing to pay up to $20,000 a year to have their children taught by part-time or temporary labor with little or no intrinsic relationship to the institution, no office hours (nor office in which to hold them), no commitments or expectations beyond the term or course?

This is no commentary on the competence or the credentials of adjuncts, but rather on their institutional deployment. It has been widely argued that increased use of adjuncts negatively affects institutional quality. To some extent that view might once have reflected the suspicion of full-timers about adjuncts' qualifications and experience. But the critique has rapidly broadened. More than ten years ago Richard J. Ernst and Larry A. McFarlane asked "Are We Shortchanging Our Students By Using Part-Time Faculty?"[12] They pointed to problems of program coordination and continuity, of integrating both teachers and students into departmental culture, and of sustaining the overall quality of instruction. Franklin and her Modern Language Association colleagues found in a 1983–84 Associated Departments of English survey "a correlation between varying ratios of full-time to part-time faculty members and a department's ability to attract majors, grant undergraduate degrees in the field, and engage in outreach and collaborative projects," including administering important writing-across-the-curriculum programs.[13] Others worry about the added burdens placed on fewer full-time faculty for advising, planning, and governance; the breaking of the significant link between teaching and research implicit in the ways adjuncts are used; the haphazard processes by which adjuncts are hired and evaluated and the lack of institutional support for their development as faculty members. Most significantly, perhaps, critics charge that widespread adjunct employment so undermines the quality of academic life, destabilizes college employment, and helps depress the economic status of the profession that it already has begun to discourage an entire generation of students from considering the professoriat as a career goal. Thus tomorrow's teachers are being turned away by today's "peculiar tenure and personnel practices," to quote the AAUP. They sum up this charge: "The creation and growth of so-called 'non-tenure-track' positions can be viewed as an institutional resignation, temporary or otherwise, from the pursuit of professional excellence."[14]

But it is not at all clear that "the pursuit of professional excellence" is a real priority at all levels of postsecondary education. That is generally the goal at elite institutions, private or public. But other priorities take precedence as one moves down the institutional ladder toward the least selective, most enrollment-driven colleges. At some point the objective becomes *not* to provide the highest quality program, but to provide a program of *sufficient* quality to meet what are taken to be the needs or "legitimate" aspirations of students likely to enroll. Both Trinity College and Hartford State Technical College are designated as "colleges." That is, a student normally has to have graduated from high school to enroll. But there the resemblance ends, as one can observe from the condition of the buildings, from the facilities, from the curricula, from the libraries—and from the personnel policies and procedures. They are, in fact, as distant from one another as Palm Beach and Port au Prince.

The sorting and acculturation processes that were once accomplished in American high schools have now been extended into the colleges as a higher percentage of each age group attends. And just as, at primary and secondary levels, significantly less money has been spent on schools serving poor and working-class constituencies, so now in postsecondary education. With personnel costs taking up to 80 percent of some budgets, adjunct employment plays a critical role in reducing per-student costs at the lower end of the collegiate spectrum. And since quality of instruction is of much less moment there than being able to respond rapidly to every shift in student/consumer demand, adjunct employment plays a critical role in program flexibility. Finally, since one does not want to project—for students directed toward lower-level technical or personal service jobs—models of self-determined, relatively unconstrained professional behavior, adjunct employment plays a critical role in screening out or controlling such models. To be sure, the vitality and interest of many individual adjunct teachers work against such objectives. But that in no way contradicts the fact that the spread of adjunct employment is no rationally correctable error but, on the contrary, a function of hard, institutional, class-conscious calculation. Indeed, as I suggested in the previous chapter, that has been increasingly true of college personnel practices in general.

I wish my colleagues trying to reform such practices the best of luck. In fact, some significant reforms may gradually be accomplished, probably through the organizing and nibbling model once advocated by Samuel Gompers: unionizing adjuncts and negotiating collective bargaining agreements. Such contracts as exist have in some measure succeeded in raising rates of pay—even converting them from a piece-work to a salaried basis. They have also been able to gain some benefits, seniority protection, and advances in hiring, evaluation and reappointment procedures—occasionally even office space and mailboxes. It may be that over time such incremental gains will sufficiently reduce the usefulness of adjunct employment that it will no longer seem so desirable to college managers. My grandmother used to say "I should live so long."

The alternative strategy remains, just as it was in the debate between Gompers and socialist leader Morris Hilquit, to challenge fundamentally the market-driven ideology of today's college managers. That may seem more than usually Utopian in the face of the movement even of most communist countries toward market initiatives. Those nations may not have produced the standard of living toward which they have aspired, but they have "provided standards of social decency and honor in work, even the lowliest"—to cite the words of Flora Lewis, no leftist she—that American society with its homelessness, waste, drugs, violence, and celebration of greed might well emulate. A great debate over the future has emerged in the Soviet Union, Eastern Europe, Nicaragua, even China; perhaps it will in the United States as well. What better place to start than with our educational system, with the question of whether our colleges shall increasingly become institutions for separating and tracking youth or a means for truly broadening opportunity and democratizing American culture.

Notes

1. The estimates vary. The most useful recent ones are those provided by Phyllis Franklin, David Laurence and Robert D. Denham of the Modern Language Association in "When Solutions Become Problems: Taking a Stand on Part-Time Employment," *Academe* (May–June, 1988). They include in the term "part-time teachers" those on full-time, nontenure-track appointments. They write:

> From fall 1972 to fall 1983, the number of part-time teachers in four-year institutions and in all fields rose 69 percent—from 75,000 to 127,000—while the number of full-time instructors increased but 21 percent—from 308,000 to 374,000. In two-year institutions during the same period, the number of part-time teachers rose 189 percent—from 44,000 to 127,000—and the number of full-time instructors increased 29 percent—from 72,000 to 93,000. . . . Estimates from the Center for Education Statistics show the total number of full-time faculty members at two- and four-year institutions decreasing from 456,000 in 1985 to 440,000 in 1986; during the same period the number of part-time instructors increased from 254,000 in 1985 to 260,000 in 1986.
>
> (p. 16)

Their figures are based upon Thomas D. Snyder, *Digest of Education Statistics, 1987* (Washington, D.C.: Center for Education Statistics, 1987), p. 158 and additional information provided by Vance Grant, U.S. Department of Education.

A sense of the sheer numbers involved may be provided by the following figures, derived from Christine Maitland, "Bargaining For Temporary Faculty," *Thought and Action* 3 (Spring 1987): 39: At the 22 California community college districts where there were, in 1985, collective bargaining contracts covering part-timers, there were in total 18,660 faculty members. Of these, 11,861, or 63.6%, were part-time. In individual districts the part-time proportion ranged from a low of 43 percent to a high of 82 percent. Maitland notes that, in 1984, California taught more than 11 percent of all the nation's college students, and that of the approximately 65,000 faculty in its three systems (university, state college and university, community college), "some 50 percent of the faculty [were] on temporary status" (p. 33). Among the community colleges' 40,000 faculty, 23,730, or 60 percent, taught part-time (p. 34).

Reporting in the *Wall Street Journal* (Sept. 6, 1986), Taeza Pierce ("Gypsy Faculty Stirs Debate at U.S. Colleges") suggested that adjuncts (as I define them) accounted for 35 percent of the faculty positions nationwide, an increase since 1970 of 22 percent.

2. A number of scholars have attempted to study this group of academics, most notably Howard P. Tuckman and William D. Vogler in *Part-Time Faculty Series* (Washington, D.C.: American Association of University Professors, 1978), much of which is summarized in Tuckman's "Who Is Part-Time in Academe, *AAUP Bulletin* 64 (Dec. 1978), 305–315. Other studies include that reported on in David W. Leslie, Samuel Kellams, and G. Manny Gunne, *Part-Time Faculty in American Higher Education* (New York: Praeger, 1982).

These studies make clear that adjuncts constitute a very diverse group, a majority of whom probably "prefer" part-time employment because they have other full-time jobs or household obligations, or need time to work on advanced degrees. The contrast between figures produced by Tuckman and Vogler and those by Leslie also suggests that both the use of adjuncts and the kinds of adjuncts available for college employment vary significantly from geographical area to area, by discipline, and by type of institution. All the studies, and particularly ones conducted by Barbara H. and Howard P. Tuckman ("Part-Timers, Sex Discrimination, and Career Choice at Two-Year Institutions: Further Findings from the AAUP Survey," *Academe: Bulletin of the AAUP* 66 [March 1980]: 71–76, and "Women as Part-Time Faculty Members," *Journal of Higher Education* 52 [March 1981]: 169–179) make it clear that proportionately, for many more women than men, adjunct positions constitute the sole source of income.

But there are a number of significant problems with these studies, including the fact that they are based on mid-1970s figures, and these in the main for strictly part-time faculty, as distinct from "off-tenure" employees. Further, these studies—particularly Leslie's—seem designed to argue against the portrait of the typical part-timer as an exploited and dissatisfied aspirant for regular academic employment. While it may be true that a majority of adjuncts—certainly a large proportion—do not fit into such a category, it is still the case that the numbers who do are very significant, and that the impact of their "irregular" employment reverberates throughout academia— a problem about which I comment below.

3. At the University of Massachusetts, the part-time minimum salary was raised from $1,500–$1,800 to $3,000 (see Arlyn Diamond, "Bargaining for Nontenure-track Faculty," *AWP Newsletter* 21 (November 1988): 11, 18. At the Community College of Philadelphia, certain benefits, elements of job security, and increases were won by adjuncts after a strike, when—much to their credit—the full-timers honored the picket lines. At a number of the California community colleges, step increases and a salary schedule have been bargained, and at a few, job security provisions and benefits have been won (see Christine Maitland, "Bargaining for Temporary Faculty," *op. cit.*).

4. This fits the generally-accepted perception that part-time adjuncts earn, in terms of direct compensation, about 25–35 percent per course of what full-timers make. See, for example, Franklin, Laurence, and Denham, "When Solutions Become Problems: Taking a Stand on Part-Time Employment," p. 16.

A 1981 study of California community colleges reported upon by Maitland maintains that "after the non-teaching assignments [holding office hours, committee assignments, and the like] were factored out and adjustments were made for differences in training and experience, the conclusion was that part-time faculty received an hourly rate of two-thirds that paid to full-time faculty" (Christine Maitland, "Bargaining for Temporary Faculty, p. 35). But what profession figures a rate of pay on an hourly basis? And how can the professional obligation entailed by college teaching be reduced simply to the number of hours one spends directly in the classroom?

Even if one accept such mendacious statistics, the fact remains that the *college spends* on part-time adjuncts a third or less what it would on full-timers.

5. " 'Two Steps Forward . . . ?' " *Academe,* (March–April, 1987): 6.

6. Franklin, Laurence, and Denham, "When Solutions Become Problems: Taking a Stand on Part-Time Employment," p. 16.

7. Arlyn Diamond, "Bargaining for Nontenure-track Faculty." p. 11.

8. See Paul Lauter and Florence Howe, "Channeling: Manhood and Manpower," *The Conspiracy of the Young* (Cleveland and New York: World, 1970), pp. 182–205. For those unfamiliar with the Selective Service's "Channeling" memorandum, dated July 1, 1965, GPO 899–125, a couple of paragraphs may be instructive, and easily translatable into today's forms of pressure:

> Throughout his career as a student, the pressure—the threat of loss of deferment— continues. It continues with equal intensity after graduation. His local board requires

periodic reports to find out what he is up to. He is impelled to pursue his skill rather than embark upon some less important enterprise and is encouraged to apply his skill in an essential activity in the national interest. The loss of deferred status is the consequence for the individual who has acquired the skill and either does not use it or uses it in a nonessential activity.

The psychology of granting wide choice under pressure to take action is the American or indirect way of achieving what is done by direction in foreign countries where choice is not permitted. Here, choice is limited but not denied, and it is fundamental that an individual generally applies himself better to something he has decided to do rather than something he has been told to do.

9. A number of writers have described a two-tiered workforce—for example, Nadya Aisenberg and Mona Harrington, writing in *The Chronicle of Higher Education.* While their analysis does underline how the exploitation of adjuncts falls disproportionately on women (who make up a large part of the lower tier), it misses the way in which a three-tiered structure operates to enhance managerial conrol.

10. That sentence begins a review by Samuel E. Kellams, one of the more active writers on the subject, of a recent management guide to *Part-Time Faculty Personnel Management Practices* by George E. Biles and Howard T. Tuckman (*Journal of Higher Education* 59 [March–April, 1988]: 236). Kellams' construction of the central issue is also telling: " . . . to balance the need for institutional hiring flexibility against the claims of equity for the part-time faculty member." When "need" is set against "claim" and "institution" against an individual faculty "member" (part-time!), is there any question where the balance will be struck?

11. Christine Maitland, "Bargaining for Temporary Faculty," pp. 34–36.

12. Richard J. Ernst and Larry A. McFarlane, "Are We Shortchanging Our Students By Using Part-Time Faculty?" in David W. Leslie, ed., *Employing Part-Time Faculty* (San Francisco: Jossey-Bass, 1978), pp. 89–98.

13. Franklin, Laurence, and Denham, "When Solutions Become Problems: Taking a Stand on Part-Time Employment," pp. 16–17.

14. " 'Two Steps Forward . . . ?' " p. 6.

Beyond Consciousness Raising: Changing Institutions

For those interested in change, raising consciousness is the critical first step, and a good deal of literary work is directed to that end. But as Frederick Douglas pointed out, it is a first step only—and often a frustrating one at that.

> As I read and contemplated the subject [slavery], behold! that very discontentment which Master Hugh had predicted would follow my learning to read had already come, to torment my soul to unutterable anguish. As I writhed under it, I would at times feel that learning to read had been a curse rather than a blessing. It had given me a view of my wretched condition, without the remedy. It opened my eyes to the horrible pit, but to no ladder upon which to get out.[1]

Ladders have been fashioned, however short and wretchedly fragile, and many have used them to scramble from the pit. But ladders do not level pits. And Douglass was quick to see that while he might as an individual escape the pit, he would never be safe until the pit itself, the institution of slavery, had been eliminated.

This chapter is not about changing individual consciousness, but about changing institutions. The beauty of institutions like slavery or patriarchy, at least for those who benefit from them, is that their perpetuation requires no conscious effort. On the contrary, though filling in the pit requires enormous collective effort, keeping it open and deep can be accomplished even while regularly denouncing its existence. Indeed, academics, none of whom ever told a "darkie" joke, few of whom would speak of a "broad," and all of whom favor equality and the Polish workers, nevertheless help maintain the pits of academic racism and sexism.[2]

My objective here is not to make a cynical point about how the road to hell is paved with liberal intentions. But after a quarter century of efforts to achieve racial and sexual equality in education, those goals do not seem in most respects strikingly nearer. The most recent report of the AAUP's Com-

An earlier version of the first part of this chapter first appeared in *Face to Face: Fathers, Mothers, Masters, Monsters—Essays for a Nonexistent Future*, Meg McGavran Murray, ed. (Westport, Conn.: Greenwood, 1983), pp. 181–190.

mittee W (The Status of Women in the Academic Profession)[3] points out, for example, that salary differentials between women and men have, in all but one rank in one category of institution, actually *increased* in percentage terms and even more substantially in real dollars between 1975 and 1988. This phenomenon cannot be explained by pointing to the concentration of women in lower ranks, at less prestigious institutions, and in part-time and temporary positions, for, as the committee points out, the situation has worsened at *all* ranks and in *all* kinds of institutions. Furthermore, while the proportion of men in tenured positions has risen from 64 to 69 percent over that same thirteen-year period, the proportion of women with tenure has remained at a static 46 percent. An earlier study pointed out that at the beginning of the 1980s, women held only about a fourth of the full-time faculty positions, were fewer than a tenth of the full professors and only a fifth of the associate professors; their salaries were overall some 18 percent less than those of their male colleagues.[4] Similarly, at the beginning of the 1960s, blacks constituted only 3 percent of all college and university teachers; by 1975–76 the proportion had risen only to 4.4 percent, mostly concentrated at traditionally black institutions.[5] In part, such results may be explained by the polite but stubborn resistance that has characterized even more academic than corporate responses to the drive for equity. But in part, too, the problem may derive from an incomplete understanding of, and therefore a strategy for compelling, institutional change.

I shall present a number of cases in point to illustrate the operation of institutional sexism. They bear, as well, on the functioning of academic racism. The first two concern regulation, especially affirmative action procedures—and the canard popular in Reaganized America of federal "overregulation." The third illustrates how traditional academic norms and standards can function to sustain discrimination. They all suggest too clearly how institutionalized discrimination can override consciously progressive intentions. For in each instance, the men involved are well aware and generally supportive of the goals of sex equity. But they remain trapped in procedures whose objective consequences are to perpetuate inequality.

My first case, then, concerns the affirmative action plan of a New York medical institution. Compiled as a two-volume work, this plan was prepared by the affirmative action officer, a person seriously interested in equal rights, indeed sufficiently concerned to devote his free time to a union conference on the subject, though he is "management." Still, the affirmative action officer serves at the pleasure of the institution's president, and his job description would more appropriately fit the title of "compliance officer." That is, his work is to ensure that the school is in compliance with the increasingly complex set of federal regulations governing reporting data—and planning for change where it is required. Among the kinds of reports required in such a plan is a "workforce utilization analysis," designed to pinpoint areas in which women or minority men are "underutilized," that is, are present in proportions significantly less than their "availability" (a subject to which I will return) suggests they should be. Now in a medical institution, the senior clinical faculty, though relatively few in number, obviously wield enormous power and prestige. If it is generally desirable to have women and minority men on the staff in all positions, it is especially so in such key posts. And, if there are hardly any women and minority men in these positions, one would assume that the institution, to comply with federal regulations—not to mention its obligations to the citizenry—would have to establish a set of "goals and timetables"; these would ensure, with more than some deliberate speed, changes in the composition of this upper echelon of the work force. But the workforce analysis showed no "underutilization"! This conclusion is not based, as it sometimes is, upon manipulation of "availability" data, suggesting that there "simply aren't enough of *them* to go round."[6] Rather, included among the clinical faculty in the analysis are all the residents, a significant number of whom are female or minority male (or, perhaps, non-American white male). Is this a falsification? No, they are clinical faculty in some sense of that term. Thus the institution is in this respect "in compliance,"[7] while meetings at which significant institutional decisions are made—such as whether to sustain, against church and right-wing pressure, an inexpensive abortion clinic—are attended almost exclusively by white men. Any questioning of the affirmative action plan becomes immediately an attack on the values of assembled colleagues: "We're in compliance—are you saying that we're a bunch of racists and sexists?" And on that note, the union president fiercely defends this management document.

The situation in this medical school is by no means distinctive. One detailed study of women in medical education reported that while about a quarter of medical students in 1981 were women (up from 9.5 percent in 1970), only 15 percent of the faculty (mainly younger) were female; that figure represented an increase of only 1.7 percent over 1968. The authors concluded "what has not occurred to any notable degree . . . and is disconcerting to all women in academic medicine—both students and faculty—is any meaningful increase in the number of women at the senior professorial ranks."[8]

A second, related case—which we might title "Regulation Stops at the Locker-Room Door"—involves a truly liberal, liberal arts institution, few of whose tenured faculty are women or minority men. Several prominent white male faculty on the key personnel committee swim or play racquetball during the lunch hour and so meet regularly in the shower or on the locker-room benches. Interestingly, it sometimes has been reported that formal meetings of that committee had an "after-the-fact" quality, as if a caucus were operating in which the issues had already been discussed and decided. Indeed, they have—in locker-room situations that lock out from the discussion certain persons: females and nonathletic males. One can even feel some sympathy for an outraged response to this observation: "Why, the next thing you know, the feds will want to regulate what we can talk about with our colleagues and wives in the gym and the bedroom."

Both of these cases do, indeed, involve the issue of federal regulation. This regulation, in civil rights areas, has become increasingly specific and detailed in the last decade. Sheryl Denbo has pointed out that Title VI of the Civil Rights Act of 1964 did not require a self-evaluation or a grievance procedure. Title IX of the Education Amendments of 1972 insisted that schools examine themselves through a formal process of self-evaluation in order to identify problem areas and to help formulate procedures for overcoming them. Section 504 of the Rehabilitation Act of 1973 took a further step: Learning from the limitations of Title IX, Section 504 required that an interested party be included in the self-evaluation process. In 1979, when the Office for Civil Rights issued regulations concerning the implementation of equal opportunity in vocational education programs, it included a provision that state inspectors go out into the field to see whether sex, race, and national origin desegregation were actually being carried out in programs and in the work force.[9]

The current fashion is to deplore these compliance requirements as "federal overregulation," and every educational administrator as well as many senior faculty can tell a favorite story about the oppressive character of "interfering" federal bureaucrats. But as Denbo's chronology shows, such regulations developed step by step in response to previous failures to achieve meaningful change. Universities in particular have learned to meet the letter of the law; indeed, they have learned to turn requirements to their own advantage. For example, when it first became necessary to employ an affirmative action officer, colleges balked, and many dragged their feet in hiring anyone or farmed the responsibility out to an already overworked (often junior and female) administrator. But the colleges quickly learned that they could hire officers who would, indeed, be compliant, and who were not necessarily advocates for change. They could be given primarily technical jobs, for example, the preparation of reports for which the parameters were already set, and their positions could be made to depend upon ensuring that the institution's legal interests were protected. Thus their energies could be channeled into activities that, while providing some small degree of change, emphasized institutional security.[10]

This process is one familiar to students of institutional change in the United States. Reforms are initiated, usually after considerable agitation, to try to correct some outstanding abuse. Often some of the agitators become those charged with implementation of the reform. They find themselves confronting persons in the bureaucracy who, often with no special malice, devise ways not only to change but also to turn whatever new reform has been enacted to their own goals. The indeterminate prison sentence, for example, was invented to encourage the rehabilitation of criminals by not imposing longer terms than would be helpful to that end. But before long the indeterminate sentence became, especially in the hands of prison officials, a powerful weapon of uncertainty through which to control convicts, who never knew precisely the length of their terms and were thus more open to coercion. The new reform has thus become defined sentences and a response to that has been pressure to increase the lengths of sentences—which will, in turn, no doubt lead to a new effort to balance punishment with rehabilitation.

The lesson to be drawn from this process is not, however, the sansculotte approach of Reaganites: "The best regulation is no regulation." Nor is it the cynicism of tired liberals: "one step forward, two steps back." We need, rather, to understand institutions as arenas for struggle, in which shifts in power come slowly; forward motion is often expressed as a series of upwind tacks; and one is always faced with measure and countermeasures. It should be no surprise that a device like a "workforce utilization analysis" would not alter the university's structure of power. That does not mean that affirmative action plans accomplish nothing. It only means that additional strategies are needed to reach into the higher echelons of the academy.

Furthermore, the real issue is not "overregulation," though no doubt every bureaucracy produces abuses of both indifference and zealotry. It is striking that in the educational community the overwhelming number of complaints about regulation concern issues of civil rights, though there are great piles of regulation about school district finances, vocational education programs, student loans, and the like. Colleges and educational agencies have learned to deal with most of these as part of their standard operating procedures, if necessary hiring extra personnel to do the job. But equal rights regulations entail—or at least imply—change, and, discomfort with change, as much as resistance or indifference to equality, is the source of complaints about "regulation." Federal regulations and such feeble enforcement efforts as there have been are quite legitimate means to help pilot institutions from the discriminatory past to a future in which such regulations will be irrelevant.[11]

Meanwhile, the problem faced by our friend the affirmative action officer and by us is solved neither by deregulation nor by abandoning to the managers the resource provided by his office. As the job has been institutionalized, it has systematically been converted from a position of advocacy for the disadvantaged to one of maintenance of institutional norms. How, then, to reinvest the position, the written materials, and the plans and procedures with the dominant concern of achieving needed change rather than legal compliance? And how can a climate of support be built for the many affirmative action officers who continue to see themselves as change agents? The precise answers to such questions will differ from institution to institution. But they are the questions that must be addressed if the pace of change is to be accelerated beyond all deliberate dalliance.

If there is a problem with rules and regulations it is probably manifest less in those promulgated by the federal government than in those, often unwritten, that control hiring and advancement at academic institutions, and this observation leads me to my third case. A former colleague at one of SUNY's university centers insists that his department is altogether free from discrimination: women and men, black and white—all are looked at and treated as equals. How, then, does it happen that almost all the senior faculty are male and white, indeed, that the department contains few women altogether though the field, psychology, is one in which women are significantly represented? That, he says, is a function of departmental standards of scholarly productivity equally applied to all comers. It is not, he argues, that women are inherently less capable than men of doing required scholarly work. But they have more in the way of competing interests, like families and equal opportunity programs, and perhaps fewer of the support systems usually provided by a wife to a young academic husband. Consequently, they produce less. Unfortunate, he continues, but surely these consequences derive from general social structures that were not invented and cannot be changed by his department. All the department can do is maintain its regular standards. After all, he concludes, it would be demeaning to women to apply lesser standards to them, thus suggesting they are incapable of measuring up to established academic norms, and unfair to students to give them less than "the best."

This argument is not presented in bad faith. Rather, it reflects both mis-information and an inadequate, but conventional, failure to examine suffi-ciently either the content of academic norms and standards or their application. Some academics might prefer a kind of mathematical formula to determine who should be hired or promoted: so many points per page of publication times a factor for the quality of the journal or press. Such a formula would, of course, invest existing norms with the imprimatur of "departmental standards." And they are hardly value free. But that is perhaps less important from the point of view of people like my former colleague than that such formulae, like standardized test scores, avoid the sticky and complex issues of balancing a variety of needs and criteria, which are generally rooted in differing values and assumptions about the role of the university. Comparing candidates within *that* context can lead to serious and bitter conflicts as my fourth case shows.

A few years ago, at a small, female liberal arts college, four men and one woman were being considered for tenure in a humanities department that had not tenured a woman for almost two decades. The four men received tenure; the one woman was fired. One of the men had written in comment about his female colleague that "she could hardly be described as a scholar, but only as a feminist." If scholarship were defined as what he and his male colleagues did, then the comment might have been regarded as an accolade, however damaging it was to her tenure fight. The men had been writing occasional, very traditional articles in minor professional journals; indeed, one of them edited a magazine concerned with such ground-breaking subjects as "Is there an American cinema?" Seeing the professional work only within the forms familiar to and supportive of themselves, this man and his colleagues failed to recognize, much less to appreciate, the particular forms feminist scholarship was then taking, especially with respect to the development of new course work in women's studies and the establishment of new, interdis-ciplinary fields of inquiry.

In fact, the problem has been less the productivity of women as compared with men—the studies show that, other things being equal, women produce as much scholarship (though whether the pace of women's and men's pro-ductivity is identical is less clear).[12] The problem is, rather, what those with power consider "merit."[13] Men in positions of authority have generally as-sumed that all areas of legitimate study are encompassed by current definitions

and existing journals in a field. In literature, for example, far more dissertations and articles continued well into this decade to be written about raked-
over and perhaps overrated canonical authors than about any women or black
male writers. That does not prove that the canonical white men are necessarily
more important or articles on them more meritorious, but only that younger
faculty and graduate students are acutely sensitive to what their tradition-
minded and powerful colleagues will deem of merit. It may make more intellectual sense to develop a path-breaking project on a forgotten but significant woman writer like Rebecca Harding Davis, Frances E. W. Harper,
Elizabeth Stuart Phelps, Meridel Le Sueur, or Zitkala-Sa than to fine-sift
once more well-established males whose writing has been the subject of dozens
of dissertations and books. But part of the function of the literary canon is
to institutionalize a set of accepted writers, largely male and white: They are
the ones contained in anthologies and taught in surveys. Work on them is
thus normative; work on anything else is peripheral and even breeds suspicion.
The impressive quality and very amount of scholarship being produced by
feminists will, in time, overwhelm resistance to acknowledging the value of
women's studies; in the meantime, however, feminists have something of the
same problem faced by Americanists in the 1920s: educating their uninformed
and occasionally hostile colleagues about the range and significance of their
work, even while they take the risks incident to producing it.

But let us, for the moment, accept the premise upon which my former
colleague in our third case based his argument: that women in his department
have produced relatively less than their male colleagues in the way of traditional scholarship. Does it follow that it is preferable to hire a person who,
apart from that, has counseled dozens of female students, served on an institution's affirmative action committee, helped establish its rape crisis center,
chaired the local NAACP, and regularly participated in panels at the con-
ferences of the National Women's Studies Association or the National Association for Ethnic Studies? What is "merit" here? What should be the
determinative standards in such a situation? For "standards" do not fall from
the sky. Rather, they are projections into academic terms of ideological assumptions about values, the role of the university, the tasks of a field of study.
Is it the role of a university simply to study and to preserve what already
exists? Or does it also have a responsibility for contributing to, even improving, what it studies? No one would seriously argue that medical research
is designed simply to examine diseases, or that if a clinical staff of a university
were itself a factor in transmitting AIDS, it has no responsibility to cure itself.
To be sure, activism—especially directed inward—cannot be the whole agenda
of an academic department. But neither is it irrelevant for a department in
the social sciences to consider changing its role in the perpetuation of a social
disease—such as racism or sex discrimination. To accept that proposition is
immediately to complicate one's standards of selection, for now one must ask
not only how many pages a candidate produces in the established journals,
not only how many pages in newly emerged journals, but a great variety of

other questions involving everything from a department's need for role models for students to the value of university—even community—citizenship, including activity on behalf of women and minority men.

Most academics have come to view such extended standards of selection as rather a dangerous swamp. And there is considerable historical reason to do so. For many years, considerations of race, religion, and gender deprived meritorious students of educational and job opportunities. *The Academic Marketplace* documented too many cases in which persons were hired because they played the recorder, because their wives gave fine parties, or because they came from "proper" backgrounds. Better "objective," meritocratic standards than religious quotas or such subjectivity. What was not seen when such meritocratic standards were erected was that they incorporated then existing assumptions of what was meritorious, from speech patterns and general knowledge to abstruse scholarship, and that they thus institutionalized existing relations of power. It was thus that my former colleague could, while supporting equal rights for women, insist upon procedures and criteria that effectively denied equal rights.

Beyond the issue of merit, whatever its basis, is the question of whether meritocratic standards are the only legitimate ones in a democracy. In the tenure case I alluded to above, no one seemed to have asked what was needed to develop a healthy educational environment for women. Was it traditional male scholars who lectured more or less wittily on the sexual metaphors of the latest literary rage or was it, rather, a risk-taking female scholar in whose classes problems of literature intersected with those of her students' lives? It may be that both are useful. But such a conclusion implies a far more complex examination of institutional mission, departmental role, and individual qualifications than the single standard of scholarly productivity—even assuming agreement about how scholarly production is to be defined.

At the beginning of this chapter I spoke of the problem of leveling the pits of sexism and racism, as distinct from helping individuals climb out of those pits. Ironically, the more racist and sexist attitudes are frowned upon as inappropriate among people like academics, the more important institutional norms become as means for maintaining patriarchal and white privilege. Such privilege, then, has accrued from the operation of discrimination; and it is in conflict with the mainstream liberal ideology of academe. For many, this contradiction between liberalism and privilege resolves into support for traditional standards or into popular hostility to government "activism" or "interference." Those who would press for change no longer confront obvious and more easily attacked expressions of prejudice, such as that in the tenure case I cited. Rather, they face much more elaborate and defensible institutional walls, which seem to those climbing from the pit to stretch ever smoother and higher.

That view from the bottom emphasizes the importance of academic programs like women's, black, and ethnic studies. For these are not only academic departments but bases for changing the larger institutions in which they are

located. It seems to me that only from such bases, and from campus organizations such as faculty and staff women's associations,[14] can helpful answers
be developed to such critical questions as these:

> Is an individual's scholarship or publication in women's studies in fact, as is
> sometimes suggested, discounted by faculty hiring or promotions commit-
> tees? Is publication in *Signs* or *Feminist Studies,* for example, taken as less
> significant than publication in the *Kenyon Review* or *ELH* [*English Literary
> History*]? Is the impressive scholarship involved in developing interdiscipli-
> nary coursework in women's studies credited, together with more traditional
> instances of professional development? Is service on the women's studies
> advisory committee considered as equivalent to service on a college curric-
> ulum committee?[15]

These are the kinds of questions that do not in the regular course of things
come before academic departments, but need constantly to be *placed* before
us. The problem becomes how to institutionalize such processes and thus to
promote real change.

I want to discuss two kinds of efforts at institutionalizing change, one
having to do with organization, the other with where colleges and universities
put money. I offer these as practical suggestions, but also because I think
they help call into question other ancient and sacred bulls.

Most institutions, and certainly almost all faculty members, are committed
to "peer review" processes in making hiring, retention, promotion, and tenure
decisions. But who are one's "peers"? This is no more an idle question in
academia than it is in the courtroom. For it has become clear over the last
decades that the constitution of juries by those who are not one's peers is a
major source of *un*equal justice. Changing the composition of jury pools does
not, by itself, ensure that justice will prevail. But it has helped limit the ways
in which lawyers can appeal to the unspoken prejudices of a homogeneous
jury; it has changed the dynamic of discussions within jury rooms; and in
significant cases it has introduced differing perspectives on events than might
be available to a monocultural group. Similar goals are desirable in academic
peer-review processes. I simply do not believe that a committee of white,
male psychologists whose work is in other fields constitutes a "peer" group
for a woman primarily specializing in the psychology of women and its practical implications for problems of family violence and child care. I do not
even believe that such a group of "peers" can with considered professional
judgment choose among a set of candidates with such credentials. Similarly,
few committees of English literature specialists can review with integrity a
specialist in contemporary Chicano writing, or, indeed, clearly pose the importance to an English department of such a discipline. But there are by now
in most institutions other professionals, in different departments and programs
or in administrative areas, who are more familiar with scholarly developments
related to women's studies or minority and ethnic studies. And if such peers
are not available *on* campus (a fact that underlines the need to find them),
they are almost certainly to be located nearby.

What blocks the constitution of truly "peer" review committees is a kind of departmental chauvinism. It is equivalent in its way to the drawing of school district boundaries—as between dominantly minority cities and white suburbs—in order to maintain segregated classrooms. The argument that such "external" members of search committees will not have the necessary professional expertise is further contradicted by the practice, almost universal in academe, of having promotion and tenure decisions reviewed by powerful, college-wide and often campus-wide committees.[16] If it is legitimate for a physicist to review the tenurability of a psychologist, it is equally reasonable for an anthropologist concerned with race and gender, for example, to be included on a psychology search panel. But furthermore, if it is an institutional priority to increase female and minority male representation on the faculty—and where should that *not* be the case?—search panels constituted entirely by men or by whites are from this perspective not only practically inexpedient but of doubtful legitimacy.[17]

That may sound harsh. But I would invite my doubting white and male colleagues to imagine themselves "on trial"—as, indeed, candidates are—before a jury (which, I suspect, could be assembled on only a handful of campuses) consisting entirely of black women.

A similar observation can be made about administrative hierarchies. Few minority or white female administrators hold upper-level management positions, especially at traditionally white colleges. Thus senior administrative councils can frequently be all white, often with a single token woman. Once again, however, this segregated outcome originates in the initial decision about who should be included within such a council, and if an administrator wishes to create a more heterogeneous group, that almost always can be accomplished by recruiting from outside the boundaries set by older definitions. That may involve, to be sure, reaching outside *both* faculty and managerial ranks, but the views and experiences of an $18,000 per year secretary may provide some much-needed light in the councils of academic privilege. The point is that segregated, homogeneous administrative committees will continue to exist only so long as those who establish them wish to keep them that way.

What is at stake is not simply a mechanical process of diversification. It is, rather, that managerial, like faculty, culture tends toward homogeneity regardless of race and gender, since so much else of day-to-day life is shared. Thus fundamental questions, or even significant practical ones—for example, whether an ice-skating rink or a child-care facility should become a fund-raising priority—are explored only in the narrowest ways, if at all. Institutionalizing diversity by reconstituting *all* committees would, I think, provide a significant step toward filling in the pits of discrimination.

One further boundary limits change—the one, often marked by physically imposing walls, separating campus and community. To be sure, that border is illusory, since American universities have for over a century been wedded to *certain* external communities: large agricultural interests, local developers, corporations that hire graduates, among others. These connections can often be valuable ones that colleges might exploit more fully—for example, to locate employment opportunities for spouses of faculty members they wish to hire. The increasingly harsh question, however, is how academic institutions can creatively interact with poor and minority communities. That interaction cannot, I think, be a one-way process by which the colleges provide self-defined "services" and personnel, including student interns; rather, what is needed is an exchange whereby such communities can become involved more directly in helping to establish the academic programs that may become valuable to them.

While my first set of suggestions involves borders, the second set focuses on money. The largest portion of an institution's funds are committed before they are raised or appropriated, of course. Funding, especially in state institutions, is significantly tighter than before, of course. Such constraints are often posed to suggest far more limited areas of discretion than actually exist in making decisions about how to spend money. To be sure, affirmative action goals of the sort I am discussing are much easier to implement in periods of expansion, but they can still be pursued in periods of fiscal constraint. For example, universities and many colleges are always starting up programs in new disciplines, like genetic engineering, brain functions, and not-for-profit management. These are, no doubt, important areas of academic work, but in the scale of institutional priorities, are they *more* important than ensuring that the faculty be more diverse? If, both for educational and social reasons, the latter is critical—especially at this depressing point in American race relations—then positions should be funded that are earmarked for minority hires. And if funds are too slim to do both, one must choose. Those who run colleges have almost always, in the past, chosen to fund new academic areas, generally outgrowths of existing disciplines and staffed by persons initially trained within them. We live with that legacy. Our grandchildren will live with it, too, if different choices are not made.

In fact, the issue seldom is choosing between new programs and minority and white female hires. Rather it is deciding to put significant available funds into serious programs for recruiting affirmative action candidates. During the 1970s, the State University of New York provided "bonus lines" for departments making minority hires. That approach significantly increased the numbers of minority faculty—until it was terminated. Trinity College has just instituted a program of setting aside a number of new lines for minority hires. The fiscal trade-off is that departments making such hires will not be able to hire replacements to teach courses if one other faculty member goes on leave.

But, complain the critics, there are not enough of *them* to go round. Even if this were true in every field, which it is not, institutions do not escape the obligation to invest in change. When, in the 1830s, Harvard College wished to have a professor of modern poetry, it hired Henry Wadsworth Longfellow . . . and then sent him to Europe to complete what amounted to his graduate training. Increasingly, a number of colleges have begun to offer predoctoral fellowships to minority scholars, both to aid in their completing graduate work and to open the possibility of their coming to teach at that or a similar institution. At the same time, UCLA has instituted a program under which as many as 200 minority graduate students have obtained full funding toward their terminal degrees. Had similar efforts been instituted during the 1960s, we would not hear complaints now about how thin the ranks of minority faculty are.

The ultimate goal of such programs is, of course, to create that academic Utopia in which they are no longer needed. In the meantime, however, institutions need to recognize the problems of isolation faced by senior women and by many minority faculty. Since they are generally so few, they are called upon to serve on endless committees and respond to problems ranging from student discipline to faculty hiring. But perhaps more difficult, they are often isolated intellectually because many colleagues do not share knowledge of, or indeed interest in, what they do or the angles of vision they have developed. Women's studies, black and ethnic studies, and related programs play a vital role, in this connection, as intellectual centers: They mount lectures and other programs, organize symposia and study groups, serve as bases for developing campus events. Their value thus extends beyond the relatively limited number of courses they provide for the curriculum. Many also have been the mechanisms to promote faculty development efforts focused on the new feminist and minority scholarship. Such programs do generate curricular change, but perhaps as important, they help the traditional faculty learn more about disciplines of particular concern to many women and minority male academics. What is involved here is the validation of professional discourses significantly different from those to which the traditional faculty have been accustomed. The continued, indeed expanded, support of such programs thus must be seen as an important component of any institutional affirmative action plan.

The variety of programmatic efforts designed to encourage and support women and minority male faculty is limited only by the imagination of those interested in pursuing such goals. The American Association of Colleges offers an "Action Manual" of programs, ranging from regular salary equity reviews to institutional child care centers to annual women's recognition days and minority cultural events.[18] The point, which college and university leaders seem only to have begun to recognize, is that generalized expressions of support for affirmative action have not, in fact, produced real change—not even in attitudes. Only concrete programs involving structural alterations will do that.

In a certain sense, the bottom line remains the institutional discourse. So long, for example, as canards about possibly "lowering standards" by hiring minority faculty pass as intelligent discussion on campuses, we have achieved nothing resembling equitable institutions. Debates over where to allocate money, discussions of minority hiring initiatives, efforts to begin facilities such as child care centers, summer institutes on, for example, the changing literary canon, are all important in themselves. And they are useful in helping to raise consciousness. In the long run, however, it is the institutional environment itself, its structures of power, and especially the presence or absence of *differing* constituencies,[19] that dominantly shapes consciousness. To get "beyond consciousness raising," that is, one must alter organization and practice.

Notes

1. Frederick Douglass, *Narrative of the Life of Frederick Douglass, An American Slave, Written by Himself* (New York: Signet, 1968), p. 55.

2. Pamela S. Tolbert similarly argues that salary inequities between male and female faculty derive largely from organizational polices and practices. See "Organizations and Inequality: Sources of Earnings Differences Between Male and Female Faculty," *Sociology of Education* 59 (October 1968): 227–236. She points in particular to the ability of organizations with dominant positions in a market, like prestigious research institutions, to indulge in "discriminatory 'tastes,' " and thus to "recruit and pay higher wages to a preferred group." At the same time, she points out, "the demographic composition of an organization can affect the nature of intergroup relations and the occurrence of discriminatory perceptions and practices" (p. 227). That is, the fewer of *them* there are, the more likely it is that the institutional discourse will be exclusive and that "discriminatory 'tastes' " will be reinforced and maintained.

Dee L. R. Graham, Patricia O'Reilly, and Edna I. Rawlings argue that "the biggest problem is that women often do not recognize when they are being discriminated against. . . . It appears that the effects of sex discrimination are institutionalized, so that most men and many women think that the status quo is inevitable and acceptable." "Costs and Benefits of Advocacy for Faculty Women: A Case Study," *Journal of Social Issues* 41 (1985): 90–91.

3. Mary W. Gray, Chair, "Academic Women and Salary Differentials," *Academe* 74:4 (July–August, 1988): 33–34.

4. These figures are those of the National Center for Educational Statistics, as reported in *The Chronicle of Higher Education* 21 (Sept. 29, 1980): 8. Cf. the discouraging report by John E. Stecklein and Gail E. Lorenz, "Academic Women: Twenty-Four Years of Progress? *Liberal Education* 72 (Spring 1986): 63–71, which suggests that "the gaps between women and men have not been reduced during the past 24 years except in a few specifics" (p. 69).

5. Robert J. Menges and William H. Exum, "Barriers to the Progress of Women and Minority Faculty," *Journal of Higher Education* 54 (1983): 125. Menges and Exum report figures regarding women similar to those I have summarized.

6. Some of the problems in the use of availability data and some solutions were presented by Phyllis Zatlin Boring in "Double Use of Availability Data," a flyer distributed by the Women's Equity Action League, June 1976.

7. Menges and Exum, "Barriers to the Progress of Women and Minority Faculty," *op. cit.,* summarize the reasons affirmative action has "accomplished less than its proponents hoped or its critics feared." These include "how hiring goals are set;" the tendency for hiring goals "to be set on an institution-wide rather than departmental basis;" where and how positions are advertised; "the criteria for evaluating women and minority candidates," and how they are played off against each other; and how "conscientious" institutions are in meeting goals (p. 129).

8. The study, by Judith B. Braslow and Marilyn Heins, was published in the May 1981 issue of the *New England Journal of Medicine* and reported upon in *The Chronicle of Higher Education* 22 (May 26, 1981): 8.

9. See Denbo Associates, "Federal Non-Discrimination Regulations and Guidelines: A Comparison of Coverage," Washington, D.C., 1980.

10. Similarly, the requirement for an affirmative action grievance procedure has, in some instances, been used to circumvent the broader and more systematic grievance procedures negotiated into union contracts.

11. I am not arguing here the merits of particular forms of affirmative action, including specific goals and timetables. That case is made with great vigor and scholarship by Richard A. Wasserstrom in "Racism, Sexism and Preferential Treatment: An Approach to the Topics," *UCLA Law Review* 24 (1977), 581–622. No doubt one could cite instances in which the effect of affirmative action rulings is to lessen the chances of successful integration. But if one rolls back federal "interference" step by step, one comes all too quickly to separate and unequal schools, male-only shop classes and gyms, and famous faculties with nary a woman or minority male among them. It is incumbent upon those who deride all regulation to establish really functional means for achieving sex and race equity. Otherwise, one cannot help but suspect that the attack on regulation is but a façade behind which lurks the defense of existing privilege.

12. To cite Pamela Tolbert's 1986 summary: "There are no significant differences in productivity between male and female faculty, as measured by number of publications, number of presentations, etc." "Organizations and Inequality," *op. cit.*, p. 234. The relevant studies cited by Tolbert include David Katz, "Faculty Salaries, Promotions and Productivity at a Large University," *American Economic Review* 63 (1973): 469–477; Marianne Ferber, "Professors, Performance and Rewards," *Industrial Relations* 13 (1974): 69–77; R. J. Simon, S. M. Clark, and K. Galway, "Women Ph.D.'s: A Recent Profile," in M. Medmick, et al., eds., *Women and Achievement* (New York: Wiley, 1975), pp. 85–110; Marianne Ferber and Betty Kordick, "Sex Differentials in the Earnings of Ph.D.'s," *Industrial and Labor Relations Review* 31 (1978): 227–238; National Research Council, *Career Options in a Matched Sample of Men and Women Ph.D.'s* (Washington, D.C.: National Academy Press, 1981). E. Goldstein, "Effect of Same-Sex and Cross-Sex Models on the Subsequent Academic Productivity of Scholars," *American Psychologist* 34 (1979): 407–410, found no difference in women's and men's rates of publication in psychology four years after their graduation. Betty J. Austin suggests in "Women Faculty and Scholarly Productivity," a paper presented at the annual meeting of the Michigan Academy of Sciences, Arts, and Letters, Big Rapids, Mich., March 1984, that while there is some evidence suggesting that women's rates of publication are lower than men's, the research evidence is inconclusive. A more technically sophisticated study by Phyllis Bronstein, Leora Black, Joyce Pfennig, and Adele White, "Getting Academic Jobs: Are Women Equally Qualified—and Equally Successful?" *American Psychologist* 61 (March 1986) concludes that " . . . There was no difference in the *rate* of publication for female and male applicants"; apparent differences in productivity were accounted for by the fact that men in the pools they examined had been " . . . in the world of professional psychology longer" (p. 319).

13. Elaine Martin suggests that, in general, women expend more effort on teaching and committee work whereas men spend more time on research and administration, the more established routes to tenure and promotion. See "Power and Authority in the Classroom: Sexist Stereotypes in Teaching Evaluations," *Signs* 9 (1984), 482–492. Her findings reinforce the question of what constitutes "merit." A similar view is presented by T. G. Turk in "Women Faculty in Higher Education: Academic Administration and Governance in a State University System, 1966–1977," *Pacific Sociological Review* 24 (1981): 212–236.

14. See Mary R. Anderson and Gloria N. Wilson, "Faculty Women's Association: An Instrument for Change," *Journal of Social Issues* 41 (1985), 73–84.

15. Florence Howe and Paul Lauter, *The Impact of Women's Studies on the Campus and the Disciplines* (Washington: National Institute of Education, 1980), p. 88.

16. Apart from such issues, those who look at the academy from outside often come to doubt the coherence of criteria used to determine tenure. See George S. Roukis, David Halpern, Robin Zeichner, "Sex-Based Discrimination in Higher Education," *Labor Law Journal* 34 (April 1983): 229–237. Cf. Menges and Exum, "Barriers to the Progress of Women and Minority Faculty," p. 130.

17. Cf. Menges and Exum, "Barriers to the Progress of Women and Minority Faculty": "Without positive efforts, illusions about compliance will combine with the values of academic culture to maintain review systems that slow women's and minorities' progress through higher education's ranks" (pp. 139–140).

18. See Karen Bogart, *Toward Equity: An Action Manual for Women in Academe* (Washington, D.C.: American Association of Colleges, 1984).

19. Cf. Pamela S. Tolbert, "Organizations and Inequality: Sources of Earnings Differences Between Male and Female Faculty," *op. cit.:* "... reduced exposure to a minority group, as a consequence of minority group size and segregation, can foster discriminatory perceptions and behavior" (pp. 233–34). Cf. Ann Fuehrer and Karen Maitland Schilling, "The Values of Academe: Sexism as a Natural Consequence," *Journal of Social Issues* 41 (1985): 39.

University Reform:
Threat or Opportunity

When you feel yourself beginning to slide down a cliff, you are not likely to think too hard about what it is you grab to stop the fall. But the choice of handholds makes a difference—the difference between continuing to plunge and holding on long enough to plant your feet. As you descend, what seems a vine turns out to be a viper, and what seems a solid trunk proves rootless and tears away.

So it is as faculty have contended with the growing shelf of studies criticizing, occasionally analyzing, and mostly prescribing for, higher education. We feel the structure, the norms of our profession, shifting and sliding beneath our feet. We reach for a handhold, a point of stability, and discover, alas, that there's little that is reliable, much that is frail and fragile.

Three of the mid-1980s higher education studies[1] were among the opening shots in what has become an extended battle over the character and quality of the institutions in which professors work, as well as over what exactly it is that faculty and staff do. One could, of course, dismiss these and more recent studies, perhaps citing their manifold banalities as sufficient reason for indifference. Or, as faculty, we could acquiesce, agreeing to such changes as the reformists are able to compel, but doing little more than what is necessary to protect our turf. Either course is rationally defensible. Neither is advisable for the academic community.

It seems to me that either indifference or generalized resistance would be mistaken—for at least two reasons. First, this has proven to be an unusually strong tide of reform, and even now, half a decade later, it seems still to be waxing. Even from the perspective of strict self-interest, not an unfamiliar ground for academics to stand upon, it would be dangerous to ignore what is a continuing effort to reshape the character of our work and lives. Second, the drive to reform college education presents faculty and staff with an opportunity to shape the direction of change, and in particular to raise what none of these reports really contends with: What political values, what economic forms, what social objectives do we really wish to pursue? And what sorts of educational programs might actually help carry out such goals?

This article first appeared, in somewhat different form, in *Thought and Action: The NEA Higher Education Journal*, 2 (Winter, 1986): 5–22.

225

My object, then, is to help arm those of us willing to enter the fray. First, I want to examine the content, the tacit assumptions, and the latent objectives of these critiques of higher education. And second, I want to propose an alternative reading of recent educational and social history partly to explain the malaise on and directed toward campuses but primarily to develop criteria by which we may judge the value of proposed reforms.

I

Superficially, these three studies resemble each other. The groups that helped produce them consisted of academic administrators, as well as some faculty, from many of that great variety of institutions hidden under the name "higher education." The three studies worked, though not deeply, with similar numbers—test score results, demographic changes in student populations, shifts in enrollments, and the like. And all reflect the widely-held perception that higher education in the United States is in a state of rapid decline.

That is a perception shared not only by the general public but, when we are honest, by most academics as well. The bill of particulars is not hard to construct: declining test scores; graduates who cannot write, who know no language but English (and that mechanically), who lack the arithmetic skills to complete an IRS 1040 short form, who know little of the history of their own—or any—nation; vocational training substituted for education yet employers who complain that their taxes do not produce a competent workforce; and parents who assert that they, never having attended college, know more than their "educated" children. We are all familiar with such catalogues and can produce our own variations and additions. Whatever their accuracy, they reflect a view of higher education more negative and sceptical than at any time in recent history. And they suggest an erosion of public support, if not for the theory, then at least for the practice of what professors do.

Unfortunately, taken in the aggregate, such lists tend to obscure the real problems of higher education, dashing together myths and realities, confusing the real agony of classroom failure with the unreal artifacts of exaggerated expectations, turning the successes of our remarkable experiment in mass higher education into "failures" (at least as measured along scales constructed at Princeton circa 1953). Indeed, one danger of examining such works together is conflating them into one undifferentiated and unmanageable condemnation of higher education.

But these are, in fact, rather different studies, with differing analyses and objectives. They conveniently arrange themselves along a spectrum from the helpful to the banal. William Bennett's paper—as its title, *To Reclaim a Legacy,* reveals—is an essay in conservative ideology, a deeply nostalgic effort to revive the consensus and the curriculum of the 1950s. The Association of American Colleges (AAC) study, *Integrity in the College Curriculum,* is at once a moralistic and a managerial treatise, directed toward coopting faculty into following the leadership so brilliantly displayed by academic administrators during the past two decades of decline. While The National Institute of Education (NIE) report, *Involvement in Learning,* shares the mainstream politics and many of the social clichés of the other pieces, it at least focuses on what is for most faculty the central issue: whether, what, and how students learn. It provides some helpful, if incomplete, ideas about the origins of the current slide and some sensitive and practical proposals for responding to student needs.

Each of these works offers, at least implicitly, different historical accounts of the roots of today's problems. Bennett blames the decay of the humanities, with which he associates the broader decline in higher education, primarily on those who teach and to a lesser degree on those who administer: "A collective loss of nerve and faith on the part of both faculty and academic administrators during the late 1960s and early 1970s was undeniably destructive of the curriculum" (p. 27). Professors, asserts Bennett, allowed their own research and intellectual needs or student preferences to substitute for what they had previously concluded students *ought* to study. In addition, more experienced senior faculty opted out of general education and broader humanities courses, retreating into their specialities and leaving students adrift with younger, untrained staff. Thus, in Bennett's view, liberal arts study lost institutional legitimacy, intellectual credibility, and pedagogical integrity. Needless to say, Bennett never examines either the historical development of the "liberal arts" or the social functions of such forms of study in the past or in the present; he simply asserts their value.

The AAC study group presents a slightly more complex historical account: It sees developing throughout this century a "dispersal of authority over the curriculum" that robbed the curriculum of its coherence and direction. The demands society in general placed on the university, the pressure for access to college education, and spiraling enrollments all played a role. But the chief villain, for the AAC, has been professorial specialization.

> Central to the troubles and to the solution are the professors, for the development that overwhelmed the old curriculum and changed the entire nature of higher education was the transformation of the professors from teachers concerned with the characters and minds of their students to professionals, scholars with Ph.D. degrees with an allegiance to academic disciplines stronger than their commitment to teaching or to the life of the institutions where they are employed
>
> (p. 6).

But the AAC panel never really examines the economic and social forces that produced academic (and other) forms of specialization; nor does it really question whether we college teachers are any longer suited, if we ever were, to be primary shapers of the values and characters of young people. And it never began to wonder why professors should be less committed to their disciplines, upon which their status and income really depend, than other relatively comfortable Americans.

The NIE group is less concerned with assigning blame for the current decline. Faculty are not under fire. Rather, the NIE study emphasizes the *changes,* social and demographic, to which colleges and universities have tried to respond—and by which they have been shaped or, depending upon one's view, victimized—during the last quarter century. The miscellany of "warning signals" cited in the NIE report are, I think, indicative both of the range of and a certain incoherence in the authors' analysis.

- "Only half of the students who start college with the intention of getting a bachelor's degree actually attain this goal."
- "Student performance on 11 of 15 major Subject Area Tests of the Graduate Record Examinations declined between 1964 and 1982."
- "Increasing numbers of undergraduates are majoring in narrow specialties."
- "Students have abandoned some of the traditional arts and sciences fields in large numbers."
- "Accreditation standards for undergraduate professional programs often stand as barriers to the broad understanding we associate with liberal learning."
- "College and university faculty have lost approximately 20 percent of their purchasing power in the past decade."
- "The proportion of faculty who teach part-time increased from 23 percent in 1966 to 41 percent in 1980.
- " . . . more and more students attend large," bureaucratic institutions.
- " . . . a funding system based principally on enrollments sends a clear message to colleges that quantity is valued over quality."

(pp. 8–12)

The authors of the NIE report see the curricular changes deplored in the other studies as products of social and economic forces—not as outgrowths of some alleged "failure of nerve" or of excessive professorial specialization. In contrast to Bennett and AAC, the NIE report rests not on a tendentious morality but on at least some historical and sociological analyses. But these are limited: They do not offer a coherent explanation of the developments I have cited, nor what at least some of these developments might offer to guide a political struggle over the future of education. For that, we need a somewhat different analysis.

II

After World War II, national policy aimed at widening higher education participation through such means as the GI Bill, the National Defense Education Act, extension of both federal and state aid programs to students and to institutions, and later, through civil rights legislation. Policymakers saw this expansion as a means for keeping surplus labor temporarily out of the job market, developing a better-trained workforce to compete with the Soviet

Union, socializing a broader segment of the populace to the cultural norms of American elites, and providing opportunities for large numbers of Americans to enter the economic and social middle-class represented by a bachelor's degree.

As unprecedented numbers arrived on campuses, and particularly as the social movements of the 1950s and 1960s opened doors for new, first-generation-to-college minority and working-class students, the traditional liberal arts curriculum came to seem not merely "less relevant" to them, but socially and historically inaccurate. As I have pointed out elsewhere, the questions "where are the blacks?" and "where are the women?" took on more force as curricular issues as they were asked with increasing power and justice in the political arena. Studying "Western culture" or "The Origins of Christian Civilization" in a narrowly orthodox fashion seemed reasonable enough in the 1950s. But if your ancestors had been kidnapped from Africa, subjected to chattel slavery, and had endured a legacy of racism sustained by "civilized," Christian westerners, that also appeared a matter worth study. So, too, did the cultural achievements, values, and social and psychological experiences of various minorities and of white women. And even how the historical aspirations and priorities of working-class people in this country differed from those of the bourgeoisie seemed appropriate to study. In a certain sense, the post-World War II extension of higher education got somewhat out of the hands of the American political and educational leaders who had initially presided over it, both with respect to the numbers coming in the doors and the unsettling of traditional curricula—even, perhaps especially, at elite institutions.

At the same time that the push toward a more comprehensive—and so more accurate—curriculum gained momentum, the political consensus that had set the United States on what seemed a road toward a New Frontier began crumbling. Indeed, the road itself disappeared in the rice paddies of Vietnam and the sand hills of Mississippi. What values American society—and therefore American education—stood for became increasingly obscure, or at least more openly conflicted. To say briefly what I have elaborated in another chapter, the social consensus that undergirded the established culture and thus the curriculum of the 1950s came apart, and the search for an adequate replacement—a search still underway—began in earnest.

As the authority of the old culture waned in the 1960s, as faculty pursued professional opportunities presented by an expanding economy, and as students increasingly came to doubt the value of what more and more seemed arbitrary requirements, academic managers stepped into the vacuum of curricular power. They brought with them business school tools arguably more appropriate to the production of consumer goods or to running a supermarket than to academe—at least as academics liked to think of it. If no consensus could any longer be established about what students *should* take, well then, what different colleges advertised in their catalogues could be determined by what the student as consumer wished (read "could afford") to buy. Whether the student shopped at K-Mart or at Nieman-Marcus would, of course, depend on the student's preference (read "class"). Faculty lines—that is, jobs—could then conveniently be allocated on the basis of enrollments. Thus came into being the enrollment-driven funding arrangements that now characterize most colleges and universities in the United States, but especially those inhabited by the newer student populations.

Academic managers were active in other areas of higher education, as well, reshaping institutions to fit the rapidly changing needs of American capitalism. Whatever role it actually played, the Vietnam War certainly marked the breakup of the American-dominated world order that had prevailed since the end of World War II. But it did not imply the final disintegration of the liberal capitalist state, as some of the more feverish manifestos of the late 1960s wished. On the contrary, American capitalism proved once again its ability to adapt to, indeed to profit from, another of the periodic crises it produces. Profits were maintained and even extended, among other things by cutting back on "nonessential" services or marginal investments, such as airline meals, free phone information, health-care benefit packages, and increasingly extended periods of education. Further, the financial burden of sustaining such services were, beginning in the Nixon administration, shifted to the middle and lower classes desiring them by, in the case of education, raising tuition and fees at public colleges, cutting back on government scholarship and loan programs, and limiting or redirecting corporate contributions. At the same time, educational workers were pushed to turn out more "products," by increasing class size, raising teaching loads, and extending terms. Even more, the period of economic uncertainty that characterized the early 1970s was made into an *opportunity* to rationalize institutions providing services to fit corporate needs better.

As the post-Vietnam War economy declined, students haunted by fears of joblessness—especially those new, first-generation constituencies—sought whatever career tracks seemed to promise secure positions after graduation. They were well aware of how fragile in a contracting economy were the tweedy dreams of becoming comfortable, "liberally educated" people. At the same time, job requirements and even names were being upgraded: mortician to "mortuary scientist," jailer to "correctional officer." What had been openings into which students moved directly from two-year terminal programs became "professions" for which one "qualified" only through elaborated requirements in four-year institutions. Colleges were thereby gripped in a vicious economic circle: As new industries demanded students trained in new skills or at least socialized through extended college exposure, managers responded with ever-new programs to which students hastened with the fervor of converts. Traditional academic areas were increasingly drained of enrollments—and steadily cut back. Resources were shifted from producing literature and history teachers, ecologists, or—in effect—social activists, to turning out mortuary scientists and corrections officers—that is, grave-diggers and jailers—undoubtedly more necessary in a period of high unemployment and downward mobility.

Four-year institutions also increasingly came to serve the "cooling-out" functions previously characteristic of the community colleges.[2] Even in elite institutions the many students (up to 60 percent in some places in the mid-1970s) who wanted to become doctors or lawyers had to be sorted out, for however wildly overdeveloped those professions, there was not room for all the competent, much less for all those wanting the prestige and income. So students, especially from the newer college populations, had to be diverted from such primary job aspirations into related, and professional-seeming, occupations like pharmacology and psychometrics. And they had to be made to believe that their "failure" to become doctors and lawyers was a function of their own inabilities, not of the class structure of American society.

In such a context, few members of the professoriat seemed to have the fortitude to assert that students *ought* to learn about American history, say, or literature—whatever else they might choose to take—much less that *all* students should have to learn about *all* American history and culture, including that of women, blacks, and other racial and ethnic minorities, and including the historical struggles over differing definitions of "life, liberty, and the pursuit of happiness." Or that students *ought* to examine the political economy and social functions of the American institutions in which they studied and would most likely be working. Or that colleges *should* be places to examine, debate and put into practice the values toward which a democratic society might aspire. An economics of education increasingly focused on technological competence usurped the place of a philosophy of education, and a kind of Gresham's law prevailed at the registration table.

For more than fifteen years I carried around with me an advertisement from *The New York Times* "Careers in Education" section. Its headline announced "Fire-eating Dragons Wanted," and it proceeded:

> One of the nation's leading career education centers will make selective additions to its faculty if dynamic, career-conscious individuals can be found for the positions. If you're content where you are or with what is presently being done in your field, you need not bother to apply—but if you have that "something extra" to offer, we may have a place for you in Correctional Services, Media Technology, Electronics Technology, Secretarial and Office Specialties, or Mortuary Science and Funeral Service. Master's degree is preferred. We are looking for people who have experience in their fields and who are on their way up—who want to accomplish something out of the ordinary.

The return address was to an academic dean at one of the better-established regional public universities—one that had, that same year, *laid off* over 100 faculty in the humanities and social sciences, including fifty-six who were tenured or on continuing appointment.

I unearth this twenty-year-old egg because it so well illustrates the central dynamic that has produced the kind of curricular catastrophe the recent studies bemoan. Not to understand the history represented by this ad is to be doomed to repeat it. The potential for repetition is clearly here—especially given the "solutions" to the present crisis proposed by Bennett and the AAC study group.

III

Common to the Bennett and AAC manifestos is a plea for the restoration of some common core of knowledge, "a clear vision of what constitutes an educated person." Their notions of what an "educated person" should know or understand overlap, but also differ somewhat: Bennett emphasizes a core of great books, encounters with the "great spirits" of the western tradition.[3] The AAC report urges that all students be exposed to a "minimum required program" embodying "nine experiences," some of which are "skills," others of which are "ways of growing and understanding." They are, to say the least, familiar categories.

- "Inquiry, abstract logical thinking, critical analysis"
- "Literacy: writing, reading, speaking, listening"
- "Understanding numerical data"
- "Historical consciousness"
- "Science"—its methods, models, values
- "Values"—the "capacity to make informed and responsible moral" choices
- "Art"
- "International and multicultural experiences"
- "Study in depth"—not "required courses or prescribed subjects," but a coherent major that focuses on "methods and processes, the modes of access to understanding and judgment"

That such an insipid list should be paraded as the goals of college education suggests how little the AAC group asked basic questions about the relationship of schooling to social priorities. The latter are never in fact considered, but only assumed.

The NIE group did not see its task as defining the "knowledge most worth having" (p. 16). However, this study, too, poses its ideal objectives for liberal education: curricular content "addressed not only to subject matter but also to the development of capacities of analysis, problem solving, communication, and synthesis," and the integration of "knowledge from various disciplines" (p. 43). Which "problems" need "analysis," what kinds of knowledge need to be integrated from which disciplines, and communicated (how?) to whom— and how the answers to such questions might shape the forms of education— the study does not address. Still, such educational platitudes are unexceptional; indeed, it is a measure of the limitations of these studies that they are assumed to need restatement. Even the premise of Bennett's curricular idea— that all students should share a common set of experiences—might not in itself evoke conflict. To be sure, his specific examples are, as I suggest in the next chapter, exceedingly retrograde. But the issue here is not Bennett's version of a cultural canon, for any progressive faculty could formulate its own healthily heterogeneous, multicultural set of readings or other experiences. In fact, significant alternatives to Bennett's nostalgic shelf have already been developed.

But there is absolutely no compelling logic to support the claim that the "right" curricular content will provide the answer to the ills that plague higher education as these are defined in such studies. The pivotal question—the question that burdens thoughtful faculty—is how to move from the aimless, disintegrated set of experiences these reports lament to a coherent educational program. But no coherent educational program can be mounted unless an academic community first comes to share a set of social goals that informs and shapes schooling. A transitional program for education, in short, requires a transitional program for society.

Bennett and the AAC list two prerequisites for reshaping the curriculum: First, faculty must put aside their commitments to specialization and departmentalism and take responsibility for the "curriculum as a whole." But because they offer no persuasive account of the historical reasons specialization developed, nor of its positive functions both for faculty careers and the national economy today, this desideratum comes to sound like a pious refrain. Second—and more importantly—administrators must seize the helm of the drifting academic ship:

> This generation of academic presidents and deans is required to lead us away from the declining and devalued bachelor's degree that now prevails to a new era of curricular coherence, intellectual rigor, and humanistic strength. ... Presidents, academic vice-presidents, and deans have the fundamental obligation to identify the curricular issues that require attention and to shape a strategy to move their faculties to responsible action.
>
> (AAC, pp. 7, 13)

There is something altogether touching in such faith in academic administrators, these renaissance gentlemen (and a few women) fully knowledgeable about changes needed in every aspect of the curriculum, these paragons of integrity immune to special interests and parochialism, who will lead faculty to renewed faith in the mission of higher education.

It is well to recall here my "Fire-eating Dragons" advertisement. College managers are not any less humane or more careerist than professors. But their *institutional* roles make them considerably more susceptible to the external pressures of the marketplace, the economy, and their governing boards. Faculty may not have been resolute advocates for continuing useful course work in history or literature or sociology, much less for envisioning needed changes in the general shape of collegiate study, but it was academic administrators who had the power—and who used it—to retrench staff in those areas and replace them with specialists in Mortuary Science and Funeral Service. Faculty may have developed excessive numbers of offerings in departmental specialities, but the proliferation of a miscellany of new *majors*, new departments, supposedly career-focused specialties (Secretarial and Office or otherwise) was generated primarily by academic managers responding to dimly-perceived (or promoted) changes in the tastes of the clientele who had come to shop at their stores. Indeed, many such managers never thought of themselves as making a "choice" between a tenured history professor and a new specialist in Correctional Services. The choices were simply made by the numbers—numbers on enrollment charts, numbers that said that American History was expendable, like PT boats or the lives of Vietnam villagers. While some senior professors at some (primarily research) universities did and do avoid general education or service courses and devote themselves to perfecting an academic language comprehensible only to a few peers, it was academic managers who developed and institutionalized the practice of hiring adjuncts, with little connection to the institution and, often, less experience in teaching as well. For all the rhetoric about better rewards for teaching, administration after administration has used the tight job market to "upgrade standards"—that is, to increase publication requirements for tenure and to restrict access to tenure tracks to fewer and fewer entrants to the academic profession. In the name of fostering "standards," in fact, management has implemented policies that increase turnover, disenfranchise junior faculty, undermine the standard of living of teachers, and ironically, demand of younger professors allegiance neither to the institution nor to their students, but to their disciplines and so to the very research and specialization these studies deplore. Such "leadership" guarantees nothing but the proliferation of another round of crisis studies midway through the 1990s.

My purpose is not to bait administrators—a sluggish game at best. On the other hand, if you had survived the Titanic, you might want to think twice before placing the tiller in hands trained at the same school. Because the Bennett and AAC papers never ask fundamental questions about the relationship of educational programs to a changing society, they can perceive no other sources of leadership than themselves, and others much like them. Thus they offer as "leadership" a kind of naive paternalism that flies in the face of history, of American industrial and academic managerial practice, and of simple common sense:

> Presidents and deans must first confront the obstacles to faculty responsibility that are embedded in academic practice and then, with the cooperation of the professors themselves, fashion a range of incentives to revive the responsibility of the faculty *as a whole* for the curriculum *as a whole.*
>
> (AAC, p. 9)

Professors, suggests Bennett and the AAC, are recalcitrant children intent on pleasuring themselves, so the academic caudillos must "fashion . . . incentives" (wonderful language) to lure them into more socially responsible behaviors.

This strategy will not work. And not just because it is rooted in such insulting condescension. The sources of faculty behavior are neither a loss of nerve nor excessive specialization—though these may be involved. Nor is the source simply professorial self-interest, though that too plays a role. Indeed, solutions to the problems higher education now confronts, as the NIE report makes clear, cannot be focused primarily on faculty behavior any more than they can be limited to curricular content. The way faculty perform is shaped in significant measure by social and institutional contexts, in particular by the fiscal and personnel policies of college managers and boards of trustees and the ways in which these policies reflect the economic and social interests of particular power elites within American society.

You can, of course, cry up administrative leadership and call for better valuation of teaching until you are hoarse. But if you do not understand why administrative leadership has taken its current path, or why teaching came to be less valued; if you have no plan at all—pious rhetoric aside—to convert college managers from part of the problem to part of the solution; if you do not perceive and look to the social and institutional seeds from which have sprung the "Fire-eating Dragons" consuming not merely academic gardens, but a world's health and treasure—well, the cries and calls will be so much Babel.

Consider narrowly the complaint expressed in the AAC report: "Professors speak of teaching *loads* and research *opportunities,* never the reverse" (p. 10). The call for attaching greater value to teaching is hardly new; indeed, it is to writing about higher education what urging obedience to the Tenth Commandment is to Sunday sermons. But why do we so seldom honor teaching *in practice,* despite the pieties and even the occasional awards? Or, to put the question practically, what in American higher educational practice must be changed if the renewal of teaching and the shift away from research priorities are to be accomplished? First, I do not think such a question can be answered in the abstract: teaching *what* to *whom* and *why?* Teaching traditional humanities courses with all their demand for and assumption about leisure time and their often unexamined privileging of elite values to working students desperate to get through academic barriers to acquire a degree can be utterly demoralizing—to both parties. This is absolutely *not* to say that such students have no rights to or needs for the intellectual worlds humane study might open to them; on the contrary. It is to say, as I argue throughout, that *what* we teach and the contexts in which we do so must be shaped by *who* we teach and particularly by the objectives of study. Are we engaged in offering a cultural veneer to students who need to understand the sources of inequality, to be inspired by others' struggles against it, to know how language encodes and is an instrument both of control and of liberation? Do we teach science courses to enable graduates to see clearly the political and ethical issues often hidden under ecological and medical decisions? Do we really engage the questions of power—its sources and its operations—that structure what is studied, who studies, and how and why? It seems to me that a "revival" of teaching depends initially on reconnecting what goes on in the classroom with the real intellectual and social concerns students face in the world.

Second, there is the question, as there always is in American society, of money. On the whole, the more you teach, the less money you make. Teaching loads in research universities are far lower, and salaries much higher, than in state universities, community colleges, and all but a few elite smaller private colleges. Are we likely to see faculty at the State University of New York's teaching institutions—the four-year and two-year colleges—paid on the same, much less at a higher, scale than those at the system's four research universities? Will we pay the teacher of three service courses and an elective each term at San Jose State anything that compares to what we pay the professor who teaches a graduate seminar each quarter at Berkeley? Will we pay the teacher of first-year literacy on a scale comparable to what we pay the graduate professor of microbiology or, heaven forbid, one of applied genetics? Or the teacher of Western, much less non-Western, Civilization on a par with the dean of parking?

But, it is said, there are compensations, the virtues of working at institutions in which commitments to student learning are valued and supported. There is merit in that argument. But it is likewise true that the faculty member who makes intense commitments to the life of one institution, and thus presumably to its students, at the expense of remaining professionally visible through research, writing, and speaking can also be digging her or his own professional grave. *The* message of the retrenchments in the 1970s was that institutions in the United States, whether Youngstown Sheet and Tube or Mudflat State University, are not loyal to those from whom they extract loyalty. Faculty who forget that message are faculty at risk.

The danger of amnesia is, however, minimal, especially since college managers and their functionaries seem not to have deviated from the last decade's iceberg course.

> . . . institutions must strive to develop a consistent philosophy that synthesizes its [sic] strategy for the 1980s. Reducing the rate of growth in faculty salaries, program discontinuance, and retrenchment should be part of a coordinated effort to adapt to a turbulent environment.[4]

The message is everywhere, reinforced by the personnel practices that have become the norm in institutions of every kind, but especially in the larger, more bureaucratic universities. Nontenure-track and part-time appointments, probationary periods that stretch to the professional horizons, repetitive reviews that emphasize a record of publication in one's field—these are the norm. Rewards for teaching are not. If faculty seize research opportunities— few enough in many humanities fields—that should not be the occasion for diatribes about our educational apostasy, but rather, for understanding how powerful are the forces driving us in that direction.

Drawing faculty toward research and publication—the real intellectual challenges aside—are not only minor matters like money, prestige, professional mobility, and other forms of access to the goods of American materialism, but actually the bottom-line question of retaining a job within academe. The plain fact is that an excellent teacher, sacked even for lack of a "tenure slot," is forever known as a sacked teacher. Fewer and fewer schools will hire such a person. And if the issue is a limited or untraditional publication record, the usual verdict of the men at the top is "good field, no hit—back to the minors or out of the game." Further, pushing faculty away from commitments to single institutions is the nature of many institutions themselves—

their paternalism, the lack of democratic practice, and the contradictions between espoused and practiced values.

It is hard for me to see how the ideological imperatives asserted by the Bennett and AAC statements will significantly alter such powerful determinants and thus establish the importance of teaching in American culture—or how Bennett's nostalgia or the AAC's miscellany of skills, experiences, and subjects will restore coherence to the curriculum.

IV

Yet changes—including some proposed in these studies—should be brought about. Where to begin? It seems to me that faculty, through their organizations—whether these are constituted for governance, collective bargaining or curriculum development—need to initiate the processes that will generate reform. The reform measures will obviously vary from campus to campus since different kinds of institutions in different areas define and interact with their communities in quite diverse ways. But whatever the process, I want to suggest six guidelines that may be helpful to pursuing that work.

1. Reform demands an integrated approach, an approach that recognizes the organic nature of the institution. That is, every proposal for change should be scrutinized with a view to its impact on the entire institution, and what in the institution must be altered fully to implement it.
2. Reforms must be concrete and practical. Noble aspirations are not enough.
3. Reforms must be serious and thorough, not cosmetic measures designed to foreclose criticism.
4. Reform must never threaten the achievements of the past two decades—especially the broadening of access to higher education and the hard-earned triumphs for at least the principle of equity.
5. Reform must include changes that substantially widen and deepen faculty control over the educational program—in a manner analogous to worker control over the workplace.
6. Reforms must help reconnect schooling with the work needed to eliminate the fundamental social problems of America: institutional racism, sexism and homophobia; the destruction of our environment; the consumption of the bulk of public resources for war and its aftermaths; the waste and terror of drug culture; and the lack of decent housing, health care, and even nourishment for a third or more of our people.

I want to examine these guidelines more fully, with some illustrations drawn from these studies, and particularly from the NIE report. These illustrations, I should emphasize, are not intended as a comprehensive survey of necessary reforms but as a set of strategies for approaching change.

1. An *integrated approach*. The NIE study provides a useful model of such thinking.

> Administrators and faculty must recognize that virtually every institutional
> policy and practice—from class schedules, attendance regulations, and re-
> search participation to work study, faculty office hours, student orientation,
> and parking—affects the way students use their time and the amount of effort
> they devote to academic pursuits.
>
> (p. 23)

It follows that the places where students work (on or off campus), the character of extracurricular or cocurricular activities, the quality of study space—
all must be examined if we are to ensure student "involvement in learning."
Similarly, curriculum changes cannot be considered independent of campus
culture—the constellation of student and institutional values. It would, for
example, be self-defeating to impose a set of core requirements if deeply
rooted and unchallenged student attitudes held them to be nothing more than
tedious hurdles to surmount to get the degree. In other words, one cannot
mandate change in colleges any more than elsewhere—one must argue and
organize for reforms, and understand that proposed reforms will not always
be adopted.

An emphasis on the organic also demands recognizing that organizational
reform is integral to improving curriculum and pedagogy. To cite the NIE
report again, many excessively "bureaucratic practices distort institutional
values and drain energy away from teaching and learning" (p. 68). A third
instance: The NIE report strongly encourages the development of procedures
to assess learning, and insists that "faculty will have to do more than they do
at present" to make these work. In the same section (p. 71), the report insists
with equal strength that "the decline in faculty purchasing power" must be
decisively reversed. While it clearly was the trend in American labor relations
of the 1980s to demand more for less, that is not a formula that will motivate
the professoriat "to do more than at present." I was, in fact, quite perplexed
in reading the Bennett and AAC statements by how little they factored into
their accounts the depressive role played by the sharp declines in real faculty
salaries—greater than in any nonagricultural profession—since the early
1970s.

The implications of such integrated thinking are crucial. The AAC report
proposes organizing change around a faculty curriculum committee working
on an administratively-generated agenda; the problem with such committees,
however, is that they function in institutional vacuums. They do not deal with
personnel procedures that drive younger faculty away from institutional commitments, with forms of organizing student life that undercut classroom efforts, and with bureaucratic structures that "drain energy from teaching and
learning." Nothing of substance will be accomplished by pouring enormous
energy into curriculum revision if student culture and institutional policies at
the heart of the current difficulties are not fundamentally altered. It seems
to me that the present atmosphere of crisis and the existence of studies that
address certain problems and name them a "crisis" provide faculty with in-
valuable opportunities for demanding the changes that we know must be

instituted, not just in curriculum but in the *contexts*—like those discussed in the preceding chapters—that shape it.

2. *Concrete* and *practical* reform. It may in the long run be necessary, or at least desirable, to revolutionize the structure of American society, not to mention academe, in order to alter education's fundamental objectives and practices. But this restructuring will not happen tomorrow, or soon. In the meantime, useful changes can be instituted today: converting fragmented part-time lines into full-time positions, providing sabbaticals and grants for the development of teaching, broadening the definition of "scholarship" in making personnel decisions to include curriculum development and other forms of academic productivity that do not necessarily lead to traditional publication. Similarly, it would be possible to use assessment procedures not to evaluate younger faculty for retention, especially in their first few years, but strictly to help them improve teaching.

3. *Seriousness* of intent. The problem of assessment serves to focus this third general consideration. The NIE report proposes, for example, that colleges consider reinstituting the comprehensive examination or some other form of *exit* assessment, more or less on the model of professional licensing exams. Such tests would appraise "an individual's grasp of principles, methods, and knowledge that should have been acquired in formal course work and related experience" (p. 46). To be sure, such tests often measure test-taking ability, not student achievement, and I would not offer them as a panacea. On the other hand, it may be that regaining public confidence will require development of some such strategy for documenting student achievement in whatever course of study a college determines to be appropriate.

But my point here is that assessment cannot be achieved by halfway measures. We need to demand of those posing general education as the core of the baccalaureate curriculum that they value the teachers of that core as highly as researchers and career specialists. We need to demand of academic administrators that they take the institutional roles of faculty seriously enough to end the excessive employment of adjuncts. We need to demand of professional accrediting agencies that they revise requirements to enable students to take the broader range of courses necessary to move away from today's excessive specialization. We need to demand of state and federal legislatures that they adapt scholarship and loan programs to enable ill-trained students to pursue longer or part-time courses of study to bring themselves up to reasonable exit standards. When the whole of the academic world begins to take change in *their* provinces seriously, we can also ask students to face their learning tasks with the commitment implied by comprehensive exams, or any other broad evaluation of their—and our—achievement.

4. *Preserving the achievements of the last decades.* This criterion stems from the observation that if, in one light, the recent period has been one of decline in colleges, in another light it has been one of expanding educational opportunities for minorities, for working-class students, and particularly for all women. I do not mean only that more students from such groups have (at

least until recently) been entering college, but that the curriculum has begun to reflect their experiences, cultures, and aspirations. One of the more deplorable sections of the AAC report implicitly pits democratization against the maintenance of quality (p. 5). There is absolutely no necessary conflict between democratization—of access *to* college and material *within* the curriculum—and quality. Quite the contrary: In discipline after discipline the impact of new departures like women's studies has been both energizing and revelatory of limitations and inaccuracies in traditional approaches.

If colleges have not adequately coped with new student constituencies, if they have failed to accommodate this new and challenging diversity, that is hardly the fault of students. The NIE study states the case extremely well.

> As higher education has expanded in recent years, entering students have become more diverse in terms of their preparation. While we would hope that the recent recommendations of various national commissions have stimulated reforms at the middle and secondary school levels that will rectify this situation, the fact is that higher education must live with this diversity for some time to come. We can bemoan the state of affairs, we can duck the problem by forbidding colleges to offer remedial programs, or we can make those programs work while respecting the standards for college-level performance that should lie behind the baccalaureate degree. The Study Group recommends the last of these options
>
> (pp. 48–49).

I wish to take this comment a step further: The Bennett and AAC documents suggest to me that in the panic for reform we can easily lose the advances in knowledge as well as in democratic education that mark the last two decades. And therefore I think we should fight measures that would attempt to return to the limited access to college or curriculum that characterized the 1950s. On the contrary, we should sustain broadened access to higher education, and continue to reconstruct the disciplines in response to the important advances made by minority and feminist scholars.

5. *Greater faculty autonomy* and *authority*. I have no illusions about the perfectibility of my colleagues, but I do believe that faculty, because of the roles they play *in* education, need to be predominantly in control *of* education. Universities today are administered on a model that reminds me of nothing so much as the Globe Theatre being run by the Coca-Cola company. The industrial model of management, whatever virtues it might or might not have in business, is singularly inappropriate to directing what goes on in the classroom. For there, as sometimes in the theater, therapist's office, or political rally, the energy of human interchange transforms fact into understanding, and even, upon occasion, understanding into wisdom. The bottom line of any educational reform is not its economy, but whether it releases that energy into the classroom or traps it, unused, within angry faculty and harried students.

After thirty-some years in the classroom, it comes to me as an inescapable fact that few systems for trapping the energy of teaching could more cunningly have been devised than today's academic hierarchies. And thus it seems to me logical to urge my colleagues to pursue changes that, in large ways and small, increase control over the educational program by those who carry it out. These range from the first tiny, elephantine steps in New York to extricate its university system from the smothering embrace of the state financial bureaucracy, to reasserting faculty control over questions of class size, room assignment, and similar considerations that directly affect modes of teaching and therefore of learning. Every faculty member can supply his or her favorite example of why this is a central issue; my own concerns a time in Maryland when I requested a library seminar room for a class so that I could seat students in a circle. When we arrived at the beginning of the term, we discovered that the chairs had been set in tight rows and bolted to the floor; I could roam, but the students were fixed in place—perhaps a physical symbol of the theory of education held by those responsible for that series of decisions. The point here is not abstractly to assert "faculty power," whatever that might mean, but to restore that critical sense of *ownership* in what our colleges actually do.

6. Reasserting the *connections of education to society*. It has been fashionable to mock the 1960s demand for a "relevant" curriculum—that is, for courses of study that addressed the major issues to which the social movements of that period directed themselves: racial and sexual oppression, the war on Vietnam. A notion of "relevance" did not disappear, but rather, narrowly construed and transformed, it was used to rationalize precisely the kind of narrow education characteristic of most "career" programs. The issue, then, is not "relevance" in the abstract, but relevance to what—to individual advancement alone, to the personnel needs of corporate America, or to constructing a humane, healthy and democratic society. It seems to me that a main point of any liberal education program is to learn from the conflicts and differences that mark the past about how power operates and may be grasped in order to shape the future. But it is precisely such questions of power that these studies evade, both in their presentation of institutional dynamics and in their ideas about curriculum. To continue such evasion, to avoid looking at the real relationships between education and other social institutions, is to render any effort at "reform" an empty and truly *irrelevant* gesture.

To me it seems that faculty and professional staffs face a time of significant choices. They can seize the moment or be seized by it, grasp the possibility to shape change or be victimized by it. These studies can represent threats. It is our task to use them as opportunities.

Notes

1. I shall here be particularly concerned with the following:
"Final Report of the Study Group on the Conditions of Excellence in American

Higher Education," *Involvement in Learning: Realizing the Potential of American Higher Education* (Washington, D.C.: National Institute of Education, 1984).

William J. Bennett, *To Reclaim a Legacy: A Report on the Humanities in Higher Education* (Washington, D.C.: National Endowment for the Humanities, 1984).

"The Findings and Recommendations of the Project on Redefining the Meaning and Purpose of the Baccalaureate Degree," *Integrity in the College Curriculum: A Report to the Academic Community* (Washington, D.C.: Association of American Colleges, 1985).

2. See Burton R. Clark, "The 'Cooling-Out' Function in Higher Education," *American Journal of Sociology* 65 (May 1960).

3. I address Bennett's curricular ideas at greater length in the following chapter.

4. Kenneth P. Moritmer and Michael L. Tierney, "The Three 'R's' of the Eighties: Reduction, Reallocation, and Retrenchment," *AAHE-ERIC Higher Education Research Report #4* (Washington, D.C.: American Association for Higher Education, 1979), p. 54. This was, I should note, written at a time when faculty purchasing power had already lost most of the 20 percent it would decline in the decade after 1972.

Looking a Gift Horse
in the Mouth

The existing monuments form an ideal order among themselves, which is modified by the introduction of the new (the really new) work of art among them.
The existing order is complete before the new work arrives; for order to persist
after the supervention of novelty, the *whole* existing order must be, if ever so
slightly, altered; and so the relations, proportions, values of each work of art
toward the whole are readjusted; and this is conformity between the old and
the new. Whoever has approved this idea of order, of the form of European,
of English literature will not find it preposterous that the past should be altered
by the present as much as the present is directed by the past. And the poet who
is aware of this will be aware of great difficulties and responsibilities.

> T.S. Eliot, "Tradition and the Individual Talent"

> There's a man goin' round takin' names,
> There's a man goin' round takin' names,
> He has taken my brother's name,
> And left my heart in pain,
> There's a man goin' round takin' names.
> Traditional, as sung by Paul Robeson

These are times which may not yet try our souls, but surely they tempt our
spirits. It was but a few years ago that the current drug czar, then chairman
of the federal agency dispensing opportunity to humanists, initiated a public
campaign to reestablish as the basis of humanistic study a five, or maybe a
two-and-a-half foot shelf of great books. These would, presumably, teach us,
or at least the youth consigned to us, the central virtues: to quote William
Bennett, "not to betray your friends, your God or your country." Across
Washington, the National Institute of Education issued a report suggesting
that American higher education suffered from a deep head cold that, were
it not properly treated, could easily develop into pneumonia. The treatment,
among other things, was an expansion of the liberal arts, and perhaps a return
to old-fashioned general education and distribution requirements. Dutifully
pursuing the theme, reports of prestigious private organizations like the Association of American Colleges sounded the trumpet of reform.

And then, as if in answer to these calls, President Reagan appointed a

Some portions of this paper were delivered, in different form at the 1984 convention of the
Modern Language Association, Washington, D.C., and were published in *Social Text* 12 (Fall
1985): 94–101. In something closer to its present form it was published in *San Jose Studies* XII
(Winter 1986): 6–19.

humanist, an academic, the very initiator of this campaign to revive the humanities and the study of Western civilization as Secretary of Education. And not, as it became apparent, to preside over the dismemberment of that federal department, but to reestablish in education traditional American virtues.

It seemed like a humanist's dream, this federally-sanctioned campaign to restore the importance of our disciplines, to "place at the heart of the college curriculum" the "study of the humanities and Western civilization,"[1] and a colleague in high place to put money behind the mouth. And besides, for many of us the very notion of reviving general education requirements, and especially the study of Western civilization, is itself appealing, regardless of money or power. So perhaps it would seem best not to look a gift horse too closely in the mouth, even if the emerging winds bring more than a whiff of sectarian values. For our survival as humanities and social sciences faculty may depend on recapturing from preprofessional programs, from our colleagues in accounting and computers and hotel management, at least a modicum of student time and credits. And, not to be altogether mercenary about it, do we not have a responsibility to educate students about values, about culture, about our "monuments of unaging intellect"? We do, indeed, I believe, nor is there anything wrong in trying to survive and to help our younger colleagues get and maintain jobs. Where, then, is the rub?

Consider Mr. Bennett's injunction, reasonable enough in its outer garb, "not to betray your friends." But who are our friends? In Central America, among the main friends of Mr. Bennett's boss were what the administration persisted in calling "freedom fighters," "Contras," the majority of whose victims in Nicaragua were innocent peasants and teachers, nurses, doctors, and community development workers. Are such thugs our friends? Was our "friend" in the Philippines the president whose chief of military staff was put on trial for rubbing out the Marcos' regime's main enemy, Benigno Aquino? Are our friends in Cambodia, whom the United States has steadily supported for a seat at the United Nations, the monstrous Khmer Rouge? The plot, then, thickens, for it seems that learning involves distinguishing friend from foe, and just who they are may well appear different if it is *The Republic* that focuses our thoughts, or W.E.B. DuBois' *The Souls of Black Folks;* Hawthorne's "My Kinsman, Major Molineux" or Richard Wright's "Bright and Morning Star;" *Leviticus, 1984,* or *The Dream of a Common Language.*

My point, to emerge from this trope, is that curricular reform, a movement back to broad, humane study as the basis for college education, is by no means an end in itself. All curricula are political. So are the most innocent-seeming of academic choices. The curriculum, like the law, embodies a set of generally unexamined values, social priorities, and definitions of personal aspiration. The yeast has been added to the dough of curricular reform; it is time, and more than time, to ask what is being baked (or half-baked) and for whom. If the undergraduate curriculum is to be reformed, if the ideas of general education and the humanities are to have more than the briefest revival, what shall be the goals, the values, the content expressed in that revival? What will sustain it? I want to suggest where some of the conflicts lie in answering such questions and to point in certain directions that may, I believe, yield more fruitful answers for us. To say this another way: It would be politically fatal to attempt to stand in the way of creative change in the liberal arts curriculum; but it would be educationally irresponsible not to inquire deeply about the directions in which change shall proceed.

I think it useful to view the current movement for reform in historical context. Many of my colleagues were, like me, educated in what seem—only in retrospect—less conflicted times. Men were men; they knew how to act the part, and if they sometimes wondered, they had (or thought they had) Hemingway and Faulkner to instruct them—or, with a different clientele, John Wayne and Ronald Reagan—or was it Hopalong Cassidy? At any rate, we placidly took and some of us eventually taught courses in the Western heritage with titles like "Great Men and Great Ideas" or "The Origins of Christian Civilization." We felt, perhaps, slightly fraudulent in such courses, some of us, but we consoled ourselves with the reflection that if we did not exactly "belong," we were at least learning to fit, more or less naturally, into our charcoal gray suits. The steady post-Second World War expansion of the economy, the GI bill, the response to the threat perceived in Sputnik, the pressure for equal educational opportunity emerging from the youthful civil rights movement—these and other factors produced the huge expansion of colleges and universities in the late 1950s and 1960s, which brought many of us our jobs and reasonably decent standards of living.

That expansion also brought to colleges very different student constituencies and, to some degree as well, their faculty counterparts. They found an educational system that did not seem to serve them well. The curriculum left them out: Western civilization was all very well, but what if its bearers presented themselves to your ancestors as kidnappers or rum-runners, or if your ancestors had developed a mighty culture while Westerners still roamed the wilds of Prussia in wolf skins? Faulkner and Dilsey were all very well, too, but maybe Richard Wright and Bigger had more to tell us about 1965. But even such curricular questions were largely irrelevant to the majority of citizens historically bypassed by higher education. To many of these citizens, it seemed you *already* had to be party to white upper-middle-class culture, had to be able to leap its hurdles, pass its tests, in order even to be admitted to the collegiate precincts of cultural apprenticeship. Perhaps admissions should be "open," access to higher learning independent of previous conditions of intellectual servitude. And besides, when it came to certain requirements, these courses in general education—whatever *they* meant by *that*—the profs themselves weren't much interested. They were too busy with their specialties, because that's the way they got ahead. Anyway, they didn't seem to agree very much about what courses like that *ought* to contain, much less what a high school graduate ought to know. One said *Samson Agonistes*, another insisted on Cardinal Newman, a third opted for *Portrait of the Artist as a Young Man,* and some young turk tossed in *Seize the Day,* altogether a sticky apple of discord.

The cultural consensus, in brief, began to come unstuck, a victim of increasing diversity in the university, as well as of mounting conflict over values and priorities in the society.

Now I would argue that the dissolution of the 1950s consensus—and I want to be clear that this is the thinnest of sketches of that process—was on the whole a good thing. To be sure, the elimination of most requirements helped to produce students who in many respects know not their right hands from their left; who wrote no tongue but English, and that indifferently or worse; who claimed they already had the education and needed from us only the degree. It also exacerbated the 1970s job crisis in the humanities by helping dry up the pool of students who came to us, however indifferently, to satisfy writing and general education requirements.

Yet and still, that 1950s consensus *was* narrow, of a piece with Jewish quotas at Columbia; the exclusion of blacks from Ol' Miss; the misogynist indifference even at Wellesley and Smith to women's history, writing, and creativity; the insistence, at Indiana, Berkeley, and Yale alike that studying French and German was necessary, but that Spanish was a language of lower degree. It was the cultural consensus of a small portion of North American society—white, male, British or Northern European in ancestry, not perhaps the Tom Buchanans of the world, but certainly the Nick Carraways. They looked for intellectual guidance to New Critics, or their gurus, like Allen Tate, who claimed that the role of "the man of letters in the modern world" was to sustain the purity of language and the sanctity of received tradition against collective society and mass culture. They—perhaps the more appropriate pronoun of thirty years ago is "we"—we, then, agreed that ideology was, indeed, at an end, together with fundamental social conflict; that poverty, "Gentlemen's Agreements," and "separate but equal" were disappearing with the expansion of mature capitalism; that in any case, socialism and capitalism would drift into marriage over the course of time; and that we would leaven, with the power of true classics, the bland but essentially healthy dough of upper-middle-class America.

Do I draw a cartoon of the fifties? Even if it were cartoonish, it retains a strong and not altogether nostalgic appeal, as the responses to Mr. Bennett's proposals—not to mention recent presidential elections—indicate. I shall outline these, as they appear in "To Reclaim a Legacy," the essay Mr. Bennett produced in November 1984, when he was still chairman of the National Endowment for the Humanities. I shall not reproduce here the paper's documentation of the decline in humanistic study; we are all sufficiently familiar with that reality of our lives. But I need to pause for an instant at Mr. Bennett's contention that a major contributing factor to that decline—indeed the only *cause* he mentions in his introductory summary—is "a failure of nerve and faith on the part of many college faculties and administrators. . . ." We have met the enemy and, in Mr. Bennett's view, he—or she—is us. Thus his paper can be taken as an effort to reinvigorate our nerve and faith, in particular our faith in the virtues of traditional approaches to the teaching of the humanities and Western civilization. His rubric for our salvation involves three components: First, the humanities and Western civilization are central to collegiate education because they voice the basic values around which American society is organized; second, a broad consensus exists about the core of humane study—about the "canon" of the humanities, the group of books, novels, essays, and poems with which an educated person should be familiar; and third, teaching that core of books and authors will, given a reasonably vital pedagogy, enable us to fulfill the functions study of the humanities is designed to accomplish in the university.

Let us begin, then, with the initial question, Mr. Bennett's and ours: Why study the humanities? His answers, spread across many parts of "To Reclaim a Legacy," are propositions with which many of us would agree: The humanities "tell us how men and women of our own and other civilizations have grappled with life's enduring, fundamental questions." What are these? "What is justice? What should be loved? What deserves to be defended? What is courage? What is noble? What is base? Why do civilizations flourish? Why do they decline?" (p. 5). And, lest these goals seem altogether too grand for Humanities 1B, Mr. Bennett added as a kind of coda in a *Washington Post* "op ed" piece that the humanities also lead to business success. "Take the time to make mankind your business," he advised students; "you will find that the humanities and other liberal arts will help you succeed, and profit, in any career or endeavor" (January 28, 1985).

Perhaps we should, then, simply be toasting to fun and profit with the humanities. Unfortunately, I am also one of those serious fellows interested in what "deserves to be defended," "what should be loved," in justice, civilization, decline, and similar weighty matters. I find very little evidence that these questions are, in fact, seriously considered in college curricula outside the areas we loosely group as the humanities. I would like to feel that my profession does speak to such issues. And yet, I feel suspicious of grand claims made for humanistic study. When it is argued that the "humanities bring together the perennial questions of human life with the greatest works of history, literature, philosophy and art," I find myself shuffling my feet and blushing. But then I reflect that the "perennial questions"—fewer in number than they may seem—are often far easier to deal with in the classroom in the abstract, than to confront the looming and unprecedented issues of our diurnal world: the threat of ecological annihilation, for example, stark hunger and homelessness amid plenty, equal opportunity for all receding like a mirage on the social horizon. I wonder, more modestly even, whether "The Origins of Christian Civilization"—as much as *I* learned teaching it at Hobart and William Smith Colleges—ever taught students not to "betray" their friends, or to widen their notions of who the friendlies were. I reflect gloomily that the twentieth century offers ample, indeed agonizing, evidence that humane study guarantees not at all the cultivation of civilized behavior. Buchenwald, the Gulag, Hiroshima, My Lai—the brutalities massive and trivial of modern life can indeed lead us to despair of the humanizing function of education altogether, to conclude that what we do in forty-five or fifty hours through a term will be little noted nor long remembered and that we had best stick to the form and allusive structure of *The Cantos* and leave questions of value and morality to the political and religious mavens who speak with less embarrassed restraint than we about them.

But surely politics is too important to leave to politicians, or morals to moralists. True, we will not end war and exploitation by teaching American Civilization 1—1A or 1B. But that is not the question. What we study and how we assess what we study are, as I have suggested, matters of politics and values, and as these shape what we study (and how), surely what we study shapes them. Let us remain wary of the more extreme claims for our profession. But the basic idea that questions of value should charge the humanities classroom is, it seems to me, vital.

Let us also accept Mr. Bennett's contention that "because our society is the product and we the inheritors of Western civilization, American students need an understanding of its origins and development, from its roots in antiquity to the present" (p. 12). Between this contention and his great books curriculum, however, lies a profound gap. First, civilization is by no means expressed solely in big books—or even in writing for that matter. This idea is, of course, familiar to those of us who teach American Studies or American Civilization. We will teach anything—as people like to say of us. The intent is both democratic and practical: To learn of the "origins and development" of our civilization we need to know what it was that those without the leisure and position to publish thought and did. Thus we seek out the testimony offered by popular and folk traditions, by material culture, and by what ethnography and anthropology can discover.

Second, the version of "Western civilization" presented by Bennett and Allan Bloom does not in fact clarify its "origins and development" (much less ours) but rather isolates it from its own historical roots and contexts. To read them, one might believe that Moses received the tablets founding monotheism straight from the hand of Yahweh and that classical Greek culture sprang directly from the head of Athena. Many students in my "Origins of Christian Civilization" course thirty years ago came away believing that Christianity replaced the Old Testament idea of justice—which they took to be "an eye for an eye and a tooth for a tooth"—with the Sermon on the Mount. But that was in part because the course never covered the "intertestamental literature" (but for the single year I describe elsewhere) in which the changing values and even the specific forms of language used by Jesus were developed within Hebrew culture. Similarly, by posing classical Greek culture as the "pure childhood," the original fount of all later Western civilization, Bennett follows in the path of those who have systematically obscured the rich Semitic and Egyptian influences that the Greeks themselves saw as critical to the development of their own civilization.[2] That is rather like obliterating the African, Asian, and Hispanic origins of significant sectors of the American people.

Such problems present a basic pedagogical issue. Do we offer to each generation of students the same set of classic texts to ensure their exposure to the ideas and, presumably, the aesthetic monuments of "our" civilization?

Or do we ask which works from the vast universe available to us speak most forcefully in *this* moment of time, to these people in this place, on precisely those questions of value that Mr. Bennett would have us address? Does what we teach change because students change, the times change, and how the past and how tradition or traditions can be grasped changes as well? Books, after all, do not live in a timeless empyrean; they were written in a particular world and they are read in a particular world. Perhaps a "five-foot shelf" served well the small elite that attended colleges half a century and more ago; might a quite differently assembled set of texts better serve today's and tomorrow's diverse students? I need hardly say that the differing strategies implied in these questions suggest quite different discussions in the curriculum committee, and lead to rather different syllabi.

In addressing this pedagogical question I have, of course, ignored for the moment the conservative function of humanistic study—conservative at least in the sense in which Mr. Bennett quotes Walter Lippmann to the effect that "a society can be progressive only if it conserves its tradition" (p. 42). My problem, English teacher that I am, arises from the lack of an "-s" at the end of that last word—"tradition" rather than "traditions." That minute but in no way trivial difference seems to me to focus a second set of issues. For underneath that missing "-s" is the question of the canon—that is, what works constitute a tradition and convey a set of shared values? What books and authors do you propose that an educated person should know? These questions began to emerge during the past decades, especially, I think, as feminist and minority critics pointed to what we might call the "dialectics of validation": That is, certain historical constructs gave importance to a body of texts, while the weight attributed to the texts sustained the very credibility of received versions of history. The search of the social movements of the 1960s and 1970s for a useable past led outside this closed circle, to works that existed often at or beyond the margins of received accounts of literary history. And, as we have contemplated writing by Harriet Beecher Stowe, Elizabeth Stuart Phelps, Sarah Orne Jewett, Charles Chesnutt, Mary Wilkins Freeman, Charles Eastman, Zitkala-Sa, Edith Eaton, Zora Neale Hurston, and Meridel LeSueur we have come to realize not only the need to construct new versions of history—social as well as literary—but the need to reconstruct our standards of excellence, our understanding of form, indeed, our ideas about the functions of literature. The question of the canon, in short, affects all the structures of literary study.

But the debate over the canon is not an academic one, although the canon is itself academically perpetuated. For the canon embodies the kinds of knowledge a society perceives as important to retain from its past in order to construct its future. That becomes clear when we look at Mr. Bennett's personal canon, the works that, as he suggests, have shaped his own values. He presented his canon with the modesty of power; it was not his purpose to "dictate anyone's curriculum," but only to respond to the curious. His was a list with which we are all familiar, virtually identical, in fact, to the curriculum of my Hobart and William Smith course of the late 1950s:

The works and authors I have in mind include, but are not limited to, the following: from classical antiquity—Homer, Sophocles, Thucydides, Plato, Aristotle, and Vergil; from medieval, Renaissance, and seventeenth-century Europe—Dante, Chaucer, Machiavelli, Montaigne, Shakespeare, Hobbes, Milton, and Locke; from eighteenth- through twentieth-century Europe—Swift, Rousseau, Austen, Wordsworth, Tocqueville, Dickens, George Eliot, Dostoyevsky, Marx, Nietzsche, Tolstoy, Mann, and T. S. Eliot; from American literature and historical documents—the Declaration of Independence, the Federalist Papers, the Constitution, the Lincoln-Douglas Debates, Lincoln's Gettysburg Address and Second Inaugural Address, Martin Luther King, Jr's. "Letter from the [sic] Birmingham Jail" and "I have a dream . . ." speech, and such authors as Hawthorne, Melville, Twain, and Faulkner. Finally, I must mention the Bible, which is the basis of so much subsequent history, literature and philosophy.

(p. 16)

I want to focus on what Mr. Bennett selects from what he calls "American literature and historical documents." It may seem ungrateful in one committed as I am to equal rights to attack this list—as I shall obviously do—particularly in view of the inclusion among Mr. Bennett's paradigmatic works and authors of Dr. King's "Letter" and speech, not to mention the creators of Hester Prynne, Nigger Jim, Sam Fathers, Dilsey, and—yes—Babo. It may sound ungrateful even after one reflects on the interesting fact that nary a single female voice seems to have emerged with sufficient force to penetrate Mr. Bennett's American Pantheon or that Spanish seems to have become a non-Western culture. But when one looks closely at that attenuated list of American fiction writers—Hawthorne, Melville, Twain, and Faulkner—these comments may not seem so ungrateful, or misplaced, as all of that.

Mr. Bennett's short list may be taken to represent, I think, a traditional conception of American fiction. I thought about this conception and the kinds of experiences and virtues it validates when a few years ago I taught Faulkner's novella, *The Bear*. I take it that *The Bear* is the kind of book Mr. Bennett would have our students read, for it is surely concerned with courage, "what is noble," "what should be loved," why civilizations decline and similar weighty matters. Indeed, it is a book about how one learns and applies courage, humility, sensitivity, and related virtues. For Ike, through whose consciousness we see events, "the wilderness the old bear ran was his college and the old male bear itself, so long unwifed and childless as to have become its own ungendered progenitor, was his alma mater."[3] It is a book, too, that renews thematic material central to other works of its tradition, *Leatherstocking, Moby-Dick, Huckleberry Finn*, among them: the white boy, orphaned, learns adult virtues from the man of color, the primitive prince, deposed but noble still, even in his degradation. I thought of such matters when I reread the opening paragraphs of *The Bear*. I want to share some of those opening paragraphs with you, as I did with my students at Old Westbury, and see if you respond to them as my students did.

The best of all talking . . . was of the men, not white nor black nor red but men, hunters, with the will and hardihood to endure and the humility and skill to survive, and the dogs and the bear and deer juxtaposed and reliefed against it, ordered and compelled by and within the wilderness in the ancient and unremitting contest according to the ancient and immitigable rules which voided all regrets and brooked no quarter;—the best game of all, the best of all breathing and forever the best of all listening, the voices quiet and weighty and deliberate for retrospection and recollection and exactitude among the concrete trophies—the racked guns and the heads and skins—in the libraries of town houses or the offices of plantation houses or (and best of all) in the camps themselves where the intact and still-warm meat yet hung, the men who had slain it sitting before the burning logs on hearths when there were houses and hearths or about the smoky blazing of piled wood in front of stretched tarpaulins when there were not. There was always a bottle present, so that it would seem to him that those fine fierce instants of heart and brain and courage and wiliness and speed were concentrated and distilled into that brown liquor which not women, not boys and children, but only hunters drank, drinking not of the blood they spilled but some condensation of the wild immortal spirit, drinking it moderately, humbly even, not with the pagan's base and baseless hope of acquiring thereby the virtues of cunning and strength and speed but in salute to them.[4]

My students—I need to tell about those New York students: Most of them were women, about two-thirds were white and one-third were black, mainly older for undergraduates, some in their forties, many with children. Largely the first generation to college—unless their children had preceded them. My students, then . . . well, they laughed. They found it all rather comical, the whiskey and the hunters and the trophies and the talk. And perhaps, perhaps at some level, Faulkner did, too, for it is certainly true that, as Faulkner created him, Ike is rather a failure at living in the world, and especially in dealing with women. Perhaps his wilderness learning isn't very helpful, the wilderness past. But then, why the fuss about learning it?

What might one make of our shared hilarity over Faulkner's mead-hall heroics?[5] Perhaps that I am waltzing my students down the garden path of barbarism. But it may also be the case that for many of us now into the second decade of the new feminist movement, the rituals of male bonding no longer retain the same force and importance, indeed, the rituals have come to appear slightly comic—except, perhaps, when they are enacted with cocked weapons, and we taste their potential for vicious display. Let me be clear: I am not about vilifying Faulkner. I have had many problems with his politics, his notions in the fifties that the civil rights movement should slow down so that the white South might reform itself; his proposition in his Nobel Prize speech that writers should stick to writing about "the human heart in conflict with itself" and avoid that central, overwhelming fact of the second half of this century—the threat of nuclear holocaust; his many degrading portraits of women, like Joanna Burden. But none of that is really at issue here.

The problem is the tradition that Faulkner stands for within his fiction, and in relation to the other writers who constitute the received canon of American literature. It is not an uninteresting and surely not a dying tradition. But it is woefully partial; it is a part, but only one part, of our Western heritage. If one evokes solely from it ideas of courage, nobility, justice, and reasons for the decline of civilization, one will arrive at ideas that are exceedingly limited, often violent, and frankly, sometimes banal. For one will not see the world coherently; one will not see even half those who are holding up the sky.

When I taught at Smith in 1965, the Freshman English course (and that *was* the nomenclature used) included Shakespeare's sonnets, *Samson Agonistes, Portrait of the Artist as a Young Man,* and two or three similar works, including Faulkner's *Absalom, Absalom.* I never could get a clear explanation of its intent from the man who designed the course, much less from the women who took it. Even then it seemed to me somehow mocking of female education. Were those the best works for that audience in 1965? By what standards? Perhaps one could ask nothing better, then. In 1991, however, one *can* ask for something different. One can ask for books that reflect the full range of human or even of Western experience, those of women as well as of men, those of *and by* people of color as well as those of whites.[6] If it does not reflect simple ignorance of the last two decades of scholarship—and I do not believe it does—what Mr. Bennett's list, what his paradigmatic figures represent, is a pretense—a pretense that the consensus or, to give it its proper name, the dominant ideology of the 1950s can be reestablished and its values recommended to undergraduates by means of newly reassembled liberal arts requirements.

But what would one expect from a man of Mr. Bennett's tradition? " 'Can't repeat the past?' " Gatsby cries incredulously to Nick, " 'Why of course you can!' "

The situation is a bit more ominous, however. For it amounts to an effort to wipe away what we have learned these past two decades. I wish to place next to the Faulkner passage one of very different content and form.

> I didn't want to go out of that filthy dollar hotel room. I didn't want to open the door and go out into the dank hall with the stinking toilet running at the end. And I didn't want to be away from the warm breast of Butch. And it seemed like he just wanted to put on his clothes and get back down on the street. We really didn't have to be out of that room till eleven in the a.m. I wanted to hide, to stay there forever. Never to stand upright in the cold air. Strange in the city to lie prone as if in a meadow along a line of sky, and feel each other near just as flesh as warmth as some kind of reaching into each other, on the other side of accidents and tearing apart and beating and collision and running into each other and blaming.
>
> I didn't feel good. I cried. Butch got mad and slapped me. My old lady used to cry all the time, he said, getting you to do what she wanted. Didn't you like it? Wasn't I good to you? My old lady is crazy too. She cries for something she can't even remember didn't happen. All women are nuts, beyond me.
>
> I hurt, I said. I didn't know it would be like this. Nobody tells you the truth. Now I could see mama and why she was hurt and why she always went back to papa, too, how she loved him in a terrible way. I thought everyone on the street would see this on me. Now I knew what they were winking and making faces about and hitting each other about and waiting for each other

on streets for. Even risking their life for each other every day. Didn't mama risk her life everytime she turned over and took her medicine as papa used to say. I would hear him say that and I would hear her cry out. I knew what that cry was. Nobody can tell you.[7]

Where in all the works of Mr. Bennett's two-and-a-half-foot shelf is the power and ambiguity of a woman's first sexual experience explored? Or is it that female sexuality, intimate violence, and how one learns of truth and heritage not in a memorialized forest but in the frosty urban jungle—is it that these are matters outside of "our" common tradition, matters insufficiently weighty to stand with the questions of why civilizations flourish, what to defend or to love, the "things that matter most"? The canon to which Mr. Bennett implicitly would have us return voices at best, a narrow version of courage and aspiration, a quite partial view of history and values; and, perhaps, turbulent and delvsory ideas about how to cure social blight—like a plague of drugs. It may well be that for our students, as for us, the "great questions" of life are addressed not in the mead hall or hunting camp but in the plain rooms portrayed by writers like Alice Cary in "Uncle Christopher's" or by Gwendolyn Brooks in *Maud Martha,* for there the issue is not finding humility despite one's gun and one's rich patrimony, but rather how, in the face of poverty, narrowness, and pride, people try to sustain human community. It may well be, too, that a meaningful path from Thoreau's "Civil Disobedience" to King's "Letter" lies (as I've suggested elsewhere) through a story like Mary Wilkins Freeman's "A Church Mouse," since mostly we and our students do not decide the fate of nations or go to jail for principle, but, like Hetty in that story, search out means, including passive resistance, to survive with dignity in the face of our weakness. And perhaps the question of justice is addressed, to students for whom family violence is far more real than slavery or a raft, as well in Susan Glaspell's "A Jury of Her Peers" as in certain more widely celebrated works.

Now in the abstract, everyone but the most hardened traditionalist will agree with these liberal sentiments. We are all for diversity, representation, inclusion—so long, of course, as we do not "compromise standards." But when we get down to cases, and in particular to the question of who gets dropped from the anthology or the curriculum to make room for Jewett or Freeman, Zora Neale Hurston or Rudolfo Anaya, Gwendolyn Brooks or Susan Glaspell, then we begin to run into tensions. For it turns out that most of us would rather fight than switch. Indeed, this issue is in curricular terms what "reverse discrimination" has become in matters of personnel action. The curriculum is not an infinitely expandable universe of discourse: There are thirty Tuesday and Thursday classes; we can, at best, imagine students reading five or six hours of work at home each week. So if one person insists on Elizabeth Stoddard, another on Charles Chesnutt, and a third on Steinbeck, who is to go? Poe or James or Hemingway or . . . well, you get the picture. I was recently at a university talking informally with a group to plan a series of programs on changing the canon, and I mentioned that I had not taught Henry James in my own courses at Old Westbury. Involuntarily, the director of the women's studies program, a fiction specialist, started: "Do you mean . . . ," she began, apprehension rising in her voice. And then she, and everyone else in the room, dissolved in laughter at the ironic demonstration of Lauter's first law of curricular momentum: Namely, whatever has been taught will continue to be taught until death, alteration of the Norton anthology, or a force equivalent to both, parts us from it.

It is precisely at this point that the voices arguing for the old, the tried, and the true—the gold and calf-bound classics—sound most seductive. "Come hither," they call. "Leave contending; be not stiff for change. Even reformers disagree. Then gather ye round what we know and share. What is, after all, the best." And now, faintly accompanying those voices, we can hear the jingle of federal gold also urging the putative classics upon us. And with a sigh of regret, perhaps, we surrender to the lure of Mr. Bennett's little list and the very real power that lies behind it.

For his is, I think, a forceful gospel. To castigate it as a snare and a delusion, an idol, however federally gilded, it will not do to play Jimmy Carter and argue that things are more complicated, that there are limits to what nerve, faith, and traditional values can accomplish, that Egypt-land, where we are, isn't perhaps so very bad, after all, after all. We need, rather, to raise an alternate standard that, if it is not precisely a pillar of fire, will at least mark the direction in which we should go.

The humanities embody, celebrate, and sometimes mourn the diversity of traditions from which American civilization has been created. To appreciate that diversity and thus to comprehend *our* civilization we must teach a broad range of works, including but not limited to classical Western texts. What these are will change with time and circumstance—nor must that be a problem. We need to embed these varied texts both in the historical world in which they were produced and also in the contemporary world in which we now read them. By so doing, we charge the humanities classroom with the energy of the real issues, the aspirations and mysteries, the pain and delight we and our students live.

Which is precisely why I would choose to teach *The Souls of Black Folks* rather than *Leviathan, The House of Mirth* rather than *Buddenbrooks,* and perhaps even *The Book of Daniel* along with *The Brothers Karamazov,* and why we need to hear the voice of Paul Robeson as well as the cadences of T. S. Eliot, the varied music of Adrienne Rich, Langston Hughes, and Ntozake Shange.

My problem with Mr. Bennett's canon, and everything that flows from it, is, then, a simple one: What the past decades of social change, what the research and pedagogy that derived from them have taught us is that the extraordinary diversity in the historical experience of people in this country cannot be represented by "*a* tradition," a narrow canon, however resounding the names that constitute and recommend it. Nor should the fact that our culture draws upon many diverse and sometimes conflicting traditions be troubling to us. To dream of creating a "common language" we must begin, with joy, at our common diversity. If we need "The Bear" and the Whale, so do we need "The Girl," "The Church-Mouse," and "The Woman Warrior," as well. Let the Bear lie down with the Church-Mouse; we may all learn from the conversation.

Notes

1. All references to William Bennett are from his "To Reclaim a Legacy: A Report on the Humanities in Higher Education" (Washington, D.C.: National Endowment for the Humanities, 1984).

2. The most provocative critique of this historically identifiable effort to erase the African and other "near Eastern" origins of Greek culture is provided in Martin Bernal, *Black Athena: The Afroasiatic Roots of Classical Civilization,* Vol. I: *The Fabrication of Ancient Greece, 1785–1985* (New Brunswick, N. J.: Rutgers University Press, 1987).

3. William Faulkner, "The Bear," *Three Famous Short Novels* (New York: Vintage Books, 1963), p. 203.

4. *Ibid.*, pp. 186–87.

5. Ann Fitzgerald suggested to me the remarkable similarity in subject, cadence, and imaginative language between the Faulkner passage and certain drinking-hall scenes in Old English poetry.

6. Barnard College's summer reading list for the class of 1993 offers a useful example. It includes works by relatively familiar writers such as Robert Coles, Anne Frank, Bernard Malamud, Toni Morrison, Alice Walker, and Virginia Woolf—but it also lists works by Sandra Cisneros, Buchi Emecheta, Joy Kogawa, Ntozake Shange, Estela Portillo Trambley, and Anzia Yezierska among the forty titles.

7. Meridel LeSueur, *The Girl* (Minneapolis: West End Press, 1979), p. 51.

Whose Culture?
Whose Literacy?

Zora Neale Hurston, the black writer and anthropologist, liked to tell a story about how she was arrested for crossing against a red light. But, she laughed, she had gotten off. "I told the policeman," she would say, "that I had seen white folks pass on the green and so assumed the red light was for me." That story has always held a particular appeal to me, since my father was color blind and could not tell red from green. He knew them apart in traffic lights, he once told me, only because one was always on top and the other on bottom.

signs, particularly: Which are on top and which on bottom; which command you to stop, and which invite you to proceed, and how that might differ, depending who "you" are. After all, schools, whatever else they do, help establish and transmit our society's cultural signals, those determinative red and green lights. Indeed, one way of understanding the curriculum is as an elaborate set of signals directing students onto the various tracks they will likely follow throughout their lives.

However that might be, it is certainly true that educational institutions always seem to be caught between two prepositions, "in" and "to." Part of our mission is to instruct students *in* various disciplines, *in* history, *in* literature, *in* physics. But at the same time, we are expected to orient students *to* the world outside the classroom, *to* its creation and recreation in the work they will perform and the ideas they will evolve. I find a tension in these prepositions between the voices of the past and the visions of the future. The dilemma may seem familiar, yet another chapter in the honored debate between the Ancients and the Moderns, between those who say "set the students' eyes firmly upon the 'monuments of unaging intellect,' " and those who say "*educere,* lead them forth, help them dream, let their 'thought be mother to the deed.' "

But to frame the issue in this binary fashion falsifies it. For the past, the

Sections of this chapter were originally part of a lecture inaugurating the Allan K. and Gwendolyn Miles Smith chair at Trinity College; other sections were delivered at the Socialist Scholars Conference, April, 1988, at Philadelphia Community College, and elsewhere.

bodies of knowledge we teach, is not something that simply exists, but rather, is something we *construct*—and we construct that past on the basis of our visions of the future. That is, we erect a building, which we call a curriculum or course of study, and bring people in to view and to use it. Of what is that building made? For whom and to what end is it built? In fact, we harvest *from* the past the materials we believe important to constructing the building in which the future will be shaped. Or, to drop the metaphors, any educational program must focus on a small selection from the vast storehouse of human experience. What gets selected is neither accidental nor inevitable, but is determined, I am suggesting, by an implicit vision of what students "ought" to know to live in the world they will inhabit.

To be sure, we don't generally acknowledge that our selection of literary texts, historical events, psychological experiments, musical compositions, and thus our curriculum, is a function of our own values and commitments. We don't normally say to students in an introductory literature course, "These are the works that a generation of critics, almost all of whom were white, male, and of Western European origins, decided are important; but someone else might come up with a significantly different list." No. We usually say "These are the major works by the major writers." William Bennett did not propose that his list of readings was especially culture-bound, much less idiosyncratic. On the contrary, he argued that his curriculum was constituted by the time-tested products of *the* great minds. E. D. Hirsch does not suggest that his 64-page list of words, phrases and names is the expression of a narrow constituency of the American populace—those, essentially, who have gone through the same system of higher education that he did. Quite the contrary, he presents his list as the inevitable, indeed natural, product of the establishment of a national culture. His list, he says, is simply "descriptive" of that culture, the cultural lingua franca of the literate.

These are, I want to suggest, ideological assertions. They recommend the texts or ideas or authors we value on the basis of "natural" selection, of historical "inevitability," of political neutrality. I want to consider such claims in two ways: first, by glancing at part of the process by which canons have been constructed in the past. I will use the development of American literature as a literary discipline to provide an example. And second, by interrogating the present moment: Why is it that the last decade is marked by efforts to "return to basics," to establish a shelf of "great books," to insist that English should be the "only" language of public discourse, to pose a definition of cultural literacy in terms of a list that "Every American Needs to Know"— to use the modest subtitle of Hirsch's book? Can we see lurking within these diverse efforts a common spirit, a common vision of the future?

I

The first thing to be said about American literature is that before 1920 it really did not exist as an academic discipline. To be sure, some classes were taught at scattered campuses, such as Penn State and Bowdoin, and a few anthologies and literary histories had begun to be published. But there was no American literature section in the Modern Language Association and no magazine devoted to the subject. Teaching or writing about it was a professionally suspect enterprise; indeed, when I was in graduate school in the 1950s, American literature was still regarded among most English professors as rather a dubious subject. But the issue is not the professional credibility of the subject; the point is that it would have been a venturesome critic, indeed, who might then have proposed that college or secondary school curricula ought to require the study of American literature. Oh, maybe *The Scarlet Letter,* an Emerson essay, and a Poe story as part of an English literature course, but surely little more, and certainly not a whole course. Nor should that come as a surprise: After all, the elevation of British literature—not to mention strange areas like Chemistry or Psychology—into a proper subject of collegiate study was of recent vintage. Before that, only the "classics," in Greek and Latin, were appropriate to a "literary" curriculum.

Even if, in 1920, some quaint college had decided to build American literature into the course of study, what constituted the subject would have borne little resemblance to today's curriculum. Melville would have been missing; Twain and Dickinson minor events; Longfellow, Lowell, and Holmes the grand canonical figures. Minority writers one would not have found, and most women would have been only at the margins. The first thing one learns about the literary canon is this: It changes. Slowly, to be sure, and often fitfully, but mutability is as much a feature of the literary canon as its presumed stability. "Permanence," as Emerson said, "is but a word of degrees."

Furthermore, the changes we see are hardly accidental products of wind and tide. On the contrary, they come about by virtue of changes in the society and politics, and through human agency. I have suggested in my case study of the 1920s and 1930s that the new canon of American literature that then began to emerge and that persisted into the 1980s was the product of a set of complex but definable forces. These helped give a determinative role in the establishment of the American canon to academicians, almost all of whom were white men of Western European extraction and upper middle-class origins. Their interests, their social vision, their desire to construct an American literature commensurate with the emerging power of the United States in the world helped define both the texts that came to constitute the canon and the sanctioned ways of reading those texts. The men—and all but one or two were men—who established what we have long called "American literature" were not content to acclaim as canonical whatever happened to float to the surface. Rather, they surveyed the creative history of this country and found within it works that fit their program for an American future. In that, they were more explicit and, I must say, somewhat more honest than today's purveyors of reading lists and cultural nostrums. They saw their task as a venture in cultural politics, and they set about it in unabashedly political ways.

One can identify four interrelated efforts: literary archaeology, theoretical reconstruction, professional organization, and institutional establishment. By literary archaeology, I mean the rediscovery and resurrection of previously lost or discounted texts. In the 1920s, the major example was, of course, Melville, who had been virtually forgotten after his death in 1892, was seldom mentioned in literary histories except as a failed writer of South Seas island tales, and who was, I dare say, never taught and seldom read. By the end of the 1920s, many critics accepted him as the preeminent American novelist. Similarly, Mark Twain passed from a crude western humorist and professional pessimist to the most influential stylist for modern writers like Hemingway.

Clearly, resurrection implied reevaluation, that is, a new set of theoretical models for understanding and "valorizing" works. I want to mention briefly three theoretical elements. The first, and perhaps earliest, entailed the denigration of the female-centered culture that had played a dominant role in the late nineteenth and early twentieth centuries. That can be represented by a passage from George Santayana's attack on the "genteel tradition" in a speech he first gave at Berkeley in 1911. Santayana converts what was initially an architectural metaphor contrasting the new, entrepreneurial American spirit with declining gentility into a proposition that gave gender to these intellectual currents.

> America is . . . a country with two mentalities. . . . This division may be found symbolized in American architecture: a neat reproduction of the colonial mansion—with some modern comforts introduced surreptitiously—stands beside the sky-scraper. The American Will inhabits the sky-scraper; the American Intellect inhabits the colonial mansion. The one is the sphere of the American man; the other, at least predominantly, of the American woman. The one is all aggressive enterprise; the other is all genteel tradition.[1]

That Santayana's formulation, as well as his contempt for what he claims is the "becalmed" and feminized American intellect, won quick and wide acceptance suggests that the power of the earlier "female world of love and ritual" (to use Carroll Smith-Rosenberg's evocative phrase) had already declined—even as women were being mobilized for the political efforts that would lead to suffrage and prohibition. Santayana's model provided a theoretical framework on the basis of which critics could depreciate certain texts, largely those of women, as "genteel," and elevate others that displayed the appropriate qualities of masculinity.

Such qualities were, in turn, given further theoretical validation by formulating the central American myth as that of the lone hero placing "sivilization," as Huck Finn called it, the world of Aunt Sally and other genteel ladies, firmly behind and confronting the dangers and opportunities of the frontier. I do not think I need at this late date to elaborate how influential this formulation became, in terms of valuing both works from the past, such as *Moby-Dick* and *Huckleberry Finn,* and then-contemporary texts, such as those of Hemingway and Faulkner. The point, however, is that critics in the post-World War I period consciously sought to establish the qualities of a distinctively American culture; these they primarily identified with this set of masculine paradigms. It took some fifty years for critics such as Kate Millett, Judith Fetterley and Nina Baym to undermine these intellectual structures.

A third theoretical element in the program of establishing American literature involved applying the modernist view of the centrality of textual complexity, narrative irony, and spiritual anxiety to evaluating literary works. Thus the one-dimensional pieties and facile rhymes that had made a figure such as Longfellow famous in the nineteenth century quickly doomed him and his fellow schoolroom poets to decline in the 1920s. At the same time, writers such as Dickinson and Thoreau, who had been accounted Yankee cranks insofar as they had been known, gradually emerged from that obscurity. Next, perhaps, to emotionalism itself, optimism became the greatest of literary offenses, the happy ending an emblem of impaired morality, and the transparent metaphor a mortal failure of taste.

But the intellectual work of resurrecting and reevaluating texts and of erecting new theories would not by itself have been sufficient to change the canon for literary study. The early professors of American literature recognized the need to organize within their profession. And so they seized the opportunity presented by a more general restructuring of the Modern Language Association in 1920 to establish an American Literature Section. Within a few years they had issued what amounted to a manifesto of their program, a book called *The Reinterpretation of American Literature*, and had begun a new professional journal, *American Literature*. These provided intellectual and social networks of support as the struggle to establish American letters as legitimate objects of study continued at every level of graduate, undergraduate, and secondary school education. Like the early advocates of black studies and women's studies in our own time, these pioneer champions of American literature were often alone in their institutions, faced with the indifference and sometimes active hostility of colleagues. The annual meetings, the new books, and the journal all served to build and sustain a political group in its struggles for recognition.

That recognition, they knew, had to come in the form of institutionalizing their new account of the culture of their country. To teach American literature they needed texts, for the most part in the form of anthologies; and so many of the small original group that began the MLA section organized and published new American literature collections. These helped in establishing courses within key institutions; those in turn legitimated other new curricular efforts. As I implied, this history, which I have most briefly encapsulated, provided us with a model for the development of the Reconstructing American Literature project. That project, of course, is part of a much larger effort to change the literary canon that emerged from the movements for social change of the 1960s and early 1970s.

Why have I devoted all this time to describing historical processes by which change has come about in a canon, in our definitions of what it is important for people to read and to know? To be sure, I think the processes are interesting in themselves. But my main concern is to illustrate the fact that however one might feel about the Bible, *literary* canons do not fall from the sky. They are constructed and reconstructed by people, people of particular stations in life, people with certain ideas and tastes and definable interests and views of what is desirable—that is, with visions of a future. Dominantly, in our time, these visions are structured in terms established by our professional divisions (and definitions) of knowledge. In short, I think the historical evidence strongly supports the idea that a literary canon is a social construction, that it changes, and that people can and do organize to effect such changes. The notion that a canon, or a list, simply exists, timeless and transcendent, independent of human agency seriously to alter it, is just one argument in a conservative political agenda. But that sharpens the question of why the "voices of the past," as I characterize them, have emerged so shrill and insistent this last decade.

II

The answer is not hard to find. When the United States emerged from World War II, it was unquestionably the most powerful nation the world had ever seen. Its factories and farms had been crucial to the military victory of the Allies. Its technology had succeeded in producing in the atomic bomb a weapon of unsurpassed terror. Unlike every other industrial power, its cities and towns were untouched by the war's devastation, and its industries quickly were able to convert their enormous productive capacities from making tanks and bazookas to making Chevies and Frigidaires. American engineers boasted of producing virtually free power through atomic fission, and social scientists talked of an era soon to be at hand when America would be virtually free of poverty and conflict, and of ideology as well—especially if loyalty programs were given scope. And as Johnny came marching home, Rosie was returned from riveting to raising babies in the newly-rising suburbs.

A quarter of a century later, the United States had essentially been defeated by a small Asian nation on the distant battlefield of Vietnam. Its factories, like its large cities, were in decay. Its monopoly on weapons of mass destruction had long disappeared into a balance of terror. The value of nuclear power, like the assumptions of a conflict-free society, like the cold-war consensus itself, had become illusory. Indeed, the fabric of American society was being shredded in harsh and sometimes violent conflicts over war, human rights, and continuing poverty. Johnny and Rosie had probably gone their separate ways—and besides, the ticky-tacky house in Daly City had begun to leak. Far from being a harmonious chorus singing "one for all, all for one," America seemed a cacophony of competing voices demanding a piece of the action.

The noise of that conflict had more or less been muted by the prosperity that extended even into Lyndon Johnson's tenure. But as economic problems increased, so did competition for jobs, places in college, and future opportunities. Measures like those we have come to call "affirmative action," which at first sustained widespread support, began to seem to some in the society as offering unfair advantages to others. And the voices saying "we want in," which had initially received great encouragement, now began to seem to many already "in" sectarian and intrusive, an expression not of democracy in action but of "special interests" demanding more than their share. The social and cultural consensus of America, which after all had been based as much on exclusion as on inclusion, had begun to unravel. In educational terms, the decline of that consensus might be represented by the general obliteration of requirements in most colleges and many secondary schools—it's hard, after all, to decide on what students "ought" to study when a society cannot agree on how or where its youth and treasure "ought" to be invested. Because it had become increasingly unclear where the United States was going *to*—Watts, Cambodia, Woodstock—it became difficult to agree upon what to instruct students *in*. Or, it might be more accurate to say, the differences in view, always there, now came more forcefully to the surface.

Furthermore, faculty faced a student body increasingly dissimilar to those of which we had been a part. The student body was older, more female, and multiracial. Indeed, in colleges it represented an historically unprecedented diversity in terms of class, national origin, race, and gender. No surprise that such students brought into our classrooms a truly remarkable variety of cultures, or that many of us, in particular traditionally-trained white men, found teaching in this new environment peculiarly discomforting. But we were not alone. Faced with such a lack of consensus, with the anxieties attendant upon a much more visibly heterogeneous society, with increased international competition for jobs, with students more various than any educational system had ever attempted to teach, many in middle America located great political comfort in conservative appeals to reestablish a "common culture," whether of "basics," "great books," the English language, or a literacy list.

III

The cultural version of this conservative theory has been tendered to the American public by the former Secretary of Education, William Bennett, and—whatever their differences—by such academic figures as Allan Bloom and E. D. Hirsch.[2] One has only to note how long books like Hirsch's *Cultural Literacy* and Bloom's *The Closing of the American Mind* remained atop the best-seller lists to recognize how this conservative cultural agenda has dominated the field. In this area as, one must admit, in many others, the progressive side has reenforced the wisdom of the old political adage that "you can't beat somethin' with nothin'." But finally, the conservative text is not the only way of reading today's cultural signs; indeed, a progressive alternative is in the process of being formulated. The debate over altering Stanford's core curriculum in a minor way to admit women and minorities symbolizes the ongoing struggle. My objective here is to join in that debate by suggesting a way of looking at the nature and functions of culture that is quite different from the way offered by Allan Bloom, William Bennett, E. D. Hirsch and others of what, echoing Emerson, I have been calling the party of the past.

The view of culture they offer begins from the assumption that it is something—a set of ideas, understandings, references, a "language"—that certain people in the past possessed and that most Americans of our "mass society" no longer own. Generally they associate this wonderful old "language," so little now in circulation, with what they term "Western civilization," and they recommend a revival of its study as a primary method for bringing a once-shared culture back into currency. In that way, they minimally believe, something of the quality of yesterday's life will be restored, a life of greater moral clarity and social cohesion, less pollution and crime, more respect—respect for legitimate authority and respect for created beauty. Thus this agenda ties Sophocles to Rodney Dangerfield, and Romeo and Juliet to the nuclear family. Maximally, advocates of this position hope, a renewal of "cultural literacy" will contribute to eliminating political alienation and poverty, not to mention rap music and teen-age pregnancy—to some commentators as closely joined as Beethoven was once supposed to be to revolutionary politics. To their credit, these critics have insisted upon the crucial link between what we study and how we live, between the content of curricula and the character of our values.

Moreover, it is not difficult to see the force of this invocation of traditional forms of culture, especially since it dovetails so well with other cherished ideas about how to restore the sense of social harmony that American society certainly lacks. In fact, it may be that the *primary* appeal of books like Bloom's and Hirsch's is not the force of their understanding of culture or even of Western civilization but their claims to be able to produce peace—or at least structure—where there is no peace. Such claims will be tested in pragmatic American fashion as prescriptions like Hirsch's are put into practice in American schools and colleges. But even in this early stage we need to ask whether the understanding of culture offered to us is deceptive, whether it atomizes student learning just as it confines teaching to drill, whether it thus inhibits the development of knowledge and, most important, whether there are other conceptions both of "culture" and of "literacy" that will serve the realization of democracy more fully in the coming years. I believe there are; I believe they emerge from the very *differences* that have made American society at once unique and disorderly. I believe that an understanding of culture rooted in difference offers hope and opportunity, rather than constraint, in a world of often fearful change. And I want to share something of that vision. But first, I want to raise some questions about the cultural conceptions that have been popularized by Misters Bennett, Bloom, and Hirsch, and here particularly of the last, since his ideas are in fact being implemented.

Many readers will be familiar with the content of Hirsch's book *Cultural Literacy,* the best-known section of which is a 64-page, double-column list of words, names, and phrases. This, Hirsch believes, constitutes a kind of cultural dictionary that—remembering his subtitle—"Every American Needs to Know" in order to communicate effectively, and thus for the society to function coherently. To catch the flavor of Hirsch's list, I opened arbitrarily to page 185 and found the following sequence of items: "lowbrow; Low Countries; lowercase; lowest common denominator; Loyola, Saint Ignatius of; Lucifer; Luddite; Luftwaffe; Luke, Saint, Gospel according to; lunatic fringe." Critics have had a good deal of fun at the expense of this list. One might point out, for example, that of things Latino Hirsch includes little more than señor, señora, señorita, wetback, "La Cucaracha (song)," and Zapata; but that he excludes Cesar Chavez, migrant worker, barrio, and La Raza. To such criticisms, Hirsch has responded in two ways: First, the list can obviously be expanded somewhat, and in fact has been. Further, if items are left out, that reflects their relative *unimportance* to what Hirsch describes as the "national culture." A "national culture," he insists, "transcends dialect, region, and social class" (p. 82), as well as race.

Nor is it politically motivated. His intent, Hirsch insists, is "to avoid any of the prescriptiveness that is inherent in cultural politics . . . " (p. 137). And this, he asserts, is a wholly neutral enterprise. As if a commitment to reproducing what is "traditional" is not political, as if a list that includes Goebbels and Goering but omits Anne Frank, that includes the Ku Klux Klan and the John Birch Society, but not the Urban League nor the Anti-Defamation League of B'nai B'rith, that contains not one woman of color among its hundreds of names is not "political," as if education is not in its most fundamental aspects a "political" enterprise. To maintain that the "national culture" represented by this list "transcends" the various particularities of class, race, gender, sexuality, or region is, in fact, to advance a political claim: that your idea of culture soars triumphantly, inevitably, above the localized grinds in which most people function. That Hirsch's list is vetted by a hundred, or even thousands, of our college-educated colleagues proves absolutely nothing except that most of us have encountered roughly the same kind of limited educational experiences as Hirsch. What he knows, we know; what we do not know—and that includes much of what our students do—he does not know either. Thus what Hirsch's list amounts to is a kind of anthropologist's cross section of the many details, trivial and otherwise, stored up in the cerebral cortexes of college-educated Americans of a certain age. But that hardly defines "culture."

Indeed, there is a much more fundamental criticism of Hirsch than the complaint of multiculturalists that his list is ethnocentric and thus flawed; if simply that were the problem, it could, as Hirsch suggests, easily be expanded. The radical criticism of *Cultural Literacy* involves Hirsch's basic understanding of culture as a kind of commodity, a set of items you possess, like family silver. Such items you can check against a master list and, if any are missing, you can go to the culture store—otherwise called a school—and possess yourself of them. From this perspective, those who own more of these certifiably cultural items are more "cultured" than those who have fewer, or whose stock consists of articles *not* marked in our society—or in Hirsch's dictionary—as items of "culture." Furthermore, these cultural items have been produced by people other than yourself; your role is simply to obtain as many as you can by purchase or perhaps by some form of labor—generally as little as possible— performed in the culture store. The nirvana of culture thus becomes the demonstrated ability of an individual to own the whole 64-page set!

IV

In proposing an alternative to this idea of culture as commodity, and thus a different perspective on our educational work, I want to begin from a central part of the Mississippi Freedom School curriculum of 1964. It may be hard, even for those of us who lived through those times, now more than a quarter century ago, to reinvoke their spirit. Certainly it was easier then to identify enemies, for what redeeming virtues could one find in the Jim Crow system, which required that black people drink out of separate fountains and wait in separate vestibules, attend separate and monstrously unequal schools, travel in segregated railroad cars or in the backs of busses? What arguments could be made for excluding black citizens from the right to vote, and, should they attempt to change that system, shooting them down in the streets of towns with names like Liberty and Philadelphia? And, on the other side, the freedom movement could invoke the rhetoric of national leadership that proclaimed "ask not what your country can do for you, but what you can do for your country," and that asserted in the very halls of the Congress "we *shall* overcome." The movement could affirm that we had a dream, not far distant, when black children and white children would study and play together, and would work and vote in a democracy newly emerged into the sunlight of equality. We could, singing together, turn toward that future.

> Before I be a slave,
> I'll be buried in my grave,
> And I'll fight for my right
> To be free.

I do not invoke these memories—for those of us old enough to remember— out of nostalgia, but because the power of such ideas does not simply evaporate in drier times. These ideas constitute a deep well-spring of idealism, a rushing of fresh waters under the arid surfaces of self-interest that have characterized this recent decade. How do we, once again, gain access to this quickening stream?

Like much else in the civil rights movement, the freedom school curriculum offers a useful starting point.[3] The mimeographed "Note to the Teacher" that all 1964 volunteers received began by pointing out that we would be working "in a non-academic sort of setting; probably the basement of a church." And our students would "be involved in voter registration activity after school." Outside resources would be few, hours irregular, conditions tense. We were urged to shape our "curriculum in light of the teachers' skills, the students' interests, and the resources of the particular community in which your school is located." Again and again this manual comes back to the inevitability as well as the importance of developing the educational program from "the students' backgrounds": "The value of the Freedom Schools," we were told, "will derive from what the teachers are able to elicit from the students in terms of comprehension and expression of their experiences." Thus freedom school education would ideally be a process of "drawing out"—*educere*—of what students had experienced but had neither expressed nor comprehended; rather than a pouring in of information and details the students had not previously known but of which we teachers had considerable stock.

The basic character of that educational program was contained in a set of questions at the center of the "Citizenship Curriculum," the real heart of the schools. The questions were:

1. What does the majority culture have that we want?
2. What does the majority culture have that we don't want?
3. What do we have that we want to keep?

To which some students added a fourth question:

4. What do we have that we don't want to keep?

These questions imply an understanding of culture, an educational program, even a pedagogy, and of course a politics radically different from that implicit in the work of Hirsch or Bloom or Bennett.

First, these questions do not ask "What does the majority culture have that *I* want?" but "What does the majority culture have that *we* want?" The distinction is critical and yet very difficult to comprehend within the framework of American educational institutions. For virtually everything in our schools and colleges, except for some team sports, is calculated to reenforce the idea of *individual* advancement, private accumulation of knowledge, grades, and degrees. In fact, I was once fired from a college for giving a collective grade to students who had worked deeply together on the main project of the course. In that process they had probably learned more than they could in any other way about the distinctions between the individualistic ethos at the heart of American middle-class culture, and the idea of collective experiences and aspirations—a set of issues central to the course. Our freedom school students were quite clear about this matter: The discrimination they encountered every day had little or nothing to do with them as individuals named Alice or Burdette or Clarie; it had *everything* to do with them as black people. And thus the question was not only the knowledge, the sense of self Alice as an individual might accumulate in her private way, but also how the social definition of her as an "ignorant nigger," or more politely a "culturally deprived" black girl, might be changed. These are issues we too need to address both as individuals and as an academic community.

Second, unlike Hirsch's cultural dictionary, the Freedom Schools asserted a fundamentally ethical understanding of education. The Citizenship Curriculum argues that while "the structure of society can be changed," "it is not simply the changing of the structure that will make a good world, but the ethical values of the individual." In discussing education, it raises questions like these:

What should be taught in schools? Do we teach myths and lies? Why? Should we? Should we train people for jobs in schools? To be good citizens? What else should we train people for? culture, resourcefulness, world citizenship, respect for other people and cultures, peace.

It suggests that teachers and students examine questions like this: "Suppose Negroes had everything that the middle class of America has . . . everything the rest of the country has . . . would it be enough?" And it urges us to "discuss 'do unto others as you would have them do unto you.' Do you have a set of values?" it continues. "Are society's laws enough? Are your own personal 'laws' important, too? Are they ever more important than society's laws?"

Hirsch would have us believe that by mastering a certain set of enchanted nouns, students shall mysteriously gain power in the world—like the Old Testament patriarch who, learning the name of God, can thus evoke God's powers. We are thus offered a tool, a cultural dictionary, when the issue is not technology, but values. The question is not simply *whether* one learns names like Goebbels, Goering, and the John Birch Society; or Anne Frank, Frances E. W. Harper, and the John Reed Clubs, but *why*. What is contested here is precisely "what should be taught in schools"—an idea of culture that perpetuates historical inequality and racism or an idea of culture that fosters change?

This question leads, in turn, to the issue of whether the very dynamics of classrooms promote or forbid change. I think that Hirsch's list says to students something like this: "I have knowledge, and power; you do not. To make it as an individual in *my* world, you need to accumulate enough of the tokens I call culture to buy in. You can do so, of course, even if you are 'culturally deprived' to begin with." What students hear is rather different, perhaps something like this: "What I experience isn't important; it's what I *don't* know that determines where I am in the world. And even if I learn all the ditsy items on that list, the people who started way ahead will still be way ahead, and I'll still be at the edges." To say it another way, a list like Hirsch's in actual classroom use amounts to a set of intellectual traffic signals—green for some, red to most. It is not a cultural means for gaining greater access to power, but a technique for classifying students as more or less marginal. The more items on the list you possess, the closer to the cultural mainstream you are; the fewer, the more at the fringes you are. And as with other commodities, possessing such items depends precisely on your position in society to begin with. As Trudy Palmer, a Stanford graduate student, recently put it, "I was expected to know all the mainstream white authors that the rest of the students were working on, while they felt no obligation to know anything about the [African-American] writers I was interested in."

Part of Hirsch's problem is that he seems unaware of the work of anthropologists and educational historians—such as Jules Henry and Michael Katz—that demonstrates how the primary lessons of school are taught by its *processes,* including those by which the curriculum is "transmitted."[4] "It is *not* primarily the message," Henry wrote in 1963, "(let us say, the arithmetic or the spelling) that constitutes the most important subject matter to be learned, but the noise! The most significant cultural learnings—primarily the cultural drives—are communicated as *noise*" (p. 290), or by what others call the "hidden curriculum." Or, as B. F. Skinner once put it, "Education is what survives when what has been learnt has been forgotten." Because he is so fixated on *content,* Hirsch cannot see how in the real school world his proposals, like similar panaceas before, become the vehicle for carrying out that hidden curriculum: teaching your place in the hierarchy, the performance of meaningless tasks determined by others, the importance of timeliness, competition within conformity, and similar behaviors desirable in a peaceable workforce.

Underlying this failure to appreciate the processes of schooling is a singular theoretical naïveté. The "national vocabulary," Hirsch maintains, does not "reflect a coherent culture of a dominant class or other group in the same way that a local dialect does. It is primarily an instrument of communication among diverse cultures rather than a cultural or class instrument in its own right" (pp. 103–104). Whatever else recent poststructuralist and feminist theory has done, certainly it has demonstrated that language—whether a literal vocabulary and syntax or a cultural "vocabulary" like Hirsch's—at once will be *both* an instrument of communication *and* of domination. That, indeed, the power relationships implicit in any vocabulary shape the kinds of communications that can occur and the uses to which they are put. It is for such reasons that Ossie Davis over a quarter of a century ago wrote an article explaining why "The English Language Is My Enemy," in which he pointed, for example, to the structures that pose as negatives words like *black* and *dark* against the positives *white* and *light.*

This is not to say that it is unimportant to know the items on Hirsch's list, including the "mainstream" writers—Plato, for example. But really to understand the values of classical Greek society, which Plato may be taken to represent, one needs also to know that it was a slave society, and to know that not as a miscellaneous fact one registers on a short-answer quiz, but to feel the meaning of slavery in society. That feeling one does not learn reading Plato, even though he was once sold into slavery. One might begin by reading Olaudah Equiano, or Frederick Douglass, or Harriet Jacobs, or Frantz Fanon, or, as I did in freedom school, Langston Hughes and Richard Wright. Or one might begin by listening to the music created by American slaves, or by trying to eradicate the still-powerful effects of slavery and the racism that rationalized it—effects that continue to deform our society. Our freedom school students, who already knew a great deal about that last, learned even more by engaging in voter registration, a "radical" effort that summer of 1964. But the freedom school idea was *not* to explain Plato through the lens offered by our students' undigested experiences, including their efforts to change their society. Rather, it was the perception that if students could first express and then understand their experiences they would establish an intellectual ground from which to examine and perhaps start to change the troubling world around them. They might also then wish to begin comprehending Plato and the culture he symbolizes. Comprehending him, too, not as a cultural icon whose abstractions one might reproduce on exams, but as a living force with whom one might argue, agree, and disagree, embrace and reject; whose decision to locate his Academy in the suburbs one might question; whose limited student body one might challenge; whose ideas one might wish to make one's own use of.

Implicit in the freedom school methodology is thus a fundamentally *comparative* strategy of learning. That signifies *neither* the clutching of Western literature as the sole determinant of "our" culture, nor its exorcism as patriarchal and racist—though often it is. Rather, a comparative strategy involves the critical examination of what both "majority" and "minority" cultures have that we want—and do *not* want. It implies an approach to minority or marginalized cultures in their own terms, and not only through the distorting lenses offered by dominant Western traditions. It offers, in fact, not the false tranquility of settled traditions, but the ferment and passion of a struggle over what shall be honored by calling it "culture" or "literature" or "history"; what shall be esteemed by describing it as canonical; what shall be dignified by including it in college curricula, reading lists, and cultural catalogues.

V

Changing what we are so willing to dignify and who constitutes that powerful "we"—that is precisely what is at contest, just as change was the objective of freedom schools, indeed of the social movements of the 1960s and 1970s. By raising the issues of social justice and political democracy, those movements also placed culture back on the agenda not, the way it seemed in the 1950s, as a settled galaxy of sublime intellects, a transcendent book list separate from politics, but as a political problem. Those of us who studied culture were increasingly engaged with the questions the movements raised—questions such as "Where are the blacks?" "Where are the women?" Seeking answers to such questions—the questions of the canon—we have been led to interrogate the very ideas of culture to which we were trained.

Those of the party of the past, like Professor Hirsch, however, suspect change. His list, he writes, aims "to represent but not to alter current literate American culture." For the notion that culture can be significantly modified is, he insists, as illusory as proposing that we drop the "s" from the third person singular verb. In fact, as I have suggested, what is illusory is the stability of culture. The question is not whether the culture changes, but how rapidly and in what directions that change takes place, who controls it, and in whose interests it occurs.

How liberating is this perception; how frightening the responsibility it entails! For if this is true—and I believe it is—intellectuals cannot for a moment evade choices and comparisons—between, say, Nathaniel Hawthorne and Harriet Beecher Stowe, between Henry James and Charles Chesnutt, between Ernest Hemingway and Zora Neale Hurston—indeed, between "literature" and the other forms of lived culture we do not dignify with that title. Thus in our curricula, our book lists, and our appointments, we are forever resetting the green and red lights of culture. That is an endless chore, but it is a precious one. For I believe such cultural work converts the teaching of humanities from a museum to a force in the world that we and our students inhabit and shall create.

It does so because such work makes us agents in the ongoing debate between the parties of the past and the parties of the future. The form of cultural study I have advanced insists precisely upon the variety of American lives. It allows us to teach the lesson of opening cultural canons so that the idea of culture is no longer restricted largely to the care of white men who claim to represent us, one and all. Perhaps we can thus learn to offer tomorrow's students knowledge of the full range of the cultures of white women, of people of color, and of today's and tomorrow's working people, all of whom together represent the rainbow spectrum of the United States—and, finally, its decisive majority as well.

As we work to extend the scope of that diverse majority culture, we must simultaneously acknowledge the limits of our roles as teachers and intellectuals; indeed, we must acknowledge the limits of culture as a form of shaping consciousness. I want to invoke here a well-known passage from Frederick Douglass' 1845 *Narrative* of his life. Douglass is discussing the effects of the critical step in his education, literacy: " . . . I would at times feel that learning to read had been a curse rather than a blessing. It had given me a view of my wretched condition, without the remedy. It opened my eyes to the horrible pit, but to no ladder upon which to get out."[5] Books generate consciousness and open the world to our inspection. But they do not in themselves *change* that world, or even offer the means to climb from its depths. The image Douglass initially offers for that—a ladder to climb out of the pit—poses the problem in individual terms, for only one person at a time can climb such a ladder. In the long run, however, as the *Narrative* dramatizes, the issue of slavery, whatever its form, will not be resolved by an individual climbing from the pit, but only by filling the pit in so that it no longer opens threateningly before our wandering feet. To that end, Douglass shares his learning with his fellow slaves on Mr. Freeland's plantation, and ultimately with his listeners and readers as well. For the object of learning, as Douglass most profoundly teaches, is not finally learning itself, or even self-advancement. It is, as the freedom schools made explicit in their name, liberation.

Notes

1. George Santayana, *The Genteel Tradition: Nine Essays,* Douglass Wilson, ed. (Cambridge, Mass.: Harvard University Press, 1967).

2. E. D. Hirsch, Jr., *Cultural Literacy: What Every American Needs to Know* (Boston: Houghton Mifflin, 1987); Allan Bloom, *The Closing of the American Mind* (New York: Simon and Schuster, 1987).

3. Much of the 1964 Mississippi Freedom School curriculum has been reprinted, together with comments by some of those who used it, in *Radical Teacher* 40 (Fall 1990).

4. Jules Henry, "Golden Rule Days: American Schoolrooms," *Culture Against Man* (New York: Vintage, 1963). See also Paul Lauter and Florence Howe, "Schools in America—The Making of Jet Pilots," *The Conspiracy of the Young* (Cleveland and New York: World, 1970), pp. 206–254.

5. Frederick Douglass, *Narrative of the Life of Frederick Douglass, An American Slave,* written by Himself (New York: Signet, 1968), p. 55.

The Book of Bloom and the
Discourse of Difference

The Lord thy God will raise up unto thee a Prophet from the midst of thee, of thy brethren, like unto me; unto him ye shall hearken. . . . [And the Lord said] I shall put my words into his mouth, and he shall speak to them all that I command him; And it shall come to pass, that whosoever will not hearken unto my words which he shall speak in my name, I will require it of him. But the prophet, which shall presume to speak a word in my name, which I have not commanded him to speak, or that shall speak in the name of other gods, even that prophet shall die. And if thou say in thine heart, How shall we know the word which the Lord hath not spoken? When a prophet speaketh in the name of the Lord, if the thing follow not, nor come to pass, that is the thing which the Lord hath not spoken, but the prophet hath spoken it presumptuously: thou shalt not be afraid of him.

                                                            Deuteronomy 18.15, 18–22

About a year ago, I received a copy of a letter that took the editor of the *Trinity Reporter,* the College's alumni magazine, to task for publishing a version of some of the previous chapter. An institution like Trinity College, the writer argued, must "unequivocally support the values and institutions of traditional Judeo-Christian culture and western European civilization." Otherwise the "elitist" and "totalitarian" political agenda, which he believed I was pushing, would triumph, to the ruination of academic freedom, our democratic way of life, and even the cultural diversity I was espousing.[1]

It its small way, this letter expressed a set of ideas in a strident tone widely heard in Reaganized America. Its best known cultural representative is, of course, Allan Bloom. Like the letter writer, Bloom sets forth a conservative answer to the questions of the canon—that is, from what tradition, or tra-

Sections of this chapter were first presented to a Trinity College symposium on Ideology (October, 1988) and were published in *Ideology and the Academy: Art, Knowledge and the Curriculum* (Hartford, Conn.: Trinity College, 1989), pp. 75–83; other sections constituted part of my Introduction to "A Cluster on Curriculum Transformation," *Radical Teacher* #37 (1989).

ditions, do "we, the people" derive? And what should be the canonical texts we ought to study, teach, and pass on to our young people? My letter writer, in brief, and Bloom, in a book of some 400 pages, argue for what they see as the key works of a well-defined Western tradition, from Plato, through St. Paul, to the American Founding Fathers. Others, like those who succeeded in reforming Stanford University's core humanities sequence in small but significant ways, propose a rather more diverse set of traditions, reaching out beyond the patriarchal or even the Western script.

Under this important but seemingly academic question of the canon lurks a more intense conflict. Indeed, the intellectual battle in which my letter writer and Bloom are enlisted has been waged in terms usually reserved for a war of succession. Stanford gets excoriated as a mutinous principality; whereas Columbia, entrenched behind its primigenial curriculum, is lauded for repelling the hordes from outside the Heights. Questions about the adequacy of the Western canon seem to get taken as doubts about the birthright of its defenders. Bloom pitches his book like an Old Testament jeremiad designed through its very denunciatory power to rescue us from imminent barbarism. The stridency of tone suggests to me that this contest involves a matter of legitimacy: At issue is not only *what* should be studied and taught, but under whose auspices collegiate study should be organized. Who, in short, has "rights" in the field? Such questions engage deeply-held feelings about place, power, and ego in institutions central to the cultural life of the nation.

But if the apocalyptic language overheats the debate, the issues are by no means trivial, either in intellectual terms or in those of public policy. On the contrary, it is true, as Bloom and others imply, that the contest involves the future shape of American society: whether or not it will reflect, and respect, *difference* as a central feature of the cultural and political landscape. My difference with Bloom is not over the importance of what is studied in schools and colleges, but over what is important. Since few of the principals in this struggle have stated the patriarchal case more strenuously than Bloom, I wish in this chapter to examine some of his arguments—in effect his prescriptions for university education and thus for American society. By contrast, I shall review some of the implications of what has been called "curriculum integration" (or "transformation"), an effort to reconstruct collegiate study and thus our culture in response to the new scholarship focused on gender, race, and class.

I

Few elements of Western tradition are as ancient, or as deeply embedded, as the idea of prophetic testimony. The practice predates even the basic moral codes, such as the Ten Commandments, and has been passed from Moses, the woman of Endor and Jeremiah, from Tiresias, Sibylla, and Cassandra, through Paul of Tarsus, Mahomet, and Martin Luther, to Carlyle and Thoreau, Karl Marx, Sigmund Freud, and Mary Baker Eddy, Marcus Garvey and Martin Luther King—not to mention Timothy Leary, Wilhelm and Charles Reich. These men (mainly) speaking what they variously construed as the inspired word, did not on the whole claim to predict the future, though they envisioned it. Rather, they denounced the corruption of the times, the falling away of the people from a state not, perhaps, of perfection, but at least of grace. And they often set themselves against the priests and scribes of their world, the keepers of tradition, the preservers of institutions. Thus they were often disturbers of the peace, that peace which is not peace, but finally accommodation.

The problem, stated in my epigraph and visualized hilariously in Monty Python's movie "The Life of Brian," is how one might know a prophet who speaks true words from the false linguists and enchanters. And this is a problem today: For a new prophet has arisen in Israel, or at least in its American branch. He has denounced our falling away from the sanctity of family; from the authority of the "old books," most particularly the Bible and Plato; and our erection of the false gods of pluralism. Today's generation, he cries out, has knowledge—of computers and of sex—but no wisdom; opinions, but no "vision of a moral cosmos;" a faddish "respect for the Sacred," but no "real religion." The people, he tells us, have become "nice," "open," but they "lack what is most necessary, a real basis for discontent with the present and awareness that there are alternatives to it" (p. 61). They have forgotten, he says, the "remarkably unified and explicit political tradition" (p. 54) established by our Founding Fathers and made manifest in the language of the Declaration of Independence. Thus the future, not just of colleges, but of American society and therefore of world order, is very much in doubt.

I am, as many of my readers will know, quoting from Allan Bloom's *The Closing of the American Mind,* a tract developed precisely in the tradition—and to its author undoubtedly in the spirit—of our prophetic ancestors. It is not only that Bloom denounces the degeneration of today's students and their falling away from the vivid educational model of the post-Sputnik era. Nor is it simply that he turns to scriptural traditions to validate his argument. But also, Bloom engages today's priests and scribes, the university professoriat, in their own Temple, contesting with them the definitions of the ideas and the literature that a doctorate of philosophy, whatever its precise content, is supposed to represent. Furthermore, Bloom appeals over the heads of these priests and scribes, speaking directly to the people of these degenerate times of the savage rock music, the homogenization of the sexes, and the emptiness of schooling that the people know, he insists, all too well already. Finally, Bloom offers both a challenge to and a hope for the future. "This," he tells us, "is the American moment in world history, the one for which we shall forever be judged" (p. 382). Purged of its cynics, its naysayers, its relativists, inspired by the model of Platonic friendship and Socratic self-sacrifice, today's university/Temple can yet help to bring forth upon this continent "a new nation, conceived in liberty and dedicated to the proposition that all *men,*" at any rate, "are created equal."

I have tried not to mock Bloom here but to offer something of the tone and spirit of *The Closing of the American Mind.* For I do not believe it useful to trivialize a book bought by a million Americans and read, at least in part, by many of them. Never mind that Bloom's logic is flawed and his history inaccurate.[2] Never mind that his dominant rhetorical tactic is the resounding overstatement. Never mind that his own prophets, as those on his right glee-fully point out, are almost all foreign to America. Prophetic testimony is seldom judged by its account of history, nor by whether its propositions follow one from the other in inevitable sequence. To be sure, prophetic testimony always claims to "speak truth to power." But in fact, its measure, as my epigraph suggests, lies in the future.

Its measure does not, I want to emphasize, depend on how accurately it "predicts" that future—as if what will happen always is created already and needs only to be envisioned. But rather, I want to suggest, its measure depends on how well it helps to *shape* that future—how well it is able to mobilize intellectual and what Bloom might call "spiritual" resources to contest *for* a future. That, in my view, is the function of ideology. And *The Closing of the American Mind,* whatever else it claims to be, is surely an ideological document.

We are then faced, I think, with the central dilemma to which my Deu-teronomic text is directed: How do we know the false prophet from the true? Is the tradition within which this book operates that of *The Greening of America,* in less than a generation now so withered, sere, and forgotten, or of *The Communist Manifesto,* alive and powerful despite the fact that it is every year proved "false" by pundits and commentators? And if the validation of such a prophetic or ideological text lies in the future, or at least in its power to help construct that future, if logic and historical accuracy are not absolutely determinative, if authority is just what is being contested, how can we judge? Are we back precisely at what Bloom condemns: relativism? That one person's truth (one man's, he would say) is no better than the next, one culture's values simply its values, and not fundamental markers *of* value? Or are there, short of a time-machine with which to leap into the future and verify a prophet's predictions, ways of testing the value, and the values, of such a jeremiad?

I want to pursue three approaches to the problem of evaluating social ideologies such as those offered by Bloom and I want to exemplify these tests by looking more closely at part of *The Closing of the American Mind.* First, I think, we need to ask whether Bloom's very forms of discourse, his language, rhetorical strategies, authorial stance, themselves imply a certain outlook and set of values. Second, ideological documents such as *Closing* incorporate or foreground certain facts and provide a framework for understanding them; but which facts do they minimize, and do their frameworks function to blind us to alternative ways of understanding such facts? And third, ideologies inscribe their vision of the future in their account of the passing moment. What, then, does the story a prophet like Bloom tells about today and yes-terday suggest about how he would construct tomorrow? Is that a tomorrow within which we would wish to live?

In examining these questions, I shall focus on Bloom's discussion of race, partly for the sake of unifying this analysis, partly for the significance of this issue to education in the United States today, but mainly because it seems to me that any examination of American society and culture must sufficiently account for this no-longer distinctively American dilemma if we are to take it seriously. For me, a critic's account of race and racism is a fundamental touchstone of the value of his or her work. This is so, I believe, not so much because, pragmatically, American society can never be at peace while racism so profoundly shapes politics and culture. Rather, as W.E.B. DuBois pointed out, the question of race is really the question of who one believes to be human, ultimately where one draws the line between those to whom we extend our deep species loyalty and those, across that divide, whom we enslave, experiment upon, or decide to exterminate.[3]

II

My first point, then, concerns the implications of the form itself. *The Closing of the American Mind* has no notes, no bibliography, no more scholarly apparatus than Plato's dialogues and the Book of Daniel, no more proof of its enormous generalizations than the word of Bloom. Much to the distress of his colleagues on the right, Bloom refers to them not at all and refers to his own mentor, Leo Strauss, only once, in passing; indeed, the book hardly cites *any* Americans, preferring the confirming observations of Tocqueville—when it seeks external confirmation at all. That is seldom and, I think, deliberate. For Bloom wishes in his book to model the ideal he espouses, and that is that the ideal man—and it *is* a male—while informed by tradition and latently charismatic, is above all else *homo rationum*. There is much in this model of Amos, crying "Woe to them that are at ease in Zion." But the model is above all Socrates, refusing to stop asking "What is truth, what is justice, what is god?"

The model is also a familiar American figure, the lone cowhand, the self-sufficient hunter, the romantic individual, standing apart from society and confronting its demons—an Ahab striking through its ambiguous masks, an Augie March for the gentiles. It is the creation of such separate, rational individuals that, for Bloom, is the true objective of education. Over against this model are the blacks. The problem with blacks in the university, Bloom contends, is that they have chosen a "group presence" (pp. 95–96), opting for separation: "Just at the moment when everyone else has become a 'person,' blacks have become blacks" (p. 92), Bloom writes. I shall pursue the racial issue in a moment, but I think it important to see how the book's form itself asserts, is designed to engender, the individualistic ideology that it is Bloom's purpose to pose against the degeneration of democratic polity and the collectivist corruption of academic life. The priests and scribes of the academy may call upon one another in multiplied citations to mask their surrender, but Bloom would have us, embracing the strength of his performance, derive from that lesson the sweet essence of good and evil.

I suggested above that a second feature of such ideological texts is that they bring certain knowledge into focus and exclude alternative conceptions. Thus, for example, Mary Rowlandson presents her 1675 captivity by Indians, her survival despite cold, disease, and lack of food, and her ultimate liberation as, in characteristic American fashion, illustrations of God's providential hand working on behalf of the white settlers of this continent. While her *Narrative* often refers to the problem she and her Indian captors have in obtaining food, it offers no way of connecting that reality to the Indians' motives for attacking invasive white settlements in the first place, nor to their willingness to ransom her for money with which they might purchase supplies. For her, the Indians *have* no fundamental motives; they are merely instruments of the white peoples' God. Inheritor of Mrs. Rowlandson's outlook, "The American Mind" has *always* been closed to certain facts and understandings, especially to those concerning people of color. In significant part, that has been a result of defining "*The* American Mind" as belonging to those, to use Bloom's words, "who populate the twenty or thirty best universities" (p. 22)—overwhelmingly white and, until very recently from his perspective, dominantly male as well. Obviously, what knowledge an ideological text makes available or obscures depends very much on the social and political interests of the groups for which it speaks. We must then ask: What are the understandings to which Bloom's book *closes* its readers and on whose behalf does it do so?

Bloom's account of the impact of racial change on the university in the 1960s provides a most useful example. The social and political pressure of the civil rights movement, of political liberalism, and later of black-power violence, he suggests, led schools such as Cornell to recruit an increased number of black students, many of whom, since they were from "inner cities," "were manifestly unqualified and unprepared" for the "great intellectual and social challenges awaiting them in the university" (p. 94). Thus Cornell, and its peer institutions, were immediately faced with a harsh choice: In Bloom's words, "fail most of them or pass them without their having learned." In structuring the choice as a dilemma, either horn of which would gore the university, and thus obscuring what the real alternatives might have been, Bloom illustrates the process I am describing. The university might, for example, have chosen to devote significant, and not marginal, resources to overcoming minority students' limited preparation, perhaps enlisting in that purpose more traditionally-prepared students enormously eager, then as now, to put their experience to use. The university might have decided to engage the issue of race as a center for its general education program. The university might also have chosen systematically to reexamine—as it has *not* even to this day—its own curriculum in light of the history and present realities of black and other minority students' lives and educations. On that basis the university might have decided what in its traditions was desirable to retain, what to critique or even eliminate, and what it wished to absorb from minority experience. Some limited gestures were made in these directions, but frankly, little was done, in part because much of the professoriat was, like Bloom, simply too ignorant of marginalized traditions and unreflectingly committed to the precedence of its own.

But more fundamental: in many institutions, the issue was posed, precisely as Bloom describes, in terms of fail or fake. The full range of alternatives was no more explored by university communities than were the alternatives to driving the Indians to desperation or extermination explored by the Puritan mainstream. To have considered these kinds of alternatives would, of course, have required a radical reexamination of institutional purpose, something to which Bloom, in the tradition of Mrs. Rowlandson's ministerial advisors, is anxious to close our minds.

Equally indicative is Bloom's selection of details in his description of the barely-suppressed violence and open intimidation that sometimes characterized the ugly struggle over black power at Cornell. The context he provides for these events in his previous chapter is Nazi Germany: "What happened to the universities in Germany in the thirties is what happened and is happening everywhere" (p. 312). Thus the intimidating black students become young Nazis and the craven Cornell administrators and faculty become the inheritors of Martin Heidegger's commitment of German universities to the Nazi cause. But of course the factual context for the black students and their allies was that of Little Rock's Central High School, of James Meredith at Ole Miss, and of Autherine Lucy at Alabama; of the murders of Medgar Evers, Malcolm X, and Martin Luther King; of the racial assaults in Watts, Newark, Detroit, and elsewhere in one hot summer after another, that were illustrated—however misleadingly—in the movie "Mississippi Burning." Bloom does not so much as mention any of this—nor the continuing war on Vietnam, whose impact on American attitudes, including those toward picking up a gun, Bloom likewise ignores. Such events Bloom no more construes as relevant to what went on at his university in 1967 than does Mrs. Rowlandson consider the alcoholism, smallpox, and starvation, consciously visited upon the Indians by Puritans, as relevant to her kidnapping. It is no apology for violence and intimidation to point out, as Rap Brown did at the time, that "violence is as American as cherry pie." It is only to say that black students did not need to look abroad for lessons in the uses of violence; indeed, the connection of education and violence—white violence—had been made for them over many years of separate and bitterly unequal schooling. Anne Moody's account of the arrest of student demonstrators protesting the murder of Medgar Evers in Jackson, Mississippi, in 1964 rings far truer than Bloom's strained comparisons with Nazi universities:

> The compounds they put us in were two large buildings used to auction off cattle during the annual state fair. They were about a block long, with large openings about twenty feet wide on both ends where the cattle were driven in. The openings had been closed up with wire. It reminded me of a concentration camp. It was hot and sticky and girls were walking around half dressed all the time. We were guarded by four policemen. They had rifles

and kept an eye on us through the wired sides of the building. As I looked through the wire at them, I imagined myself in Nazi Germany, the policemen Nazi soldiers. They couldn't have been any rougher than these cops. Yet this was America, "the land of the free and the home of the brave."[4]

It is perhaps true that Bloom's experience of Cornell in 1967 was inscribed for him in terms derived from Kristallnacht. But in constructing a history of those events for today's readers, Bloom's choice of details, his omissions, and his framing of the available choices offer a lesson in ideological foreclosure. It might, in fact, provide a useful text for students, who need to become familiar with how such processes of selection and structuring are designed to limit how they can look at the world and what, therefore, they might see. What is at stake, however, is not just an historically accurate account of race and the university in the 1960s; for, as Bloom says, the "severing of the races in the intellectual world" of the university carries over into the larger community (p. 93).

I want to follow this discussion of the relationship of black people to colleges and universities during the past quarter century in order to pursue one further matter concerning how prophet Bloom's account of the past and present reveals the kind of future that he wishes us to help him construct. Bloom presents the problem of race as an anomaly, "the one eccentric element" in his portrait of the dissolution of older distinctions of ethnicity, class, and gender among today's students. For blacks have, in his view, *chosen* separation. To be sure, he agrees, "any part of the large community in a pluralistic society" has the "right" to "separate itself." But in so doing, "the movement of the blacks goes counter not only to that of the rest of society, and tends to put them at odds with it, but also to their own noblest claims and traditions in this country" (p. 93). Thus does Bloom blame the victims of segregation for its perpetuation and assert his paternal knowledge of what are black people's "noblest claims and traditions." He also presents "the rest of society" as functionally homogeneous, speaking a monologue that he claims to represent; thus he tries to obliterate the real differences of gender, ethnicity, race, and religion, not to mention sexual preference, that have marked American society and culture and that quicken them today. Further, by insisting that social "movement" is toward homogeneity, Bloom suggests the "deviance," the *rightful* marginality of those for whom the dominant discourse presents—as another form of nationalist dominance once did for Jews, Gypsies, Slavs, and homosexuals—not simply no shelter but a substantial threat.

Bloom roots the rise of what he holds to be black separatism in events that took place in universities, and particularly at Cornell, late in the 1960s. The advent of black power, he argues, rescued universities from the supposed dilemma of fail or fake by proposing separatist black studies programs as second-rate homes for inadequately-prepared black students. Thus was created a "shadow of the university life," marked by racial quotas, "racially motivated hiring" of implicitly unqualified black faculty, fake grades, separated facilities, and everywhere hypocrisy (p. 95). By suppressing the accomplishments of black studies, Bloom offers just enough truth, or rather half-truth, in his account of separate and unequal education *within* the university, the recruitment and ultimate graduation of ill-prepared students, the occasional building of small, squalid affirmative-action empires, to lend his history a spurious currency. What he omits, first, are the similar, but less observable, abuses among the white majority, the inadequate students pushed along, the promotion of sycophants rather than scholars, and the establishment of corrupt administrative empires. Racial issues have had nothing to do with the increased number of firings of white college presidents for lining their own pockets.

Primarily, however, Bloom ignores—or rather rejects—the enormous achievement in the last two decades rooted in black studies: that is, the process initiated by minority and feminist scholars of rethinking university curricula, supposedly objective standards of scholarship, and unexamined conceptions of knowledge. Essentially, he rejects *difference* not only as an important analytic category but as a valid feature of American society.

My point here is not to question the accuracy of Bloom's history, which is at once idiosyncratic and a product of racially exclusive thinking. Rather, I wish to ask: What are the implications for the future of his account of yesterday and today? It seems to me he is, in effect, calling for the virtual elimination of black and Hispanic students from the elite universities. For the fact of the matter is that the primary and secondary schools have succeeded in so miseducating black and Hispanic students that a majority do not even graduate from high school now, and of those who do, a relatively small number have been taught the traditional skills, but more to the point, the familiarity with academic culture, Bloom poses as the sine qua non for admission to his university. I imagine he would argue that improvement of the lower school system will, over time, eliminate the de facto separate and unequal education that now prevails in the United States. But that is to assume that the public schools have, up to now, "failed" in their mission. If, on the contrary, one sees the public schools as having succeeded all too well in their task of separating and stratifying the population, and of shifting blame for class and race segregation to supposed individual inadequacies or deviant group characteristics, there is no reason to believe that they will prepare minority students more adequately in the future than they have in the past.

Furthermore, since Bloom offers no insight as to the successes of minority and feminist scholarship and curriculum development, only exaggerated portraits of failure, one must conclude that his future university would have no room for their discomforting reconstructions of knowledge, for their decentering of biblical, Platonic, or even Bloomian authority. Because Bloom can hear only a cacophony in the many different voices now speaking within the university, he constructs his story as a choice between a Babel and a monologue, *his* monologue. But these are not the limits of choice. The issue is not, on the one hand, abandoning choice for an inane relativism in the face of multiplicity or, on the other, embracing the one true god and his prophet. Like many prophetic books in the past, Bloom's objective is to make it appear that choice is so delimited, and thus to perpetuate a single form of worship.

In fact, I want to suggest, college is precisely the place in which many gods, many cultures compete for allegiance, and in which students examine, and perhaps develop, the values on the basis of which they begin to choose systematically and coherently among those gods and cultures.

III

One critical alternative to Bloom's monologue is being developed across the United States today in what have been called "curriculum integration" or "curriculum transformation" projects.[5] The stated purpose of such projects is to change regular departmental and general education courses to reflect the new scholarship of the last two decades centered on questions of race, gender, sexuality, ethnicity, and class. These projects usually entail bringing together groups of perhaps a dozen or twenty faculty interested, even mildly, in altering their course curricula, working intensively with them in a "faculty development" seminar format that features extensive reading in recent feminist and minority scholarship, and then supporting them—sometimes with funds or released time—as they apply what they learn to transforming their own courses.

This effort has been rapidly spreading. At virtually every unit of the California and New Jersey college and university systems, for example, such projects have been organized, generally with some funding from central state sources. At the 1989 National Women's Studies Association meeting, almost 300 people attended a preconference day devoted to strategies for carrying out such projects. And now, even the prestigious research universities, like UCLA, encouraged by substantial foundation funding, are taking up the work. But to see these solely as efforts to alter somewhat a dozen or twenty discrete courses at perhaps a couple of hundred American campuses is, I think, to miss something more fundamental about them. To be sure, that objective is itself valuable and significant. But there are higher stakes.

Bloom and other right-wing critics have directed a major part of their fire against the retreat from professorial definition of what students *ought* to know, represented by the virtual ditching of college requirements two decades ago. That, conservatives argue, was a fundamental, indeed a deadly error. It substituted "doing your own thing," whether at the level of student choices about what to take, or professors' decisions about what to offer, for the considered judgment of an academic community. Paradoxically, and correctly I think, a similar critique has been posed from the "left," represented here by these curriculum transformation projects. They do not argue, like Bloom and William Bennett, for a return to the "classic" curriculum of the 1950s. But they do assert that there *ought* to be at least some commonalities to what students study.

But *what* commonalities? And how will these be arrived at? In answering these questions—and they are organically related—the network of curriculum transformation projects offers what I think constitutes *the* most fundamental alternative to the right-wing program. In response to Bloom's implicit contention that classically-ordained academics—like himself—ought to be empowered to resurrect an older, time-tested curriculum focused on the classic works, curriculum transformation projects have been designed to bring together the most diverse set of "players" the academic community can offer at the table where curricula changes will be designed. Many of them are younger; generally they include many of the relatively few minority faculty members as well as most feminists. Indeed, the need to have a diverse group has been used to encourage flagging university affirmative action efforts.

Implicitly, the argument being made by these projects runs something like the following: Students ought to base at least part of their study on the perception and consequences of *difference;* indeed, responsibly preparing students for the future involves educating them in and about diversity as well as commonalities. After all, while this may have been the "American century," as people like Bloom feel, tomorrow's world—even tomorrow's American college—is likely to be ever more heterogeneous, more taken up with exploring, understanding, indeed with celebrating difference. The precise translation of this educational imperative into curricular terms will vary depending upon local conditions and the distinctive strengths and needs of a particular institution. What would be sensible at Trinity College would not work at San Jose State University, nor would San Jose's mix fit comfortably at Virginia Polytechnic University. At some institutions a requirement that all students take at least one course focused on issues of race and/or gender might be appropriate; at another, such issues might best be built into a number of general education courses; at still others, the primary vehicle might be altered departmental courses. The curricular model follows from the primary process of deciding upon a core of ideas—of historical experiences, social analyses, and literary texts—not narrowly construed, but centered on difference.

Further, these projects have assumed that no one individual, nor any small group of homogeneous individuals, can work out the translation of that core idea into curricular practice. On the contrary, successfully accomplishing that primary goal depends on bringing to the table those who in experience and specialized knowledge represent difference and can help hammer out its curricular meanings. The curriculum transformation projects thus model *processes* themselves central to constructing new common curricula: In place of purely individualistic enterprise, the patriarchal Bloomian monologue, they substitute a degree of collectively-developed efforts in curriculum organization and in faculty development. The goal of these projects is thus not only a *product*—a new core of study and/or changed courses—but also institutionalization of a *process* of incorporating diversity into academic planning. Implicitly, that curricular process requires a more systematic pursuit of affirmative action in hiring in order to overcome the rather obvious contradictions in most colleges between the academic study of difference and its implications for staffing.

Seen thus, the underlying agenda of the curriculum transformation movement involves a growing effort of minorities, feminists, and their allies to contest for power in defining collegiate educational programs.

IV

This contest seems to me inevitable: For economic, social, and educational reasons the day simply of doing one's own thing is passing. In the past, new curricular initiatives, such as black studies or women's studies, have been accommodated in higher education as add-ons. That is less likely today. For public institutions have not been very successful in competing against crime, drugs, health care, teen pregnancy, and homelessness for state, let alone federal, dollars; increasingly, even state institutions have been turning to private sources of funds. And independent colleges have more sharply privatized soaring educational costs by radically raising tuition and fees. In this context, political and educational leaders stress the need to cut "fat," often by eliminating "duplication" or otherwise streamlining the curriculum. Such economic considerations inflect the ideological debates over curricular content and organization with a certain urgency.

But even if colleges were as financially comfortable as they were in the 1960s, there would be strong social and educational reasons for seeking to establish such a common core of learning. American society seems to have taken an increasingly dogmatic turn. We have grown accustomed to the way in which what used to be called "tolerance" is now denigrated. Indeed, Bloom uses the word "nice"—tolerance drained of muscle—almost as a pejorative. As a Republican candidate, the President feels constrained to evoke a "kinder, gentler" America—precisely because it isn't. *The New York Times* mourns the bullying tone of Supreme Court decisions, especially regarding abortion— the debate about which takes on increasingly apocalyptic qualities. Racist incidents have increased on once-progressive university campuses, physical attacks on gay men are again spreading, rape has by no means decreased, domestic violence seems so commonplace it is hardly reported in crime statistics, joblessness, especially among black youth, seems an accepted fact of life, and city-dwellers appear more inured to homelessness and thus more indifferent to its victims.

These seem to me the epiphenomena of a society under stress, a society whose capacity to produce, and especially to produce problems, has far outstripped the ability of its structures to control production or to resolve its problems. One of Marx's major insights concerned the way in which the enormous productive power generated by capitalism inevitably overtook the social forms created to direct it. A primary political question was therefore evolving forms of social organization able to sustain and yet control the forces of production. Northern societies today have generated enormous and internationally distributed wealth. They have also generated *more* poverty in the Third World and thus an increased flight of distressed people to imperial centers such as the United States, Great Britain and West Germany. They

have created more, and more dangerous, pollution—acid rain, ozone deple-
tion, oil spills, nuclear waste—far more internationally distributed. And a
climate of gloating nationalism, often masking what once would have been
called piracy, has emerged as the dominant character of international relations. Meanwhile, domestically, American society has generated homelessness unprecedented since the great depression; a feminization of poverty that
even more deeply institutionalizes it; an economy in which the greatest growth
industries are junk bonds and cocaine; a tide of waste and pollution fouling
beaches, lakes, and forests; schools that, according to the head of the American Federation of Teachers, fail to educate some 80 percent of their students;
and a system in which more black men are in jail than in college. If these
problems, which I offer as symbols, are understood not as accidents or mal-
adjustments of the economy, but as some of its *products,* undesirable to be
sure but products nonetheless, then we might conclude that once again the
forces of production have outstripped the capacity of our forms of social
organization to direct them.

When such contradictions intensify, so too does social friction, between
classes certainly but among different racial, ethnic, and language groups as
well. That is because significant numbers of people, even those relatively well
situated, sense the world around them as out of control and its previously
accepted norms as "inoperative." Capitalism teaches us that we are masters
of our fate, and most people in our culture come to believe that. Yet what
is it possible even for comfortable individuals to do when syringes wash up
on our beaches and water from the highest streams in Colorado needs to be
boiled; when substance abuse is a way of life, high and low; when crime,
petty and not so petty, emerges as an inarticulate form of social protest—
much as in the mid-nineteenth-century Britain described by Engels? And for
those pushed to the fringes by the movement or disappearance of jobs, by
corporate stock manipulations, by housing gentrification, by illness, despair,
and ignorance, and by bureaucracy itself, what meanings can traditional social
norms maintain? Naked power rushes in when social norms disintegrate; and
such power, raw or cloaked, alone comes to define the relations between
people and groups.

Obviously, no college curriculum—Bloom's or those being developed by
curriculum transformation projects—can resolve such conflicts. Perhaps only
the most thoroughgoing transformation of the systems of economic decision-
making and the structures of society will do so. But that does not say that
what we teach our students and how we do it is irrelevant even to the most
radical social changes. Here I agree with Bloom: What we do in colleges
today significantly shapes what will be done in the world tomorrow. The
question then becomes how will tomorrow's curricula—and especially any
common core—be defined, by whom, and to what ends? Do we wish to entrust
tomorrow to a man on a white pedestal like Allan Bloom? Is his individualistic,
authoritarian discourse one that includes or excludes us? Does his monocultural construction of the present moment, or of the past, offer confidence
about how he would structure tomorrow? Is his enterprise of returning ed-

ucation to the limits—wide but very real—of Plato and Alexander Hamilton one in which we want to enlist?

Or do we see greater possibilities in the project represented by curriculum transformation groups? Does their effort at inclusiveness, at starting at points of difference, at arguing precisely the legitimacy of authorities, provide a model of a hopeful democratic, participatory process? Does the account they offer of past and present, rooted as it is in the heterogeneous experiences and cultures examined by recent feminist and Third World scholarship, yet predict a more coherent if less one-dimensional path into the future? Is its effort to broaden everyone's education—even Allan Bloom's—one that commands our attention as citizens and compels our interest as intellectuals? In whose university would you rather teach—or study?

Many of my colleagues would, I am aware, vote for Bloom. It is always easier to do what has always been done: The old models lie open before us, like road maps of familiar territory. But that is precisely the problem: All over the world today—from Gdansk to Buenos Aires, from Tiananmen Square to Soweto—societies are struggling to devise forms of economic and social organization that cope with what I have called the vast new international forces of production. The old maps do not describe that new territory very well, much less a world in which power might be distributed more evenly, south and north, among people of color and whites, among women and men.

In a society under stress, the preachers of the older, simpler, traditional forms of worship will always have an audience anxious to turn away from needed but fearful changes. We like to hear people whose voices have become troublesome being urged—if not commanded—to return to their old places. Furthermore, the old rituals are not without virtue. But to renew their power, they must, like the healing ceremony enacted in Leslie Marmon Silko's novel *Ceremony,* be reinvested with what a changing culture truly creates. As that most American of prophets, Walt Whitman, tells us, creation is not over.

> There never was any more inception than there is now . . .
> Urge and urge and urge,
> Always the procreant urge of the world.
> Out of the dimness opposite equals advance, always
>   substance and increase, always sex,
> Always a knit of identity, always distinction, always a
>   breed of life.

The real challenge lies not in closing the American mind to distinction, but in listening to the choir of its urgent voices—coming to hear, to understand, to enjoy, and finally to knit our identity from that discourse of difference.

Notes

1. My correspondent will no doubt be pleased to know that part of this chapter, too, was published in a pamphlet issued by the college.

2. Without belaboring the obvious, one might, for example, point to Bloom's claim

that the American constitution condemned slavery. On the contrary, Article IV, section 2 explicitly provides for the return of fugitive slaves. And, of course, there is the notorious "three-fifths" provision in Article I, section 2. Bloom further asserts that the Founding Fathers promulgated a "remarkably unified and explicit political tradition" (p. 54), and thus he ignored the profound conflicts between libertarians and radicals like Jefferson and Paine, and conservative elitists, like Hamilton and Madison. In teaching, as a matter of fact, what students find striking are precisely the *differences* in content and personae between the "Federalist Papers," on the one hand, and texts like "Common Sense" and Jefferson's *Notes on the State of Virginia* and his letters to Madison, on the other. The recognition and reconciliation of these and other such differences offer a far more interesting historical problem than the assertion of a false unity.

3. I think particularly of a passage in DuBois' "Of Work and Wealth" in which, after discussing the need to eliminate profit and interest from economic relations, he adds:

> What we must decide sometime is who are to be considered "men." Today, at the beginning of this industrial change, we are admitting that economic classes must give way. The laborers' hire must increase, the employers' profit must be curbed. But how far shall this change go? Must it apply to all human beings and to all work throughout the world?
>
> Certainly not. We seek to apply it slowly and with some reluctance to white men and more slowly and with greater reserve to white women, but black folk and brown and for the most part yellow folk we have widely determined shall not be among those whose needs must justly be heard and whose wants must be ministered to in the great organization of world industry.... [N]o real reorganization of industry could be permanently made with the majority of mankind left out. These disinherited darker peoples must either share in the future industrial democracy or overturn the world.
>
> W. E. B. DuBois, *Darkwater: Voices from Within the Veil*
> (New York: Schocken, 1969 [1920]), pp. 101–102.)

4. Anne Moody, *Coming of Age in Mississippi* (New York: Dell, 1968), pp. 280–81. Ironically, the analogy to Nazi Germany had been posed in the 1964 Mississippi freedom school curriculum . . . to help black students, as well as white volunteers, understand American racism. In *Three Lives for Mississippi* William Bradford Huie further pursues the analogy between the "good Germans," who watched the concentration camps being built, and the "good Mississippians," who by refusing to speak out against Klan terrorism effectively gave it the blessing of community sanction.

5. One might point to a variety of other initiatives, involving core curricula, reading lists for incoming students, and community internships, among other efforts.

Index

127, 130, 155, 156, 159, 268
Jacobs, Philip, 170
James, C.L.R., 142
James, Henry, 8, 24, 34, 48, 54, 64, 68, 69, 71, 74, 75, 80, 93, 99, 100, 106, 110, 115, 116, 122, 129, 133, 146, 162, 163, 166, 186, 253, 269, 278
Jameson, Fredric, 137, 152
Jefferson, Thomas, xiii, 286
Jehlen, Myra, 170
Jewett, Sarah Orne, 25, 31, 42, 45
Jewish culture, 51
Jewish quotas, 246
Johns Hopkins University, 133–35, 139
Johnson, Charles S., 82
Johnson, James Weldon, 25, 31, 42, 45
Johnson administration, 140, 261
Jones, Gayl, 77, 130
Jones, Howard Mumford, 26, 35, 43

Kallen, Horace, 164
Kampf, Louis, 19, 143, 152, 170
Karcher, Carolyn, 171
Katz, Michael, 267
Kellams, Samuel E., 209
Kelley, Edith Summers, 38, 102
Kennedy, John Pendleton, 29, 115
Kessel, Barbara, 19
Kessler-Harris, Alice, 46, 153
King, Katie, 132
King, Martin Luther, 117, 118, 156, 250, 253, 274, 278
Kingston, Maxine Hong, 52, 77, 83, 84, 147
Kirkland, Caroline, 51, 55, 57, 111, 114, 117, 122–25, 130
KNOW, Inc., 145
Kogawa, Joy, 255
Kolka, James W., 186, 196
Kolodny, Annette, 55, 116, 131
Kreymborg, Alfred, 25
Kroeber, Karl, 96

Lanier, Sidney, 24, 26
Lanser, Susan Sniader, 46
Larsen, Nella, 39, 130, 164, 169
Latino, 161, 165, 264
Lawrence, D. H., 5
Lazarus, Emma, 25
Leary, Lewis, 5
Left, the, ix
Leisy, Ernest E., 26, 35, 43
Lentricchia, Frank, 20, 46, 138, 151, 152, 163, 164
Lerner, Gerda, 37
Lerner, Laurence, 135

Lerner, Max, 5
Leslie, David W., 207, 208
LeSueur, Meridel, 9, 58, 93, 102, 127, 150, 159, 249
Letters, 48, 50, 56, 64, 65, 71, 77, 103, 105, 110, 111, 122, 125, 126, 175, 246, 260
Levertov, Denise, 76
Levine, Lawrence, 85, 93, 96, 113
Lewis, Sinclair, 43
Lewis, Wyndham, 104
Lewisohn, Ludwig, 38
"Life in the Iron Mills," 59, 116, 147
Lincoln, Abraham, 26
Literacy, 26, 51, 52, 76, 81, 83, 98, 129, 155, 156, 161, 163, 169, 232, 236, 256, 257, 262, 262–64, 270
Literary canon, 104, 105, 167, 216, 221, 258, 260, 261
Literary history, 50, 53, 54, 57, 59, 100, 116, 119, 162, 163, 164, 165, 167, 249, 259
Littlefield, Daniel, 147
Locke, John, 159
Loggins, Vernon, 31
London, Jack, 41
Longfellow, Henry Wadsworth, 24, 26, 72, 220, 258, 260
Lorenz, Gail E., 222
Lowell, James Russell, 8, 24, 26, 43, 83, 258
Loy, Mina, 163
Ludwig, Richard K., 5
Lu Hsun, 142

McCall, Joseph Darryl, 47
McFarlane, Larry A., 205
McIntosh, Peggy, 100
McKay, Claude, 25, 42, 45, 109, 163
McKenna, Teresa, 91
Macmillan *Anthology of American Literature*, 100
Macy, John, 22
Madison, James, 286
Maier, Robert H., 186, 196
Mailer, Norman, 100, 101, 103
Maitland, Christine, 204, 207, 208
Malamud, Bernard, 255
Malcolm X, 156, 278
Malcriado, El, 67
Mao Tse-tung, 157
Marginalized culture and literature, 49, 50, 52, 59–62, 64, 65, 67, 69, 70, 71, 74, 77–80, 82–86, 121, 126, 129, 147, 148, 160, 161, 164, 165, 167, 269, 278
Market; marketplace, x, xi, 107, 141, 146, 175, 179, 181, 192, 194, 201, 202, 206, 217, 228, 233, 234